The Indian Great Awakening

The Indian Great Awakening

*Religion and the Shaping of Native
Cultures in Early America*

LINFORD D. FISHER

OXFORD
UNIVERSITY PRESS

OXFORD
UNIVERSITY PRESS

Oxford University Press, Inc., publishes works that further
Oxford University's objective of excellence
in research, scholarship, and education.

Oxford   New York
Auckland   Cape Town   Dar es Salaam   Hong Kong   Karachi
Kuala Lumpur   Madrid   Melbourne   Mexico City   Nairobi
New Delhi   Shanghai   Taipei   Toronto

With offices in
Argentina   Austria   Brazil   Chile   Czech Republic   France   Greece
Guatemala   Hungary   Italy   Japan   Poland   Portugal   Singapore
South Korea   Switzerland   Thailand   Turkey   Ukraine   Vietnam

Published by Oxford University Press, Inc.
198 Madison Avenue, New York, New York 10016

www.oup.com

Oxford is a registered trademark of Oxford University Press

Library of Congress Cataloging-in-Publication Data
Fisher, Linford D.
The Indian great awakening : religion and the shaping of native cultures in early America / Linford D. Fisher.
p.   cm.
Includes bibliographical references and index.
ISBN 978-0-19-974004-8 (hardcover : alk. paper) 1. Indians of North America—New England—Religion.
2. Indians of North America—New England—Social life and customs. 3. Christianity and other religions—
New England—History. 4. Christianity and culture—New England—History.
5. New England—Religious life and customs. I. Title.
E78.N5F56   2012
974.004′97—dc23   2011042931

3 5 7 9 8 6 4 2

Printed in the United States of America
on acid-free paper

For Jo

CONTENTS

ACKNOWLEDGMENTS

Every historical project likely has an archival "Aha!" moment. Mine came in June 2010, when I was in the Hamptons on Long Island, New York, trying to track down what seemed to be impossibly elusive shreds of evidence regarding Montaukett and Shinnecock engagement with Christianity in the 1740s. After a series of dead ends, I was fortunate enough to be referred to Hedy Boyd of the First Presbyterian Church of Southampton, not far—in the colonial period and now— from the Shinnecock Reservation. The archival room in the church was sweltering, making me all the more eager to finish and take advantage of the other attractions the Hamptons are known for. But then, there it was. In the very bottom drawer, covered by folders with untold miscellaneous financial records and pamphlets from the church's 350-year history, I spotted a bound volume that looked promising. Fishing it out from beneath the stacks of other ephemera, I was initially disappointed to discover that the handwriting inside was a neat, cursive, nineteenth-century script on lined paper. *Darn.* Too late for my purposes. I flipped to the title page and read, "History of the Shinnecock Church." *Wait.* I began reading and quickly realized it was the history of an Indian church I had never heard of, led by Indian ministers who were similarly unknown to me. *Peter John. Paul Cuffee.* The next day I was standing in front of the present-day building of this Indian church whose congregational history wound back over three and a half centuries.

Reconstructing the lifeworlds of mostly nonliterate people requires imaginative historical detective work. Tracking down new pieces to this puzzle—such as the Shinnecock Presbyterian Church—was part of the many joys and challenges of this project. In the pages that follow, I have utilized the writings of Natives themselves whenever possible—petitions, letters, sermons, journals, wills, autobiographies, hymns, essays, books, land deeds, and oral histories. In many cases these documents were dictated to a literate colonist and then "signed" (usually with an "X" mark) to indicate agreement, although as Native literacy rates rose marginally throughout the eighteenth century, documents penned and fully signed by Natives became more common. More broadly, however, I have gleaned snippets from non-Native sources, such as court records, the letters and diaries of colonists, newspapers, records of colonial and state assemblies, depositions, legal petitions, land deeds, wills, church records, probate records, and the records of various missionary societies. Even outside of the documentary evidence, when possible I have analyzed objects and leaned on the findings of archaeologists and anthropologists. On the whole, although there are always gaps in the available sources, I continue to be amazed by the volume of information—no matter how fragmentary at times—relating to Native groups in early America.

This book could not have been written without the help of many generous individuals. I owe an ongoing debt to David D. Hall, Jill Lepore, and Laurel Ulrich, who have continued to shape this project even after guiding it through its various stages in graduate school. Along the way, I have greatly benefited from conversations with and help from fellow historians and scholars including Ted Andrews, Brandon Bayne, Kate Grandjean, John Grigg, Jason Mancini, Daniel Mandell, Robert Orsi, Daniel Richter, Neal Salisbury, David Silverman, Nancy Shoemaker, and Doug Winiarski. Present-day members of some of the Indian nations under consideration in this book helped me gain a better understanding of the past through the present, including Melissa Zobel (Medicine Woman) and Faith Davison (now-retired archivist) of the Mohegan Nation; Tall Oak Weeden of Narragansett and Mashantucket Pequot ancestry; and Laughing Woman, Cheryl Allen, Fatima Dames, and Wayne Reels of the Mashantucket Pequot Nation. This book was also shaped by feedback received while I presented portions of this project at the American Historical Association, the American Society for Church History, the Annual Conference of the Omohundro Institute for Early American History and Culture, the Boston Area Early American History Seminar at the Massachusetts Historical Society, the Religious History Colloquium at Vanderbilt University, the American Society for Ethnohistory, the Early American History and Culture Seminar at the Newberry Library, the Boston Area American Religious History Group, the Medieval and Early Modern History Seminar at Brown University, the Early American Workshop at Harvard University, and the North American Religions Colloquium at Harvard Divinity School. Two chapters appeared elsewhere in different forms: a shorter version of chapter 4 was published in *Ethnohistory* (2012); a shorter and different version of chapter 7 can be found in Gregory Smithers and Brooke N. Newman, eds., *Native Diasporas: Indigenous Identities and Settler Colonialism in the Americas* (Nebraska, forthcoming).

This project could not have been completed without generous fellowships, including the National Endowment for the Humanities /Massachusetts Historical Society Long-Term Fellowship; William Hutchinson Fellowship, Harvard

University; Gilder Lehrman Summer Fellowship; Phillips Fund Grant for Native American Research, American Philosophical Society; Kate B. and Hall J. Peterson Fellowship, American Antiquarian Society; and the Dean's Fellowship, Harvard Divinity School.

Along the way, numerous libraries and institutions graciously allowed access to materials that made this project possible, and their knowledgeable and helpful staff members gave freely of their time to help me track down necessary sources and references. Included are Guildhall Library, London (Stephen Freeth); London Metropolitan Archives (Wendy Hawke); Connecticut State Library (Bruce Stark); American Antiquarian Society (Jackie Penny); Massachusetts Historical Society (Elaine Grublin, Anna Cook, and Conrad E. Wright, among many others); New England Historic Genealogical Society; Gilder Lehrman Library; New York Historical Society; Rare Book Room, Columbia University; Hamilton College Archives; Connecticut Historical Library; Rhode Island Historical Society; Presbyterian Historical Society; Library of Congress; Special Collections Research Center, College of William and Mary; Houghton (Thomas Ford), Widener (Pam Matz), Lamont, and Andover-Harvard libraries at Harvard University; Mashantucket Pequot Museum and Research Center (Jason Mancini and Kevin McBride); Long Island Room, East Hampton Public Library; First Presbyterian Church of Southampton (Hedy Boyd); Long Island Room, Southampton Library; First Presbyterian Church of Southold; Southold Free Library (Dan McCarthy and Melissa Andruski); Kingstown Congregational Church; the Pettaquamscutt Historical Society; the Newberry Library; Rauner Library, Dartmouth College; Lilly Library, Indiana University; John Carter Brown Library; and the John Hay Library, Brown University (Holly Snyder).

Throughout, Susan Ferber at Oxford University Press went above and beyond in her role as editor with her encouragement, enthusiasm, input, and general support. It is hard to imagine a more careful and supportive editor, for which I am incredibly thankful. Rick Stinson and the production team were equally efficient and helpful. A few friends and colleagues gave valuable time to read the entire manuscript as I was wrapping up revisions: Ted Andrews, Akeia Benard, Jo Fisher, Ray Fisher, Kate Grandjean, David D. Hall, Paul Harvey, Jason Mancini, David Silverman, Mark Valeri, and Conrad E. Wright; others kindly read portions of the manuscript, including Chris Beneke, Ken Bishop, Ann Braude, Mark Breneman, Joe Grady, Karl Jacoby, Anna Lawrence, Elaine Peña, Bill Simmons, David Spader, David Watermulder, and Jeff Wilson. Thanks also to Lynn Carlson, who skillfully and efficiently produced the maps in this volume; Erin Calfee for her excellent and cheerful research help in the summer of 2010; Amy Remensnyder for the Latin translation; and my colleagues in the Department of History and elsewhere here at Brown, who have been wonderfully warm and supportive.

To my steadfast parents, Daniel and Priscilla Fisher; my inspiring siblings—all eight of them; my parents-in-law, Daniel and Erma Wenger; and the rest of my immediate family I owe a debt of love and support that I too often take for granted. To our children, Eden, Elliot, Helena, and Harrison, I owe a world of thanks for making my life unspeakably rich and for providing a welcome and playful balance to the academic life. Last, but most important, it is impossible to tabulate the innumerable ways, big and small, that my talented and incredible wife, Jo, has supported this project over the years. She patiently read and corrected draft upon tedious draft and endured long days and even weeks of single parenting during research trips while effortlessly maintaining a busy household. I could not have done this without her support, love, and encouragement, and likely would not even be writing this had she not planted the seeds of academic pursuits in me more than fifteen years ago.

The Indian Great Awakening

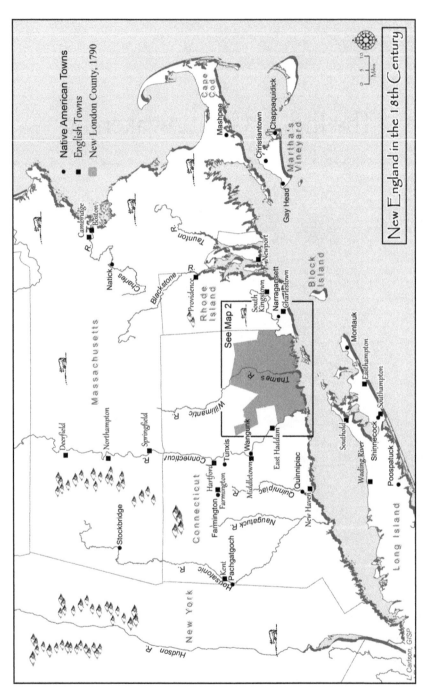

Map 1. New England in the Eighteenth Century. Map by Lynn Carlson, Geographic Information System Professional, Brown University.

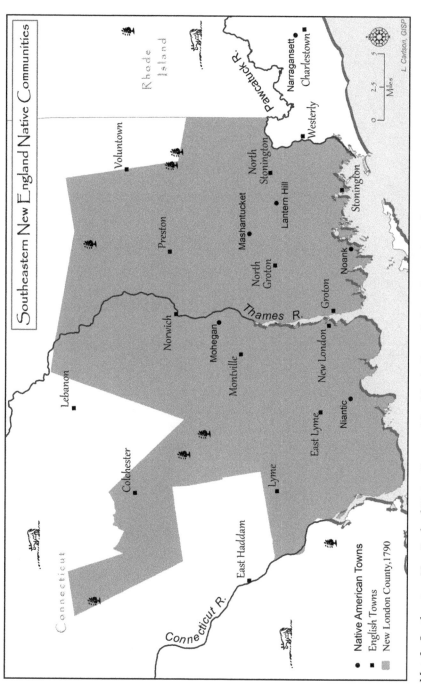

Map 2. Southeastern New England Native Communities. Map by Lynn Carlson, Geographic Information System Professional, Brown University.

Introduction: Bear Paws and Bible Pages

Religious conversions can be powerful. History is replete with stories of prominent individuals who converted to one religion or another, including the Apostle Paul, the Roman Emperor Constantine, his mother Helena, and Saint Augustine to Christianity; and, more recently, Malcolm X and Islam Yusuf (Cat Stevens) to Islam, Glenn Beck to Mormonism, and celebrities such as Madonna to Judaism, Richard Gere to Buddhism, and Tom Cruise to Scientology. However, the *idea* of religious conversion is also powerful—at times even more powerful than the reality itself. The idea of conversion and the imaginative possibilities therein have launched a thousand ships—in some cases, literally, although not all at once—in the hopes of spreading a particular set of practices or system of belief and, in the process, to eradicate perceived falsehood, heathenism, and paganism. Usually contained within the idea of conversion is an *ideal* of conversion that presumes a particular narrative, including a religious experience that leads to the rejection of one way of thinking or living and the embrace of another way altogether.[1]

In most cases, however, religious change is more ambiguous than either the idea or the narrative ideal of religious conversion conveys. This is particularly the case in colonial contexts, or in situations where missionaries offer a competing set of religious beliefs and practices as part of an imposing, conquering presence, whether, for example, in the medieval Mediterranean (Islam) or early modern Americas (Christianity). Contemplating the proffered religion becomes considerably more complicated as the balance of power tips less and less in the favor of the indigenous population. Especially in these contexts—those marked by an obvious imbalance of power—religious decisions are not transparent; in most cases they are multivalent, ongoing, rarely final, and difficult to interpret.[2]

Consider, for example, the following story from colonial New England, the time and place with which this book is concerned. In 1990, archaeologists in Connecticut working with the Mashantucket Pequot Nation made a fascinating discovery. During the careful unearthing, analysis, and reburial of nearly fifty Pequot graves dating back to the late seventeenth century, they found remains of an eleven-year-old Pequot girl who had died sometime between 1683 and 1720, elaborately dressed and positioned in traditional Pequot manner—in a circular grave, on a bed of woven grass, her legs and arms tucked up in a fetal position, on her right side facing eastward, with the axis of her spine pointing to the southwest. A variety of funerary objects were in the grave with the young girl's remains—most of them articles of everyday life that reflected her recent transition into young adulthood: a pestle, pothook, and an iron hoe.[3]

The surprising item among the funerary objects, however, was a small cloth bag, or medicine bundle, that contained the skeletal remains of the front left paw of a bear and a folded page with faint printed letters on it. Taken individually, the objects seemed simple enough to investigate. The bear paw—a rather unusual funerary object for Indians of southern New England—likely symbolized the belief that the bear, as a powerful being, was capable of helping the young girl make the transition between this world and the next. The folded paper had been preserved because it and the cloth bag were in direct contact with an iron cup, which fossilized the cloth and paper into iron salts known as a pseudomorph. As a result, enough text was visible for bibliographers to determine that the page fragment was torn from a small-format King James Bible printed between 1669 and 1680. The original text from Psalm 98 read:

[1]O sing unto the LORD a new song; for he hath done marvellous things: his right hand, and his holy arm, hath gotten him the victory.

[2]The LORD hath made known his salvation: his righteousness hath he openly shewed in the sight of the heathen.[4]

Either object alone would have garnered little interest in an otherwise unexceptional grave. Bundled together, however, the Bible page and bear paw raise a host of questions. How did the Bible get into Pequot hands? Did the girl assemble the medicine bundle, or did her parents or relatives? Is it even possible a sympathetic colonist passed along the Bible page to the grieving parents for comfort? And what about the Pequot girl herself? What was her experience of colonialism? What kinds of changes in family structure, cultural ceremonies, and methods of subsistence had imposed themselves on her community as a result of the coming of the English? What did she make of the Bible page (assuming she was familiar with it)? On the surface, the page itself seems to have been used as a talisman, as having power in itself, and represented the kind of salvation and protection that English colonists often spoke of when they read and preached from their holy book.[5] And yet the specific content of the selected verses—unless selected completely by accident, which seems unlikely—clearly referenced both salvation and the "heathen," which opens up the possibility that literacy and biblical understanding potentially played at least some role in its use.

Then again, even if this particular Pequot girl had achieved a rudimentary English literacy—a rarity for Natives in southeastern New England through the early eighteenth century—the particular use of the Bible page in its ripped out, fragmented form, differs dramatically from typical and "orthodox" Euroamerican ways of using the Bible. Even taking into account the possibility of full literacy, the medicine bundle seems like a broadly inclusive approach to the question of efficacious oversight in the afterlife, a sincere hedging of bets.

This Pequot medicine bundle opens up many of the broader themes and interpretational puzzles that drive *The Indian Great Awakening*. The simultaneous presence of the Bible page and bear paw represents the multitude of surprising and interesting ways that American Indians interacted with European religion and culture during the colonial period. Although a first impulse might be to interpret the medicine bundle through the lens of conversion—that is, to ask whether this Pequot girl converted—this is in some ways the wrong question, driven by Western, Judeo-Christian notions regarding conversion.[6] A more historically attuned and ethnographic question might be, What did this Pequot girl find interesting or useful about what the missionaries had to offer?[7] Keeping this Native-centered question in mind is essential for considering religious engagement in colonial contexts. Native individuals and communities often found missionaries, education, and Christian ideas and practices interesting and useful, but this interest and utility were almost always filtered through the realities of colonialism and a deep and abiding concern with retaining Native land and preserving community sovereignty and autonomy. Nonetheless, this Pequot medicine bundle also signals that lived, even metaphysical, concerns guided decisions about religion. Undoubtedly, some American Indians throughout the entire colonial period and beyond found solace in Christian teachings, even as they wrestled with the seeming hypocrisy of many white colonial Christians.

The pages that follow recount the stories of Native American communities in southeastern New England between 1700 and 1820. The main actors in this unfolding drama are Indian individuals from communities in Connecticut, Rhode Island, Long Island, and western Massachusetts—Mohegans, Mashantucket Pequots, Lantern Hill/Eastern Pequots, Niantics, Narragansetts, Tunxis, Wangunks, Mohicans, Montauketts, and Shinnecocks—who in the seventeenth century had shown little interest in the religion and culture of the European colonists during the first wave of evangelistic attempts. At the heart of this story is a sustained—even if irregular—engagement with Christian practices and European cultural offerings, often in the form of proffered education and evangelism, as the presence of the English-language Bible page in the medicine bundle illustrates. This book highlights the spectrum of responses that emerged out of these encounters, particularly as they played out over many decades.[8] Native communities were not monolithic in their views of what precise shape their relationships with European leaders, customs, and religions should take, just as Euroamericans varied greatly in their goals and expectations for Natives.[9] What unfolds is a tale of ebb and flow, engagement and disengagement, affiliation and deaffiliation, which varied by individual and community. Additionally, this book situates these religious decisions in the lived, on-the-ground realities of eighteenth-century Native lives. Religious engagement, this book argues, must be understood in the fullest possible context of local colonial interactions and the broader, transatlantic tugs of imperial power.[10]

With this in mind, what follows is an investigation into the social sources of religious and cultural engagement, or at least the broader social and cultural contexts in which religious changes are debated, considered, enacted, adapted, and even retracted. Building upon the notion of religion as lived—that is, intertwined with the messiness of ordinary life—this story keeps in tension the material and spiritual aspects of Native lifeworlds, namely, everyday concerns like land and subsistence as well as more explicitly "religious" considerations, such as Christian practices and interior processes of religious change.[11] Without ignoring the realities of Native religious experience and, in some cases, the emergence of indigenous Christianities, this book suggests that interior processes never occur in a vacuum, and the broader social and cultural contexts cannot be neglected, especially in colonial situations marked by an obvious imbalance of power.[12] As much as possible, Native interactions with Christian practices and ideas are narrated in a way that reflects Native modes of religious engagement, which tended to be more practical and provisional. Native religious engagement usually defied the more totalizing and complete notions that often frame the word "conversion," which too often imposes Eurocentric ideas about religion on Native populations.[13] Accordingly, in the pages that follow, the words "religious engagement" and "affiliation" are used to capture this dynamism and inherent instability, rather than "conversion."[14] Without intending to completely replace the notion of religious conversion, such words allow for discussion in temporally and historically specific ways about what individual Natives actually did instead of speculating on interior processes. Affiliation also allows for the dynamic, on-and-off ways in which Natives selectively pursued education or church membership, but then in many cases deaffiliated or made different choices over time. The concepts of affiliation and religious engagement also better reflect the frame of reference that non-Christian cultures—like that of Native Americans—had regarding religious choices, namely, more in terms of testing, sampling, and appending to existing customs and practices, rather than conceiving of religious change in terms of a wholesale renunciation of one set of ideas in favor of another. Finally, these concepts are more value-neutral and allow for the interpretive ambiguity that often reflected reality, as in the case of the Pequot medicine bundle or in Natives requesting education or joining a church.

The chronological scope of this book is intentionally broad. Tracing Native religious engagement over the course of a century allows for the observation of trends over generations as well as the particularities of individual decisions. The story begins in the opening decades of the eighteenth century with a "second wave" of evangelistic attempts by Euroamericans between 1700 and 1740 toward unevangelized communities in southeastern New England (the "first wave" consisted primarily of the efforts of John Eliot, Thomas Mayhew, Jr. and Sr., and the New England Company, a London-based missionary society, in the years before King Philip's War in 1675).[15] Central to this second wave was a renewed strategy for southeastern New England that emphasized the education of Indian children.[16] As it turns out, education greatly interested Natives, even if they did not initially see any benefit in professing Christianity itself. In the 1720s and 1730s, Native communities in southern New England welcomed schoolteachers onto their lands, sent their children to English schools, and generally took part in whatever material benefits the missionaries offered, such as food, blankets, and clothing.[17] Such educational attempts, however, were considerably complicated by the simultaneous and contentious controversies over land and an internal struggle for leadership and control within Native communities.[18]

Native religious engagement prior to 1740, therefore, is essential to understanding Natives' involvement in the Great Awakening. The "First Great Awakening," as it was later called, was a series of loosely interconnected Christian (and primarily Protestant) revivals that took place in British North America, the Caribbean, the British Isles, and parts of Continental Europe in the 1730s and 1740s.[19] It was a time of heightened spiritual awareness and cultural ferment, with thousands of people showing up to hear local, regional, and international preachers who adopted a more engaging, extemporaneous style of preaching that emphasized personal conversion and relatively unmediated spiritual experiences. Although the actual events and results of these revivals were contested—by observers then and by historians ever since—in some locations, particularly in New England, these movements empowered the unlearned laity, including women, Indians, and blacks; gave a new sense of spiritual authority to anyone who had experienced a dramatic new birth; and divided churches over such religious experiences, which in many cases led to new, "Separate" churches.

American Indians participated in many of these revivals during the Great Awakening—indeed, their involvement is part of what made the Awakening great—but these participations and their various meanings are arguably the most misunderstood episodes in Native lives in eighteenth-century New England.[20] The revivals of the Great Awakening offered Natives an opportunity to participate in a seemingly new and egalitarian expression of Christianity and to join local churches. Even so, Natives responded to the revivals in a wide variety of ways that ranged from complete indifference to a seemingly wholesale embrace. A variety of records from New Light (pro-revival) and Separate churches reveal the spectrum of responses by Natives, indicated by various kinds of participation and affiliation that included adult and infant baptisms, being received into full communion, giving relations of grace (testimonies of salvation), and owning the covenant (assenting to a church covenant that described particular beliefs and a commitment to the church community). More conspicuous, however, are the absences of many Natives—at times, the majority—from these church records; these absences reveal the very different ways in which some Natives responded to the opportunities afforded by Christian affiliation. Even among those who did affiliate, Natives did not always maintain the same levels of affiliation over time, opting instead (at times) to deaffiliate completely and in some cases to join the more unofficial network of Christian Indian Separate churches conducted by unlicensed Indian ministers that emerged in the 1740s. Indian Separatism was a thriving, largely underground, post-Awakening movement that provided several decades of cultural connectivity and intertribal fellowship for Christian subsets of Native communities.[21] Thus, Christianity and Indian churches became important within Native nations, but not in the way English ministers and colonial officials had hoped.

The years following this Indian Great Awakening reveal a fascinating third attempt to evangelize and educate Natives of southern New England. Despite an emerging culture of Indian Separatism in many Native communities after 1750, colonial ministers and missionaries were convinced the Awakening had failed and attempted to continue in their efforts to evangelize these same Native groups. This re-re-evangelization came, once again, primarily in the form of proffered schools and sermons. More than before, however, Natives in the post-Awakening period asserted their own autonomy and control over education and preaching. Schools for Natives proliferated across southern New England between 1750 and 1775. The largest ones were on Native reservations and— whenever possible—taught by Natives. Whites, too, tried to control these educational efforts. At least two schools experimented with the boarding school model, one started by John Sergeant at Stockbridge, Massachusetts, and the other founded by Eleazar Wheelock in Lebanon, Connecticut. The boarding school experiments were not particularly well received by most Natives or effective for New England Natives. Wheelock only trained approximately thirty New England students at his Indian Charity School between 1754 and 1770; Indian schools in Stockbridge, Mashantucket, and Narragansett had that many students in just one year.

Widespread frustration and resentment on a variety of fronts in the 1760s and 1770s prompted one particular subset of Native Christians to attempt to move away from New England in the 1770s. The removal of the Indian Charity School by Wheelock to Hanover, New Hampshire, in 1770, with the founding of

Dartmouth College was one factor, but others were equally important, including issues of dispossession and deep internal divisions over tribal leadership and membership. Although the Revolutionary War delayed the plans for relocation, in 1784 and 1785 a small group of New England Natives moved to Oneida country in New York state and founded a Christian community called Brothertown and another similar town, New Stockbridge, nearby.[22] Nonetheless, the vast majority of New England Indians, including many of the tribal and Christian leaders, remained in New England and pursued other avenues for legal justice and community sovereignty.

The post-Revolutionary War era of New England Indian life saw a fourth phase of attempted evangelization of these same groups, especially the Narragansetts.[23] As missionaries soon found out, the Narragansetts living on the reservation in Charlestown, Rhode Island, in 1810 were in some ways more Christianized than their forefathers had been in 1710, but the situation was complicated. The Narragansetts had a church, but only a few Narragansett adults attended each week. Most of the Narragansett Indian children were illiterate and virtually none of them could recite basic foundational elements of Christianity (such as the Lord's Prayer). And yet at least a few of the older adults could narrate some of the history of their Christian affiliation that—as they told it—started with the era of the Great Awakening. And, as was true one hundred years prior, Narragansetts still preferred education for their youth rather than sermons for the adults. Viewed through the lens of this broad time frame, then, the Indian Great Awakening is merely one of several points of transition in the long eighteenth century and part of a broader series of cultural and religious changes that were always ongoing and provisional.

Indian Separatism in southern New England shared similarities and differences with other pan-tribal movements in the eighteenth century, particularly those that involved elements of nativism—a call to a recovery of Native traditional practices and a rejection of European cultural and religious influences. These nativist movements began in the early 1740s in the mid-Atlantic and Midwest and resurfaced in a variety of communities through the early 1800s.[24] Native prophets and visionaries like Neolin (Delaware) and Pontiac (Ottawa) gave inspiration for and leadership to movements that resulted in violent conflicts between Euroamericans and Natives from a wide range of Native nations. Although there are a few common elements between Indian Separatism in New England and the nativist impulse—shared disillusionment, promoting separation from Europeans—in practice the two were very different. At no time during the Native Separate or Brothertown movements was military resistance ever discussed as an option, nor were there any visions of or conversations with the Master of Life, the Indian deity from whom Neolin and other prophets received instructions. Furthermore, Indian Separatism (and especially Brothertown) was an explicit embrace of an indigenized version of reformed Protestantism and European-style cultural practices like individual property ownership and agricultural surplus production, not a rejection of Christianity and Euroamerican culture.

Taken together, the various threads of argumentation in this book suggest a rethinking of the timeline, mode, and extent of Native Christianization in early America. Native American engagement with Christianity was a contested, multigenerational process that had at its core an interest in education and was framed by concerns for the ongoing loss of land and a slowly eroding sense of cultural autonomy. Applied more broadly, this book is a call for the recovery of the full range of social and cultural interactions between colonial and indigenous populations as they play out over time regarding the issues of religious and cultural change. Illuminating discoveries like the Pequot medicine bundle with its Bible page and bear paw reveal that religious engagements and affiliations are ambivalent and need to be situated within the wider, oppressive, and ambiguous context of colonial pressures and social life. There are certainly unique particularities in the eighteenth-century New England context, but the dialectical engagement with Euroamerican religion and culture over the course of many decades and multiple generations in this particular region has wider resonance in colonial and missionary contexts worldwide.[25]

But this book is also about the writing of history. It has been difficult for Americans to find a meaningful way to recognize and understand Native persistence, presence, and activity in our collective history between King Philip's War (1675–1676) and the Indian Removal Act (1830). Such omissions were not possible in the eighteenth-century northeast, when questions about Native presence, land rights, sovereignty, and religious practices embroiled entire towns, colonies, and regions and made headlines on both sides of the Atlantic. The forgotten stories retold in this book should hopefully prompt consideration about how they fell by the wayside in the first place.

1

Rainmaking

The Pequot River was rising.[1] The cause, torrential rain, was natural enough. The timing of the rain, however, may have been supernatural, since it came shortly after local Connecticut colonists prayed and fasted for it. That alone would not have been so unusual except that the English prayers were preceded by the repeated attempts of local Mohegan holy men, or shamans, to make it rain. Having suffered through a long August 1676 drought that dried up their corn and withered their fruit trees, some Mohegans sought out James Fitch, the local Congregational minister in Norwich, Connecticut, desiring that he would "seek to God for Rain." Fitch jumped at the opportunity and quickly called a public day of fasting and prayer, undoubtedly desiring to bring life-giving rain to not only the barren countryside but also to his unfruitful missionary attempts among the culturally resilient Mohegans. In order to remove possible ambiguity regarding the source of any imminent rain, Fitch queried Uncas, the Mohegan sachem notoriously uninterested in Christianity, "whether if God should send us Rain, he would not attribute it to their Pawawes?" No, Uncas assured Fitch, the shamans had "done their Uttermost, and all in Vain." To be absolutely certain, however, at Fitch's request Uncas agreed to give "a great speech to the Indians" stating clearly that "if God should then send Rain, it could not be ascribed to their Pawawing, but must be acknowledged to be an Answer of [the English] prayers." In a staging that could hardly have reflected more the biblical showdown between Elijah and King Ahab and the prophets of Baal, Fitch was confident of success, not only because he believed the English God to be more powerful, but because twice before he and his congregation had sought God "by Fasting and Prayer," and both times the rain came. And so it was again. The first day of the public fast started like the other days: hot, dry, and clear. By nightfall, however, the clouds began to gather. On the second day Uncas gave his promised speech to all the Indians as the clouds thickened. On the third day there was "such a Plenty of Rain" that the "River rose more than two Foot in Height."[2]

This story—with all of its likely embellishments—represents the complexity of seventeenth-century colonist-Indian relations, particularly around issues of religion and perceived spiritual power in a broader context of colonial conquest. On the surface, the story line is simple enough. In a typical power encounter replicated throughout history in a variety of global geographic contexts, Christianity is demonstrated to be superior to local, indigenous religious rituals. Christians produce what Natives cannot through their petitions: rain. Nonetheless, the various tensions and factors involved reveal a lot about the modes of religious and cultural interaction between colonists and Indians. The scene related here unfolds in August 1676, the same month in which the English military leader Benjamin Church and his troops and Indian allies hunted down and killed the Wampanoag sachem, Metacom, or King Philip, thereby bringing to an end the fourteen months of vicious conflicts between the English and Indians in New England known as King Philip's War. Although the Mohegans had sided with the English—thereby escaping the vast numerical losses and enslavement the Narragansetts, Nipmucs, and Wampanoags suffered—this power encounter regarding rain played out in the dark shadow of unspeakable violence and massacre. In some ways, the success of Fitch and his congregation in this instance could be read as the spiritual triumph over New England Natives, even as King Philip's War demonstrated—though barely—the military dominance of the English. In truth, however, whatever minor "victory" this rainmaking was for the English, the Mohegans—even as English allies—and other Native groups in Connecticut, Rhode Island, and on Long Island continued to keep English ministers and evangelists at arm's length in the seventeenth century.

Archaeologists relate that ancestors of the seventeenth-century New England Natives first arrived in North America between 12,000 and 20,000 BCE, having crossed over a land bridge at what is now the Bering Strait, and migrating south and east over the subsequent millennia, eventually populating the two continents that later became known as North and South America. Native American traditions teach, however, that each Native nation was created on the particular lands their ancestors occupied, land that was given to them by the Great Spirit. In the centuries prior to contact with Europeans, American Indian life and culture was dynamic and surprisingly interconnected across the vast geographical expanse of North America. Major urban centers, such as Cahokia (near present-day St. Louis), were strung across the Midwest, usually grouped around important waterways, such as the Mississippi River.[3] In the southwest, the Anasazis developed far-reaching and intricate systems of trade with other Native groups. Important cities, such as the one located at Chaco Canyon (in present-day New Mexico), illustrate the architectural complexity of Native cultures.[4] Along the winding waterway later called the Ohio River, mound-building Natives constructed elaborate effigies of animals to house their dead, to mark the landscape, and to create ritual community space.[5]

In the years prior to contact, life for eastern woodland Algonquians in the northeast corner of North America—which include the Native tribes of southeastern New England—was marked by seasonal migration, extensive trading networks, agricultural prowess, and seasonal rhythms of the hunt.[6] Native American chiefdoms claimed and utilized vast swaths of land. Individual bands of Natives formed community and social hubs that moved seasonally between the coast and inland locations, following long-established traditions of utilizing the coastal waterways for clams, fish, and other seafood during the summer, and leaning heavily during the long, cold winter months on lengthy hunting excursions and the corn, beans, and other vegetables they had grown in the summer and stored for later use. Native homes, called wigwams, were rounded structures made of bent saplings and covered with bark and animal skins, and ranged considerably in size and use. A hole at the top let out smoke from the fire that, in the wintertime, kept the wigwam as warm as any English hut or house, as later colonists would attest. Regionally, Native groups formed a dynamic network of trade and exchange that kept a steady stream of goods and products flowing from the coast to bands farther inland, and vice versa.

Native Americans in the coastal northeast first discovered Europeans on their shores a few decades after Columbus mistakenly landed at San Salvador in 1492. One of the first recorded contacts occurred in 1524, when the Italian explorer Giovanni Verazzano, sailing under a French flag, explored the coast of what later became known as New England, including the Narragansett Bay. During the next century, Natives on the coast increasingly dealt with the seasonal presence of fishermen and traders from France and England, and, starting in the early seventeenth century, the more permanent presence of the Dutch along the Long Island Sound. Early English efforts at establishing a permanent colony focused farther south, first at the failed Roanoke colony in present-day North Carolina in the 1580s, and later at Jamestown, Virginia, in 1607. Fishermen and merchants established little villages along the northeast coast from present-day Newfoundland to Cape Cod by 1620, when the Pilgrims—separating Puritans, really—landed on the eastern coast of Cape Cod and eventually settled in a vacated Patuxet village at Plymouth. Within the following two decades, English presence in "Newe-England" increased dramatically, with the founding of Salem (1626), Boston (1630), Hartford (1636), Providence (1636), and New Haven (1638) as principal outposts.

For the first decades of European colonization in New England, American Indians far outnumbered their hairy and seemingly effete European counterparts, despite the fact that some New England Indian communities lost between 60 percent and 90 percent of their members, largely due to "virgin soil" epidemics that accompanied European expeditions and trade in the sixteenth and seventeenth centuries.[7] In the early years of colonization, Europeans lived at the periphery of powerful Indian chiefdoms and received or stole corn, venison, and knowledge of the new world that allowed the colonists simply to survive.[8] Over the course of a hundred years, two devastating wars, disease, and massive colonial expansion decimated Indian populations, vastly reduced Indian landholdings, and reversed the patterns of dependence in favor of the colonists. The Mohegan population alone dropped from several thousand men, women, and children to less than five hundred between the early seventeenth century and 1730.[9]

Native Lifeways

Despite Euroamerican assumptions at the time of contact, northeastern Algonquian communities had a rich and complex system of beliefs regarding the spiritual world and its relationship to the physical world, a cultural ethic of right and wrong, and ideas about the afterlife. At the most basic level, Native Americans did not separate out something called "religion," nor did they have ideas about the world that might resemble a creed or systematized belief system—or any other religious convention like written scriptures that contemporaries might have identified with European religions. Native religious traditions were virtually synonymous with their cultures.[10] Ideas about the earth, humans, animals, nature, and the gods, as well as the relationship between these various components, were intertwined with the daily rhythms of life and lived out in ways that seemed nonreligious to many Europeans. The world Indians inhabited was full of spiritual forces and meaning that shaped lives, events, and rituals. Daily life— cooking, eating, hunting, singing—could potentially be infused with spiritual significance. In the 1730s, John Sergeant observed an elaborate ritual at Stockbridge performed prior to skinning and preparing a freshly killed deer, in which the deer was cut into quarters, a prayer was offered by the shaman (who was promptly paid), and then the deer was boiled and consumed. Such customs, the Mohicans explained, were taught to them by a hero and prophet of long ago who also showed them how to make and use snowshoes.[11] Nature, too, was full of gods and spiritual forces who directed events and influenced Indians' successes or failures.[12]

Algonquians in southeastern New England believed in a great God they called "Cautantowwit," as Roger Williams noted in 1643, who was responsible for creating the lands the Natives called home.[13] According to creation stories passed down orally through the generations, Cautantowwit also brought forth humankind, first creating a man and woman out of stone but, being dissatisfied, "broke them into pieces, and made another man and woman of a Tree," from whom all of humanity flowed.[14] Cautantowwit's "Court" or residence was in a southwesterly direction, and it was from Cautantowwit's fields that corn and beans first came.[15] The spiritual and material realms were intertwined, however, by the governance of other-than-human forces or beings who had charge over specific aspects of the world. A robust panoply of such beings—gods, as Williams called them—governed all aspects of human life and included "the gods of the four corners of the earth," "a god over their corn, another over their beans, another over their pumpkins, and squashes, &c."[16] Other powerful beings watched over their wigwams, women, children, fire, sea, wind, day, night, and each of the four seasons. Although Cautantowwit was the "one great and good God, that was over all the rest of the gods," Natives also believed in a "great evil god," variously called Mutcheshesunnetooh, Chepi, or Hobbomock, who they thought to be an "evil power" and "mischievous." The relationship between the Indians and these powerful beings was dynamic: "to these gods they call for help under every difficulty," the eighteenth-century Mohegan minister Samson Occom mused, "and to them they offered their sacrifices of various kinds."[17] In addition to these other-than-human beings, Natives believed more generally in a manifestation of spiritual power that could appear in any form, which they referred to as "manitou." Natives ascribed as "manitou" anything excellent in humans, animals, or the physical world including, as Williams noted, "every thing which they cannot comprehend."[18]

Also serving as mediators between the seen and unseen worlds were "powwaws" or shamans, spiritual leaders ("priests," as Williams called them) to whom Native communities looked to divine the will of the gods with regard to individual and community decisions as well as explanations of natural and supernatural events including sickness and drought.[19] Shamans attained their spiritual power and community status through a dream in which "Chepian appears to them as a servant"; once visited with this vision, shamans were empowered to perform supernatural acts, conduct healings, and advise the sachems in matters of importance. Although dreams and visions were not the exclusive domain of shamans, the revelations received gave them insight and direction for leadership. Shamans served as community leaders, offering invocations at various feasts and dances and performing intricate public rituals and dances. Likewise, shamans served important roles in times of illness and attended to sick individuals with traditional remedies drawn from nature combined with specific actions, incantations, and prayers, which often had the intended effect of driving out the illness.[20]

The gods (and even Chepi) might appear in various forms; often these became the basis for "images"—carved statues of animals or human figures—kept by Native leaders and shamans. Indian shamans consulted their images on behalf of individuals or the entire community in an attempt to "know the minds of their gods" regarding what should be done in various circumstances, whether "to make a dance or a feast, or give something to the old people, or sacrifice to the gods."[21] During later periods of evangelization and Christianization, missionaries demanded that Native converts destroy these wooden and stone gods in an attempt to eradicate traditional Native religious practices, although neither the persistence of such practices nor the attempts to eradicate them in English colonial contexts compared in intensity to the persistence or eradication attempts in certain areas of Spanish colonial South America.[22]

Colonists, when they recognized Native religion at all, accused Indians of serving the devil, as early reports from New England suggest.[23] Although this is clearly in part a caricature from a religiously narrow European perspective, Natives often attempted to placate both "good" and "evil" gods in an effort to maximize the desired outcome, as the Pequot medicine bundle (mentioned in the introduction) suggests. During a drought in the 1730s, the Narragansetts held a "great Powaw" for several days. When a local colonist went to them and "rebuked them as serving and worshipping the Devil," an elderly Indian shaman "readily owned and justified it," explaining that "all the Corn would die without rain" and Chepi, "the Evil Power," was to blame, so praying to him made perfect sense. "If I was to beat you, who would you pray to?" the powwow asked; "to me, or to your Father Ten miles off? You would pray to me to leave off and not beat you anymore: so we pray to the Devil to leave off affecting us with Evil."[24] Similarly, Mashantucket Pequot oral tradition relays that during the colonial period Natives would leave offerings of corn, beans, and nuts in a deep pit to appease Hobbomock, whom they believed inhabited the lower regions of the earth.[25]

Regardless of the source, both Indians and colonists alike regarded Native shamans as possessing real power—even as quasi-magical cures, remedies, and divining abilities among whites were regarded as real (even if officially prohibited) by English colonists. The presence of European Christians in many instances prompted contestations between old and new sources of spiritual power, as in the Fitch-Mohegan rainmaking showdown in 1676. Similarly, John Sergeant noted of the Mohicans in western Massachusetts that although the Indians loved to boast of the "great Feats" their shamans could perform, they admitted that they "had no Power over Christians." Sergeant himself recognized the possibility in real-world power possessed by the shaman but personally supposed the Natives to be "very much impos'd upon by such kind of Pretenders."[26] The eighteenth-century Mohegan minister Samson Occom believed that shamans sometimes would merely "pretend" that they could divine the will of the gods through the images; yet with regard to casting spells or "poisoning one another, and taking out poison," Occom heard firsthand from people who had experienced such things that it was "no imaginary thing, but real." Poisoned or bewitched individuals either felt pain immediately or a growing sense of pain over time "till they are senseless, and then they will run mad. Sometimes they would run into the water; sometimes into the fire; and at other times run up to the top of high trees and tumble down headlong to the ground, yet receive no hurt by all these." For

Occom, this was all plausible, given the widespread belief (and the testimony of the shamans themselves) that Indian shamans "get their art from the devil," either through dreams and visions or "by the devil's immediate appearance to them" in different shapes. "I don't see for my part," Occom reasoned, "why it is not true, as the English or other nation's witchcraft, but is a great mystery of darkness."[27]

Eastern woodland Algonquians clearly had ideas about an afterlife. Upon death, Indian souls traveled southwest to Cautantowwit's house, to be reunited with the souls of their forefathers. On Long Island, the Montauketts believed that after death "their souls go to the westward a great way off, where the righteous, or those who behaved themselves well in this world, will exercise themselves in pleasurable singing and dancing forever, in the presence of their Sawwonnutoh or their western god, from whom they have received their beans and corn, their pumpkins, squashes, and all such things." The "wicked" go to the same place, "but they are to be exercised in some hard servile labour, or some perplexing exercise, such as fetching water in a riddle, or making a canoe with a round stone."[28] Other Natives believed that "bad" individuals would also travel to the southwest and knock on Cautantowwit's door "but he bids them quatchet, that is to say, walk abroad, for there is no place for such; so that they wander in restless want and penury."[29]

The most common collective ritual in Native communities was the feast or dance. Although lacking overt "religious" purposes (from outsiders' perspectives, at least), these community gatherings were held at regular times throughout the year—in the early spring, late summer, and during the winter—as well as when necessitated by internal or external events or activities—sickness, drought, war, death, or marriage. Colonial visitors to these events often misunderstood the ritual dancing, songs, and regalia they observed, variously interpreting them as pernicious or even dangerous (both in terms of spirituality and warfare). Local colonists, even into the eighteenth century, often erroneously assumed animal sacrifices to be taking place at such events. In approximately 1718, a ten-year-old English youth attended several Indian powwows at Mohegan (one of which was a "New Corn Feast") that lasted all night but did not, he later reported, include any sacrificing of animals.[30] No matter what the specific occasion, it is clear that Native gods and spirits were invoked by the powwows for goodwill and success. Among the Mohicans and Housatonic River Indians, the Keutikaw was a dance that concluded the year-long period of mourning for someone deceased. Friends and community members would make short speeches and then give presents that were intended to help make up for the loss of the family member. After this extended time of speech-giving and gifting, the whole community would "eat together, and make Merry."[31]

Although it is commonly assumed that the process of colonization, warfare, and disease dismantled Native traditional structures of belief and practice—even as early as 1676 (the end of King Philip's War)—it seems rather that Native ritual practices went underground in the face of persistent colonial presence, and, over time, Natives learned simply to hide whatever traditional beliefs or practices the community at large held.[32] During the summer of 1735 William Treat went to visit the Wangunk Natives near Middletown, Connecticut, and stumbled upon a series of Native rituals and community events that he was not expecting. Upon arriving on a Saturday, he learned that the Wangunks were hosting a regional "Great dance" with Niantics and Mohegans in attendance. Treat had already served among the Wangunks as a missionary for the prior half year, so his presence as a known missionary created tension since the Wangunks assumed—correctly—that he had come to preach to them. Some Niantic and Mohegan Indians came and promised that if he would leave them, they would come and hear him preach the next day. Accordingly, Treat left and went to the agreed-upon house the next morning, but no one was there. Treat wandered around the Wangunks' village and discovered that an Indian child was sick and offered to help. The Natives forcefully told Treat that he was not welcomed in the wigwam or anywhere nearby while they tended to the sick child, but that if he would remove himself to a small orchard a ways away, "they would Speedily Come to me and they would hear me preach." Treat withdrew and waited, but instead of any Natives coming to him, they instead started another ritual ceremony, this time a "powwow" intended to "know of the Devil" if a previously deceased Indian had been poisoned by another Indian. Once again, Treat reported "Grunting, Groning, Sighing," and Natives beating their breasts. "I Cannot Express the forlorn, dollerous noise that they then made," Treat recalled. Convinced that "the devil would speedily make his appearance," Treat took it upon himself to break up the powwow, which made the Indians understandably furious. Once again Treat was told that if he would go off a distance, they would come hear him preach. Again he removed himself; again he waited in vain. Treat reported that he broke up the powwow repeatedly until at last they gave up and sat quietly while he preached to them. Whether or not the encounter—as narrated by Treat—had such an ending, the episode demonstrates the ongoing vitality of Native ritual practices in ways that were intentionally hidden from and in direct competition with proffered Christian modes of religious being.[33]

Often escaping the notice of colonists, Natives reshaped the physical landscape around them in ways that held special meaning for individuals and communities. In addition to "earthen fortifications and burial mounds," northeastern Algonquians "painted prominent rocks, carved trees, and erected posts to mark an important path, the grave of a celebrated warrior, or the site of some great accomplishment in hunting or war."[34] Hundreds of stone mounds and stone rows still exist all around New England, as do specially placed large stones, either upright or at an axis with lunar or solstice views or angles, much like the mounds of the Ohio River valley. Some stones contain rudimentary etchings or markings, while others have been smoothed in certain places, reflecting either practical or ritual activity. When John Sergeant traveled with some Mohicans in western Massachusetts in 1734, they passed a "large Heap of Stones"—ten cart loads' worth—which the local Indians created by adding a stone or two when passing by. When pressed as to why they did it, most of the Indians informed him "their Fathers us'd to do so, and they do it because it was the Custom of their Fathers." Sergeant's Indian interpreter, Ebenezer, however, thought that it was "design'd to be as an Expression of their Gratitude to the supream Being, that he had preserv'd them to see the Place again."[35] Intentionally altered trees, carefully constructed stone forts, and underground stone chambers all indicate pre-contact activity that—in the case of religious rituals—was often intentionally hidden by Natives or went unrecognized by Euroamericans in the colonial period.[36]

Pervading all of Indian life was an emphasis on the community. The family served as the most basic block of social organization, although Indian families were built—and dismantled—in ways that defied European family logic. Native men—especially leaders—took more than one wife, often with a somewhat hierarchical preference between them. As in many polygamous cultures, wives were symbols of status in addition to practical help in raising the many children that often resulted from such arrangements. Native marriage ceremonies could range from simple to ornate and complex, but in some communities, at least, it took very little to dissolve the resulting union. John Sergeant explained of the Mohicans in the 1730s that the dissolution of Native marriages was "very common," and in most cases, the children and all household items remained with the woman except the gun, "for that is the Man's Livelihood."[37] Indian communities were also intricately interconnected through marriage and kinship in ways that usually defied "tribal" boundaries. The seventeenth-century Mohegan sachem Uncas, for example, was arguably part Mohegan, Pequot, and Narragansett. Intertribal marriages were probably in part strategic, but were not enough to prevent maritally related communities from waging war against each other. Uncas himself married first the sister and then the daughter of Sassacus, the Pequot sachem, against whom Uncas rebelled when he joined with the English in the Pequot War (1636–1638).[38]

Land

One of the primary points of interaction between American Indians and Euroamericans from the opening years of contact—and indeed, up through the present— involved land. Land was far more central to the "ceremonies of possession" of the English than in other early modern empires in the New World, including the

Dutch, the Portuguese, the Spanish, and the French, in part because of English interest in individual land claims and large-scale migration and colonization.[39] Consequently, controversies over land—and the resources on it—permeated almost every sector of the Indian-Anglo relational frontier.[40] The problems largely stemmed from vastly different ways of conceptualizing and using the land. Although Roger Williams reported in 1643 that Indian communities were "very exact and punctuall in the bounds of their Lands, belonging to this or that Prince or People," even Williams recognized the cultural differences that existed in terms of land use and transfer.[41] Native ideas about land were linked to conceptions of "collective sovereignty," that is, recognizable rights to the use of particular swatches of land and the resources on them usually controlled by the tribal or village Indian leader, or sachem.[42] English colonists tended to have a very specific concept of legitimate individual land ownership that was often linked to the idea of "improvement" and continuous occupation of the land. If land was not visibly occupied or if its inhabitants were not using it in a seemingly profitable way—clearing, planting, grazing domesticated animals, and building fences and permanent buildings—then the land was going to waste.[43] The idea of seasonal hunting or living grounds and a hunter-gatherer model of subsistence with small-scale agriculture that did not include domesticated animals or observable patterns of crop rotation as practiced in Europe was one that most Europeans either did not understand or did not see as an appropriate use of the land.[44]

English settlers in Boston had not bothered to purchase from Natives most of the land they settled on, in part because they saw no need to (and had a royal charter to prove their right). Although the presumption of royal land grants from distant European kings and queens had at times been vigorously contested in the sixteenth century (particularly by the Dominican Bartolomé de las Casas), one of the first Euroamericans in New England to really question the legitimacy of English settlement on Indian lands was the infamous dissident Roger Williams, who in 1633 wrote a scathing treatise against the Massachusetts Bay Colony and its magistrates, which among other things challenged the concept of a royal land grant.[45] How could the king grant land that was never his in the first place? How indeed. The General Court's answer to Williams's diatribe was to banish him from Massachusetts in 1635 for this and other infractions, even as they began to think more pragmatically about land deeds and sales.

Very quickly in New England, then, a precedent was set for obtaining a land deed from the Indians. All English colonists needed was several Native individuals with some semblance of community power who would grant them land in written form (drawn up by colonists, of course) to convey a sense of legitimacy among fellow colonists and governors, interested parties back in London, and competing empires in New England, like the Dutch.[46] Over time, the granting of lands as an executive privilege by Indian sachems—as encouraged by the English—became a point of frustration and tension within Indian communities, especially as sachems sold tribal lands out from under their own people to pay personal debts. Throughout the seventeenth century, hundreds of individual land grants were given or sold to countless colonists by Indian sachems, colonists serving as Indian guardians, and the general assemblies of various colonies, despite attempts by Indian communities and English colonial governments to restrict who could sell land.[47] Over time, the issue of land got wrapped up in another controversial development in New England: the evangelization of American Indians.

Seventeenth-Century Evangelistic Attempts

By the time the English successfully established their first settlement in the Americas at Jamestown in 1607, the Spanish already had a century of colonization and evangelism under their belts. For the most part, the proudly Protestant English were excruciatingly aware of the Spanish Catholic precedents and, despite protestations to the contrary, leaned heavily on them when it came to fitting Natives into a theological-cultural-imperial framework.[48] Throughout the colonial period, Protestant English ministers, merchants, and promoters of colonization also self-consciously imagined themselves in direct counterdistinction to the colonizing and evangelistic efforts of the French and French Jesuits along the Saint Lawrence River in present-day Canada. Nonetheless, despite the charter statements and sermonic exhortations in New and Old England regarding colonial responsibility to the Indians, evidence of intentional missionary activity by colonists in Virginia, Plymouth, or Massachusetts Bay before the 1640s is scant. This is partially because the early colonists, including New England settlers, believed that simply setting the example of a godly, charitable, and civilized lifestyle would eventually win the Natives to European Christianity.[49] Although dozens of Natives, particularly those who served—either willingly or unwillingly—as laborers, servants, and slaves in English households, would have had ample opportunity to observe the rhythms of English religious practices in person, such exposure produced few baptisms or professions of faith, or few that were publicized, at least.[50] Additionally, given the precariousness of the colonies themselves in the first few decades, the colonists were consumed with trying to establish their own presence and dominance in New England, a process that included a violent conflict with—and attempted extermination of—the Pequots in Connecticut in 1636–1638.[51]

No concerted effort was made to evangelize local Natives on their own lands until the 1640s, even though by then the English were well known either by trade or by warfare to every major Native group in Massachusetts, Rhode Island, and Connecticut. Roger Williams had spent time among various Indian communities in the 1630s, first voluntarily among the Wampanoags near Plymouth, and later, among the Narragansetts in present-day Rhode Island, although he generally declined to actively evangelize the Natives he encountered.[52] The Roxbury, Massachusetts, minister John Eliot was therefore one of the first colonists to take active and long-term interest in the evangelization of Natives. Eliot began learning the Massachusett language sometime in early 1640 and in September or October of 1646 attempted his first sermon among the Natives just west of Roxbury. Despite a clumsy beginning, between 1646 and 1675 Eliot founded fourteen Indian "Praying Towns" throughout Massachusetts, in which he gathered Christianized Indians into highly organized towns designed to inculcate European cultural, religious, and agricultural values. Thomas Mayhew, Jr., on Martha's Vineyard similarly began an evangelistic mission around the same time, a missionary program that spanned generations of both missionaries and Christian Indian families.[53] Praying towns like Natick (established in 1650) were controversial from the beginning. Although the idea seems to have been proactively embraced as early as 1646 by some Massachusett Indians as a strategic way to secure a stable land base, in negotiating the land grant Eliot and the Massachusetts General Court usually required the local Natives who moved to the newly organized praying towns to sign away all current and future rights to vast tracts of land, which immediately opened up more land for colonial development.[54] The results were mixed, however, as the long history of Natick illustrates, with ongoing land sales and dishonest dealings slowly whittling down the actual amount of land in Indian possession through the eighteenth century.[55]

In the late 1640s, Eliot's descriptions of his work prompted interest among wealthy humanitarian Christians in London. This was in part due to Eliot's relentless self-promotional efforts through the so-called Eliot Tracts, a series of reports on the successes and setbacks of the evangelistic enterprise in New England.[56] These tracts, more often than not intended for readers in Old England, relayed with relative candor the long and halting process through which Eliot and others tried to refashion Indian spirituality in their own image. To support these ongoing efforts, a London-based missionary organization, the Society for the Propagation of the Gospel in New England, was created by an act of English Parliament on July 27, 1649.[57] The society members were "entirely Puritan and predominantly Independent" and primarily drawn from the merchant class.[58] The purpose of the society was to raise money, ostensibly for the much-publicized missions to the Indians already taking place in New England, but the first decade was marred by questions of money that disappeared or was not properly accounted for. In 1660, the Restoration, the crowning of Charles II, and the Act of Oblivion dissolved the society, and it was not until

February 7, 1662, that Parliament granted a new charter for "the Company for the Propagacion of the Gospell in New England, and the parts adjacent in America," which by the eighteenth century was often referred to as the New England Company (NEC).[59] The money raised in England for the Christian evangelization of Native Americans in the New World was administered in New

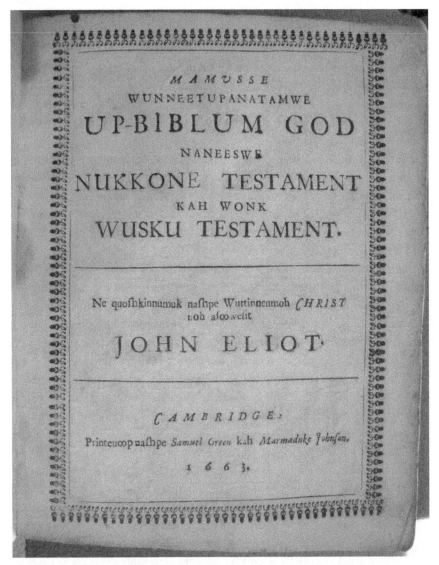

Figure 1.1. Eliot Bible, Title Page. Mamusse wunneetupanatamwe Up-Biblum God naneeswe Nukkone Testament kah wonk Wusku Testament ne quoshkinnumuk nashpe Wuttinneumoh Christ, by John Eliot. Cambridge: Printed by Samuel Green and Marmaduke Johnson, 1663. Courtesy of the Massachusetts Historical Society. Photograph by the author.

England by a board of commissioners that met in Boston, usually referred to as the Boston Commissioners. The NEC's focus was relatively narrow, both with regard to geography and mission, for its missionaries sought only to convert the American Indians within the colonies of New England. The NEC most famously supported John Eliot and Thomas Mayhew Jr. and Sr. in the seventeenth century but additionally sponsored dozens of other missionary efforts throughout the seventeenth and eighteenth centuries in almost all of the New England colonies and New York. One of the crowning achievements of Eliot and the NEC was the so-called Eliot Bible, a Massachusett-language Bible that was the product of eight years of translation by Eliot, who leaned heavily on his Montaukett Indian servant, Cockenoe, and the Narragansett Job Nesutan in the process.[60] In short, the NEC quickly became the financial backbone of almost all missionary efforts in New England undertaken by Congregationalists prior to the American Revolution.

Though most evangelizing efforts took place in Massachusetts, it wasn't as though Connecticut and Rhode Island were unimportant to the NEC. Quite the opposite, in fact, since lands claimed by both colonies were home to two of the largest Native communities in New England, the Mohegans and the Narragansetts. Both communities, however, showed considerable indifference to more than a passing engagement with missionaries. The Mohegans especially received sustained attention in the mid-seventeenth century from the NEC, which paid Congregational minister William Thompson to provide regular lectures to the Pequots and then to the Mohegans between 1657 and the early 1660s.[61] The Reverend James Fitch, minister in Norwich, Connecticut, first preached to the Tunxis near Hartford in 1670, and when he moved to Norwich began to receive £31, 10s from the NEC each year to preach to the Mohegans. Every other week Fitch traveled from Norwich to the Mohegan tribal lands to deliver a lecture on basic Christian beliefs. And for a while, the Mohegans welcomed him into their community. Things changed quickly, however, when Uncas and the other Mohegan leaders realized "that religion [i.e., European Christianity] will throw down their heathenish idols, and the sachems' tyrannical monarchy: and then the sachems, discerning this, did not only go away, but drew off their people, some by flatteries, and others by threatenings."[62] Such threats notwithstanding, Fitch was able to attract the attention of thirty Mohegans over the period of a year and a half who desired to have their children instructed and who agreed to be taught by Fitch on Sundays.[63] Where gentle persuasion failed, the Connecticut General Assembly turned to legislation. In May 1675 the Assembly passed ten "Laws for the Sayd Indians to Observe" (like Massachusetts had done thirty years earlier) that included prohibitions against powwowing, adultery, stealing, speaking against God, and breaking the Sabbath. Most telling was the eighth law, which required that "ready & comely attendance be given to heare the word of God preached by Mr. Fitch, or any other minister," and empowered local constables to round up the Indians, force them to attend, and punish those who misbehaved or refused.[64]

Additionally, John Eliot reported to the Commissioners of the United Colonies in 1671 that Fitch also was working with "Mr. James"—Thomas James, first minister of the Congregational church of Easthampton—on Long Island to coordinate religious instruction for the various Indian groups there and was making long-term plans to send a missionary to the Mohawks in New York.[65] James, with his linguistic fluency, evangelistic itinerancy, regional diplomacy, and sponsorship from the New England Company, extended into Long Island the work of Eliot in Massachusetts and the Mayhews on Martha's Vineyard. In 1667 he reported to Connecticut governor John Winthrop, Jr., "I am busy in Indian affairs from one end of the Island to the other."[66] Although these efforts in Rhode Island, Connecticut, and Long Island did not amount to much in the long term (Fitch reported that the Indians on Long Island did not have "any inclination to learn the knowledge of God"), eastern Massachusetts and Plymouth presented a different story. By 1674, Eliot and the NEC could boast at least 4,817 "praying" or Christianized Indians and six gathered Indian churches in Massachusetts and Plymouth colony including Cape Cod, Martha's Vineyard, and Nantucket.[67]

Whatever missionary program there was and whatever "success" might have been touted were severely challenged by a massive conflict that erupted in New England in 1675–1676.[68] In response to long-standing political subordination, dispossession, and evangelization, the Wampanoag sachem Philip (Metacom) and his Indian allies attacked more than half of the ninety-two colonial towns in New England, virtually decimating twenty-five of them.[69] Colonists responded in kind, burning Indian villages to the ground and killing and enslaving any Indians they could find, including women, children, and the elderly. King Philip's War was a war that forced most parties to take sides—a war that pitted Indian against Indian and Christian against Christian. The war began when the body of John Sassamon, a Harvard-educated praying Indian, was found under the ice of a local pond—murdered by King Philip's men, a mixed Indian-English jury later decided—and largely ended when Alderman, an Indian soldier fighting for the colonists, killed Metacom.[70] While Wampanoags, Massachusetts, Narragansetts, Nipmucs, Pocomtucks, and Abenakis all fought against the Euroamericans, the Mohegans, Pequots, Mohawks, Christian Wampanoags, and a smattering of other Christian Indians from a variety of Native groups fought alongside the New England colonists and aided them in countless ways as spies, interpreters, messengers, and assassins.[71] The trauma of war was a momentous rupture in the lives of both colonists and Indians; approximately 5,000 Indians and 2,500 colonists were killed, and many more Indians were forced into servitude in Euroamerican households or shipped to the Caribbean as slaves.

King Philip's War is often seen as the fairly decisive end to the Indian missionary program in New England.[72] It is true, in part, that the war laid bare the thinly veiled hostility that the average colonists had for all Indians, even—and in some cases, especially—praying ones. Mary Rowlandson was far from alone in her palpable distain of supposedly praying Indians when she noted that the residents of Lancaster, Massachusetts, "were slain and mangled in a barbarous manner, by one-eyed John, and Marlborough's Praying Indians."[73] Aside from the acts of slaughter and destruction perpetuated by colonists and Indians alike, the worst casualties, perhaps, were the thousands of Christian Indians who had adopted Christian practices and largely grouped themselves into the fourteen or so praying towns across Massachusetts, Cape Cod, and Martha's Vineyard. As hostilities peaked in the winter of 1675–1676, five hundred or so praying Indians were rounded up for the "protection" of both colonists and praying Indians and shipped to Deer Island in the Massachusetts Bay.[74] Supporters of praying Indians, like John Eliot and Daniel Gookin, were threatened with their very lives by their Indian-hating neighbors. Due to the increasing animosity of settlers toward all Indians, "praying" or not, many of the books, Bibles, and tracts translated into local Indian dialects were gathered up and destroyed by Indians and English alike. When two Dutch travelers, Jasper Dankers and Peter Sluyter, visited John Eliot in 1679 and asked him for an Indian Bible, Eliot told them that "in the late Indian War all the Bibles and Testaments were carried away and burned and destroyed," and he had not been able to save any for himself (although future reprinting remedied this loss).[75]

Nonetheless, missionary activity continued after the war, in part perhaps because humanitarian-minded sponsors in London could not comprehend from afar the cultural shock and devastation the war brought. The money still flowed, and Eliot and others tried hard to put it to good use. In 1680 Eliot reported to Robert Boyle, the NEC governor, "The Lord's work still goeth on among them," and four years later, Eliot gave a lengthy, upbeat description of a typical local Indian church service.[76] In 1686, just one year after the printing of 2,000 second-edition copies of the Indian Bible, Eliot happily told Boyle, "Our Indian work yet liveth, praise be to God; the Bible is come forth, many hundreds bound up, and dispersed to the Indians, whose thankfulness I intimate and testify to your honour."[77] Even on his deathbed, Eliot's optimism overcame his realism when he noted, "There is a Cloud, a dark Cloud, upon the Work of the Gospel among the poor Indians, the Lord Revive and prosper that Work and grant it may live when I am dead."[78] The "Work of the Gospel" hardly needed reviving, however; the combination of international warfare and metropolitan humanitarianism ensured that it was never extinguished. Far from being abandoned, the evangelization of New England's Indians continued on almost as before even following King Philip's War. There were setbacks, to be sure—the fourteen praying towns in Massachusetts were reduced to four, for example—but overall the New England Company kept a steady supply of missionaries, ministers, and schoolteachers in local Indian communities during the decades following the war. This was particularly true of the regions that had largely remained unaffected by the fighting, namely Cape Cod, Martha's Vineyard, and Nantucket.[79]

One small gauge of the ongoing vitality of the post–King Philip's War missionary enterprise is the Indian-language publications produced in this time period. Prior to 1675, a total of sixteen books, pamphlets, and tracts were translated into local dialects by John Eliot, Thomas Mayhew, and Abraham Pierson, and then printed and circulated to the various Massachusett, Nipmuc, Penobscot, and Wampanoag communities throughout New England. Between 1676 and 1721, however, more than twenty-one items were published, twelve of which appeared between 1700 and 1721. Some of these items were reprints or second and third editions of material previously put into print—Eliot's Bible, the Psalms, and Lewis Bayly's *The Practice of Piety*. But as many as thirteen of the twenty-one postwar publications were entirely new translations, and some had been composed by individuals with the explicit intention of evangelizing Natives. In 1698 a series of sermons by Boston minister Increase Mather was translated by Samuel Danforth and published as "Masunkkenukeep Matcheseaenvog Wequuetook kah Wuttooanatoog. . . .; Greatest Sinners called and encouraged to come to Christ, and that Now, quickly." In 1700, a treatise for Indians composed by Cotton Mather was translated, published, and circulated: "Wussukwhonk En Christianeue asuh peantamwae Indianog . . .; An Epistle to the Christian [or praying] Indians, Giving them a Short Account, of what the English Desire them to Know and Do, in order to their Happiness."[80] As measured by Indian-language publications, then, King Philip's War did not slow down the missionary project. Neither, in fact, did Eliot's death in 1690, since by that time the NEC employed at least three additional missionary-translators: Samuel Danforth, Grindal Rawson, and Experience Mayhew.[81]

Early Eighteenth-Century New England

King Philip's War did, however, set into motion a long-term shift in the broader dynamics of Indian-colonist relations in southeastern New England, although these changes unfolded slowly in some areas. Having essentially solved the "Indian problem" in their immediate midst, the New England colonies were free to expand and grow, which they did. New London, Connecticut, with its ample harbor, by the early eighteenth century was quickly becoming a center for international trade, joining Boston and Newport in allowing New England as a whole to stand as a minor outpost of growing importance within the larger British empire that sprawled throughout the Atlantic world. Towering ships bulging with wares made frequent stops at New England's ports en route to and from London, Scotland, Ireland, Spain, France, Portugal, Holland, the Canaries, Barbados, Nevis, St. Christopher, and Jamaica, in addition to North American destinations such as Newfoundland, New York City, Virginia, and Maryland. By 1730, Connecticut alone boasted 38,000 Euroamerican inhabitants "of both sexes and all ages" and approximately 1,500–2,000 Native Americans, in addition to the "700 Indian and negro slaves" serving in households across the state.[82]

Religiously, New England was solidly Protestant, reformed (Calvinistic), and mostly Congregational in polity through most of the colonial period, although over time a relative Christian religious diversity formed a vibrant undercurrent in the form of Presbyterians, Anglicans, Quakers, Free-Will Baptists, Rogerenes, Moravians, unitarians, universalists, Free-Thinkers, Deists, and—eventually— Jews and Catholics. Rhode Island quickly developed a reputation in the seventeenth century as the most religiously tolerant colony in the northeast and accordingly attracted a wide diversity of Quakers, Baptists of various stripes, Jews, Congregationalists, and Anglicans. The eastern portion of Long Island, on the other hand, was largely Presbyterian, despite the fact that it was initially settled by New Englanders.[83] In spite of the water separating the two regions, the eastern end of Long Island was culturally more part of southern New England than it was New York and remained a strong point of cultural, religious, and kinship connection for Indians and English alike.[84] Connecticut and New Haven (a separate colony until 1662) were settled by Congregationalists from Massachusetts, although the tenor of early eighteenth-century Connecticut Congregationalism tangibly demonstrated the increasingly blurred line between Congregationalists (who historically favored congregational autonomy) and Presbyterians (who favored regional and structural oversight of local congregations). The Saybrook Platform, adopted by Congregational churches in Connecticut in 1708, gave a nod toward Presbyterian polity by creating "consociations" of regional oversight and ministerial associations.[85] Central and western Massachusetts were often in line with ecclesiastical and social development in Connecticut, primarily due to the ease of travel and trade along the Connecticut River, where key families dominated local social and ecclesiastical happenings.[86]

As a result of disease, warfare, and the immensely one-sided process of colonization, by the end of the seventeenth century Indian communities that were politically independent prior to colonization experienced a slow erosion of their political autonomy and geographical influence even as they retained to a surprising degree their cultural vitality.[87] But Indians persisted. All across New England, Natives continued to live together on reserves of land that allowed them to simultaneously practice older patterns of traditional medicine, small-scale agriculture, hunting, and fishing, and to maintain regional networks of kinship, all while simultaneously taking advantage of labor opportunities and market resources that growing English towns afforded. As land became more scarce, older patterns of hunting and gathering gave way to farming, seafaring, manual and unskilled labor, various trades, the production of baskets, brooms, and spoons, and—perhaps more perniciously—various forms of servitude.[88] In some cases, Indians were forced by economic realities to change their ways of living. In other cases, however, Indians semi-voluntarily adopted European cultural conventions

Table 1.1. **Estimated Indian Populations in Southeastern New England, c. 1725**

Native Community	*Location (nearest English town)*	*Approximate Population*
Connecticut		
Mohegan	South of Norwich	350
Mashantucket	Ledyard	322
Lantern Hill	Stonington	218
Niantic	East Lyme	163
Wangunk	Middletown	32
Tunxis	West of Hartford	30
Weatinock	New Milford	49
Pachgatgoch	Kent	500
Misc. communities at New Haven, Sharon, Potatuck, and Turkey Hill		100
	Connecticut total:	1,700–1,800
Rhode Island		
Narragansett	Charlestown	400–500
Block Island	Block Island	30
	Rhode Island total:	450–550
Long Island		
Montauk	Easthampton	100
Shinnecock	Southampton	100
Misc. Indian communities on central and eastern Long Island		200
	Long Island total:	400

of dress, language, and even habitation. Although for centuries Indians of New England had lived in various versions of tentlike structures made of animal skins and wood, by the eighteenth century some Natives started to build English-style houses. Such developments were irregular, however, and the precise moment of these changes among specific communities is still uncertain. Well into the 1730s, Mohegan Indians—even leading Indian families—were still living in wigwams. As seasonal patterns of migration became impossible over time, permanent English-style houses became more attractive, not only as a way to more securely mark one's land, but also for more durable protection against temperature changes and the elements. Such buildings were costly, however. In 1748, a Farmington Indian named Cusk began building a wood frame house, having "a Desire to Live in that forme that the English do," but ran out of money. In order to finish the project, he asked permission from the Connecticut General Assembly to sell one acre of his land, which was granted.[89]

Despite the increasing economic disparity, Indians and Euroamericans continued to live side by side in eighteenth-century New England, with conflicts, tensions, and lawsuits occasionally punctuating the normal rhythms of life.[90] And—like neighbors were prone to do in the eighteenth century—Natives and colonists dragged each other to court for a variety of reasons: nonpayment of debt, violence, threats, theft, and land disputes. Native experiences confusingly vacillated between interactions with local structures of colonial and imperial justice that at times made real efforts toward upholding Native rights regarding land and property, and semi-private interactions with colonists who were set on bilking Indian individuals and families at every turn. Constant bickering about land, fences, and the destruction of crops led to some heavy-handed moves on the part of local towns. Several times between 1720 and 1745 the trustees of Easthampton ordered several men to go to Montauk to kill the Indian dogs that were apparently killing the sheep of colonists (who were, in turn, probably encroaching on Montaukett land).[91]

Additionally, two intertwining difficulties brought on by colonialism continued to plague Native communities: alcoholism and indebtedness. Although Indian men as drunkards was a widespread colonial stereotype, behind the racial tropes lay a lived reality that affected Native leaders and, most often, Native women and children. When Pachgatgoch men came back to the reservation late at night after long days of working and drinking in nearby Kent, Connecticut, Indian women were so afraid of physical violence that they occasionally took refuge with the Moravian missionaries until morning.[92] Over the course of the eighteenth century, most leaders of Native communities—whether Christianized or not—worked to reduce the availability of alcohol on Native lands. Such efforts, even when coordinated with magistrates and legal structures, were an uphill battle, since local colonists had much to gain and little to lose from continuing to sell rum and hard cider to Indians. Alcoholism was often, although not always, related to indebtedness. In the absence of a consistent coinage or paper currency, early Americans largely worked off of a system of credit, nonmonetary exchange, and barter. Native individuals quickly racked up considerable debts to various colonists—farmers, traders, store owners—for items of daily life, European goods, and—inevitably—liquor. In the case of tribal leaders or Natives with access to land, selling land was the quickest way to get out of debt. In situations where there was simply no exchange of goods to satisfy debts and no lands to sell, many local colonists hauled Native individuals into court, where they were sometimes fined even more money, sent to prison, or perhaps even forced to physically work as a servant to pay off a debt. Sometimes, however, colonial governments stepped in. In 1718, the Rhode Island General Assembly passed an act that protected Natives from being sued for reasons of indebtedness. The Assembly justified its decision since it recognized that colonists "out of wicked, covetous and greedy designs, often draw Indians into their debt, and take advantage of their inordinate love of rum, and other strong liquors, by selling the same to them, or otherwise to take advantages, by selling them other goods, at extravagant rates, upon trust, whereby said Indians have been impoverished."[93] Nonetheless, in both cases, Natives worked with colony and local governments to find solutions and protect their communities.

In 1698, the NEC administrators in London who relied upon annual reports from the Boston Commissioners and missionaries for updates wanted a more concrete way of gauging the success of their collective evangelistic efforts. To provide a more accurate tally, the Boston Commissioners sent Grindal Rawson and Samuel Danforth on a month-long visitation throughout Massachusetts to take an informal survey of the presence and spiritual vitality of American Indian communities. Their report was surprisingly positive. All across Eastern Massachusetts, including Cape Cod and Martha's Vineyard, Rawson and Danforth reported many Indian ministers and "rulers" or elders, Native schoolmasters and teachers, and more than thirty indigenous congregations ranging from 3 to 120 participants subsisting within larger clusters of Indian towns. Schools and churches operated side by side in many towns, mostly run by Natives. At Nukkehkummees, near Dartmouth, Massachusetts, the Indian minister William Simons reported "forty communicants" drawn from surrounding Indian towns. Simons preached twice each Sunday to a congregation of 120 adults and children, and the children—most of whom could read—attended the school during the week.[94]

Strikingly absent from Rawson and Danforth's 1698 report were the geographic regions comprising southeastern Connecticut, Rhode Island, and Long Island. Rawson and Danforth were not sent there because the NEC already knew how many Christian Indian congregations existed in that area: zero. In part because of the vibrant cultural practices and kinship networks in southeastern New England—despite the real pressures of land loss and wider cultural changes—these Native groups showed little interest in the evangelistic overtures of English colonists through the opening decades of the eighteenth century. The Mohegans remained unimpressed with Fitch's rainmaking. Perhaps in part because of this 1698 report, however, previously unevangelized Native communities in Connecticut, Rhode Island, and Long Island began to occupy the sporadic attention of colonial officials and agents for missionary societies, which sparked a renewed evangelistic effort that over time dramatically refashioned Indian-Euroamerican relations in the following century.

2

Evangelizing

The sachem's son seemed bewitched. Observers noted that the eight-year-old Niantic youth had been "in a very Strange Condition" for four days, biting his tongue and writhing about, making it difficult for those attending him to hold him down. The problems had started months earlier, when the Niantic sachem Mahomet II brought his son to Mohegan in 1733 to the house of the English missionary and schoolteacher, John Mason, "to be instructed in Reading." The Niantic youth ran off with some Mohegan friends and was soon taken back to Niantic by the boy's mother, who was apparently estranged from her husband. Mahomet II's son later showed up at Mohegan again, this time brought by Ben Uncas III, the Mohegan sachem's son, who had found the Niantic boy in New London and decided to bring him again to Mason. A few days later, Mahomet II's son participated in a "Dance" at Mohegan, immediately after which he became gravely ill and began acting strangely. A Niantic shaman who was present convinced the boy's grandmother that the youth was under a spell and, at the grandmother's request, performed a series of rituals to relieve him from it. Going to the sick child, the shaman removed the boy's outer garments and "pulled out of the Belly [of the youth] a leather string, about 3 Inches long, in which there was tied some Hair." Believing there was more of the same still in the youth (and partially to convince some of his skeptical onlookers), the shaman "pulled out another out of the small of his Back near as long as a Man's Finger, which also had some Hair, and a Wampampeag [Wampum, or a carved shell bead] tied to the middle, and there was Several knots tied in the string." Then things got out of control, and quickly. The flesh surrounding where the string, hair, and beads had been pulled "Quivered much," and the strings of leather themselves "moved about" without any visible human agency. Within a matter of minutes, the child died, and the shaman "was immediately taken with great Trembling," got deathly ill, and those around him were unable to find a cure. Disturbed, Mahomet II, who had been out hunting, and the boy's grandmother went to see John Mason. Both were "amazed" and pondered the possible source of such bewitchment. The grandmother, however, was more bluntly suspicious: she "wondered the child should Die in Such a Manner so soon after it was put to school."[1]

This grand internal struggle over cultural accommodation with English colonists opens a window onto the processes of religious engagement that were beginning to take place among Native communities in southeastern New England in the 1730s. Although over the course of the seventeenth century many Indian communities in Massachusetts had adopted Christian religious practices and gathered into praying towns with viable Christian churches, in Connecticut the story was different, largely due to the creative efforts of the "first" Uncas, the seventeenth-century Mohegan sachem, who ensured, according to contemporary observers, that the Mohegans remained "averse to entertain Christian religion."[2] This religious intransigence persisted, so the story goes, until the Great Awakening of the 1730s and 1740s, when suddenly the Mohegans— along with most other previously un-Christianized communities in southern New England—joined English churches in large numbers.

This vignette illustrates, however, that engagement with Christian ideas and practices by unevangelized Native communities in Connecticut, Rhode Island, western Massachusetts, and on Long Island began earlier, lasted longer, and was far more interesting than a narrative of sudden conversion can adequately explain. Even something as seemingly innocuous as receiving basic education in the English language was contested within Native communities in the opening decades of the eighteenth century. Mahomet II's son was caught between his mother and grandmother—both of whom resented the educational intrusion—and his father and Mohegan playmates, like Ben Uncas III, who thought it worthwhile to make distinct accommodations with the English colonists in the hopes of improving their own situation. In this particular instance, the results were inexplicably tragic—despite the powerful recourse to traditional remedies and practices—and the grandmother laid the full blame at the feet of the colonizers.

This particular encounter was hardly unique. The first four decades of the eighteenth century were marked by a slowly unfolding series of exposures to Christianity that involved both a renewed emphasis by the English on evangelizing Indian communities and an active seeking out of education by these same Natives, often resulting in dissension and disagreements in families and communities. By the 1720s, things had shifted in Native communities that made education for their children an attractive option for some families, opportunities that were almost always sweetened by the material benefits and potential political alliances that education, schoolteachers, and sponsoring societies brought. Such religious and cultural decisions were embedded within a larger lived reality of cultural engagement, adaptation, and accommodation that included ideas about labor, land dispossession, kinship, and strategies for survival.

Renewed Evangelistic Attempts

The opening decades of the eighteenth century were a time of momentous change for Native communities in Connecticut, Rhode Island, and Long Island. In many ways, Indians occupied an increasingly difficult cultural position: they were generally poor, illiterate, and of a lower social class, and yet they held a disproportionate amount of land population-wise, aroused the occasional fear of local colonists, and garnered the constant attention of colonial officials. Colonists tended to have two completely contradictory ideas about their Indian neighbors. On the one hand, they were increasingly seen as a social menace, drunkards, and generally lazy. On the other hand, many Indian communities were still respected for their skillful knowledge of the land, their ability to hunt for days in the forest with few provisions, and—most important—their ability to fight effectively in times of war. In August 1712, for example, Connecticut governor Gordon Saltonstall ordered a scouting party of fifteen men, "half of which" he desired to be Mohegan Indians, to investigate "some sculking Indians" near the towns of Colchester and Lebanon.[3] In short, Indians were both loathed and needed, disrespected and feared.

It was under these circumstances that missionary societies and governments made a renewed and sustained attempt in the early eighteenth century to Anglicize, civilize, and convert to Christianity the Natives within their colony boundaries. The benefits of such deep cultural changes were widely touted. Christian Indians would be loyal, honest, hardworking, sober, and—perhaps most telling—submissive, all of which would make them better neighbors, laborers, and servants. A surprisingly large network of ministers, magistrates, and metropolitans in New and Old England, for a variety of humanitarian, religious, and political reasons, devoted large amounts of time and resources to evangelizing New England's indigenous peoples. Such renewed attention prompted suspicion among Indians in some locales, however. When Massachusetts and the New England Company (NEC) suddenly provided for the Mohicans in the western portion of the colony in the mid-1730s a minister, schoolteacher, and a newly established Indian town, one of the sachems, Umpachenee, said he "wonder'd they had been neglected so long, and desir'd to know the true Spring of the great Favour, so suddenly shown them."[4] At the heart of such suspicions were usually legitimate concerns about the potential loss of land involved when English ministers and settlers showed up.

This early eighteenth-century renewal of Indian evangelization in Connecticut, Rhode Island, Long Island, and western Massachusetts took place on a stage that was both intensely local and surprisingly international. At the broadest level, the late seventeenth century and early eighteenth century marked a period during which New Englanders began to look in a more sustained way at the possibility of expanding territorial control and cultural influence beyond the peripheries of English settlement. This was in part, perhaps, a luxury afforded by the defeat of the Narragansetts, Wampanoags, and their allies in King Philip's War. It was also prompted by the various military campaigns against the French and their Indian allies in King William's War (1690–1697) and Queen Anne's War (1702–1714). One distinct element of securing allies, increasing territorial reach, and promoting ever-expansive avenues of trade was to evangelize politically and militarily powerful Native groups in northeastern Massachusetts (present-day Maine), western Massachusetts, and New York. In a lengthy report by the Lords of Trade on the British colonies in North America in 1696, the evangelization of the Haudenosaunee, or the Five (later Six) Nations of the Iroquois Confederacy, in particular was listed—using NEC funds—as an activity "of the greatest importance" in securing alliances with the Iroquois and allowing the English to gain the upper hand over the French in the region.[5]

Motivation for renewed interest in Indian evangelism was also prodded along by religious competition in the form of an Anglican missionary society to the west in New York and the ongoing presence of Catholic priests to the north and northeast. Indian warriors in French Canada especially were notoriously believed to be under the direction and influence of Catholic missionaries; occasional frontier raids like the one on Deerfield, Massachusetts, in 1704 only strengthened this conviction.[6] When the French Jesuit priest Sebastian Rale began having moderate successes among the Wabanakis along the Kennebec River in southern Maine starting in 1694, Massachusetts officials tried over time to outperform him by sending their own missionaries to the region and engaging in public debate with him regarding the "errors" of Catholicism. The intensely political nature of Joseph Baxter's mission—Baxter agreed to serve as a missionary in 1717 for £150—was hard to miss. In August 1717, Massachusetts governor Samuel Shute accompanied Baxter and some NEC commissioners to Arrowsic Island at the mouth of the Kennebec River to first sign a treaty with the Wabanakis and then to introduce Baxter as their minister. When Baxter proved ineffective as a missionary and an insufficient counter to Rale, the Presbyterian minister James Woodside took his place. He was dismissed in 1720 in part because, as the prominent Boston judge and NEC commissioner Samuel Sewall reported, the Indians were "in such ferment about their Lands, lest the English should entirely engross them."[7] When the Wabanakis began demanding greater land rights from the English, seemingly at Rale's instigation, Massachusetts troops stationed nearby raided Rale's mission village of Norridgewock in a failed attempt to seize him. In retaliation, Wabanaki Indians began raiding English towns, occasionally with the company of Rale. Irate, Massachusetts governor William Dummer sent 208 soldiers to Norridgewock in 1724 where they decimated the Catholic missionary village and killed Father Rale.[8]

Similarly, in New York, the NEC and New England colonial governments tried to minimize French territorial control and trade influence while outpacing the efforts of Jesuit priests and Catholic ministers and—after 1701—the presence of Anglican missionaries. To this end, the NEC (with encouragement from the bishop of London and magistrates from New York and Massachusetts) sponsored several missionaries in New York with an eye toward exerting influence over the Haudenosaunees west of Albany. As early as 1693 the NEC engaged Godfrey Dellius, a Dutch Reformed minister residing in Albany, New York, paying him £40 per year to evangelize the surrounding Native groups, including the Mohawks. Despite the annoying presence of a French Jesuit named Millet, Dellius reported that he had translated half a dozen Psalms and the Ten Commandments into the Mohawk language.[9] His dismissal in 1698 (for secretly securing a land grant from the Natives) caused the bishop of London to lament to the Council of Trade and Plantations in 1700 that Dellius was the "only man that understood how to converse with the Mohocks."[10] Undeterred, the NEC soon funded additional ministers, including Daniel Bondet in 1698 and John Lydius of Albany and Bernard Freeman of Schenectady in 1700.[11]

One additional point of motivation for the NEC, however, came from a source closer to home, namely, the creation of the Society for the Propagation of the Gospel in Foreign Parts (SPG) in 1701. The SPG was simultaneously the NEC's twin and its foil. Founded by the Anglican Thomas Bray, it too was created by an act of Parliament but operated as an unofficial organization of the Church of England with the strong and ongoing support of the archbishop of Canterbury and the fund-raising networks of the Church of England at its disposal. The SPG grew out of an earlier society formed by Bray in 1698, the Society for the Propagation of Christian Knowledge (SPCK), which had as its mission the religious education and uplift of Anglicans in the British Isles and broader British empire (including the American colonies, the Caribbean, and even India).[12] The SPG's mission was much broader than that of the NEC, however, for part of its aim was the return of Dissenters and, in the New England context, Congregationalists, back into the Anglican fold, something it attempted with relatively little success. The SPG did, however, from the very beginning fund and send missionaries to parts of New York and specifically to Native nations there—territory many New England Congregationalists found irksomely close to their own.

More generally, however, some rather internationally minded ministers were aware—painfully so—that other European empires touted far greater successes among indigenous populations in the New World. Boston minister Increase Mather expressed hope to Massachusetts magistrates in 1693 that the French efforts "to proselyte the heathen unto popish idolatry, may not exceed our endeavours to engage them unto the evangelical worship of our Lord Jesus Christ."[13]

"The Spaniards, have done a great deal to bring the Indians in Peru and Mexico to their Religion," Solomon Stoddard lamented in 1723, "And the Portugueze, to bring the Indians in Brazil, and the Indies, to theirs. And the French, are diligent in Canada, and elsewhere, to gospellize them. And do we sit still, without any hearty Endeavours for the Salvation of the Heathen among us?"[14] Similarly, Cotton Mather saw New England's evangelization project on the far-larger stage of an emerging Protestant missionary impulse that had at its root an anti-Catholic motivation with a focus on non-Christian groups around the globe.[15] Mather corresponded regularly with August Hermann Francke, a well-known Pietist minister and professor at the University of Halle, and watched with great interest as Bartholomew Ziegenbalg and Heinrich Pitschau were sent from Halle to the Danish colony of Tranquebar in India in 1706.[16] Mather also expressed a strong desire "to learn the Spanish Language" in order to "transmitt Catechisms, and Confessions, and other vehicles of the Protestant-Religion, into the Spanish Indies," a goal he later accomplished. Mather's evangelistic zeal was usually intertwined with imperial aspirations, for in this same journal entry he explicitly connected his bilingual evangelism with "taking Possession of those [Spanish] Countreyes."[17]

With regard to the Native nations in southeastern New England, most of the renewed evangelistic impetus seems to have come from those outside Rhode Island and Connecticut, primarily from Boston and London, and—not surprisingly—from individuals intimately related to the New England Company. Accordingly, on September 30, 1706, even as Connecticut governor Fitz-John Winthrop and the Connecticut magistrates were nursing their wounded pride over the Crown's rebuke in the 1705 Mohegan land hearings (in which the queen of England demanded that the colony of Connecticut return land to the Mohegans), Increase Mather, Samuel Sewall, Cotton Mather, and other NEC commissioners in Boston added insult to injury by writing to Governor Winthrop, chastising him for the "body of Indians within the very bowels of your Colony, who to this day ly perishing in horrid ignorance and wickedness, devoted vassals of Satan, unhappy strangers to the only Saviour." The commissioners encouraged the Connecticut magistrates to "renew" their attempts, and promised to provide any necessary financial support.[18]

Mather and the NEC broached the topic of Indian evangelism to colonial officials repeatedly from 1700 to 1725.[19] The efforts of the NEC commissioners extended beyond the bounds of New England proper, across the Long Island Sound into New York. In 1713, Mather suggested to New York governor Robert Hunter that the Long Island Indians should be instructed in Christianity, and four years later, in 1717, Mather wrote a letter to the various ministers on Long Island, encouraging them "to do their best for Christianising the Pagan Indians there, whose children are now generally in English families."[20] Despite these efforts, soon after the formation of the Long Island Presbytery in 1716, the Congregationalist NEC seemed to be less interested in sending missionaries to that region.[21]

One of the more creative plans the NEC proposed was to use literate, Christian Indians to evangelize other Indians. In March 1702, Mather put together such a plan to reach the "Salvages in the eastern Parts of the Countrey" (i.e., Maine), but when his plan was actually enacted a few years later, the Indian missionary was sent west, not east. In November 1705, Japeth, a Christian Wampanoag minister at Christiantown on Martha's Vineyard, was requested by the commissioners of the NEC to visit the Narragansett, Pequot, and Mohegan Indians "and reside a convenient while among them."[22] No concrete outcome of Japeth's tenure in Connecticut and Rhode Island was reported.

Building on this somewhat inconclusive missionary experiment, in 1713 and 1714 the NEC commissioners sent their star English missionary from Martha's Vineyard, Experience Mayhew, on two separate evangelistic journeys among the un-Christianized Natives in Rhode Island and Connecticut in an attempt to gauge their spiritual receptivity. For both journeys, Mayhew sailed the twenty miles west from Martha's Vineyard to Rhode Island and wound his way seventy or so miles westward to Lyme, Connecticut, and back home again. Such a trip was surprisingly effective in terms of coverage, for along the way Mayhew was able to visit at every major unevangelized Native community in eastern Connecticut and Rhode Island: the Narragansetts, Lantern Hill Pequots, Mashantucket Pequots, Mohegans, and Niantics. At each of these locations, Mayhew conversed with local colonial religious and political leaders, inquiring about any existing evangelistic efforts. He also met with any and all Indians from each community who would come hear him, leaning heavily on several interpreters. Unsurprisingly, Indian reception was tepid at best. When Mayhew pressed Ninigret, sachem of the Narragansetts, to "consent that this people should hear me open the mysteries of Religion to them," Ninigret retorted that Mayhew should "make the English good in the first place: for he said many of them were still bad." Even Mayhew's own Christian Wampanoags from Martha's Vineyard, according to Ninigret, were resented in Rhode Island for theft. At a joint meeting of the Eastern and Mashantucket Pequots, Mayhew preached a long sermon on the basic tenets of Protestant Christianity and especially "asserted & proved the being of one great God that made the world," but the Pequots "tho't the mention of that unnecessary, because they said they knew that as well as I."[23]

One year later, on his follow-up trip in 1714, after Mayhew preached for an hour and a half to the assembled Mohegan Indian sachem's council, he found that Ben Uncas I and the other councillors did not deny "the truth of Religion" in general but rather the "necessity of it": "Some of them said they did Acknowledge that there was a God and did worship him, but as several nations had their distinct way of worship, so they had theirs; and they Thought their way was Good, and that they had no reason to alter it."[24] Later on the same trip, as he passed through Stonington, Mayhew held a Monday meeting with fifty local Pequots, with some eminent men of the town in attendance. After a two-hour sermon, an elderly Indian man got up and, after first trying to discourage the Indians present from listening to Mayhew, admitted that he did not disbelieve all of it: "I own, said the old man, that there is a God, and I pray to him in my way, having by the English learned something of him."[25]

One source of this basic indifference to Mayhew's message was the recent and ongoing controversies over land. During the 1714 trip, the Mohegans told him outright "they could not see that men were ever the better for being Christians, for the English that were Christians would cheat the Indians of their Land and otherwise wrong them."[26] Among the Pequots, especially, Mayhew reported after the same trip that some recent dispossessions—in this case, a prime section of coastal land called Noank—and the ensuing court cases "proved a very unhappie obstruction in my way, and produced in the Indians a greater aversation to the English and their Religion than otherwise they would have had."[27] In one respect, however, Mayhew reported a glimmer of hope. In almost every Indian community, he found Natives who desired to learn how to read and write, and who said they would allow a Christian minister in their communities to teach them these skills. These two important factors—one negative (land), and one positive (education)—definitively shaped English missionary approaches to Connecticut and Rhode Island Indians in the twenty-five years prior to the Great Awakening. In an attempt to convert these Indian communities, missionaries worked to undo the bitterness of land injustices and pursue their one possible inroad: the education of Native children.

The efforts of Mather, Sewall, NEC commissioners, and local ministers—along with political developments north and west of New England and the activity of the Anglican SPG—eventually began to shape local legislation. In October 1717, the General Assembly of Connecticut passed an "Act to promote Civilization and Christianity among the Indians."[28] In it, they decided that "drunkenness and idleness may well be looked upon as among the strongest chains that hold them fast, in their ignorance of and prejudices against the religion of the gospel," and passed several laws targeting each vice. To reduce drunkenness, the General Assembly levied a fine of 20 shillings on those "convicted of selling any Indian strong drink." Dealing with idleness, however, was more difficult and required a more totalizing "reformation." The General Assembly recommended that the Indians be "by easy and agreeable methods, brought off from their pagan manner of living, and encouraged to make settlements in convenient places, in villages after the English manner." Each family who agreed to gather in a town settlement would be given "suitable portions of land" that "should descend from the father to his children, the more to encourage them to apply themselves to husbandry and good diligence therein." Two judges of the Superior Court were charged with the responsibility of identifying a suitable tract of land (New London was recommended, most likely near the Mohegan territory) and "forming a village of the said Indians there, and bringing them to such civil order, cohabitation and industry, as may facilitate the setting up of the gospel ministry among them."[29] No outcome of this very Eliot-esque praying town experiment in Connecticut was recorded, and it was likely never enacted.

This 1717 act also indicates that colonial officials were finally beginning to recognize the insurmountable offense that simultaneous land dispossession and evangelism posed for most Indians. One of the proposed measures in the act was aimed at securing and preserving Native lands, since to "have their Tillage preserved from Tresspasses is the Liklyest way to put them into circumstances in which they may more Easily be prevailed with, as to the great design which is proposed of perswading them to receive the Gospell."[30] In time, even the usually optimistic Boston commissioners for the New England Company caught on. On September 9, 1720, Samuel Sewall wrote to NEC president Robert Ashurst that "for the present there seems to be no way left open for the Word of God to have a free course among them; the Indians are in such a ferment about their lands, lest the English should entirely engross them. 'Till their Spirits are calm'd respecting this momentous affair; there is no likelyhood that any successfull offer of the Gospel of Peace can be made unto them."[31] A decade and a half later, however, progress on this front was still slow. In 1734, George Griswold, minister of the church in Lyme, complained to the Connecticut General Assembly that the Niantic Indians there "seem to be prejudiced against receiving the gospel, upon the account of some wrong done to them by the English, as is supposed by said Indians," to which the assembly responded by assigning a committee to "inquire into the wrongs complained of by said Indians," but, most important, to "take all prudent care that the said Indians be quieted in their just rights to their lands."[32] From the Natives' perspective, contestation over land and ideas about religion were inextricably connected, even more so because the religion of the swindlers and the religion of the evangelists were one and the same.

Indians Desiring Instruction

Despite this flurry of activity, however, renewed evangelistic attempts would have likely come to nothing had not Native groups shown an active interest in education. By the 1720s, various Indian communities across southern New England were beginning to see advantages to literacy and wider selective English cultural appropriation in the service of their own communities. Education and religious instruction, then, were not just merely imposed from the outside. Indian communities actively sought out ministers and teachers, recognizing within English literacy and religious instruction a means of empowerment, although such decisions were often contested from within each Indian community, as illustrated by the contestation over the education of Mahomet II's son.

Starting in the 1720s, Native communities slowly began inviting Anglo-American ministers and missionaries to reside on their lands. In Connecticut, the Mohegans requested English instruction in the early 1720s. In May 1723, the General Court approved John Mason to live on the Mohegan reserved lands and to take "care of the said Indians, to protect them from wrongs, to set up a school among them and acquaint them in the Christian religion." Although the details of Mason's early educational efforts at Mohegan are unclear, from very early on they garnered intertribal interest and attendance. Within two years, for example, on July 1725, seven Mohegan and one Niantic tribal leaders gave mini-speeches of gratitude that John Mason recorded and passed along to the NEC commissioners. Every single speech (some only a few sentences long) specifically thanked either John Mason or the "gentlemen in England" for the care taken in the education of their children. Cauchegon, for example, said he "thanks all the English Gentlemen both in old England and New that Such Care is taken to Instruct Their Children and hope there will be Care taken for ye and for them." Similarly, the new Mohegan sachem Ben Uncas II stated that he was thankful that "Capt Mason takes Such Care of them for to Instruct them." These educational efforts among the Mohegans also spilled over into other communities, primarily through existing kinship networks. Amauhzeen, the sole Niantic representative, said in his speech that "altho he doth not Live att mohegan yet his Children and grand-Children do and Leaves them with Capt Mason to Instruct them."[33]

As a result, Mason happily reported to Governor Joseph Talcott in 1725 that "the Mohegans have Manniefested their desire that their Children may be instructed in the Christian faith," and in 1726 he made a formal proposal to the NEC commissioners of needed items to run a more official school.[34] For the first few years, Mason taught his Indian pupils "in his own hut," but in 1727 a schoolhouse was built and Mason moved in as the schoolmaster. The building measured twenty-one by sixteen feet and had been erected by the colony at a cost of £60. Within a year, however, Mohegan girls became jealous of the educational opportunities offered to their siblings and relatives. "The Females begin to think it hard that They are not taught," Adam Winthrop reported to the NEC, "so that some girls are likely to be received in Short time."[35] Mason was so successful—and the NEC so desperate for missionaries—that although his early annual salary was £15, by 1728 he had successfully demanded an impressive £100 each year for his services.

Mason, the Connecticut magistrates, and the NEC designed the school at Mohegan to accomplish the dual goals of educating and civilizing. In part, providing food, clothing, and housing for each Indian student was a way to convince parents to send their children away for weeks at a time. The budget that Mason submitted in 1726 reveals just how this school attracted students. First—and likely most important—he requested lots of blankets for the sachems and councillors of the Mohegans, Pequots, and Niantics: stroud blankets (high quality) for the three sachems and ordinary blankets for others. Mason also requested separate line items for clothing and food for the Indian students, along with funds for the "boarding of 8 of 'em removed from their parents for 1 year."[36] In fact, Mason's school functioned as a small-scale regional boarding school; by the late 1720s, Mason boasted a dozen Mohegan boys with seven or eight Pequot and Niantic children expected to arrive later that year.[37] In 1733 the NEC decided there was room for a second missionary at Mohegan and accordingly hired Jonathan Barber for £100 per year to live near and preach to the Mohegans.[38] Even the help of other Christianized Indians was once again solicited. In 1732, at Mason's suggestion, Thomas Pegun, a Christian Indian from Natick, Massachusetts, was sent to the Mohegans "to introduce among them family worship and the observation of the Lord's Day."[39]

At the same time the Mohegans were entertaining Mason and Barber on their lands, the Narragansetts were similarly pursuing Euroamerican instruction and religious influence. In 1727 the General Assembly of Rhode Island—at the request of the Narragansett sachem Charles Augustus Ninigret—carved out twenty acres of Narragansett land in Westerly "for the erecting thereon a house for worship, according to the form of the church of England."[40] The Anglican minister Ninigret had in mind was the Irish-born Scottish Presbyterian turned SPG missionary/minister James McSparran, who in 1721 had been sent to the "Narragansett territory" in Rhode Island—which in the 1720s referred to basically all of southern Rhode Island—with instructions to minister to both colonists and the four hundred Indians in the area.[41] McSparran served at a small church building, called St. Paul's, in North Kingstown, which had been erected in 1707 and ministered to a mostly Anglican community of colonists.[42] Ninigret over time came to appreciate the presence of McSparran in the vicinity, which led to the grant of twenty acres, twenty-five miles west of St. Paul's, on Narragansett Indian land. A small, wooden church was built on the property, situated north of the "post-road," approximately half a mile from Ninigret's house. A small number of Narragansetts attended this Anglican outpost church for much of McSparran's thirty-seven-year tenure at St. Paul's (1721–1757), which undoubtedly made Congregationalist ministers in neighboring Connecticut more than a little jealous, considering their prior (although limited) efforts among the Narragansetts and their general dislike of Anglicanism.[43]

In part to directly compete with what was perceived to be an unwanted Anglican intrusion, local residents in Westerly petitioned the Boston commissioners of the New England Company for a minister to the Narragansett and English populations. The commissioners recruited Joseph Park, who in 1733 consented to serve for five years to both local white colonists and any Indians who would attend.[44] In 1734 a multipurpose meetinghouse was built in Westerly, on the land of Colonel Joseph Stanton, five miles from the Anglican Indian church. Half of the Westerly meetinghouse was reserved for the Indians and the school Park operated for them, all funded by the NEC. Park facilitated the education of Narragansett children in a variety of ways, including sending some to local English schools, teaching them in the meetinghouse, and instructing a few in his own home.[45] Over time, some Narragansetts and Eastern Niantics found Park's church—operating in direct competition with McSparran's—the more appealing option, and on May 5, 1742, during the Great Awakening, a church society was officially formed at the Westerly meetinghouse, with Park ordained minister over it three months later.[46]

By 1734, almost all of the major remaining unevangelized Native communities in southern New England had requested education in some form. On November 5, 1734, NEC treasurer Adam Winthrop wrote an effusive letter to Joseph Williams in London, updating him on all the various efforts of the NEC. The year before, two missionary ministers—Park and Barber—had settled among the Narragansetts and Mohegans. "This year," Winthrop reported, the Housatonic Indians in western Massachusetts "have signified their desire of being taught to read, and to receive the Christian Religion." A similar request had come from the Pequots in Connecticut "who are likewise willing to receive instruction, & the English Inhabitants are willing to set apart a considerable share in their meeting-house to the use of the Indians." The Pequots requested a school to be set up among them, and one was also planned for the Niantics. Moreover, the "Indians also at Hartford & Farmington in Connecticut express an inclination to be taught to read, and to be instructed in the principles of Religion towards which they never had till lately the least disposition."[47] A similar request for an English minister came from colonists on Block Island just off the coast of Rhode Island, who promised that, should a minister be sent, they would set aside some room "for the accommodation of the Indians there."[48] In response to this surge in Native interest, the NEC commissioners and local officials rushed to employ nearby ministers to provide instruction and sermons to these Indian communities—or, as was the case in some locales, to increase the level of instruction already offered. The Reverend Samuel Whitman intensified his efforts among the Tunxis in Farmington; Richard Treat taught the Wangunks in Middletown; Joseph Mayhew, a recent Harvard College graduate, was sent to Block Island and was paid an annual salary of £60; Joseph Park continued his religious instruction of the Narragansetts in Westerly; and John Mason and Jonathan Barber continued on at Mohegan.[49]

Massachusetts ministers and NEC commissioners were especially delighted to discover a new receptiveness to education and Christian instruction by the numerous Mohicans along the Housatonic River in western Massachusetts. One of the chiefs, Kunkapot, informed Ebenezer Williams in the early 1730s that he was "inclin'd to embrace the *Christian* Religion" but had two concerns. First, he was afraid that "if he became a *Christian*, his own people would discard him," and second, he was bothered by the "ill Conversation of *Christians*" which he judged as bad as "if not worse than that of the *Heathen*."[50] Even so, concerns for literacy and education were central to the Mohicans' requests. Kunkapot especially "shew'd himself very desirous of having a *Missionary* sent among them, that their Children might be taught to read."[51] The NEC hired John Sergeant—then a student at Yale—as a missionary and Timothy Woodbridge of Springfield to serve as a schoolmaster for their children and instruct the Indians "in a Catechetical Way."[52] Sergeant's ordination at a large ceremony at Deerfield, Massachusetts, on August 31, 1735, highlighted the imperial importance of his mission. It was placed at the conclusion of a huge regional conference between the Massachusetts government and the most important nearby Native nations. A large number of Mohican and River Indians were present, along with Governor Jonathan Belcher and a "large *Committee*" from Belcher's council and the House of Representatives. The *New England Weekly Journal* covered it as a major news event, sure to interest a large and transatlantic audience.[53]

Sergeant's Stockbridge mission was unusual in that from the beginning a few Natives immediately opted to receive baptism (requests for education rarely translated into baptisms prior to the Awakening in southeastern Connecticut). By late 1735, Sergeant reported having baptized forty individuals, including adults and infants.[54] From the beginning, however, education was a large component of the plans for Stockbridge and, in fact, what Natives hoped to get out of it as well. Woodbridge started the school in early 1735 and by the end of the year had forty students in regular attendance.[55] Sergeant and Woodbridge had the additional financial assistance of Isaac Hollis, a generous benefactor in Old England, who in 1736 gave money to clothe, feed, lodge, and instruct an additional twelve Indian boys.[56] Hollis's students first lived with Sergeant starting in January 1738, but within a year he persuaded most of them to instead be housed in local English households.[57] By 1737 the Massachusetts colony had financed the building of a meetinghouse and a schoolhouse in Stockbridge. The meetinghouse was large—thirty by forty feet—and intended to house both the Indian and nascent English populations.[58]

Stockbridge—when it was officially incorporated as a town in 1736—was essentially a replication of Eliot's praying towns almost a century prior with a few modifications. Native communities agreed to give up vast tracts of prime territory in exchange for a smaller, bounded swath of land on which to build a new, colony-sponsored Christian Indian town. As in the seventeenth century, such transactions must have been viewed as an excellent bargain for the English and a not entirely unfavorable arrangement for some Indians who hoped to gain education, political protection, and an accrued regional prominence through associations with English traders, missionaries, and families. Nonetheless, some Mohicans were incensed by such proposals, fearing that "the English had some ill Design upon them."[59] An arable tract of land ten miles square was eventually agreed upon by the Indians, who—not without some complaints—moved their families, wigwams, and possessions to their new town in May 1736. Even though the exchange was overtly unfair—fifty-two square miles given up for ten square miles—Samuel Hopkins and other English observers thought it a reasonable exchange for the "Favour bestow'd" in the form of education, Christianity, and civilization.[60] Over time, Stockbridge's Indian population grew rapidly, from a few families in 1734 to 218 families in 1749, as additional Mohican families came to settle within its boundaries. The presence of English families—strategically placed among the Mohicans to provide cultural modeling—also ballooned over the course of the eighteenth century, which in later decades led to acrimonious disputes.

From the beginning, Sergeant wanted to educate Indian girls as well as boys. His initial proposals in 1738, however, were rebuffed by the Mohicans themselves. This was perhaps because his education proposals consisted of sending a dozen Indian girls to English households—to be supported on the NEC's dime—in the hopes that they might become acquainted "with the *English* Language and Manners."[61] Sergeant eventually found two parents willing to co-operate, and in the summer of 1738 two Indian girls were sent out. The plan failed, according to Sergeant, "Thro' a childish Fondness for Home," since "they would not be contented to stay long enough where I sent them, to obtain any Good by it."[62] The money was in place, but the Indians were unwilling, in part, perhaps, because the Indian girls were likely treated as servants in the English households to which they were sent.

Similarly, in Connecticut, in response to the professed desire of the Pequots in 1734 for the education of their children, the NEC sprang into action. The New London minister Eliphalet Adams held "frequent lectures" among the Pequots from at least 1735 onward, including them in his occasional itinerant journeys into Indian country.[63] Eliphalet's son, William Adams, also preached to the Mashantuckets starting in 1735 for two years, and around the same time John Morgan served as a schoolteacher at Mashantucket.[64] Some local English churches agreed to cooperate, in part because of the extra money given to the church and minister as a result. As early as October 16, 1734, the North Groton

Congregational Church voted that "the Pequit Indians shall have the Liberty of coming into our meeting house to heare the Gospell preacht."[65] Among the Eastern Pequots, the Reverend Nathaniel Eells of East Stonington and the Reverend Joseph Fish of North Stonington both provided educational support and occasional lectures from the mid-1730s on. By 1738 many Pequot children attended the Stonington school with English children, supported by the NEC, which allowed one shilling per week per child.[66] In the years preceding the Great Awakening, the NEC funded at least nine individuals to provide part-time educational and evangelistic services to the Mashantucket Pequots. During and after the 1740s, it hired as many as sixteen Natives and colonists to do the same.[67]

With such a noticeable surge of interest among Native communities, it is no wonder that in May 1736 the Connecticut General Assembly noted that "of late the Indians have desired to be instructed in the Christian religion" and accordingly mandated that "at the next publick Thanksgiving that shall be appointed in this Colony, there shall be a contribution attended in every ecclesiastical society or parish in this government," to be used for the "civilizing and Christianizing of the Indian natives in the Colony." The General Assembly additionally set aside £15 to be given to Thomas Lee of Lyme and Stephen Prentiss of New London so that they might hire "some suitable person to instruct the said children to read, and also in the principles of the Christian religion."[68] Governor Talcott reported later that same year, "Our School of Indians at Niantik prospers."[69]

In the late 1730s, the presence of yet another missionary society, the Society in Scotland for the Propagation of Christian Knowledge (SSPCK) expanded the proposed scope of evangelization, although—unlike the SPG—the Presbyterian SSPCK provided a welcome opportunity to partner with the New England Company in terms of funding missionaries. The SSPCK seemed especially interested in Native communities along the Delaware, Susquehanna, and Hudson rivers in New Jersey, Pennsylvania, and New York, as well as on Long Island. Such ambitions provoked interest among NEC missionaries, including John Sergeant, who in the early 1740s first talked about and eventually visited the Shawnees in northern Pennsylvania and southern New York.[70] As Sergeant found out, however, the Shawnees exhibited none of the openness to Christianity that the Mohicans had a decade earlier. "The Indians have one Way of honouring and pleasing him [God], and the White People have another; both are acceptable to Him," a Shawnee chief bluntly told Sergeant in 1741.[71] Sergeant reported that the Shawnees had "strong and invincible Prejudices against Christianity" and blamed it on the Senecas in New York, who, he was told, gave the Shawnees their current land and "charg'd them withal never to receive Christianity."[72] From the 1740s through the 1770s, however, the SSPCK would serve as an important source of income and support for schools and churches on or near New England Native lands.

Educational Content

It is understandable that Natives in southeastern New England desired education. After all, they did not have to look far—merely north to Natick or east to Martha's Vineyard—to notice the relative autonomy afforded other Native nations through Native schools, churches, and literacy in general. The irony of such requests for education, however, is that—despite Native desires to the contrary at times—New England educational practices and content had long been based on a thoroughly reformed, Protestant, and Christian curriculum.[73] *The New England Primer*, the basic educational tool used by schools all across New England in the colonial period, was infused with Christian ideas, right from its famed opening line for the letter "A": "In *Adam's* Fall /We sinned all."[74] Even a 1720 edition of the bilingual *Indian Primer*, published in the Massachusetts language (and therefore not entirely serviceable for educators to the Mohegan-Pequot-speaking Indians in Connecticut and Long Island), after giving the basic alphabet, vowel clusters, and syllable breakdown for long words, turned directly to the Lord's Prayer and a lengthy exposition of it.[75] Similarly, the surprisingly large Indian library of the NEC in the 1710s hints at the thrust toward religious education of the society. A February 1708 inventory revealed, among other things, 60 "Indian Catechises," 427 copies of Lewis Bayly's *The Practice of Piety* (1611), 292 copies of Thomas Shepard's *The Sincere Convert*, 265 copies of Mather's sermons on John, 563 copies of *Confession of Faith* (in English and Massachusetts), and 688 copies of Cotton Mather's 1700 treatise titled *An Epistle to the Christian Indians* (also printed in both languages), besides another 1,400 copies of the *Indian Primer* that lay unbound in boxes.[76] Only a few efforts were made to publish tracts in the Mohegan-Pequot language spoken by the Natives in southeastern Connecticut and on Long Island, likely because they themselves could not read it (even though if it was read to them, they might have grasped phonetically the rough meaning). The one major exception to this was a 1721 translation into Mohegan-Pequot of the Lord's Prayer, commissioned by Connecticut governor Gordon Saltonstall.[77]

Consequently, educational success was measured in terms of proficiency in religious literature and Christian ideas, no matter how foreign these were to Indian children. Constant repetition and recitation of religious ideas and phrases—mostly in English—over the course of months and years often made those ideas seem a little less strange. On May 2, 1728, John Mason took seven of his Indian students to the Reverend Eliphalet Adams in New London, and Adams was surprised to hear them read from their "Psalters and some in their Primers." "They can spell very prettily," Adams marveled, "and some of them can read pretty tolerably without spelling." They could also recite "the Lord's Prayer, the Creed and the Ten Commandments very readily," along with portions of John Cotton's 1646 catechism, *Milk for Babes*.[78]

Indian education also included elements in the realm of orality that lie beyond historical recovery. Indian children weren't just taught to read English; they were also taught to read and speak it with a distinctly Euroamerican intonation. When Benjamin Lord, the minister of Norwich, observed some Mohegan school children brought to him by Mason, he reported to the NEC commissioners that "their dropping of the Indian and falling so readily into the English tone and pronunciation to such a wonderful degree of conformity made me think they might quickly become great proficients in the language and manners of the English."[79] The education that Natives embraced, then, was for many colonial leaders a comprehensive, far-reaching way of producing literate, Christianized, and culturally Anglicized Indian men and women.

Educational Strategy: Indian Children

Native interest in education for their children actively shaped colonial strategies for education and evangelization. In a September 1725 letter to NEC treasurer Adam Winthrop, Governor Talcott of Connecticut, encouraged by a warm reception among the Mohegans and Niantics, put in print his recommendations for making the education of children more central to the New England Company's evangelistic efforts. The first step was to gradually wean Indian children from their traditional cultural practices through schools run on Native reserved lands. "I am reddy to think it best to bring them up from their own habits and Customs," Talcott wrote, "& it must be by degrees. If about 20 or 30 of their Children might be kept to School, separate from their parents and under good government, Mixt amongst English Children, it may be best: and then the Indian Girls must allso be taught if it may be by School dames." In smaller Indian communities, where it was not worth the expense of a meetinghouse and a paid Anglo minister, Talcott thought it best to "get all their Children that can be to live with the English, and our Laws will oblidge them to teach them to read."[80]

In May 1727, the General Assembly made more explicit its educational targeting of children by requiring all persons in Connecticut who "hath taken, or shall take, any of the Indian children of this or the neigbouring governments into the care of their families" to "use their utmost endeavour to teach them to read English, and also to instruct them in the principles of the Christian faith by catechizing of them, together with other proper methods." Selectmen and grand jurors in each town were charged to "make diligent inquiry" that Indian children in English homes were thus instructed and given the power to fine negligent masters or mistresses forty shillings, to be given to the local town school.[81] Such an emphasis on civilization was seemingly a direct legacy of the aftermath of King Philip's War. When Edward Randolph was sent to New England in 1676 to assess the causes behind the colonists' conflicts with the local Indians, he was plainly told by some that the war was partially due to an "impudent zeal in the magistrates of Boston to christianize those heathen before they were civilized and enjoining them the strict observation of their laws, which, to a people so rude and licentious, hath proved even intolerable."[82] The lesson had been learned. Evangelization alone was insufficient, and even dangerous. Although civilization had long been part of the NEC evangelization strategy under Eliot, the Mayhews, and John Cotton, Jr., it received greater emphasis in the decades after King Philip's War, particularly with reference to Indian children.

In the decade or so following Talcott's 1725 proposals, letters and reports from NEC officials and local missionaries and ministers indicate that this emphasis on Native children was somewhat successful in producing literate, partially Anglicized Indian youth. The Farmington minister Samuel Whitman, for example, reported in January 1735 that "It is with no small pleasure that I can observe to you that the zeal of our Indians especially of our younger ones after learning & the knowledge of the christian religion still continueth & increaseth." The all-encompassing nature of English education was revealed in ways of measurement that Whitman highlighted: "the little knowledge they have gotten, has a good influence on their morals, & does lay some restraint on the elder ones, who are accustomed to do evil." The program for Indian education in Farmington included the full range of ages. The smaller children (eleven in the summer of 1734) were "kept in school" during the summer, while the older ones—by order of the Connecticut General Assembly—were taken in and cared for by Anglo families during the winter months and sent to the local "public school." According to Whitman, the attendance of the Indian children at school was "steady" and their "proficiency equal to that of the English children."[83]

Although the general task of Indian education proceeded apace, the NEC commissioners usually invested more in a few Indian boys, in the hopes that they would become ministers and educators to their own communities.[84] Perhaps the biggest "success" story of the 1730s in this regard was John Mettawan, a Tunxis youth who, like John Sassamon a century prior and Samson Occom a decade later, demonstrated an exemplary capacity for classical learning and spiritual leadership. Tunxis children since the 1720s had sporadically been allowed to attend local English schools, and it is possible that Mettawan would have done so.[85] Mettawan was approximately eighteen years old when he was identified by the local Farmington Congregational minister, Samuel Whitman, as a potential schoolteacher, if not minister. Whitman took him into his own home for a personalized tutorship, and in May 1733 secured for him "a Homespun Coat, Jacket, and Breeches, two Shirts, Stockings, Shoes and Hat."[86] Mettawan quickly responded to Whitman's care and instruction, and by 1736 Adam Winthrop, the NEC treasurer, reported that Mettawan had been baptized and received as a member into Whitman's Congregational church in Farmington. Of the several Indian youth receiving targeted, individual instruction in the 1730s, Winthrop reported that Mettawan was "very conspicuous not only for his application to his Studies, but also for his religious Disposition."[87]

Mettawan's educational progress during this time was masterfully demonstrated in a neat, handwritten letter in Latin he sent to the NEC commissioners on January 6, 1736:

> To the very distinguished and eminent lords, worthy of all praise and honor, to whom has been committed the task of propagating the Christian faith far and wide among the pagans in these American lands.
>
> Most excellent and eminent lords, I give thanks to God, great and excellent, who called me forth from pagan darkness into the light of the Gospel, and I render thanks to you for the immeasurable and unmerited benefits that you bestowed upon me, an Indian, although I am unknown to you. God, as I hope, will recompense you with most abundant rewards. I wish to fear God and to obey his commands. I honor all my superiors, but I especially bestow my love upon my benefactors. I greatly love good learning, and I love my people and my compatriots and I fervently desire their salvation. I hope, if it pleases God, to be an instrument in accomplishing this.
>
> I am the obedient servant to your honors, and forever obliged to you for many great favors.
>
> John Metauan.
>
> Farmington, the sixth day of January, year of Our Lord 1735/6.[88]

Mettawan's education thrust him into a greater leadership role among the Farmington Indians and, despite his clear association with Christianity, was viewed by the Tunxis in quasi-traditional ways in terms of leadership and knowledge. Whitman reported in January 1737 that Mettawan "is much respected by the Indians & consulted by them as an Oracle in difficult cases."[89] In the summer of 1737, Mettawan took over the education of Farmington Indians from Whitman and organized the construction of an Indian schoolhouse. Although Whitman took much of the credit for this development, the Tunxis built the physical school building themselves, "at their own charge" and "according to the Indian mode."[90] John Mettawan was designated the schoolmaster, and in the first summer and fall, before cold weather forced him to close the

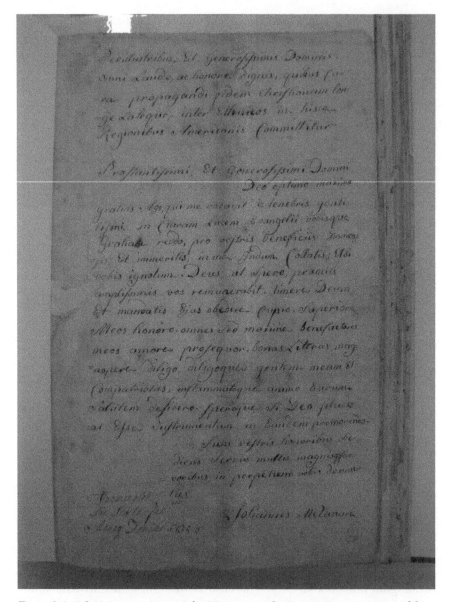

Figure 2.1. John Mettawan Letter. John Mettawan to the Boston Commissioners of the New England Company. Adam Winthrop to Robert Clarke, March 7, 1734, NEC LMA, Ms. 7955/2, 109. Courtesy of the New England Company. Photograph by the author.

school for the winter, he averaged fourteen or so students, for which he received £10. Whitman occasionally dropped by to catechize a few students himself, and he reported to the NEC that Mettawan kept the school "well and faithfully and as good orders in it as in any English School."[91] Mettawan's service continued into at least the early 1740s, giving many colonial officials, missionaries, and ministers hope that, with some more perseverance their efforts just might pay off.[92]

Native Responses and Motivations

Although Indian communities demonstrated an increasing desire for instruction in the English language in the 1720s and 1730s, not all Indians sought out education for the same reasons, even as not all Euroamericans desired to give it for the same reasons. Some Indians undoubtedly sent their children to school—and even sought out education themselves—for rather individual reasons, such as personal curiosity, prior exposure to the world of print and texts through labor in an English household, or other kinds of contact with English neighbors. Perhaps some Indians desired instruction because they saw in it, not unlike some non-Indians, a means of potential social improvement. In many other cases, interest in English education was practical and rooted in the material and political worlds in which they lived. Indian leaders often viewed the presence of an English schoolmaster or missionary on their lands as a means of increasing their own importance within the Native community and even in the region. Where the English missionaries read interest in education as the first step toward Christianity, many Indians—especially leaders—sought such associations with an eye toward the building of alliances and a way to create networks of support and practical aid in a rapidly shifting world. Additionally, Natives quickly learned that offers of education came with a good many material benefits, such as clothing, books, food, and money for building new structures on tribal lands.

Indians in the colonial period were often attracted to education and even European Christianity for practical reasons and were far more focused on the efficaciousness of religious practices than they were with the abstract "truth" of them.[93] European cultural and religious practices could be tried out, adopted, and then discarded if they were deemed irrelevant or incapable of bringing real change to local situations. This is basically what the Mohegans told Experience Mayhew in 1714—that their fathers had tried Christianity fifty years prior but had not found it worth the effort and gave it up. The practical benefits of Christian instruction were, after all, precisely what the colonists increasingly highlighted for Natives. Norwich minister James Fitch, while preaching to the Mohegans in the early 1670s, gave the thirty or so adult Indians who would come listen to him three hundred acres of his own land (and some from the town of Norwich) "and made it sure to them and theirs, so long as they go on in the ways of God."[94] Similarly, when Mayhew was told by the Pequots in 1713 that they, too, had knowledge of God and a sense of right and wrong, Mayhew and a local minister, James Noyes, switched tactics. Instead of asserting the uniqueness of

Christian revelation (which the Pequots said they already had a sufficient version of), they instead focused on the tangible benefits of adopting Christian practices. Noyes, for example, told several stories of "God's hearing and answering Prayers," particularly in times of near-death experiences and in times of severe agricultural duress, when prayers to God brought much-needed rain. Mayhew also chimed in, adding some "remarkable Instances of God hearing the prayers of Christian Indians, who now worship him." Noyes and Mayhew continued, describing in detail "how much better the Indians lived who serve the true God than they [the Pequots] did." Christian Indians "kept coews & oxen & sheep," Mayhew asserted, "and went in good apparel after the manner of the English." After two hours of this spiritual bribery, the Pequots were still noncommittal, although they did voice an openness to learning to read and write.[95]

Colonial governments and missionary societies, too, spent thousands of pounds to ensure that the material benefits of Christian affiliation were tangibly felt by offering "encouragements" like blankets, hats, clothing, and even food and extra money for parents who would permit their children to be instructed.[96] In 1692, John Usher suggested to the NEC that "presentts of Laced Coates Shooes stockins hatts & shirts with a Small Sword and belt" should be given to important Native sachems from the king as tokens of the "justice" they could expect as "his Majestys subjects."[97] Proffered material items often came with strings attached; in the case of John Mettawan, the NEC agreed to fully clothe him "in the English fashion" if he agreed to be "bro't up to Learning and be a Minister." If he did not agree, the offer of clothing was to be rescinded and Mettawan would receive only a large blanket.[98]

Consequently, Natives often became experts at milking the system. Indian individuals and families well understood the practical value of entertaining missionaries and even showing up at local English churches. When Samuel Woodbridge, the minister in Hartford, Connecticut, tried to convince some of the Indians living in the area to attend his church, they told him that if they had proper clothing, they might do so, and said that they were also interested in learning how to read. Woodbridge suspected that the Indians were using him to get new clothing but nonetheless urged the Boston commissioners for the NEC to provide some material encouragement as requested. Accordingly, the NEC sent ten blankets and twenty primers for the Natives "upon their engaging to attend Publick Worship, and to be instructed in reading."[99] Similarly, Samson Occom recalled that as a child in the 1720s he and other youth attended sermons in part to receive the blankets that were passed out.[100]

Even more than tangible goods, however, was the tantalizing suggestion—often implied and at times explicitly stated—that if Indians submitted to instruction and professed Christianity, they would win the sympathy of powerful men who could help them in their ongoing struggle to retain their lands. In 1714, for example, after Mayhew preached to the Pequots, they thanked him for coming but "objected as a great discouragemt to them the Injuries wch they supposed were done them by the English, with relation to the Lands." Mayhew declined to intervene personally but informed them that "if they became true Christians that was the way to have God and Good men become their friends, and plead their cause for them."[101]This was no small promise to Native groups who tried at every turn to protect their rapidly shrinking land base and must have served as a powerful motivating factor for at least some. Consequently, Native groups repeatedly leveraged offers of education toward the pressing issues of dispossession. In September 1735, some Mashantucket Pequot leaders expressed outrage over land loss and linked it directly to the way it might affect the rising generation's ability to do the very things the missionaries and colonists desired, namely, pursue educational opportunities and adopt various elements of European culture, such as embracing Christianity and building English-style houses: "It makes us Conserned for our Children what will be Com of them for thay are about having the gospell Preched to them, and are a Learning to read."[102]

Overall, however, requesting education in the 1720s and 1730s was not a wholesale embrace of a totalizing cultural transformation on the part of the Indians but a careful and selective engagement with particular offerings that met Native community needs and personal desires. Consequently, Natives continued to show a clear preference for education over evangelism when given the choice. In July 1732, Eliphalet Adams addressed a large gathering of Mohegans, Pequots, and Niantics (with translation by Thomas Avery, John Mason, and Captain Morgan), offering once again to have more settled missionaries among them, along with schools, where they were not already in place. The Native responses illustrate the depth of their cultural memory when it came to Christianization, reaching back into the 1660s. The gathered Indians politely reminded Adams that "Mr. Fitch of Norwich had formerly preached to them, but they never well understood it; they were afraid they should not understand it now, and wished that the preaching might be deferred till they were able to understand it." Nonetheless, the Natives affirmed their desire for ongoing education and resolved to keep on sending their children to Mason's school at Mohegan.[103]

Additionally, requesting an English schoolteacher or showing up for monthly lectures was not the same as renouncing traditional practices. For example, most Natives were quite willing to listen to English missionaries and teachers wax eloquent about the particularities of reformed Protestantism and even affirm the truth of them in a nonexclusive way. At the same time Mohicans were entertaining English ministers and missionaries and receiving baptism, they were also relying upon traditional avenues of knowledge and community discernment, primarily through powwows. In mid-January, 1735, after the "Drinking and Frolicking" that normally concluded a regional meeting of Natives along the Housatonic River, two Indians were "seiz'd with a violent Fever" and died suddenly. The other Indians present suspected they were poisoned; Sergeant credited it to their practice of dancing around a hot fire and then running—drenched with sweat and stripped naked—to roll around in the snow outside the wigwam. Convinced of something more pernicious at work, some of the local Mohicans decided to seek the help of a shaman to "apply some invisible Power for the Discovery of the Murderers." On February 21, a month after the deaths, Kunkapot and forty other Mohicans gathered in the wigwam of Umpachenee to have a "Pawwaw" in hopes that the murderers might reveal themselves to the Indian shamans/medicine men who conducted the ceremony. The Mohicans were seated around the periphery of the wigwam with several fires and an empty space in the middle reserved for the shamans. The meeting opened with the assembled Indians rapping two sticks together and singing while the oldest shaman engaged in prayers and enquiries. After an hour of this, the shaman got up, threw off his blankets and skins, and performed a dance with his eyes closed, dancing from one end of the wigwam to another. The meeting lasted all night, with the four shamans taking turns dancing and praying, all interspersed with ritualistic pipe smoking and occasional collective dancing. Woodbridge, of course, was horrified to observe this and did not pass up the opportunity to let them know "how sinful & displeasing to the great God" this ongoing kind of activity was.[104]

Nonetheless, some Natives were increasingly willing to conform to the Christian ideals and standards the missionaries set out for them, even if it meant altering traditional practices. On a chilly day at Mohegan in November 1734, Mahomet II's wife and infant child both perished in a tragic wigwam fire. The remains of the infant were extracted from the ruins of the wigwam and placed in a coffin, along with the body of its mother and a variety of funerary objects, including strings of beads (wampum), gold jewelry, and a decorative plate, all reportedly "of considerable value." After several days of mourning among the Mohegan community, the bodies of the mother and child were taken five miles north to the Mohegan royal burial ground in Norwich, Connecticut. The next day, on November 11, 1734, as a large crowd of Indians and curious colonists gathered to watch the interment, the mother of Mahomet II's deceased wife sent for Benjamin Lord, the minister of Norwich, to counsel and to pray with them. Lord obliged, but also took the opportunity to lecture the relatives of the deceased "concerning the Impropriety of burying their Treasure with their dead" and to advise them to take out the funerary objects. Surprisingly, they complied. The relatives removed the objects and proceeded to bury the two coffin-encased corpses "with their usual decency, care and exactness," in the words of one English observer.[105] The use of a coffin *and* funerary objects is evidence of Native cultures in motion, much like the Pequot medicine bundle. The fact that the Indians sought out Lord's counsel and prayers and removed the objects at his recommendation indicates a growing willingness to at least publicly conform to English ideas about the afterlife and caring for the deceased.

Ben Uncas II, Contested Sachemships, and the Mohegan Land Controversy

One excellent window into this process of religious engagement in which religious, political, and practical concerns were inextricably intertwined is the sachemship of the Mohegan Ben Uncas II. He became famous for being the first sachem of the unevangelized Native nations in southeastern New England to profess Christianity in 1736. Far more than a simple "conversion," at that very moment he was neck deep in a heated, prolonged controversy that included Mohegan land, rightful Mohegan sachemship, allegiance to the English, and ideas about religion.[106] Simultaneously, English missionaries and ministers were making ongoing attempts to Anglicize the Mohegans and convert them to Christianity. Although these various struggles were mostly local and regional in nature, they took on international importance when the Mohegans inserted themselves into transatlantic power structures and a far larger debate about indigenous rights in the Americas by appealing directly to the British monarchs. Intertwined with these political and social concerns were Ben Uncas's seemingly sincere interest in education, social reform, and his own personal spiritual transformation.

Ben Uncas II's leadership at Mohegan got off to a highly contentious start in 1725 when he was controversially elected sachem after his father's death. His election came on the heels of the even more disputed election of his father, Ben Uncas I, in 1723. After the 1723 election, John Uncas, Jr. (who likely should have been elected sachem, or perhaps Mahomet II), uprooted and moved half a mile down the road, taking a sizable number of the Mohegans with him.[107] Consequently, two distinct Mohegan communities, Ben's Town and John's Town, existed on the west shore of the Thames River.[108] The divisions among the Mohegans had their origins in decisions over who should be sachem, but they quickly became about other things, too, such as accommodation with the English on a variety of issues, including education, religion, and cultural practices like dances.

From the beginning, Ben Uncas II embraced the English presence and cultural offerings, including education. In addition to welcoming John Mason and Jonathan Barber onto Mohegan lands, Ben Uncas II and his wife, Ann, personally attended lectures, sermons, and reading and writing lessons offered by Mason. In the late 1720s, Ben Uncas II sent his own son, Benjamin Uncas III, to receive educational and religious instruction, first from John Mason, and then—in 1729—from Eliphalet Adams, the minister of the church in New London.[109] In 1731, the commissioners for the New England Company reported that Adams was starting Ben Uncas III down a rigorous educational path "in order to qualify him for a preacher to said Indians, which both his Father and he are desirous."[110] Following this, the boy went to the Reverend Oliver Peabody's house in Natick to continue his training, but the NEC commissioners soon reported that Ben Uncas III, "not having a Disposition to Learning, but rather choosing a trade," was instead indentured to Thomas Russell of Sherburn, Massachusetts (a small village near Natick), to learn the art of cordwaining (shoemaking) for two and a half years.[111] Nonetheless, starting in 1739, Ben Uncas III's education paid off as he was appointed schoolmaster at Mohegan, a position he held until he was elected sachem in 1749.[112]

Ben Uncas II himself seems to have undergone some sort of spiritual transformation in the mid- to late-1720s. Governor Talcott wrote to Eliphalet Adams in 1728 that Ben Uncas II "hath a while since in a time of sickness been very much awakened and concerned to think what would become of him if he should die in his state of ignorance and sin." When he recovered, he went to visit Talcott "for some instructions in religion," which Talcott obliged as best he could given their mutual "unacquaintedness with each others language."[113] As early as October 1733, John Mason reported to Governor Talcott that Ben Uncas II was "of late greatly Reformed," along with "some of his People." "He has himself, and his Wife, of late began to learn to Read," Mason observed, "and they give their Minds to learning, and have for the time they have been learning made great progress."[114] On May 5, 1734, Benjamin Uncas II and twenty Mohegans accompanied Jonathan Barber six miles north to Benjamin Lord's Congregational church in Norwich, where they attended the "Publick Worship" at Lord's church "with such a decent Gravity and Fixedness" that was observed by all in attendance "with Thankfulness and Pleasure."[115]

Over time, Ben Uncas II had tried to influence the Mohegans in ways that resonated with the moral sensibilities of the English missionaries. Just three years prior to his official profession of faith, Ben Uncas II complained in 1733 to the General Assembly that the sale of "strong drink" to the Mohegans "impoverished" their "estates," "debauched" their manners, and rendered his people "more untractable to receive the Christian faith."[116] As anticipated, the General Assembly responded by passing an "Act for the more effectual Preventing the Selling of Strong Drink to the Mohegan Indians." More surprising, however, was Ben Uncas II's public foreswearing of certain traditional practices. In September 1733, the Mohegans hosted at least two large dances within a few weeks, and both times he refused to join in them, which prompted a mini-showdown within the Mohegan community. Upon learning of his refusal to join, Ben Uncas II's mother and others came to try to persuade him to join. His response seemed unequivocal: since he was "going to be a Christian" and the Mohegans had a minister among them, he would no longer attend the dances. When some of the Mohegans warned him that he might be "slighted" if he refused, he retorted: "he did not care for them, and that he wronged no Body in refusing and he said that he would not have any thing to doe with their Dances more, Because that they were very hurtful to them."[117] Other sachems had demonstrated similar refusals to participate in traditional community activities after the arrival of missionaries. Shortly after Sergeant arrived among the Mohicans in western Massachusetts, Kunkapot and Umpachenee similarly pledged to "keep clear" of the drunken four-day "Frolicks" that the Mohican community still participated in.[118] Nonetheless, at Mohegan, Ben Uncas II was taking a gamble by so solidly allying himself with the missionaries. In October 1736, Ben Uncas II further cemented his commitment to the Christian religion and to the English colonists by declaring that "he doth embrace the Christian religion" in such a way that the news was sure to reach the General Assembly and governor of Connecticut, which it did. The General Assembly reciprocated by sending him a coat and a hat, along with a lovely new English-style gown for Ann.[119]

Although Ben Uncas II's public commitment was partially a natural extension of his prior interest and activities, the timing demonstrated that he was well aware of the political significance of such a profession. One hugely important context for all of this was the Mohegan land controversy (or Mason Case, as it was sometimes called).[120] This seventy-year-long (1704–1773) land case had as its roots some seventeenth-century land grants between the Mohegan sachem Uncas and the colony of Connecticut. By 1662, the colony recognized that Mohegans possessed a large square-shaped tract of land in east central Connecticut by a "Native Right."[121] The problems really began in the 1690s and the early 1700s, when Connecticut began selling off portions of these same lands to form additional towns. In response to a petition in 1704 from the Mohegan sachem, Owaneco, Queen Anne formed a royal commission to investigate the case. When the queen's royal commissioners—all from Connecticut and Massachusetts— met in 1705, they sided with the Mohegans and ordered the colony of Connecticut to return all contested land immediately.[122] Not surprisingly, the governor of Connecticut and his agents vigorously refuted the decision, refused to give back any land, and instead appealed the decision directly to the queen. Although the Mohegans petitioned Connecticut for justice from time to time, no land was returned. The case remained unofficially unresolved and the dispossessions continued, despite a brief revisiting of the case by the colony of Connecticut between 1719 and 1721.[123] Instead, Connecticut courted Mohegan sachems who seemed unlikely to press for a reopening of the land case, including Ben Uncas I and II.

In part because of his willingness to completely drop the Mohegans' land claims against Connecticut, by the 1730s Ben Uncas II was becoming increasing unpopular at Mohegan. To bypass Ben Uncas II, in early 1736 John Mason, Samuel Mason, Augh Quant Johnson (often called Cato), and Mahomet II (who had lost at least two sons by this point, one by reported bewitchment and another in a fire) traveled to London to press for land justice and to reopen the Mohegan land case, with Mahomet II claiming to be the rightful sachem. Ben Uncas II's standing at Mohegan hit an all-time low when, at a "black dance" on September 10, 1736, a large number of Mohegan, Pequot, and Niantic Indians voted unanimously for Mahomet II. Since Mahomet II was in England, the Natives decided that his cousin, Ann, should rule until his return.[124] Local colonists who attended this intertribal meeting of Natives later testified that all present gave sustained and verbal opposition to the sachemship of Ben Uncas II.[125] However, both Mahomet II and John Mason died in England, leaving only Samuel Mason and Cato to carry the good news back to New England that George II had called for a retrial of the Mohegan land case.[126] Within a month of the black dance and the Mohegans' public rejection of Ben Uncas II's leadership, Ben Uncas II publicly professed Christianity, in part to guarantee the ongoing support of the Connecticut magistrates. Such a strategy worked, for despite his almost universal rejection at Mohegan, he remained the sachem through the successive land controversies at Mohegan and the additional challenges to his leadership until his death in 1749.

Because of the successful petition of Mahomet II, Cato, and the Masons, the Mohegan land case was officially reopened in May 1738. The agents for Connecticut did all they could to make Ben Uncas II look like the rightful sachem, including parading him into court dressed in special English clothes commissioned and paid for by the colony and undoubtedly playing up his recent profession of faith.[127] The John's Town Mohegans, on the other hand, held a large dance with the Niantics and possibly Pequots at Mohegan on May 22, and the next morning they traveled to Norwich to prepare for the imminent opening of the Mohegan land controversy hearings. The Mohegan land controversy was far from a local event or limited to the Mohegans. Every major Native group in the region was represented in the audience—the Mohegans, Niantics, and Pequots, with the Narragansetts also likely in attendance for part of the time.[128] They took great interest in the proceedings and listened intently, using an interpreter when necessary, simply because so much was at stake. A victory for the Mohegans would have increased the possibility of other Native groups pursuing similar suits. After nine days of hearing testimony from all sides, the case was ultimately decided against the Mohegans. The Mason family and the New York commissioners protested, however, and a retrial was granted for a future date.

Ben Uncas II, meanwhile, continued to pursue his rather pragmatically sincere practice of Christian affiliation in the hopes of courting of Connecticut officials' favor in the land controversy. This helps explain why, in early 1739—a full year before the first sustained religious commotion in the area—Ben Uncas II approached the New London North Parish church and requested that it might physically move its meetinghouse closer (within half a mile) to the Mohegan villages so that the Ben's Town Mohegans could begin attending regularly. In the end, a mutually agreeable new location for the North Parish could not be decided upon, despite the financial support of the NEC commissioners and the formation of an official committee to determine an appropriate location.[129] Nonetheless, when David Jewett was installed as minister of the North Parish church in New London on October 3, 1739, he almost immediately began preaching regularly to the Mohegans, and Ben Uncas II was undoubtedly among those who walked the extra mile or so to worship each week.

There was one additional, if inadvertent, outcome of the struggle over Mohegan land in the 1730s. In the aftermath of the Mason/Mahomet II debacle—in which an NEC missionary stirred up enormous controversy at Mohegan by reopening the Mohegan land controversy—the NEC and its missionaries became far less willing to pursue land justice alongside evangelistic and educational efforts. Although clearly the NEC still saw dispossession as a major roadblock to evangelization, when faced with the possibility that Mason might have partially used the Mohegan case for his own gain (at least as described by the Connecticut magistrates) along with the pressure placed on the NEC to not support Mahomet II, the NEC had backed down and never fully recovered its ability to assert that respect for land rights must accompany offers of Bibles and primers.[130] Colonial and town governments, too, recognized the problem and were required by law to support local land claims in the courts, but in subsequent years they rarely linked land rights with evangelization as had Talcott and other magistrates in the 1720s.

The experiences of Ben Uncas II and the other Natives in southeastern New England prompt a consideration of the layered, sociocultural contexts in which religious engagement and—ultimately—religious change occur. Social factors like land loss, internal tribal disputes, and desire for education can never fully explain the decisions people make, but such factors are always relevant. Although Natives at first seemed resistant to Christian instruction in the opening decade of the eighteenth century, by the 1720s and 1730s this began to change as Indian leaders and individuals grew increasingly interested in the services provided by English missionaries and ministers. But such religious engagement was rarely universal, and families and communities were divided over education, leadership, and cultural accommodation.

These persistent and contested evangelistic efforts, however, seemed to produce results on only a small scale and primarily among youth, although the reluctant son of Mahomet II and the accommodating Ben Uncas III demonstrate that even the younger generation exhibited differing responses. Partially in response to these efforts, a few Indians began joining English churches in the 1720s and 1730s, but the results were not as great as the NEC commissioners and local ministers had hoped. Contrary to beliefs that indigenous interest in education during the colonial period was often a byproduct of "conversion" among Natives, in this particular region interest in education was part of a broader pattern of religious and cultural engagement that preceded religious affiliation.[131] This process was, in fact, exactly what the NEC commissioners and Connecticut magistrates hoped and strived for, since education was a central component to civilization, which in their minds was an important prerequisite to conversion.[132] What they did not always realize, however, were the ways in which controversies over land, along with Natives' own ideas about the purpose and meaning of religious education and practices, would shape the outcome of these educational attempts in the decades to come.

3

Awakening

It started as a rumor. Something strange was happening among the English. Mohegan artisans heard about it when they traveled to neighboring New London, Norwich, and Lyme to peddle their baskets, brooms, and other wares. Indians who labored for a pittance or less on local farms, in sawmills, and in households heard bits and pieces of what was happening from exuberant co-workers and masters. Long, intense meetings, "extraordinary Ministers Preaching from Place to Place," they were told, were all creating a "Strange Concern among the White People."[1] Some of the Indian youth, like the sixteen-year-old Samson Occom and his sister Lucy, perhaps drawn by curiosity, might have even sneaked into local churches during the spring of 1740 and watched with fascination a service like the one described by Joshua Hempstead one year later in New London:

> When Mr. Davenport had dismissed the congregation some went out and others stayed; he then went into the broad alley [aisle], which was much crowded, and there he screamed out, "Come to Christ! Come to Christ! Come away!" Then he went into the third pew on the women's side, and kept there, sometimes singing, sometimes praying; he and his companions all taking their turns, and the women fainting and in hysterics. This confusion continued till ten o'clock at night. And then he went off singing through the streets.[2]

The reports of unusually vigorous preaching, sermons full of vivid imagery of the burning fires of hell, urgent calls to make a decision to follow the Christian God or burn forever in those fires, and—even more shockingly—scenes of white people crying out loudly in anguish, writhing on the ground in pain, shaking uncontrollably, and lying prostrate on the floor as if dead all must have intrigued the local Indian populations. Compared to the relatively staid, orderly world of read sermons, monophonic lined-out songs from the Psalter, and a sharp demarcation between minister and layperson, these meetings must have come across as a marked change in the local religious culture—a carnivalesque environment with reversals and opportunities in abundance as well as a vivid demonstration of the experiential reality of the English God.[3]

By summer, the excitement had spilled over onto the Mohegan reservation in the form of itinerants of various stripes—ministers and "Common People"— who came to hold services among the Mohegans on their lands. For some Indians—as for many colonists—attending occasional revival meetings became a feature of community life. Revival services were, after all, quite entertaining. And sometimes even moving. Samson Occom recalled that at one of these meetings, he was "convicted," after which he "went to all the meetings I could come at."[4] Similarly, Samuel Ashpo and dozens of other Mohegan men, women, and children went out of their way to hear English revivalists, local ministers, and self-appointed laypersons who aped the better-known itinerants like George Whitefield.

The apparently sudden religious interest of the Mohegans is one of the best-known examples of what has been otherwise generally assumed of Indians in southern New England in the 1740s: that they converted, en masse, during the First Great Awakening.[5] The most important source of this narrative of the sudden conversion comes from Samson Occom, who described Mohegan participation in the Awakening more than twenty-five years later. In his account of his spiritual journey, Occom emphasized that he was "Born a Heathen and Brought up in Heathenism" and "Livd a wandering life," while his tribe "Chiefly Depended upon Hunting Fishing & Fowling for their Living and had no Connections with the English" except when trading "Small Trifles" with them. The Mohegans, according to Occom, "Strictly maintain'd and followe'd their Heathenish Ways, Customs & Religion." The English ministers and schoolteachers who occasionally showed up, according to Occom, were entirely ineffective. Of the school, Occom insisted, "I believe there never was one that ever Learnt to read any thing," and despite all the sermons, "all this Time there was not one amongst us, that made a Profession of Christianity."[6] According to Occom, onto this landscape of bleak, unreceptive "heathenism" burst the revivals. Within a year, Occom went from "heathen"—by his own description—to "converted."

Occom's characterization of the Mohegans as heathens and his own rapid spiritual transformation often have been taken to stand in for all Natives in southeastern New England.[7] Although there is no reason to doubt Occom's own religious experience, his descriptions of the Mohegans in the 1720s and 1730s simply do not correspond with other extant records, nor was his experience necessarily typical. Occom's depiction of the Mohegans as steeped in "heathenism" prior to the Awakening stands in sharp contrast to an account given in 1736 by Ben Uncas II, when he thanked Connecticut governor Joseph Talcott for "making way for & promoting the Knowledge of God & Jesus Christ amongst us,

& for the Education of our Children yt we may be no Longer the Heethen that know not God."[8] Occom completely ignores the way in which education was requested by and—in time—run by the Mohegans themselves; starting in 1739, for example, the schoolteacher at Mohegan was none other than Benjamin Uncas III, the sachem's son. Occom's 1768 autobiographical account was written long after the actual events and was intended to prove to his Euroamerican doubters that he had actually been a "real" (wild) Indian at one time. To highlight his own religious transformation, Occom clearly minimized both the Mohegans' prior exposure to Christianity and the depth of the Mohegan community's connection to surrounding English towns.[9]

The participation of many southern New England Natives in the Awakening during the 1740s was a continuation of, not a break with, prior religious engagement and strategies of creative cultural and religious adaptation and survival. This point is worth lingering over because the trope of the sudden conversion obscures the far more interesting ongoing processes of religious engagement and cultural change. It was precisely *because* Pequot, Montaukett, Niantic, Narragansett, and Mohegan communities had been broadly exposed to English religion and culture that participation in the Great Awakening held any attraction at all.[10] Although they might have initially shown up to view the spectacle of revivalism, many of them soon found in revivalistic evangelicalism creative possibilities for their own communities. The "Indian Great Awakening," then—while not discounting supernatural explanations or professions of belief given by its participants—was a logical but not inevitable result of three prior decades of renewed attempts of the English to evangelize their Native neighbors and the Indians' increasing attempts to procure education, literacy, and acceptance into the larger Euroamerican colonial society.

The First Great Awakening

What historians call the "First Great Awakening" consisted of little more than a loose collection of local revivals that were preached, promoted, celebrated, and experienced in the 1730s and 1740s throughout the wider British Atlantic world, including Great Britain, the British North American colonies, and parts of the Caribbean.[11] Revivals in their various manifestations—unconnected as they often were—involved Baptists, Congregationalists, Moravians, Presbyterians, and even Anglicans and helped form new movements, such as Methodism and the Separate movement in New England. Such experiences created a transatlantic culture of revivalism—both in experience and in print—that accordingly tended to form expectations and cultural scripts for those involved.[12] Seasons of local revivals took place across New England and the mid-Atlantic region in the seventeenth and early eighteenth centuries, but what unfolded in the 1740s surpassed prior revivals in terms of geographical and denominational spread, the kinds of experiences reported, and the realignment of denominations in the aftermath. Although New England ministers participated in the regional revivals that emanated out of Jonathan Edwards's church in Northampton, Massachusetts, in the mid-1730s, things did not reach a fever pitch until the early 1740s. English revivalist George Whitefield's tour of New England in 1740 exemplifies the overwhelming popularity of the extemporaneous sermons; heartfelt exhortations toward personal, experiential redemption; and, perhaps above all, the spectacle of the revival participants, including shaking, fainting, crying out, and even laughing, all under the influence, they claimed, of the Holy Spirit. Everywhere he went, Whitefield drew enormous crowds, with reported numbers ranging from several thousand to more than 20,000 on the Boston Common on Sunday, October 12—no small feat for a city of approximately 16,000 men, women, and children.[13] Although Whitefield's personal presence in southeastern Connecticut was minimal, New England ministers often followed newspaper reports of his activities and were influenced by Whitefield's emphases on extemporaneous preaching, the necessity of a new birth, and personal piety.[14]

New London County, Connecticut, quickly became the center of much of the extreme sort of revivalism common during the Great Awakening.[15] As the revivals moved through various stages of intensity, local differences of opinion crystallized into published disputes over the necessity and meaning of a certain type of new birth religious experience. In the earlier phase of the revival, even prominent conservative ministers throughout New England welcomed the perceived and much prayed-for renewal of their congregants that the revivals represented.[16] As the revivals were taken in more democratic, anti-authoritarian, and experience-based directions, a spectrum of responses to them emerged, including antirevivalists who opposed the revivals (often called Old Lights); moderate revivalists (or moderate New Lights) who embraced the Awakening but shied away from certain, more radical practices; and radical revivalists (or radical New Lights) whose passion for stirring up crowds and practice of naming ministers as unconverted worried antirevivalists and moderate revivalists alike.[17] Ministers who welcomed the revivals early on but later did not approve of what they saw as unnecessary excesses suddenly found themselves tagged as "Old Lights," publicly challenged by radical "New Lights" and, in some cases, even voted out of their churches.

In most cases, however, New Lights in local churches were a minority and lacked the power to oust their supposedly unregenerate ministers; in these cases, they began forming their own churches and became known as "Separates."[18] As early as November 1742, a split had taken place in Eliphalet Adams's church in New London, and more schisms quickly followed.[19] In virtually every town in New London County, new Separate churches split off from existing Congregational churches during the 1740s. Within six years, approximately twenty new congregations were formed. Dozens more Separate churches gathered, either temporarily or permanently, out of other congregations in Rhode Island, Massachusetts, and New Hampshire.[20] Some Separates over time began to doubt the need for infant baptism and instead found more sympathies with local Baptist congregations.[21] Not all New Lights were Separates, and not all Old Lights were antirevival, but the divisiveness of the revivals often forced people to take harderline positions than they actually held.[22]

Indian Communities and the Awakening

All of this created a euphoric and contentious moment in the southern New England religious culture into which some Native individuals and even subsets of Native communities were drawn.[23] Natives participated for a variety of reasons. First, and most simply, there were more—and more interesting—services to attend. Meetings took place at traditional venues and times like Sunday mornings in churches, but also out of doors, by ponds and rivers, and on town greens and in barns, during the work day or all night. Additionally, they were marked by riveting, extemporaneous preaching, an invitation to direct spiritual experiences, and an open invitation to repentance and the new birth. Additionally, dozens of smaller prayer and revival services took place, often without the sanction of an official minister, as blacks, Indians, and women—individuals who otherwise were barred from most church leadership—gave powerful testimony to their spiritual experiences. New places, faces, ministers, and ideas created new potential religious contexts that provided an attractive alternative to the normal Sunday morning services.

Natives also participated more in these gatherings, in part because New Light ministers paid more attention to them. Chief among them was James Davenport and a small circle of radical New Lights, including Andrew Croswell, John Owen, George Griswold, Joseph Fish, and Eliphalet Adams, who made special visits to Native communities in the late 1730s and early 1740s. Despite the fact that Davenport eventually caused more harm than good in Jonathan Parsons' West Lyme Parish church, Parsons was quick to praise Davenport for being "a great Blessing to many Souls; but especially to the Mohegan and Nahauntuc [Niantic] Tribes of Indians," for although "much Pains had been taken to win them to embrace the Gospel before, yet nothing seem'd to have any considerable Effect 'till Mr. Davenport came among them."[24]

Although Davenport had a traditional start to his ministerial career at Southold, Long Island, by 1740 he had adopted a more direct and confrontational style, due in part to Whitefield's influence.[25] With his anti-authoritarianism and his social subversiveness, Davenport quickly became perhaps the most colorful—and divisive—figure of the period, along with Andrew Croswell (Groton, Connecticut), Gilbert Tennent (New Brunswick, New Jersey), and even George Whitefield.[26] Tennent, Croswell, and Davenport especially became notorious for urging laypeople to force out ministers who could not recount a conversion experience, encouraging congregations to form their own associations, and telling lay men and women—particularly those of color—that they, too, had the right to preach the gospel.[27] In every town they never missed the opportunity to rail against the established order and proclaim the importance for individuals to experience the conviction and love of Christ in an immediate, unmediated way.

Additionally, these radical New Lights tapped into and contributed to an emerging hymnody drawn from personal experience rather than the Psalms—a feature of revival services that had unmistakable drawing power for Natives, as later traditions of Indian Christian practice indicate.[28] In radical New Light circles, hymns were not just sung in churches; they were raucously belted out by rowdy crowds of worshippers at all hours of the day and night as they marched down streets of urban centers all across New England. During a preaching tour of the Boston area in early 1742, for example, Croswell led a group of worshippers through the streets of Plymouth, Massachusetts, at 11 o'clock on a Saturday morning, singing hymns on their way to a meeting that lasted until 9 P.M., during which time, in the words of Josiah Cotton, "such was the noise thro distress & joy real or pretended, that the Ministers neither preached nor prayed, but Mr. Croswell went about the Meeting house Crying mercy, mercy, mercy."[29]

Davenport's influence in New London County peaked—and declined—in 1743. On Sunday, March 6, of that year, he and some New Light Separate friends, following instructions Davenport said he "received from the Spirit in Dreams," started a huge bonfire at the New London town wharf and began tossing into it the books of revered Puritan divines, past and present. Up in flames went works like "Beveridge's Thoughts on Religion, part of Flavel's Works . . . one piece of Dr. Increase Mather, one of Dr. Coleman's, one of Dr. Sewall's, and Dr. Chauncy's Sermon against Enthusiasm," and all the sermons of New London minister Eliphalet Adams that could be found.[30] The next day, another bonfire was planned, this time fueled by items Davenport found emblematic of the "heinous Sin of Idolatry": "Wigs, Cloaks and Breeches, Hoods, Gowns, Rings, Jewels and Necklaces." For many New Londoners, this was the last straw; on Monday a "mob" prevented Davenport and his followers from actually burning the collected idolatrous items. Local authorities dispersed the New Light leaders and ensured that no more bonfires were lit.[31] Davenport returned to Long Island and was later persuaded to write a lengthy retraction of his excesses.[32]

It took more than boisterous singing and renegade bonfires, however, for American Indians to be drawn to New Light revivalism, although certainly such activities sparked interest. Natives were drawn, in part, because Davenport and other New Lights went out of their way to preach a compelling message of immediate religious experience to any and all Indian communities they could find. And, given their success in attracting Natives, clearly something in their presentation of this version of Christianity struck a chord with many Indian listeners.[33]

It is clear that the revivals of the late 1730s and early 1740s intensified the already existing concern for Native souls among the ministers like Davenport in southeastern New England and that many Indian individuals, in turn, were attracted to their distinctive practices of Christianity. In most cases, the revivals did not originate from Indian communities per se, but rather within the larger English society with which Natives were inextricably linked. Griswold reported in Lyme East Parish in 1744 that "God made use of the Concern in some to create a Concern in others"—an apt way to describe the way in which interest in religion and revival enthusiasm traveled along preexisting routes of cultural exchange and mimesis: kinship, trade, employment, and communal activities.[34]

To better explain the nuances of Native participation in the revivals, what follows is a description of the engagement within each Native community in southeastern New England. Each Native community experienced revival services in slightly different ways and at different times, although rarely in complete isolation from other Native groups. Even so, Native engagement with the revivals themselves was not universal or even community-wide. But within each community, a subset of the population did attend services and pondered the meaning of the revivalists' message for their own lives and communities.

Mashantucket and Lantern Hill

The Mashantucket and Lantern Hill Pequots had been broadly exposed to Christian teaching and education in the 1730s. A smattering of Mashantuckets had also attended the North Groton Congregational Church as early as the mid-1730s. Despite these efforts, John Owen and Andrew Croswell reported to the General Assembly that as late as the summer of 1741 the Pequots in Groton "Remained in heathenish Darkness, Debauch'd in life and manners, and utterly Averse to all manner of learning"—an assessment which, however misleading and biased, did accurately reflect the Pequots' lack of interest in joining English churches up to that point.[35]

The Awakening came to the Pequots, as in other locales, in the form of local New Light ministers, including the Stonington Congregationalist ministers Joseph Fish, Andrew Croswell, and John Owen, and the radical New Light itinerant from Long Island, James Davenport. In the summer of 1741, Davenport made a tour of New London County, stirring up dissension and religious fervor in each town. Davenport's meetings, widely attended by Indians, blacks, and white colonists alike, garnered controversy and praise. For five nights in July 1741, Davenport held revival services in Groton. The last of his services held there was an outdoor spectacle near the First Congregational Church on Thursday, July 23, that drew a thousand listeners and lasted until two o'clock in the morning, with small groups remaining "all night under the oak tree & in the meeting house."[36] The next day he moved on to Stonington, where he preached in the newly constructed, cavernous two-level First Church of Stonington.[37] There, as in most places Davenport preached, his theatrical methods attracted large crowds that responded with conviction and feeling to his message. Joseph Park, a missionary to the Narragansetts in Rhode Island, described how Davenport and a large group of people approached the church, "in solemn Procession singing an Hymn." Park—himself affected by Davenport, and having good reason to render Davenport's methods harmless—reported in *The Christian History* that Davenport "preach'd a plain and awakening Sermon, from John 5.40. I heard nothing extraordinary, but the wholsome Truths of the Gospel, and expected no extraordinary Effect, when to my Surprize their was a Cry all over the Meeting-House." When Park asked a few people about "Meaning of their Out-cry," they told him it was because of a "deep Conviction of Sin."[38] Another observer noted that after Davenport's sermon "mighty works" followed (probably meaning bodily manifestations like shaking, etc.), in addition to hundreds crying out.[39] So popular were Davenport's meetings that when Joshua Hempstead went on Saturday, July 25, to Stonington to mow his hay fields, he found all his hired hands were in town listening to Davenport.[40]

When Davenport preached to a sizable crowd "under the Trees" next to the East (Third) Stonington church on Sunday morning, July 26, minister Nathaniel Eells and his congregation joined the service. Things soon got uncomfortable when Davenport began—in what was quickly becoming a trademark tactic—to very pointedly suggest that Eells might not be converted. Disgusted and offended, many people present thought Davenport was too "Severe in Judging & Condemning Mr Eells," and "withdrew into the meetinghouse" where Eells preached his normal Sunday morning sermon while Davenport continued his service for a large crowd outside.[41] Regional newspapers reported that as a result of Davenport's preaching in Stonington, Groton, and Norwich, one hundred people converted, including some "Negroes" and approximately "twenty Indians."[42] No indication is given regarding how such conversions were manifested or gauged, but they likely hint at a larger presence of Natives than the twenty who had in some way professed Christian belief.

According to Stonington ministers John Owen and Andrew Croswell, the first signs of a large-scale awakening among the Pequots came shortly after Davenport's visit, around September or October of 1741, when the Pequots became "Generally much Concern'd about their Souls" and "Deeply convicted of the Dreadful Sinfulness of their hearts."[43] As a result, by May 1742, Owen and Croswell reported that fifty Mashantucket Pequots "constantly attend the preaching of the word" and were "Generally Reformed as to their beloved Sin of Drunkeness." Thirty of them, Owen and Crosswell affirmed, "are Much Inclind to Learn to Read." A similar account was given by the Pequots themselves in a May 5, 1742, petition to the Connecticut General Assembly. The document, signed by forty-one Pequots from Groton, provided a small window into the religious happenings in their community. "Of late we have been much concern'd about our souls," the Pequots wrote, "& to know wt we may do to please the Great god, who we are Sensible is very angry with us for our wickedness and drunkenness our Sabbath breaking & idleness & some of us we hope have believed on the Lord Jesus Christ." "Our Knowledge is but very little," they confessed, but "we want to learn to read the Bible and to have our Children learn to read it too, & thereby learn to know more of the Great God & what He would have us to do in this world that we may live with him in the next." The petitioners also informed the General Court that they had appointed a schoolmaster and desired of the General Assembly some money with which to support him.[44]

Although it was perhaps Davenport who first gave various Indian communities a compelling vision for what Christianity might mean or do for them, the work was carried along and encouraged by local ministers, overseers, and self-appointed missionaries. In the case of the Pequots, Andrew Croswell seems to have been at the forefront of the efforts. Croswell, a 1728 graduate of Harvard College, had been ordained at the Second Congregational Church in Groton on October 14, 1736. Not only did he defend James Davenport in print in the *Boston Post Boy* in 1741, Croswell also took the Pequot petition to the General Assembly in May 1742. The minister of the First Church in Groton, John Owen, was similarly involved in a variety of ways. And, according to the 1742 Pequots' petition, Captain John Morgan and his son had both been holding meetings among the Pequots "almost every Sabbath to the Conviction and awakening of many."[45]

Niantic

As with the Pequots, local ministers noted that the Niantics had both preachers and a school set up among them in the years prior to the Awakening. By some assessments, however, it was to "little good Effect," at least in ways measured by colonial magistrates and ministers, namely, religious conversions and evidence of cultural conformity. By 1741, however, the Reverend George Griswold had different news to report. In the East Parish of Lyme, Connecticut, Griswold stated that it all started not with George Whitefield's 1740 tour of New England—during which only three Lyme residents converted—but rather with a series of meetings in April 1741 held by Gilbert Tennent, the itinerant preacher from New Jersey, and Jonathan Parsons, minister of the first parish church in Lyme. When Tennent first preached in Lyme on April 1, 1741, one of Griswold's parishioners reported to Eleazar Wheelock that "the Common Conversation almost universally changed[;] the things of God and the other world is now all the talk[;] a Generall Concern about such things seem'd to spread almost over the whole parish in a weeks time."[46] On April 14, 1741, Griswold attended an evening meeting in the house of Jonathan Lee, where "the Word fell with great Power on sundry, who were deeply wounded under a Sense of Sin and divine Wrath," so much so, in fact, that "some had Fits, some fainted." In the wake of this outbreak of "religious Concern," Griswold set up weekly lectures, evening lectures, and other frequent religious meetings, conducted in traditional meetinghouses as well as in private homes. A strong sense of conviction was manifested by "Out-cries, Faintings and Fits" that became almost the signature mark of a revival. The youth of Lyme, as in other towns, seemed particularly affected and pleaded with Griswold to preach a sermon to them on May 14.[47] During his address to a "great assembly" in Lyme, all heaven broke loose: his hearers' "knees smote one against another. Great numbers cried out aloud in the anguish of their souls. Several stout men fell as though a cannon had been discharged, and a ball had made its way through their hearts. Some young women were thrown into hysteric fits."[48] This time of community renewal lasted through June, during which Griswold "had Reason to hope that about forty Persons experienced a saving Change."[49]

No Indians in Lyme professed Christianity as a result of the spring 1741 revival, although it is not difficult to imagine that some attended the many and intriguing meetings. After experiencing the intensity of a revival in his own church, however, in June or July Griswold offered to go and preach to the Niantics, but "not receiving any Encouragement from them that they would come hear" him, he decided against going. In August 1741, Davenport, not waiting for an invitation, held a series of long meetings among the Niantics on their own lands, during which some of them, Griswold reported, "were hopefully converted by his Ministry, and some others awakened." Although Davenport soon moved on, Griswold took over as he had opportunity and noted that the "religious Concern not only continued among them, but increased for a considerable Time." A number of Niantic individuals began attending Griswold's church, and some of them altered actual behaviors, such as reforming their "excessive Drinking and Sabbath breaking." By June 1744, he reported that "there are twenty or upward of this Tribe of Indians that have been hopefully converted." Of these, Griswold noted, they "seemed to live near to God, and to have much of the divine Presence with them."[50]

Mohegan

At least a small portion of the Mohegans—likely all from Ben's Town—had been attending the New London North Parish church during the 1730s, particularly after the arrival of minister David Jewett in 1739. Additionally, during that decade dozens of Mohegan youth had attended Jonathan Barber's school. Building on this prior engagement with Christianity, in the early 1740s the New Light revivals presented new and different opportunities for many Mohegans. As early as 1740, the Mohegans began to hear the "Strange Rumor" of "Extraordinary Ministers Preaching from Place to Place." Nonetheless, Jewett's church— only a few miles from Mohegan lands—was a bit of a latecomer to the revival scene. Not until 1741 did the full revival touch the North Parish church and—by extension—the nearby Mohegans. Once again, James Davenport was eventually involved.

Jewett took part in the East Lyme revival as a guest preacher in George Griswold's church in early May 1741. Griswold, flush with his own revival successes, returned the favor and preached two sermons at Jewett's church later that month. Griswold reported a steadfast attention to his preaching at Jewett's church, although he did not see any "visible Appearance of remarkable Concern" that had marked his own revivals. The trouble started when James Davenport preached in Jewett's New London North Parish church in late July 1741. As Davenport had done with Nathaniel Eells in Stonington a month prior, Davenport declared Jewett to be unconverted when Jewett refused to give a narration of "the Work of God's Spirit on his Heart." The congregation was thrown into turmoil for the next five months, with part of the congregation threatening to separate and start their own church since they, too, believed Jewett to be unconverted. Resolution came late that year when a major revival took place in Jewett's church under Griswold's guest preaching in December 1741, during which time Jewett finally experienced a personal renewal that made him far more zealous than before.[51]

It is likely that some Mohegans were in attendance for these various events and services, undoubtedly even Ben Uncas II and his family, given their negotiations regarding moving the church building in 1739. More broadly, Samson Occom's descriptions of the Awakening itself makes clear that a subset of the Mohegan community found the revival services intriguing events since they were sometimes held out of doors and involved an ecstatic, emotional element that was not part of the normal order of service in English churches. As a result, Mohegans of all ages likely showed up at a variety of church services over a year-long period and saw different types of Christian expression and practice on display. Some—like Occom—likely took the messages to heart, pondering for months and days their own religious condition and the ultimate destination of their souls. Through these efforts, Occom reported, "it pleased the L[or]d, as I humbly hope, to Bless and Acompany with Divine Influences, to the Conviction and Saving Conversion of a Number of us." Occom himself "was one that was Imprest with the things, we had heard," and felt "convicted" and "Continued under Trouble of Mind about 6 months." Finally, at the age of seventeen, Occom recalled that he had "a Discovery of the way of Salvation through Jesus, and was enabled to put my trust in him alone for Life and Salvation," at which time "the Distress and Burden of my mind was removd, and found Serenity and Pleasure of Soul, in Serving god."[52]

It is surely the case that the Mohegans' experiences of the revivals varied widely, and Occom's embrace was only one of many pathways chosen. After the initial surge of Indian interest in the revivals, George Whitefield also held a great meeting with the Mohegan, Pequot, and Niantic Indians near Norwich in early August 1745, but this visit merely built upon preexisting Native interest in the revivals.[53]

Montauk and Shinnecock

In August 1741, around the same time Davenport was stirring up the Niantics near Lyme, evangelistic services were taking place among the Montauketts and Shinnecocks on eastern Long Island. On August 5, 1741, Presbyterian missionary Azariah Horton, employed by the Society in Scotland for the Propagation of Christian Knowledge (SSPCK) for £40 per year, set out from Jamaica, New York, on western Long Island, for a two-month preaching tour among the various Indian communities of Long Island.[54] He stopped first at Rockaway, where he found thirty or so Indians who were "willing to hear, and ready to receive Instruction." Horton obliged in a sermon in which he "set before them the Sin of their Natures, that this exposed them to God's Anger and eternal Displeasure. And, briefly, to show them the Way of Reconciliation by Jesus Christ."[55] Horton continued eastward, arriving at Easthampton and then, on August 14, at the seasonal Montaukett community at Naapeck, roughly halfway between Easthampton and Montauk, which lay fourteen miles apart.

During the ensuing two months, Horton traveled back and forth between Montauk, Naapeck, Easthampton, Shinnecock, and Sebbonneck (close to Southampton), exhorting any groups of Indians he could find, holding larger meetings in Indian wigwams, and preaching to English and Indians in Euroamerican meetinghouses. Among the Indians of eastern Long Island, he reported unprecedented evangelistic success and sustained interest in the Christian gospel. At both Montauk and Sebbonneck, Indians came out in droves to hear Horton preach: more than seventy on August 23; fifty on the 25th; forty on the 26th, and as many the following day. Although the Natives preferred public meetings, according to Horton, he often spent time between lectures visiting door to door—or, more accurately, "from Wigwaam to Wigwaam"—asking direct questions to individuals and families about their spiritual conditions.[56]

The most interesting thing about Horton's itinerations, however, is that in the Indian communities on the eastern part of Long Island he found Natives who were either already "awakened" or had experienced some level of conviction from hearing other ministers and itinerant preachers. During his time at Naapeck, Horton met with twenty Natives on August 14, 1741, and in particular spoke with one Indian woman who gave him "a satisfactory Account of a saving Conversion from Sin unto God." She explained to Horton that at first she felt "a lively Sense of her actual Sins, and bewailed them exceedingly," but that "the Lord Jesus appeared to her exceedingly lovely; and that the Load of Guilt she felt before, was now gone; and that she felt Light."[57] In the evening of August 27, Horton reported meeting three girls who told him "the Lord Jesus Christ had eased them of the distressed Burden they felt" and went around singing a hymn written by the English hymnist Isaac Watts entitled "The Blessed Society in Heaven." The girls knew the song "partly by Heart, having heard some English People often sing it, and when they could not remember the Words, they kept the Tune along."[58] Clearly Horton was not the first one to inform these Natives of their supposedly lost condition. At most sermons, according to Horton, at least a few Indians were "awakened"; others were "filled with deeper concern"; and still others gave evidence that they had "passed through the Pangs of the New Birth." On September 2, 1741, Horton preached to forty Indians at Sebbonneck and reported that "some that were concerned before, brought under deeper Impressions of their guilty sinful State; one awakened; many made something thoughtful about their Souls."[59]

Not all Indians who were "savingly converted" had been previously well versed in Christian ideas, however. One woman approached Horton after a meeting in Southampton on September 3 and confessed that although "she had no Thoughts of another World a few Days before, now told me her Heart was sick and heavy."[60] On October 1, 1741, Horton reported that another woman at Sebbonneck who had "lived altogether among the Indians" and "was never concerned before" was "brought under dreadful Distress indeed, and continued about an Hour, as near as I can judge, and then appeared to be very joyful."[61] The few situations like this caused Horton to speculate that such converts had received their teaching directly from "the Almighty Spirit of Christ."[62]

The receptivity of the Montauketts and Shinnecocks on the eastern part of Long Island is all the more striking when compared with Horton's entries regarding the Indian communities of western Long Island. These western Long Island Indians did not give any initial evidence of spiritual agony or awakening to their supposed hardness of heart. Horton reported them to be generally open to what he had to say, but they responded much differently to his sermons than did the Montauketts who exhibited broad prior exposure to and acceptance of Christian ideas and practices. The most obvious explanation is that, similar to conditions in other localities in Connecticut and Rhode Island, the combination of the education of Indians and occasional lectures by local ministers and interested persons ensured that the Indian communities on eastern Long Island were familiar with the basic ideas of a fervent, reformed Christianity before Horton ever arrived. Davenport had come to Southold, just northwest of Easthampton and Montauk, in 1738 and had periodically held lectures and meetings among the Indians in the region, especially following a 1740 meeting with George Whitefield in New York. The Montaukett Indian minister Cyrus Charles, reflecting thirty years later on the events of the early 1740s, recalled that it was Davenport who came and "preached Jesus Christ to them." Davenport could not speak the Montaukett language, and many of the Montauketts were similarly unable to understand his sermons. Nonetheless, Charles reported, "the Holy Ghost interpreted it to our hearts."[63] Additionally, for two months prior to Horton's arrival in August 1741, Easthampton congregant Jacob Wickham had taken it upon himself to meet with the Shinnecock and Montaukett Indians each Sunday, during which time he would read the Bible to them, talk to them "in the best Manner he was capable," and pray with them. Horton reported—while careful not to undermine his own importance—that Wickham's "Endeavors, thro' God's Help, were attended with some Success."[64] Horton also credited the Reverend Jedediah Mills (Ripton, Connecticut), along with Davenport, with aiding in the conversion of nine Indians on Long Island before Horton's arrival in 1741.[65]

Among the Montauketts in particular, Horton's labors seem to have gotten a tragic boost. During a visit in February 21, 1742, Horton noticed that it was a "Time of Sickness among these Indians"; three persons died in one week and others grew dangerously ill. Horton hoped that the illnesses would be "a happy Means of awakening Christless *Indians*, to deep Concern for their own Souls, and to make speedy and diligent Preparation for the Time of their Departure hence!"[66] One Indian woman at Montauk publicly blamed Horton for the spate of illnesses, stating that the "Meetings were the Occasion of the sore Sickness and many Deaths which they were visited with."[67] Nonetheless, Horton spent many days talking with sick and dying Indians, and these various deaths and the deathbed speeches of a few Indians provoked an even greater attentiveness to Horton's message.[68] On March 22, 1742, Horton spent time with a dying Indian man, who, just before death, spoke to his gathered family and "begged them to take Care of their Souls Salvation."[69]

Although it is unlikely that the Montauketts "renounced all their heathenish idolatry and superstition" as a result of these revivals as some suggested, 1741 does seem to have been a pivotal year in the lives of some Natives on Long

Island.[70] Horton reported that as a result of the revivals, a number of Natives from various communities chose to travel long distances—up to sixteen miles— to attend weekly public worship services in English churches.[71] Horton himself made six missionary trips back and forth on Long Island between 1741 and 1744 and until his departure in 1751 continued to provide sermons, oversight, and spiritual leadership to the Montauketts and Shinnecocks. Other itinerant ministers occasionally passed through Montaukett and Shinnecock villages, preaching to any Natives who would assemble, as David Brainerd did at Montauk on Wednesday, March 9, 1743.[72]

Narragansett

In many ways, the Narragansetts were the last Native group in the region to experience the revivals. Building on the slow warming toward Christian ideas and practices over the course of the eighteenth century, the experiences of the revivals piqued the interest of many Narragansetts. Given their close proximity to Stonington in Connecticut, some of the Narragansetts would have undoubtedly attended revival services or at least heard about them, but there is little indication that anything changed as a result. In early 1743, however, the tide shifted. On Sunday, February 6, 1743, a number of Pequot Indians traveled from Stonington to visit the Narragansetts near Westerly, Rhode Island. In the evening, after holding the usual Sunday evening service at his own church, New Light Congregationalist minister Joseph Park rode out to meet with the combined group of Pequot and Narragansett Indians. The meeting started with a prayer, in which Park noted that "the LORD gave me to plead with him that his Kingdom might be seen coming in Power among the Indians." A hymn followed, during which "the Glory of the LORD was manifested more and more"; a "Spirit of Prayer and Supplication was poured out" upon the "Enlightened" among them, and "a Spirit of Conviction upon the Enemies of God." By this time, the meeting had taken on a life of its own; when Park tried to preach his sermon on 2 Corinthians 6:2, he reported that he was not able to continue "by Reason of the Outcry." Park contented himself with offering a few words of exhortation and stayed with them until late in the night. The Narragansetts and Pequots, however, "continued together all Night, and spent the most of the next Day and Night together."[73]

According to Park, this meeting marked a significant turning point in his attempts to evangelize the Narragansetts. Although previously he could convince only ten or twelve Indians to attend his church services, by September 1743, seven months after the meeting, he reported closer to a hundred in regular attendance, six of whom had received baptism.[74] Indians were not only baptized; Park was convinced some were also transformed. In the wake of the religious revivals,

Park reported that at least some of the Narragansetts had "forsaken their Dances and drunken Frolicks, appear sober and serious," and adopted a variety of Christian practices and rituals that they had heretofore resisted. "They flocked more to the House and Worship of God," Park reported, "than they were wont to do their Frolicks," and "very diligently attend the preaching of the Word of God and Prayer."[75] The revival spilled over into local Native households and communities where they "set up the Worship of God in their Families; praying and singing God's Praise" and held "frequent private Meetings among themselves for Prayer and Praise, and Conference; particularly stated on Sabbath Day Evenings, and Wednesday Evenings." Natives who embraced the revivals quickly became evangelists, too, attempting to "bring over such as oppose themselves; by setting forth the Evil of their Ways, in which they used to walk with them, and the Comfort and Sweetness of a divine Life"; in larger meetings the Christian Indians "plead[ed] with their Brethren to come over on the Lord's Side."[76]

Such religious transformation also worked wonders in changing what Park called the "outward as well as the inward Man"—welcome news to his ministerial colleagues and sponsors in Boston and England. "They grow more decent and cleanly in their outward Dress," Park rejoiced, and "provide better for their Households, and get clearer of Debt." Most of all, converted Narragansetts began to win the war against the "Sin of Drunkeness," as some Indians were reported to "have no Desire after strong Drink, but loath it; others that a little Dram satisfies and refreshes them more than to guzzle it down as they used to do." Drunkeness and quarrelling—common English stereotypes of Indian activity—now brought "great Sorrow of Heart" to the newly converted. These awakened Indians, in fact, put Park and other whites to shame with their "Zeal, and fervent Charity among themselves." Although new in the faith and largely illiterate, Park declared that "they may well be called experienced Christians; and are Examples of Faith, Patience, Love, Humility, and every Grace of the Spirit of God."[77]

Certainly some of these rosy descriptions were merely wishful projections of what Park and others hoped would be the long-term results of the revivals. Nonetheless, the February 6, 1743, meeting with Park and the Pequots was an important moment in the Narragansetts' religious engagement. These same Narragansetts, however, had been cued for more than twenty years to the practices of reformed Protestantism, and the apparent embrace of Christianity by some of them cannot be understood apart from this prior exposure, or apart from the influence of the awakened Pequots who had traveled to the Narragansetts, most likely with the specific intent of encouraging them to consider the spiritual, practical, and cultural opportunities Christianity afforded. Additionally, the experience of the Narragansetts is a reminder that interest in the revivals was not universal. In addition to what likely amounted to "traditionalist" factions on almost every reservation (as evidenced by the contestation over religious practices in the 1730s), at Narragansett especially a group loyal to the sachem existed that seemed to prefer at least ongoing symbolic alliance with the local Anglican minister. Consequently, the revivals that took place at Park's Congregational church had little drawing power for this population of Narragansetts.

Other Indian Communities

Portions of other Native communities throughout southern New England participated in varying versions of the Awakening, even those on the farther outreaches of colonial settlement. On May 13, 1742, the Pachgatgoch Indians near Kent, Connecticut—just miles from the New York border—wrote to the Connecticut General Assembly describing their spiritual situation. There were "about Seventy Souls of us poor natives who are now Awakened," they reported. "Many of us to See a necessity of Being Taught the word of God and the Gospell of Jesus Christ in order to obtain Eternal Life through Him." Once again, education was central to their concerns. The Pachgatgochs requested of the Assembly a schoolteacher to have their children "Taught to Read the English Tongue" and a minister "to preach the Gospell of Jesus Christ unto us; and Instruct us in the Principles of the Christian Religion."[78] New Light minister David Brainerd preached to the Pachgatgochs on August 12, 1742, as did a few other local English ministers.[79] But when the Assembly failed to send someone who would live among them, the Pachgatgochs took matters into their own hands and invited the Moravians from nearby Shekomeko in New York to live with them, which they did starting in early 1743.

The Moravians arose within German Lutheranism under Philip Jacob Spener in the seventeenth century, and their religious practices blended pre-Reformation spirituality and seventeenth-century Continental Pietism. They were best known for their emphasis on the blood and wounds of Christ and a warm, heart-centered religious community. The Moravians, drawn by their increasing commitment to worldwide evangelism, first arrived in the American colonies in 1735 and were initially viewed with immense suspicion. The Moravian presence in western Connecticut during a time of religious and military turmoil alarmed Connecticut officials, who promptly arrested and marched them to Milford for a week-long trial. Although the Moravians were partially acquitted of some of the charges—they were proven not to be Catholics with insidious designs—they were nonetheless warned out of Connecticut under the threat of a hefty fine.[80] Not everyone despised the Moravian presence among the Indians, however; John Sergeant at Stockbridge approvingly noted in May 1743 that "a *Moravian Missionary*, not far from hence, has to Appearance had a wonderful *Success* among a Number."[81] As the diaries of the Moravian missionaries to the Pachgatgochs indicate, itinerant ministers drifted in and out of the

Pachgatgoch Native community for several decades, offering sermons and coming to inspect the work of the Moravians, who had returned there a few years after their expulsion.[82]

In some more remote areas, individual families and communities took advantage of the renewed interest in their well-being by requesting educational and material aid. In 1741 Hachet Tousey (Atchetoset), living in the Shepaug region of West Woodbury (southwest of Farmington), petitioned the Connecticut General Assembly, declaring his intention to "embrace the christian faith" and desiring that six of his eight children might be educated and financially supported by the colony. Twenty pounds were given to satisfy Tousey's request, and local magistrates were instructed to see that his children were put into schools and fed.[83] Such charity cases built on earlier educational practices in Connecticut, in which Indian parents had the satisfaction of seeing their children fed, clothed, and housed by English schoolteachers and ministers.

The communities of Indians around Farmington, Connecticut, also reported periods of religious revival. In early 1743, John Mettawan, the educated and Christianized schoolteacher and informal minister to the Farmington Indians, reported in a letter, "There is a disposition among them to embrace Christianity: about 20 of them have been baptized & in some there is an appeearence of vital piety & religion." Additionally, the school that he had been keeping since 1737 was thriving, and many students were advancing in literacy and religious instruction. "Some can read well in the Bible, others in their Testaments, others are in their Psalter, others in their primmers, and a list of the books needful is herewith sent." Mettawan acknowledged the role of the New England Company in these developments, noting, "We don't only thankfully acknowledge your past care, and bounty but pray the continuance of it."[84]

Even more than any other recently evangelized Indian communities in Connecticut, Rhode Island, or on Long Island, the Mohicans at Stockbridge, Massachusetts, experienced the Awakening as merely a continuation of what had already been started half a decade prior to 1740. The Northampton revivals (1734–1735) were taking place at the same time Sergeant and Woodbridge were first preaching to and teaching the Housatonic Indians near what became Stockbridge, but virtually none of this revival influence comes through in the records.[85] The Stockbridge community—Indians and English—participated in the revivals of the 1740s, however. On May 20, 1743, Sergeant rejoiced that "of late a Reformation is very visible among us."[86] In August he reported that one of his Indian students had proved "very helpful among the young Indians in a general religious Concern that has of late prevailed among them."[87]

These various collected accounts of Native participation in the Great Awakening confirm that previously un-Christianized Natives in southeastern New England participated in the First Great Awakening, but these events represented neither a sudden intrusion of Christian ideas into the lives of Natives nor a reversal of former disinterest in Christianity. Rather, it was a fairly natural extension of two full decades of Native individuals and communities engaging with Christian ministers, educators, ideas, and practices. Educational opportunities co-existed with revival services during the Awakening, as just one sign of this continuity. David Brainerd paid an English woman to hold a school for Pachgatgoch children near Kent in 1742.[88] Azariah Horton hired a literate Indian woman to teach English to Native children near Quaog on Long Island in the winter of 1743–1744.[89] Before an official school was set up among the Narragansetts, as early as 1744 Joseph Park and the NEC employed a Narragansett woman to "keep School in a Wigwam," where she taught Native children to read.[90] Samson Occom, similarly, set up a small school during the winter of 1747–1748 at Mohegan.

Certain aspects of the revivals were new, however, and proved to be immensely popular among particular subgroups of Natives within each Indian community. The boisterous singing, extemporaneous preaching, explicit licensing of individual ecstatic religious experience, and overall framing of anti-authoritarianism in favor of individual expression and religious authority are part of what gave the revivals such traction among Indians and whites alike. The question, of course, is how this effusive moment played out over time in the lives and communities of Native Americans, particularly with regard to local Euroamerican churches.

4

Affiliating

The church service lasted far longer than usual. But Irene Doit didn't mind, despite the songs, sermons, liturgies, hard benches, and lengthy stretches of speaking in the English language that, while not exactly unfamiliar, were all things she was still getting used to. She was, after all, receiving baptism on that balmy sixteenth day of June in 1742. The entire North Stonington Congregational Church was tangibly abuzz with the unprecedented events of the past few weeks and months, and Doit herself was lost in the crowd that day as a spectacular throng of seventy-nine people made formal Christian affiliations on what the minister Joseph Fish declared to be a "great and glorious day of Grace." Despite the crowd, Doit likely still stood out as one of only five Indians paraded before the congregation. Sixty-six of the seventy-nine individuals gave testimonies of faith and were received into full membership; the remaining thirteen, including all five Natives—Doit, Charity Phagens, Sarah Simons, Sarah Putak, and Peter Quahaug—merely received baptism. Doit had likely met separately with Fish in the preceding weeks to ensure that her affirmation of faith was acceptably sincere. No narration of grace was necessary, at least not publicly, for what amounted to a partial membership in the North Stonington Church as a result of owning the covenant and receiving baptism. Nonetheless, it was a formal affiliation that set her apart from most of her Pequot friends and neighbors.[1]

A decade later, however, Doit was no longer a member of Fish's church. Doit became pregnant under suspicious circumstances in 1751 and made several accusations about the child's father that that are not recorded but seem to have involved rape or other wrongdoing. During the delivery of her illegitimate child in 1752, Anna Frink, an Englishwoman who was present, rather inopportunely asked Irene "whether she had not Injured the Truth In her Accusation, Respecting the Father of her Child," and counseled her that it was "better to go back than to persist in Falsehood." Doit, exasperated at being accosted during childbirth, retorted that she "had gone too far to go back," which Frink and others thought sounded suspiciously close to an admission of lying.[2] Having caught wind of this exchange, the North Stonington Church ordered a full investigation

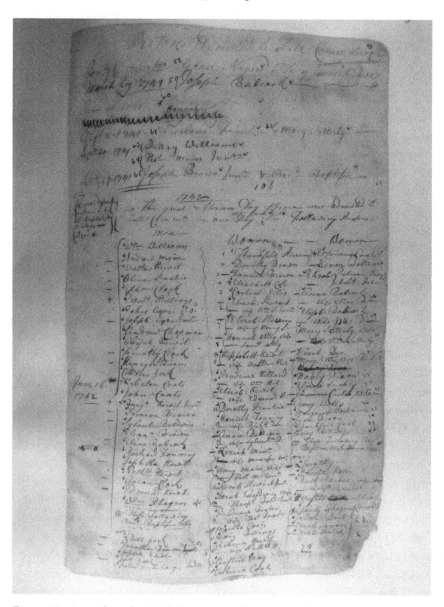

Figure 4.1. Image from the North Stonington Church Records. Entry at top of listing reads: "1742 In this great & Glorious Day of Grace was admitted to Full Commn in one Day viz: June the 16 the Following Persons." Seventy-nine persons are listed, of whom sixty-six joined as full members and thirteen were baptized, including four Indian women listed in the bottom right corner (Charity Phagens, Irene Doit, Sarah Simons, and Sarah Putak). At the bottom left one Indian man is listed as having received baptism as well. North Stonington Church Records, CSL, 1:9. Courtesy of the Connecticut State Library. Photograph by the author.

and on July 6, 1752, decided that Doit was guilty but offered her a full return to "Charity & Privledges" if she would publicly confess her sins. Unsurprisingly, Doit did not make a confession and does not appear again in the church records.[3]

Although it is difficult to measure what Natives *believed* about Christian doctrines, it is somewhat easier to investigate what they *did* in the years immediately following the Awakening. One concrete way to measure action—in this case, public rituals, which, in turn, shed light on more obscure interior processes—is by examining the baptismal and church membership records of specific Congregational churches that were within close geographical proximity to individual Indian communities. Natives, like their Euroamerican counterparts, often expressed faith commitments by formal associations with churches, as Doit did, but it is important to trace how these associations unfolded over time.

Judging by the records, "affiliation," rather than "conversion," seems a more precise way to describe the relationships of Native Americans to white colonial churches during the Great Awakening and to more accurately represent how Natives might have understood such relationships. Conversion often implies a unidirectional, total, complete, and usually permanent transformation from one religious "state" of being to another, whereas affiliation is one element of religious engagement and reflects an elasticity in religious association as lived, which was often provisional and changeable. Although adult Indians might have sometimes "converted" in some sort of abstract sense, this information is not usually recoverable. In most cases, Natives who found the revivals and particular aspects of Christianity attractive affiliated with particular colonial churches in one or more of three very specific ways: (1) attending a local English church (a fairly anonymous level of affiliation); (2) receiving baptism and becoming a "partial" member of a local English church; or (3) owning the covenant (and perhaps giving a confession of faith), thereby becoming a full member.[4] Additionally, Indians could affiliate in two related ways: they could present their child or children for baptism (which required a parent to be at least a partial member) or they could marry in an Anglo-Christian fashion, in a local church with the ceremony performed by an English minister.[5] Indians who affiliated in all of these ways could also deaffiliate, though such a deaffiliation need not be read as a spiritual falling away. Many Indians—like some colonists—tried Christian affiliations and practices for a while. Practices that could be adopted could also be dropped without "conversion" or its apparent opposite, "apostasy" or "deconversion," taking place.[6]

Church affiliation is an imperfect gauge of the religious sentiments and practices of Indians, but it is at least one step closer to observing in a measurable way public engagement with Christian ideas and practices—engagement that, as Doit discovered, came with an immense amount of community oversight and spiritual policing. What affiliations mostly measure is the degree to which an

Indian felt that having formal ties with an English institution was important, meaningful, or viable. Nonetheless, a close examination of church records in the years preceding, during, and after the peak of the Great Awakening reveals patterns of Native affiliation that involved fewer Indians and for a shorter period of time than has been previously acknowledged, and for reasons that are far more complicated than appear on the surface.

Parsing "Conversion"

During the Awakening, revivalists in the British Atlantic World used a variety of terms to designate the various expected and predictable stages people moved through en route to a conversion experience. Ministers recognized that the pathway to salvation was marked by discernible signs in at least three distinct stages: "first, fear, anxiety, and distress at one's sinfulness in the sight of a holy God"; second, "absolute dependence on the sovereign mercy of God in Jesus Christ"; and third, a "sense of relief from their distress under conviction of sin and their joy at being accepted of God."[7] To be "awakened" was often the beginning, not the end, of the process; to be awakened was not to be saved but merely to be made aware of one's sinfulness and hardness of heart. The vocabulary of awakening had many synonyms: one could be "awakened," "concerned," "wounded," and "touched," all without experiencing "conversion."[8] One of the innovations of New Light revivalists was the dramatization of the conversion process, along with the collapsing of the time frame of conversion generally expected among Anglo Protestants in New England in the preceding century.[9] Many individuals received conviction of sin and assurance of salvation in a short time period. Both the conviction and the assurance could be noisy, showy events.

In reports, letters, and journals produced during the Great Awakening, Indians were widely reported to have experienced the full range of this morphology, including having been "hopefully converted." Scholars, following assessments of eighteenth-century ministers and missionaries, have too often read Indian participation in the Great Awakening as "conversion," perhaps assuming that the narrated experiences of the eventual Mohegan minister, Samson Occom, and the reports of missionaries and ministers reflected the religious experience of all Natives.[10] Understanding what a broader spectrum of Indians thought about the issue of religious change is difficult. Natives rarely wrote or relayed what affiliation or "conversion" might have meant in this time period (examples of this become more common in the later eighteenth century as literacy rates rose). Hints of possible differing ideas about what "conversion" meant come from the seventeenth century, however. John Eliot, the lifelong Massachusetts-based missionary, when attempting to translate the title of Thomas Shepard's classic work,

The Sincere Convert, into the Massachusett language, chose to use *Sampwutteahae uinnuppekompauaenin*, which literally means "man who stands turned-about."[11] Eliot's reliance on a lengthy descriptive phrase to describe conversion suggests that eastern Algonquians—unsurprisingly—did not have a corresponding concept in their experiential religious vocabulary.[12] Native Christians influenced by Eliot, however, having been exposed to Christian ideas (including conversion), did make reference to their religious change, but often in terms that made more sense to them. Contrasted to Eliot's "turned-about" notion of conversion, for example, is the Pennacook tribal leader, Wannalancet, who, after months of evangelistic attempts by John Eliot and Daniel Gookin, finally confessed in 1674 that he was willing to "leave my old canoe, and embark in a new canoe."[13] Such a metaphor encapsulates both the change and continuity perhaps envisioned and practiced by Christianized Natives.

In the eighteenth century, one striking model for thinking about the meaning of "conversion" for Native Americans comes from a story attributed to Occom in the mid-1770s and told to a primarily Indian audience. In a sermon, illustrating what Occom called "traditionary religion," he told an anecdote of an old Indian who "had a knife which he kept till he wore the blade out; and then his son took it and put a new blade to the handle, and kept it till he had worn the handle out; and this process went on till the knife had a half dozen blades, and as many handles." "Still," Occom insisted, "it was all the time the same knife."[14] One of the eighteenth-century meanings of "traditionary" given by the Oxford English Dictionary is "one who maintains or accepts the authority of tradition"; in this case, the tradition would be, of course, Native religious lifeways. In this powerful anecdote, Occom reveals the tensions and continuities in the process of generational religious transmission and no doubt saw himself as the son in the story, adding blades and handles to what his own forefathers had given him. It is surprising that Occom would describe his own religious outlook in this way, since he is often represented as the most thoroughly Anglicized and Christianized of Indians in eighteenth-century New England.

Although the particular brand of eighteenth-century Christianity most Indians were offered tended to see religious ideas as competing and exclusionary, Occom's metaphor suggests that Indians had long incorporated new ideas and practical skills alongside old ones, often without intending to drop, remove, or alter the existing ones. This would strongly suggest that Natives, whether individually or communally, rarely "converted" in some sort of totalizing way, as is often assumed.[15] In adopting Christian practices, and even in making professions of Christian faith and receiving baptism, Indians did not "commit cultural suicide, to cease to be an Indian."[16] Instead, Indian approaches to religion were incorporative, and Christian beliefs—like blades on Occom's knife—could have been appended in provisional and incomplete ways, without intellectual or religious discomfort, no matter how foreign this possibility might have appeared to Euroamerican missionaries. This distinctive Indian approach to new or contrasting ideas about the world was one of the first things Roger Williams noted. When Williams challenged eastern Algonquian creation stories in the 1640s with the Christian six-day version of divine creation, Natives responded by affirming that "they deny not that English-mans God made English Men, and the Heavens and Earth there," and that "their Gods made them and the Heaven, and the Earth where they dwell."[17]

A broader, Native-centered understanding of religious engagement also shifts away from questions regarding "authenticity" as it related to "conversion"— something eighteenth-century ministers and even some later historians worried about—particularly whether the experience of the Awakening produced "bona fide" Christians.[18] Such questions artificially proscribe the boundaries of historical inquiry, obscure the different choices Natives made, and ignore the important reality that many Natives did not think in terms of a totalizing, Euro-Christian religious "conversion." Natives conceptualized their association with Christian idioms, practices, and rituals in surprisingly dynamic terms. The point is not to argue that Natives who adopted Christian practices were *not* Christians but rather to highlight the spectrum of possible responses Natives could and did choose—decisions and actions that fluctuated and were always related to other lived realities, whether social, economic, or political.

Even in cases where Christian ideas and practices became deeply meaningful for individual Indians, these were not necessarily conceptualized and lived out in ways completely parallel to the varieties of Euroamerican experiences. Even as written texts—such as scripture—can be and have been understood in vastly different ways, meanings inscribed in rituals might have varied greatly between the minister and the parishioner, the Anglo and the Native. The meanings, then, of the various rituals of affiliation should not necessarily be exclusively read through the lens of European Christianity. Baptisms that in the eyes of ministers represented spiritual rebirth, a token of religious commitment, and a basic assent to reformed Christian doctrines might mean all this to Indian participants, but they could also be related to ideas of protection, access to education, and cultural uplift. The possible meanings were endless for Natives, ranging from fully shared with colonists to fully divergent.[19]

Church Records and Native Affiliations

A more Native-centered approach to the question of religious engagement involves looking at the specific ways that Natives affiliated with local colonial churches during and after the Awakening. The Great Awakening did not mark the first time Natives attended English churches, but it did bring about a noticeable upswing in formal Native affiliations. American Indian baptisms and membership admissions in the record books of specific New Light churches provide one concrete way to gauge the scope and meaning of the Great Awakening. The records of the First, Second, and East Congregational churches in Stonington, Connecticut (close to the Lantern Hill Pequot reserved lands), offer such an opportunity, as the ministers of all three churches in the 1740s embraced the revival and experienced significant increases in baptisms and memberships among Anglos and Indians alike.[20] While these church records are only one window into the meaning of the Great Awakening among Native communities, they are nonetheless surprisingly helpful in answering questions related to who was involved and when.

In these churches there were 128 instances of Indian affiliations between 1730 and 1750—meaning adult baptism and owning the covenant (partial membership), infant baptism, full membership (could take communion), or marriage.[21] The actual number of Indians involved was approximately 108, since at least 20 Natives affiliated in more than one way (baptism *and* marriage, for example). Of these 108 Natives (presumably Pequots), 62 were adults and 46 were children. Forty-four adults received baptism but only eighteen joined one of the three Stonington churches as full members. All forty-six children received baptism. Eleven Native marriages took place during this twenty-year time period, mostly distributed between 1738 and 1747, with a slight concentration of them occurring between 1742 and 1744. Somewhat surprisingly, only five of the Native individuals involved between 1730 and 1750 were listed as servants in the church records, which indicates that the vast majority of these affiliations were relatively uncoerced. Although there is a definite gender imbalance in adult Indian baptism and full membership (twenty-three men; thirty-nine women), it is not as large as one might expect. In colonial New England's Congregational churches women had long comprised the majority of full members—between 54 percent and 84 percent, depending on the church.[22] Indian membership trends in the 1740s also followed this pattern, with more women affiliating in general, and in more ways (baptism, full member, and bringing their children for baptism, for example). However, adult female Indian affiliations in the three Stonington churches only accounted for 63 percent of Indian affiliations in this time period, which placed this gender ratio at the lower end of the broader colonial spectrum.

From these Stonington church records, several important patterns emerge. These records confirm that, like Euroamericans in this same time period, Indian Christian affiliation was sometimes a family affair. Married Indian couples who joined as members often brought their young children for baptism. In other cases, members of extended families affiliated at the same time. Between June

1741 and July 1742, fifteen members of the extended Garret family affiliated with one of the three Stonington churches, five of them doing so on the same day at the First Stonington Church. Similarly, Robin Cassacinamon (II) watched as his entire nuclear family (wife and four children) was baptized on June 14, 1741, at the First Stonington Church. Cassacinamon himself, however, held off for another eight months before receiving baptism on February 14, 1742. As with the Mohegans, when members of the Pequot tribal leadership formally affiliated with Christianity, their actions had an impact on subsegments of the community. Just three months after receiving baptism at the First Stonington Church, Robin Cassacinamon's name was listed (along with the names of forty other Pequots) on the May 1742 petition to the Connecticut General Assembly in which they stated that some of them had "believed on the Lord Jesus Christ" and desired to have more instruction.[23] Such a family-centered practice of Christian ritual would have warmed the heart of the Boston Congregational minister Increase Mather, who observed in 1678—although certainly not with American Indians in mind—that God had drawn the line of election so that "it doth (though not wholly, and only, yet) for the most part, run through the loins of godly Parents."[24]

These records also reveal that the timetables of the levels of affiliation varied greatly (baptism versus full member). In many cases, Indians were baptized, made a profession of faith, and joined in full membership in one day. Such was the case with Gideon and Judah Harry, a Pequot husband and wife who joined as full members on April 18, 1742. In other instances, individuals were drawn to the church and baptized, but only later joined as full members. Tobiah Sockient, for example, was baptized as an adult at the First Stonington Church on July 12, 1741, thereby making him a "partial" member of sorts. Eight months later he was received into the same church as a full member.

Perhaps the most important thing these records clearly indicate is the striking timeline of Indian Christian affiliation. Using these records, a basic chronology of Indian affiliation in Stonington can be reconstructed. American Indian affiliations of any sort were rare in the 1710s and 1720s, picked up gradually in the 1730s (twelve in all three churches), spiked in 1741 and 1742, dropped off sharply by 1743, and by 1750 had returned to only sporadic affiliations with the exception of marriages, of which there were a handful—rather inexplicably—in the 1750s and 1760s. Of these 128 Indian affiliations, a clear majority of them (84) took place in a concentrated year and a half period between June 1741 and October 1742, which seems to be the high point of the Indian participation in Stonington. In some senses, this merely confirms what historians have assumed all along: that Indians in southeastern New England flocked to local churches during the Awakening. Taken together with the larger context of the eighteenth century, however, these church records underscore that the spike in affiliations

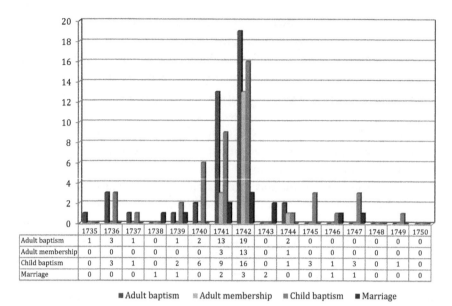

	1735	1736	1737	1738	1739	1740	1741	1742	1743	1744	1745	1746	1747	1748	1749	1750
Adult baptism	1	3	1	0	1	2	13	19	0	2	0	0	0	0	0	0
Adult membership	0	0	0	0	0	0	3	13	0	1	0	0	0	0	0	0
Child baptism	0	3	1	0	2	6	9	16	0	1	3	1	3	0	1	0
Marriage	0	0	0	1	1	0	2	3	2	0	0	1	1	0	0	0

■ Adult baptism   ▨ Adult membership   ■ Child baptism   ■ Marriage

Figure 4.2. Native Affiliations with the First, Second, and East Stonington (Connecticut) Congregational Churches, 1735–1750.

in 1741 and 1742 did not simply appear from nowhere. There was a buildup in terms of Indian interest in Christianity and a basic literacy concerning Christian ideas that made involvement in the Awakening a religiously and culturally attractive possibility for some individuals. The fact that there were twenty-three affiliations in these three churches in the decade preceding 1741 is significant and parallels similar evidence among other communities of increasing engagement with English Christianity prior to the Great Awakening.

More notable is the drop-off of Indian affiliations after 1742, and especially after 1750, which calls into question the long-term meaning of the Awakening in American Indian communities. Although it is not possible to definitively say whether or not every Indian who affiliated remained in English churches, the records strongly suggest that institutional affiliation did not always last long, or at least not at the same levels of intensity. The main evidence for this is twofold. First, the number of adult Indians being baptized or admitted to full membership in the Stonington churches drops off sharply after 1742, even though the overwhelming majority of the Pequot adults had not yet joined in full membership. Second, even though several Indian children were brought forward for baptism between 1744 and 1750, after 1750 the baptism of Indian children ceases completely. No Indian child was baptized in a Stonington church from 1750 through the early 1770s. Compared with the forty-six Indian children baptized in the Stonington churches during the previous twenty years (1730–1750), this represents a dramatic drop in the willingness of Indian parents to present their children for baptism.

What does this all mean? One possible interpretation is that although many Natives participated in revival services, most of them never internalized core Christian doctrines in the same way as some eventual Christian Indian leaders, like Samuel Niles, Peter John, Joseph Johnson, or Samson Occom.[25] Some Natives simply stopped attending any Christian religious services and abandoned Christian practices they had once found meaningful. Joseph Fish observed this among the Narragansetts in Rhode Island. In 1768, during one of his monthly preaching visits, Fish visited William Sachem, a Narragansett man aligned with the sachem's party in the ongoing land controversies, and reported that William had "got a hope of Grace, in Former times but for Years past lives poorly." Fish reproved him "for not reading the Bible (as he Says he Can read it Well,) in his Family daily." Knowledge of the Christian faith was not the problem; neither was literacy. William had just grown disinterested. Exasperated, Fish "endeavoured to Awake him to a Sense of his Duty and Danger," but to no apparent effect.[26]

In other cases, some Native men and women were forced out of local churches in the years after the Awakening when they failed to conform to European Christian sexual and social norms.[27] Such was the case with Irene Doit. So, too, with Mercy Laten, who was accused of "the Sins of Drunkenness & Fornication," and Hagar, a "Molotto," was accused of "Fornication" by the North Stonington Church in 1746. Instead of submitting to the church leadership, they refused to show up and make the requisite confession of wrongdoing, so on December 1, 1746, they were both "Judged & Declared Guilty of Contempt of the Authority of Christ in his Chh" and suspended from fellowship.[28] The same fate befell Mr. Palmer's servant, "Indian John," who had joined the First Baptist Church of Groton in June 1764.[29] Less than a year later, on February 22, 1765, John was brought before the church members and confessed "that he had been out of the way being at the Ferry setting & Drinking with bad Company & that he used bad words at home." The church forgave him after his apology and promise of "Reformation." A year later, however, on April 5, 1766, John was again called before the church, but this time he did not show. John did come to a second meeting called just five days later, on April 10, in which he was asked to "Tell honestly how it was with him and Give an Account of his Conduct." John refused, however, and instead insisted that they tell him "what they had heard." Four people then stepped forward (all suspiciously related—with the last name Burrows) who said that they heard Indian John "Make a gam[e of] Religion and the Worship of God and Said Sometimes he Did not believe their was any God." The Burrowses testified they also witnessed him drunk, claimed that he often would "Curs and swear by his makers Name," and frequently took part in the "Playing of Cards." Having heard the charges, John confessed the accusations to be "just and true" but—particularly with regard to playing cards—he declared "it is no harm" and refused to demonstrate the repentance demanded of the church. The church members pleaded with John to see the error of his ways "in Order to Reclaim him" but when he remained "obstinate" and unrepentant, they proceeded to "Withdraw their hand of Fellowship from Sd John and Deliver him up to the Visebell [Visible] Kingdom of Satan for the Destruction of the flesh that, the Spirit May be saved for the day of the Lord Jesus."[30]

Other individuals were accused of nonattendance over time, along with allegations of other kinds of misconduct. In the North Groton Congregational Church, Indians Mary Johnson, Sarah Tervis, Dido Mezen, and Dorcas, along with several black or mulatto individuals (Ackery, Bristol, and Phebe) were all charged by church members of various wrongdoing over the course of several years (in Mezen's case, "for long sinfully neglecting the public worship & ordinances of God, for drunkenness, & disorderly behavior") and eventually suspended from fellowship when all but Johnson refused to show the desired repentance and confession. Johnson, who had been accused of "lying, in saying & spreading a false report" regarding fellow churchgoer Thomas Wells, made a full public confession on October 19, 1745, and was that same day voted by the church back into full communion.[31] The process of expelling Natives from English churches, while seemingly not part of some proto-racist master plan, was surprisingly widespread and lasted at least into the 1770s.[32]

Added to all of this was the harsh and persistent reality that despite formal Christian profession and affiliation, Natives were treated with the same level of contempt and marginalization within the physical church spaces as they were without. Most New England churches were rather hierarchical in the arrangement of social classes (which in many cases involved the purchase or rental of pews and pew boxes by those who could afford them) as well as divided by gender (men on one side and women on the other). Despite the seemingly inclusive rituals of Christian initiation like baptism and church membership, the ongoing relegation of people of color to physical peripheries—rear, sides, and galleries—in English churches continued to remind Indians of their racially inferior status, even in the professed embrace of Christian fellowship.[33] Extra requirements for baptism and membership created additional obstacles to entry and ongoing participation. Ben Uncas II, for example, was "propounded for Baptism" on October 17, 1742, a recommendation that was accompanied by an extra requirement designed to deal with what colonists viewed as the Indians' worst vice: a "Confession of Excessive Drinking" that was "Read & accepted" by the congregation.[34] A deep and persistent prejudice pervaded English-Indian relations in churches and added to the many reasons some Natives had for feeling disillusioned with English churches and even Christianity itself.

Another explanation for the short-lived involvement of Natives in Anglo churches, however, is that over time Indian Christians voted with their feet and favored either Anglo Separate churches or—over time—Indian Separate churches. Evidence of such "Indian Separatism" abounds, especially from the mid-1740s onward.[35]

All this highlights an important point however: many of the Indians, perhaps even a substantial majority of them, chose not to publicly identify with Christianity at all during this time period, or at least not in this particular set of events in the early 1740s.[36] Getting a firm sense of the percentages of the larger Indian population that these affiliations represent is often difficult since population estimates of these Indian groups vary widely. Nonetheless, it might be helpful to apply a given metric to existing estimates. Using the population estimates reported by Governor Talcott of Connecticut in 1725, 20 percent can be added to them to account for individuals missed in the estimates.[37] If adults comprised roughly two-fifths of the population, Native affiliations can be compared in a fairly standardized way to the Indian population as a whole in particular communities. In 1725, Talcott reported 218 Lantern Hill Pequot men, women, and children on their reserved lands; adding 20 percent raises the total to 261, or approximately 104 adults and 157 children. This means that slightly more than half of the Lantern Hill Pequot adults—62 of the 104—affiliated with the church in some way between 1735 and 1750, and only 17.3 percent of the adult Indian population became full members of the church. And Stonington was a town that actually saw a lot of Native baptisms and memberships; some towns saw far fewer among even larger populations of Indians, such as Groton and New London.

Due to poor recordkeeping in some churches in eighteenth-century southern New England, it is not always possible to tabulate the kind and number of affiliations in other churches as in Stonington.[38] Nonetheless, a few English ministers proudly published the numbers of Indians who affiliated with their respective churches during the Awakening. George Griswold reported in the *Christian History* that he had received "into the communion of the church" thirteen Niantics between March 7, 1742, and May 8, 1743.[39] Applying the formula above to Talcott's 1725 estimates, there might have been 192 Indians on Niantic lands, 77 of whom were adults. The thirteen Natives Griswold reported who had joined as full members account for 17 percent of the Niantic adult population. Even taking into consideration the possible tabulation inconsistencies at every point, these affiliations represent approximately the same percentage among the Niantic population as among the Lantern Hill Pequots.

Conversely, in Rhode Island, Native affiliations with the New Light Congregational church constituted a larger percentage of the Narragansett population than among the Pequots. By February 1744, Joseph Park joyfully noted that sixty-four Narragansetts had "professed Subjection to the Gospel of Christ."[40] Using estimates that placed the Narragansett population at 400 and applying the formula explained earlier brings the total number to 480, 192 of whom were adults.[41] This means that approximately 33 percent (64 of 192) of the Narragansett adults affiliated through full membership—16 percent more than among the Lantern Hill Pequots.[42] It is interesting to note, however, that affiliation with the Anglican church on Narragansett lands (present by the sachem's invitation from 1727 onward) was entirely nonexistent, according to the records. James McSparran, the Anglican minister who was based in North Kingstown but made at least monthly trips to the Narragansett Anglican church, recorded not even one instance of Narragansett Indian affiliation from 1727 through the end of his ministry in Rhode Island in 1757. The consistent non-Indian affiliations he recorded at this same church in Narragansett territory indicates that the church was indeed active but that whatever number of Narragansetts may have attended simply did not feel compelled to make any sort of public commitment to the church or the Christian faith.[43]

On Long Island, the story was quite different from the Congregational churches in Connecticut and more like McSparran's church on Narragansett lands, but for different reasons. Although there are fairly complete records of the East Hampton Presbyterian Church, which was the closest English church to the Montauketts, and although Natives seem to be consistently marked in the records when they do appear, there are simply no Indian affiliations at all between 1727 and 1751. This is the case even though from 1746 onward the church had as its minister Samuel Buell, who was active among the Native populations and concerned about their evangelization (and, indeed, preached the ordination sermon for Samson Occom in 1759).[44] A partial explanation may lie in the relative geographical isolation of the Montauketts, who had to travel a full sixteen miles from their reserved lands to the East Hampton church. Additionally, given their relatively poor treatment by local officials, such affiliation might have been wholly undesirable. The church closest to the Shinnecocks, the First Presbyterian Church of Southampton, does not have extant records prior to 1785, so it is impossible to gauge affiliations there.[45]

Indians on Long Island were still receiving baptism, however, and even owning the covenant. The unique thing about Long Island Natives is that very nearly 100 percent of the Native rituals of affiliation during the Awakening (and thereafter) were performed on Native lands and, over time, in conjunction with nascent Native congregations. Although these Native churches have amorphous beginnings and virtually no written records until the nineteenth century, the journals of SSPCK missionary Azariah Horton record what is undoubtedly the majority of Native awakenings and affiliations on Long Island in the early 1740s.[46] Between August 1741 and March 1744, Horton recorded eighty-seven instances of what he deemed a conversion, thirty instances of adults owning the covenant and being baptized (both at once), and forty instances of children receiving baptism.[47] Horton estimated the total populations he served to be 400, both "young and old," which, applying the above formula, means approximately 480 Natives he was dealing with, or 192 adults and 288 children. Therefore, "conversions" constitute 45 percent of the adult population as a whole, but the actual rate of affiliation was only 15.6 percent (30 out of 192). As a proportion of the total child population, the number of baptized children was 13.8 percent. These numbers fall into the low end of the spectrum of affiliations compared with the other Native populations, but they still seem to follow the basic pattern of affiliation among Indian communities in terms of far more adults "converting" than affiliating. The gender dynamic also seems a bit accentuated on Long Island, with twice as many women as men reportedly converted (fifty-six women; twenty-eight men; the gender is unclear for three additional individuals). Similarly, nineteen women owned the covenant and were baptized, but only eleven men did so. In most cases, it was the mother who brought forward her children for baptism, although fathers did, too, at times.

Stockbridge, too, was a bit different simply because so many Natives received baptism prior to 1740, before the Great Awakening even began. Sergeant reported baptizing forty persons—adults and children—within the first few months of his time among the Mohicans in 1734.[48] Additionally, Stockbridge was unique in that it was set up more along the model of a seventeenth-century praying town, with its initial membership and later accessions of Indian families being primarily limited to Natives who had explicit interest in Christianity or some level of affiliation with what was widely advertised as a Christian/converting/civilizing/educating project. Sergeant admitted as much in January 1747, when he reported that "Our Numbers increase from Time to Time by the Addition of new Families, especially of those who are kindly dispos'd to Christianity."[49] Even so, while the levels of affiliation are higher than in other areas, they are still far from universal. By the time of Sergeant's death in 1749, there were 218 Indians at Stockbridge. Of the 218, only 129 had received baptism, although Timothy Woodbridge's report does not distinguish between adults and children who were baptized. Of the approximately eighty-seven Indian adults at Stockbridge, only forty-two were communicants, meaning that even at Stockbridge—the eighteenth-century equivalent to Natick under Eliot—only 48 percent took the final step of full membership.[50]

Interpreting Affiliations

The question, of course, is whether these numbers represent higher or lower than expected levels of involvement. On the one hand, for almost 60 percent of adult Lantern Hill Pequots to be affiliated with Anglo churches in some way between 1735 and 1750 (including marriages) seems quite high. On the other hand, the numbers of Natives who joined in full communion were surprisingly low— probably around 25 percent on average (although this figure ranged from 17 percent to 33 percent in the Pequot, Niantic, Narragansett, and Long Island communities under consideration here; Stockbridge is the outlier for the reasons outlined above).[51] Compared with the rather limited affiliations prior to the 1740s, these numbers would have indeed represented a marked change and a reason for local ministers to tout some measure of "success." But given the commonly held assumption that the Great Awakening caused entire Indian communities to convert at once (or nearly so), these numbers are unexpectedly low.

It is unsurprising, then, that ministers and missionaries complained about what they perceived to be a frustrating trend of noninvolvement commingled with sporadic participation. Despite his apparent success among the Narragansetts, Fish soberly admitted that "the Evidences of Grace do not appear so clearly in many of them." Similarly, Griswold lamented of the Niantics in Lyme that even among those who he hoped "experienced a saving change," some "are not as yet joined with any Church."[52] Even John Sergeant at Stockbridge lamented the seemingly "little Fruit" of his labors in January 1747. "Some of those who have appear'd the most promising Converts," Sergeant complained, "have, to my great Grief, and, some Times, even to my Astonishment, strangely fallen away, which has almost wholly discouraged my further Attempts." Of the thirty-five Indian full members in his church, Sergeant had to place five or six of them "under a temporary Suspension from the Communion."[53]

Even more revealing of the rather low levels of long-term affiliation with Euroamerican churches, however, is the degree to which evangelism continued on much as before in many Native communities just ten years after the Awakening. Jacob Johnson, the English minister in North Groton, was sponsored in the mid-1750s by the NEC to deliver monthly evangelistic lectures to the Pequots. During this time, he preached sermons that, by his reports, were much more geared to listeners who had never affiliated in the first place. On one such occasion, for example, he reported informing the Pequots how "the Gospel was to be preached & published to all Nations; especially the Gentiles, and those affar off," and he had now "come to preach it to them."[54] It was like the Pequots were being preached to for the first time. Again.

All this is not to discount the possibility of long-term, meaningful engagement with Christianity itself. For some Indians, Christianity clearly became an important part of their lives over time. Native preachers, ministers, and missionaries who were trained by Eleazar Wheelock and sent to serve across New England and New York testify to the way in which Christianity served a vital role in the lives of some Natives. Reading through the letters and sermons of Samson Occom in the 1760s and the diary of the Mohegan leader Joseph Johnson from the early 1770s, it is obvious that Christianity had become for Occom and Johnson a whole new way of finding meaning and order in the world they inhabited, even as they continued to operate in their traditional Native circles and communal rhythms.[55]

For other Natives, affiliation with white churches—and even Christianity itself—might not have proved so fulfilling in the long term. It is difficult to know how long Natives remained active members in the local English churches they joined during the 1740s. The perception of local English ministers was that things did not last long in general. This certainly seems to be true for many of the Niantics. Despite the optimism of the 1741 Davenport-led revival among the Niantics, by 1744 George Griswold admitted that "the great Sense of divine Things seems to be in a great Measure abated among those Indians as well as among the English." In particular, the Niantics who Griswold at least thought had been reformed by the revivals were now "returning to their old Habit of excessive drinking."[56] Although Azariah Horton's journals from 1741 to 1744 are filled with glowing reports of his successes among the Montauketts and Shinnecocks on Long Island, in his 1751 resignation letter to the SSPCK he lamented regarding the evangelization of the Long Island Indians that "the obstructions, as yet, are unsurmountable; and I believe nothing but the interposure of an almighty and gracious God will effectually remove them."[57] Even after a decade of working among the Montauketts, Samson Occom in 1761 admitted that "they are not so zealous in religion now, as they were some years ago."[58] Similarly, a decade after the Awakening, in 1755, Jacob Johnson, the minister of the North Groton Congregational Church, perhaps frustrated by the Pequots' unresponsiveness to his preaching, reported that the religious fervor among the Mashantucket Pequots "provd But Temporary, & Short lived."[59] Such comments were possibly part of the articulated cyclical revival pattern of awakening and deadening (revival, after all, presupposes a spiritual drought), but Johnson's observations might also reflect the very real frustrations of trying to continually reshape Pequot religious practices in ways he deemed acceptable.

For a surprisingly large minority of most Native communities—and in some cases the clear majority—however, affiliation with Anglo-Christian churches apparently had no drawing power at all. This can be seen most clearly in the absence of Natives from the church records. Other examples, however, surface from time to time. When Azariah Horton made his second trip among the Montauketts in 1742, one particular Indian woman who was "very resolute" in her "Indian Way of living" warned those who attended Horton's services that "their Meetings were the Occasion of the sore Sickness and many Deaths which they were visited with" (although Horton reported that she was later "awakened"). Even those who affiliated with Christianity often did not feel obligated to take on the Euroamerican culture in which Christianity was packaged and at times wondered at the price Christianity exacted on their communities.[60] In the 1760s, Mary Occom, a Montaukett and wife of the Mohegan minister, Samson Occom, continued to look favorably on Montaukett customs despite her own Christian leanings and marriage to the best-known Indian preacher in New England. David McClure reported in 1772 that she refused "morning and evening" to sit at the table with the family; she insisted on wearing traditional Indian clothing; and when Occom addressed her in English, she responded in her Native Montaukett language, even though she could "speak good english." Mary Occom apparently did not object to living in their comfortable two-story English-style house on Mohegan Hill and undoubtedly attended the Christian services held by her husband at Mohegan.[61] Additionally, although Occom apparently had his younger children at home "in subjection," the ones who had grown up and moved out "adopted the wild & roving lives of Savages," turning their backs on the Anglicization and Christianization that their father embraced.[62]

Hints of ongoing traditional practices and folk remedies among Christianized Natives surface occasionally in the records. When Azariah Horton was itinerating among the Shinnecock Indians in Southampton, Long Island, in September 1741, he reported conversing with an Indian woman who "had the Possession of two wooden Gods" that Horton "could by no Means persuade her to part with." The woman insisted "that she did not worship them, but kept them, because her Father gave them to her; the other Indians said, they had no Concern with them."[63] The Pachgatgochs near Kent, Connecticut, welcomed the Moravian missionaries, and a sizable number accepted baptism; but they were so insistent upon spending regular time in the sweat lodges (a cultural practice with explicitly religious overtones) that the Moravians were forced to plan their religious services around the sweat lodge schedule.[64] Ezra Stiles, commenting in 1762 on the Indian practice of ritually piling stones at particular places to remember the dead, noted that "the Inds. continue the Custom to this day, tho' they are a little ashamed the English should see them, & accordingly when walking with an Eng. they have made a path round at a quarter Mile's Distance to avoid it."[65] Mary Cooper, an Oyster Bay, Long Island, resident recorded that on August 5, 1769, she used the services of an "old Indian" known for his abilities to "let fortans [tell fortunes]" using "charmes to cure tooth ach and drive away rats."[66]

The question still remains, however: Why did any Indians choose Christian affiliation at all during this period? Interpreters of Indians and the Great Awakening have suggested that Indians and blacks were drawn to the New Light revivalism of Davenport and Croswell because of its emotionalism, robust singing, appeals to unmediated revelation, and parallels with traditional shamanism.[67] Similarly, others have argued that Mohegan, Pequot, and Niantic listeners might have recognized in Davenport a means of critiquing the established order and claiming religious authority on their own terms and based on their own experiences.[68] Many of these explanations are important and certainly accurately describe the experiences and motivations of some Natives in this time. As a total interpretation, however, it seems incomplete. Motivation for Native involvement in the Great Awakening appears to have been locally specific, to have varied from individual to individual, and to have played out in particular ways over time. Additionally, these explanations do not adequately consider counterexamples, such as why some Indians (such as Ben Uncas II) affiliated with English churches prior to the Awakening, why the Narragansett ruling families chose (and continued to choose into the 1760s and beyond) Anglican association— although not affiliation—over New Light revivalism, why so few Natives actually affiliated as full members with English churches, or why Native affiliation in local Congregational churches dropped off precipitously after the Awakening. The Natives seemingly self-consciously allied themselves with particular Christian churches or groups, even if only in the short term. How can this be explained?

Although it is difficult—and perhaps even misleading—to generalize too much, when one takes the long view of Indians and Christianity in the eighteenth century, it becomes clear that, especially among the leaders of Native communities, Indians expected affiliation with Christianity to *do* something for them, whether spiritually, politically, or materially. Indians sought out education and ministers and—in some cases—joined English churches, all prior to the Awakening. During the Awakening, this interest was intensified and resulted in a smattering of formal affiliations with local, New Light English churches. But the drop-off of Native affiliations after 1742 indicates that something did not turn out as planned.[69] Read this way, Native affiliation in the Great Awakening seems less like a momentous point of religious and cultural disjuncture for Indian communities—wholesale conversion—and more like one more step in the ongoing, decades-old engagement with Christian ideas and Euroamerican culture, all with an eye toward community and cultural survival and revitalization.

This religious engagement through affiliation had various manifestations. One was akin to the "family strategies" exhibited by English colonists in the colonial period, in which affiliation was seen as granting greater access to Euroamerican offerings such as education and financial support.[70] This seems particularly true with regard to the baptism of children, which may also explain why more Indian women than men joined English churches. In a few cases, Indian adults bringing children forward for baptism state very plainly their motivations: to procure education for the child. Two examples of this can be found in the New London records—both of which, incidentally, involve the grandmothers. On March 16, 1729, an Indian named Rachel brought her grand-child, William, to be baptized by Eliphalet Adams in the New London First Congregational Church. The church records explicitly state that she "engaged for his education"—meaning, apparently, that for her, baptism represented a potential means of access to the educational care and support she desired for her grandson.[71] Similarly, on October 18, 1741, the widow Mary Manwaring brought her "spurious" grandchild, Valentine, to Adams for baptism, his mother "not being capable." Once again, the records indicate that the child was "engaged by grandmother for education."[72] More broadly, however, colonists in this time period often sought membership in local churches in order to have their children baptized. Among Anglo-Christians, at least, this was in part due to a growing belief among the laity that there was ritual efficacy in baptism, and the belief that—ministers' assurances to the contrary—baptism "offered their children protection against damnation."[73] Such beliefs may well have been partially adopted and in some cases enhanced among Native communities, who would likely have been even more prone to believe in the power of rituals than their Protestant counterparts. Christian affiliation, then, had a multiplicity of possible meanings that spanned both practical and spiritual concerns.

In other cases, it is clear that Native individuals and communities leveraged Christian affiliation with regard to situations and concerns central to Native communities and existence. Even as the Mohegan sachem Ben Uncas II had professed Christian belief in 1736 during a challenge to his leadership, six years later he made this Christian affiliation more explicit during the height of the Great Awakening and the reopening of the Mohegan land case. On October 31, 1742, he, his wife, Ann, and their four children, Benjamin Uncas III, Lucy, Esther, and Mercy, "made profession of faith & were baptized" under the watchful care of Eliphalet Adams in the Congregational Church in New London, Connecticut.[74] Six months later, on May 4, 1743, in Greenwich, Connecticut, the land controversy was reopened by newly appointed royal commissioners. The pinnacle of the proceedings, however, was when Ben Uncas II—through an interpreter, surprisingly—appeared in person with his son, Ben Uncas III, to address the commissioners and the large crowd that overflowed out of the capacious Norwich meetinghouse. Dressed in clothes suitable for fine English gentlemen—once again made especially for the occasion, compliments of the Connecticut taxpayers—the Uncases arrived at the meetinghouse prepared to argue their case with two visible signs of their vested Native power: a Bible and a brass hawk.[75] The Bible—a copy of the "Eliot Bible," from 1663—the elder Ben explained to the court, was "translated into Indian" and had been given to the Mohegans eighty years prior, "sent by the late great king Charles the Second, &c. unto the then chief Sachem of the Moheagan Indians [Uncas], which hath always been delivered unto the chief Sachems successively at their instalment," and accordingly was given to Ben Uncas II in 1725 when he became sachem after his father's death. Ultimately, the point was well taken; the importance of a Bible-wielding, Christianity-professing Indian sachem who was also, conveniently enough, firmly allied with colonial governments was not lost on the royal commissioners, particularly given the context of King George's War and the ongoing need to maintain Mohegan—and more broadly, Native—loyalty against the French and their Indian allies. In the end, the royal commissioners decided once again in favor of the colony of Connecticut—and, by extension, Ben Uncas II and his Indian Bible. No land was returned to Mohegans, although the case would be reopened in the 1760s as a result of a successful appeal.[76]

Other Native communities, too, pursued explicit identification with Christianity for political and community purposes. In May 1743, just a year and a half after Davenport's series of meetings among the Niantics and within days of the

Figure 4.3. Eliot Bible, Side View. Mamusse wunneetupanatamwe Up-Biblum God naneeswe Nukkone Testament kah wonk Wusku Testament ne quoshkinnumuk nashpe Wuttinneumoh Christ, by John Eliot. Cambridge: Printed by Samuel Green and Marmaduke Johnson, 1663. Courtesy of the Massachusetts Historical Society. Photograph by the author.

last of thirteen Indian members owning the covenant in Griswold's East Lyme Church, the Niantics submitted a lengthy complaint to the Connecticut General Assembly. Their English neighbors, they claimed, had over time illegally taken possession of two hundred of the three hundred acres allotted to the Niantics, using the grassy acres to feed their cattle and horses and the wooded ones to fuel the profitable demand for New England timber. The Niantics asked the Assembly to intervene—a plea submitted countless times by Native communities throughout southern New England for more than a century. The Niantics' petition, however, was striking: they stated that they "wish to live more like Christian people, to keep cattle, sheep, and swine, and if the grass is theirs, they wish to have it."[77] The Niantics' self-identification as "Christian people" clearly increased the sense of injustice and placed more pressure on colonial officials to rectify the situation.

The same held true for the Mashantucket Pequots, who similarly complained to the Connecticut General Assembly on April 28, 1741, that, despite an agreement with the colony in 1731 and 1732 regarding their land at Mashantucket, the committee set up to oversee their lands had dealt fraudulently with them, not leaving the proper amount of land for firewood and, even worse, they had "ploughed considerable of sd Land and have built houses thereon which they had no right to do." The Pequots therefore requested that they "might be restored to the injoyment of there Land that they may be able to attend the Preaching of the word of God and to have their Children School'd which tis imposable to attain to So Long as their Land is taken away from them."[78] Likewise, in their petition on May 5, 1742, in which the Pequots described their recent interest in Christianity, one of the main purposes of the petition was to request new overseers for their lands. After describing their interest in Christianity, the Pequots moved to the ongoing issue of land dispossession: "We are thankfull to your Honors for your Care of us in appointing men to take care of us & our lands from time to time. But those men your Honours employed last year tho honest men yet they live a great way from us & know very little of our affairs & upon that account are not likely to be so beneficial to us." Instead, the Mashantucket Pequots suggested Captain John Morgan and his son, since they already demonstrated care and sympathy for the Mashantuckets through holding weekly religious services on their lands.[79]

In many instances, then, Indians used their newfound status to their own advantage and attempted to use their connections with revivalist ministers to secure greater legal leverage and improved social standing. This idea that Christian affiliation might have real-world benefits regarding things that mattered most to their own communities—including justice in their land claims—seems in some cases to have been one of the strongest motivations for Native participation in the First Great Awakening, particularly for Native leaders. New Light ministers paid great care to the Indians, provided them with food, clothing, and education, and were seen as powerful allies for Native individuals and communities who felt marginalized.[80] Ironically, this motivation for joining churches roughly corresponded with reasons some Massachusett Natives gave for praying to John Eliot's God almost a century earlier. "I prayed," John Speene confessed in 1659, "because I saw the *English* took much ground, and I thought if I prayed, the *English* would not take away my ground."[81]

As some Native individuals and communities discovered over time, however, in many cases New Light interest in Native land rights was only soul-deep. From the Indians' perspective, at least, New Light ministers were unwilling or unable to influence colonial governments to actually do much to halt the continual land loss. These same communities that had experienced the Great Awakening realized that their newfound association with Christianity did little to increase the respect of their Anglo neighbors or significantly improve their ability to shape their circumstances. From the perspective of the Indians, their "Christian" neighbors still let their cattle graze on Indian fields, built fences and constructed houses to claim more Native land, fabricated deeds of sale or lease, and refused to leave when the time on an agreed-upon lease had expired. In return, Indians still complained to local officials and the Connecticut Assembly, but usually stopped invoking Christianity when they found it ineffective. On May 13, 1747, Joseph Wuyok "and the rest of the Pequod Living in sd Groton" complained to their overseers that neighboring colonists had recently fenced in some fertile Pequot lands formerly used for planting.[82] Similarly, on May 2, 1749, the Niantics at Black Point complained yet again to the General Assembly, this time for being denied access to the fertile herbage lands at the center of their reserved lands.[83] Not once did either petition mention Christianity.

As the realization of these unfulfilled expectations began to sink in, Native individuals and communities continued to respond to European Christianity in various ways. Some rejected it completely, despite their broad and long exposure to it. A few still desired to have their children educated but did not personally pursue Christian affiliation for themselves or their children. And, although the exact proportion varied by community, by the 1750s a sizable minority in each of the Native communities in southeastern New England continued to profess an increasingly indigenized version of Christianity. These subsets of Indian communities increasingly shifted from a Christianity-as-practical-aid model—in which ministers and missionaries were allies—to a Christianity-as-revitalization model. Learned Christian practices and models of church organization (and the legitimacy and social power that accompanied them) were used in the service of the Indian community in creating new visions, new opportunities, and—most of all—a new sense of what it meant to be Indian (although certainly both models existed side by side in many cases).[84]

The Indian Great Awakening did mark a wider interest in official American Indian affiliation with English churches. But this interest varied greatly within Indian communities, as did interest in Christianity itself. For some individuals, the change was tangible and long lasting. For others, it was rather an experimentation with strategies for colonial survival. Certainly nothing like wholesale tribal adoption of Christianity took place, at least not all at once in the 1740s.

The point here is not simply that some Natives used Christian affiliation for practical purposes. Rather, some Natives found religious affiliation and—more broadly, participation in the revivals—meaningful *and* useful. Native affiliations were necessarily embedded with meanings that were different from those of white affiliations, simply because of their social and theological position as colonial subjects and religious others. Throughout, for those who did affiliate, practical approaches to Christian affiliation were mingled and intertwined with the inner, personal, and subjective elements of religious experience and practice. But as Irene Doit and others found out, such affiliations did not always prove satisfying in the long term. Even as these larger frameworks of power shaped Native understanding and experience of the Christian faith, they could not and did not render the revivals or Native religious experience irrelevant for a substantial minority of Native communities. For at least a core of these Natives, the various challenges and disappointments of Christian affiliation did not cause them to completely reject the newly incorporated Christian practices and beliefs. Indeed, there is good evidence that these practices remained meaningful, even as they were appropriated, reimagined, and applied to their own Native communities, mostly outside the reach and influence of English institutional Christianity. If one result of the Awakening was low levels of affiliations, short-lived institutional interest, and broader noninvolvement on the part of Natives, another result was the beginnings of a Native Christianity pursued and practiced by subsegments of the New England Native population.

‖ 5 ‖

Separating

Bernhard Adam Grube wasn't sure what to think. On September 7, 1759, a rather unusual group of American Indians arrived at the Native town of Pachgatgoch in western Connecticut where Grube—a Moravian—served as a missionary. Despite the tumultuous and dangerous times the French and Indian War had brought to the New York region, Grube could tell immediately he had nothing to fear from the Indians—eleven women and six men—who showed up, "all dressed well in English style." But what did they want? His answer came soon enough as the curious Indians proceeded to hold an impromptu service with the Pachgatgochs who were present. Their "so-called preacher" stood up, read a passage from the Bible, and proceeded to speak for an entire hour "half in Indian and half in English" about the suffering and death of Jesus. Grube reported the sermon to be in general agreement with Moravian principles and that many Pachgatgoch Indians were attentive and moved to tears by the preacher's exhortations. That afternoon, Grube sat down with the group to learn more about where they had come from. The Indians, as it turned out, were a mixed group of Tunxis and Mohegans from Farmington and the New London area who were traveling to New York. The preacher was the Mohegan Samuel Ashpo, a self-professed Separate Indian minister. When pressed about their own spiritual journey, Grube reported, "they told me of their awakenings, [and] that they had been baptized by the Presbyterians but were then expelled again by them. At this they joined the separatists, but now they had separated themselves from them as well and were on their own."[1] The New England Separate Indians held true to form, holding three to four church services apart from the Moravians each of the three days they stayed at Pachgatgoch before continuing their travels.

The presence and activity of this roving, evangelistic Indian Separate Christian group are important for understanding the religious and cultural changes among subsections of New England Native communities in the 1750s and 1760s. Although English ministers continued to talk about Native groups as ripe mission fields in the years following the Awakening, Christianity had in some cases already taken root in rather indigenized forms and through networks that were largely invisible to outside observers. The ongoing religious education of the Indians and the religious revivalism of the 1730s and 1740s produced a sufficient interest among the Indians in many communities to make them begin to consider ways in which they could make the ritual of weekly worship services better fit their own needs, especially as white churches felt less welcoming. The English Separate movement encouraged by radical New Light revivalists such as James Davenport and Gilbert Tennent during the Great Awakening offered a model of retaining Christian practices while dropping more conventional institutional affiliation, an option that Christian Indians increasingly chose in the years immediately following the Great Awakening.

The result was an "Indian Separatism" in which Native Christians conducted religious services on their own lands, run by Indians and primarily for Indians. In most cases, this resulted in the formation of an Indian Separate church that, no matter how informal or unofficial, provided an attractive alternative to white churches for Natives in each Indian community who continued to find the practice of Christianity a meaningful part of their lives. Indian Separatism was rather fluid in practice, partly because it was more a general attitude about Indians' relationship to English structures of ecclesiastical authority than a clearly defined policy. Indian Separatism also emerged more strongly and quickly in some locations than in others and did not really reach its fervent, intertribal peak until the 1760s and 1770s. Nonetheless, Native Separatism was more widely in operation on Native lands between 1750 and 1770 than has usually been recognized. While not universally agreed upon or adhered to, Indian Separatism became for the Natives who did profess Christianity a new way of conceptualizing their place in the colonial world and strengthening existing connections between communities, as well as providing space to cultivate their own set of religious practices.[2]

The idea of having separate Indian meetings was not entirely novel nor was it only tied to the radical New Lights during the Great Awakening. Natives in New England had been gathering apart from their white counterparts for more than a century to elect leaders, prepare for war, deal with communal issues, create alliances with neighboring tribes, hold dances, or commemorate important festivals in the lunar year. In the 1720s, Indian dances were so common and raucous in Rhode Island that in 1729 the General Assembly encouraged and empowered towns to make laws "for the better regulating of such Indian dances" and imposed a fine of up to forty shillings for selling "strong liquors" at such gatherings.[3] Dances and other such meetings were often viewed with suspicion, particularly in areas less populated by colonists. When the Paugussett Indians of New Milford in southwestern Connecticut began holding a series of dances in August 1725 and "painted themselves as is usual for Indians to do that design war," the Connecticut General Assembly immediately passed a resolution that all Indians in the New Milford region who were found to be painted after August 21, 1725, would be "taken for enemies and proceeded against as such."[4] For this reason, in the eighteenth century local officials usually required Indian communities to request permission in advance to hold a larger meeting and to explain its purpose. Local officials usually also sent a non-Indian with some fluency in the local Indian languages to attend the meeting and report any unusual activity.[5]

Most interesting, perhaps, was the intertribal nature of many of these meetings. When Charles Augustus Ninigret, the Narragansett sachem, passed away in 1735, an enormous crowd of fifteen hundred Natives from across southern New England gathered for a funeral dance.[6] As missionary presence increased, Natives had good reasons to try to hide certain kinds of meetings, like dances. When Middletown minister Richard Treat went to a Wangunk village in the late summer of 1735, he found a large intertribal dance in process with Natives "Singing, dancing, yelling, humming, &c." Treat, spotted as an intruder, reported that several Indians demanded to know why he had come and told him to "begone." Predictably, Treat tried to break up the intertribal gathering, hoping to "prevent no little wickedness which they are Commonly Guilty of at Such times."[7]

Separate Christian Indian worship services, then, were in part an outgrowth of prior, corporate rhythms of Native communal life, in some cases perhaps constructed specifically as an alternative—at least early on—to Indian dances, which in many communities were relished for their late nights and drunkenness. Separate Indian church meetings had the added benefit of the absence of direct colonial oversight since they were smaller and relatively benign. Indian Christian meetings operated either unbeknownst to local officials or with their tacit permission, particularly in areas where there was not an "official" (English-ordained) Indian church or minister. Christian Indian communities were certainly influenced by English New Light Separates, but—as with other elements of Christianity—Separatism perhaps took root so readily among Christian Indians because it was so similar to strategies of adaptation and survival already being practiced in Native communities.

Indian Separatism was born when, in the years following the Awakening, Natives who had affiliated with local English congregations simply stopped attending. Sometimes this was because of internal squabbles in white churches. The Awakening itself, after all, had deeply divided Euroamerican communities and left some Natives with a sour taste in their mouths. On July 19, 1742, for example, the moderate New Light Eliphalet Adams preached a sermon at Mohegan, as he had done for years. When Adams invited the more radical New Light David Jewett to offer the closing prayer, Jewett instead used the prayer as an opportunity to openly chastise Adams for his sermon, which Jewett felt was "dangerous & hurtful to souls." Adams, deeply offended, complained about Jewett's actions to the ministers in the New London County Minister's Association, who dryly noted that, as a result of such incidents and divisions, the Indians were "likely to be stumbled."[8] They were right. Jacob Johnson, minster at the North Groton Congregational Church, reported that many Pequots who had affiliated in the early 1740s left when the church experienced a schism a few years later.[9]

Another related and important reason Indians increasingly eschewed Anglo services and churches was the bewildering proliferation of competing versions of the Christian life. The Mashantucket Pequot sachem Charles Skuttaub over time, according to Johnson, had grown "averse to any Religious Meetings," simply because he was being pulled in four different directions: Skuttaub told Johnson the Anglicans "say they are Oldest, & Rightest, & I must come to them, the Presbyterians Say we are Right, & you must come to us—The Separates Say we are certainly Right & all others are wrong, & therefore you must be sure to come to us," and additionally, Johnson wanted Skuttaub to attend his Congregational church. "Now where shall I go?" asked Skuttaub. Quite simply, "No where"—to no Euroamerican service at all.[10]

One of the most important reasons that Natives deaffiliated from English churches was differences over religious practices, particularly the presence or absence of a more free-flowing, spirit-led worship experience. Such was the case with Sarah Putak, a Pequot woman who separated from the North Stonington Church in 1746. Putak began attending the North Stonington Church early in the revivals, perhaps sometime in 1741. On June 16, 1742, Sarah was admitted into full communion—along with a large number of colonists and four other Indians. Between 1742 and 1746 she began attending a local New Light Separate church instead of the North Stonington Church where she was a member. In January of 1747, when the North Stonington Church demanded to know why she and others had been absenting themselves from church, Sarah stated that her reason for separating was "That the Pastor Denies God, and others Preach as they used to do when I first went to meetings, But I cant come here, for God Calls to go & hear others."[11] Implicit in Putak's comments is a reduction in religious fervor at the North Stonington Church, which she found instead at the North Stonington Strict or Separate Congregation, where she joined as a member on November 12, 1746.[12]

But more often than not, Natives soon found English Separate churches stifling as well. "Indian Betty" (presumably a Mashantucket Pequot) gave a public profession of faith before the elders and church members of the First Baptist Church of Groton on September 5, 1762, and was baptized and received into church fellowship. Less than two years later, however, Indian Betty, or Sister Betty, was brought before church elders in April 1764 for, among other things, her erratic behavior at a particular worship service, where she "fell down on the floor as she was in a trance and afterward got up and said she had seen her father and he said she might return and be faithfull a while and then hee would come and fech her." Tension had likely been building for a while, since Sister Betty was also charged with threatening to "go and join to the indine [Indian] church and she did not know what the church would think of it nor did not care." Although a month later Sister Betty made the requisite public confession and was received back into fellowship, less than a year later, in February 1765, she was once again brought before the church, accused of various sins and shortcomings, confessed them, and was restored to fellowship. Nonetheless, shortly thereafter she was listed in the records as having "gonof"—undoubtedly having made good on her threat to join the Indian church instead.[13] If these examples are any indication, it seems that after the fervor of the revivals lessened and many English church services lost their spontaneous, spirit-filled edge, many Natives who had interest in Christianity stopped attending these churches in favor of something more informal—or "spirit"-filled—happening either on their own reservations or at other Separate churches, particularly if they felt (through physical seating arrangements and censure) discriminated against in or forced out of white churches.

The precise progression of Indian Separatism—from English Congregational churches to English Separate churches to Indian Separate churches—as described to the Moravians by Ashpo in 1759 was also observed by the Groton minister Jacob Johnson in 1755. Indians had joined his church in the early 1740s and largely left during the split later that decade. Some of these Pequots dropped all Anglo Christian affiliation entirely—or "dropped away to Some of their former heathenishness," as Johnson stated it—while others followed local English Separates who had formed their own New Light church. Most Pequots soon left the English Separates, too, and therefore ceased all affiliations with English Christian churches. Some of these Pequots still seemed interested in Christian sermons and lectures, since even in this "degenerate State" of nonaffiliation, Johnson observed, Natives "would Some Times go to hear the Separates; & Sometimes come to hear me." Even when Pequots did show up at Johnson's lectures on their own lands, it was "with a great deal of Indifference, & Carelessness," since they greatly preferred "to hear the Separate Lay Exhorters." After a while, the Pequots apparently "wholly left" the Separate exhorters, too. The result was that by 1755, Johnson simply could not convince the Pequot Christians to come worship with his English congregation on Sunday mornings.[14]

The reasons Johnson observed for the Mashantucket Pequots' refusal to attend reveals the intense, complicated, and overlapping ways in which religious engagements continued to play out in the years following the Awakening. First, according to Johnson, the Indians' "Natural Temper & genius" was to blame—a phrase he left unparsed; second, the Indians had been "led away by the Seperates" and therefore had somehow become disillusioned with English churches as a whole; third, "because they have mett together among themselves, & Carried on Religion in their own way on Lords Days"; fourth, the influence "of Evil Councellors," likely Native traditionalists who were dissuading Indians from attending English churches; fifth, "their Old Natural fondness for Liberty, & Jealosie left in Some way or other they Shoud lose it & become Slaves & tributary"; and sixth, "they imagine the White People are Enemies to 'em; And have got Possession of Some of their Land & hold them out of their rightful Possession, & design to dispossess them of all their Lands & so turn them adrift, or make Servants of 'em."[15] This astonishingly candid list reveals the deep and abiding suspicions, fears, and resentments that framed the interactions between Christian Indians and local whites in the years following the Awakening. Natives who had experienced English churches had largely become disillusioned and fearful that Christianity and church membership was merely a way to reduce the Indians to servitude and dependency and to entice them to give up more of their lands. Many Natives realized that their Christian affiliation changed little in terms of the larger colonial dynamics of oppression and power, and they responded accordingly.

As a result, the English Separate movement in and of itself did not automatically have the drawing power one might expect. Existing records do not record more than a trickle of Indians in and out of these churches, perhaps in part because they tended to be even more demanding in terms of social and sexual norms, as well as more vigilant in casting out members who lapsed. Page after page of the church records of the East Lyme Baptist Church, for example, is devoted to meetings in which individuals were brought before the church and charged with various offenses.[16]

Clear preference for Native Christian meetings and, conversely, the increasing aversion of some Natives for Euroamerican church services and lectures, can be found among other Indian communities as well. North Stonington minister Joseph Fish, who was paid by the NEC to provide monthly lectures and other pastoral services to the Lantern Hill Pequots in the 1750s and 1760s, reported to Andrew Oliver in 1762 that the number of Pequots attending his lectures on their lands was highly irregular. "The principal Cause, I apprehend," complained Fish, "has been, their great Fondness for the Indian Teachers." The Lantern Hill Pequots had been influenced by "their Brethren . . . the Narragansetts" who, Fish reported, "seldom think it proper to hear Me." To make matters worse, the Narragansett Separates consistently showed up on the same day Fish was trying to preach to the Pequots and usually persuaded most of the Pequots not to attend.[17] The rather unwelcome presence of Separate Narragansett Christians on the very days Fish was trying to win over the Pequots proved irksome and was undoubtedly what prompted the NEC to pay Fish to deliver monthly lectures among the Narragansetts just two years later, in 1765.

Indian Separatism, however, was sparsely documented, in part because it remained a somewhat underground movement (whether intentionally or not). One way into this little-known world of New England Indian religious life is through the lives of three Native Separate leaders—Samuel Niles, Samuel Ashpo, and Samson Occom—as well as an examination of the broader phenomenon of Indian Separate churches and the general shape of an emerging Native Christianity. For centuries prior to the arrival of the Europeans, Indian shamans interpreted events and provided moral guidelines for their communities, just as European ministers had done for their people. Native leaders who adopted Christian practices often continued this traditional leadership and were central to the ongoing self-definition of Indian identity and practice in the decades following the Awakening. New rituals were added, and old ones retained or infused with new meanings. In many cases, the Christian practices that Indians adopted were the ones that most closely corresponded to prior Indian practices.[18] The irony of the development of local Indian churches is that the very institutions that were supposed to help turn Indians into faithful English subjects in the end were used by Indians to create semi-autonomous space within which they could monitor their own spiritual lives, exercise a great deal of autonomy, and strengthen intertribal connections.[19]

Samuel Niles

Perhaps the most illuminating example of organized Indian Separatism is the Narragansett Indian Church and its eventual minister, Samuel Niles.[20] Divisions at Narragansett over questions of Christian practice and polity illustrate how individuals and subgroups thought about and engaged Christianity in differing ways, sometimes oppositionally vis-à-vis non-Indians, but at other times as a point of leverage or separation among factions within their own Native community, largely over the issue of land ownership and leadership succession.

Samuel Niles was born in c. 1701 into a family on Narragansett reserved lands in Rhode Island.[21] Not much is known of his childhood, but it seems Niles was born too early to take advantage of educational opportunities offered by the NEC missionary Joseph Park. Even once Park arrived, it is possible that Niles, as a Narragansett shaman and a representative of the more traditionalist faction of the Narragansetts, would have initially opposed his presence. This changed over time, however, and by the early 1740s Niles was more open and apparently interested in the emerging Christian revivalism. He eventually gave a profession of faith in the Westerly church, was baptized by sprinkling, and began to regularly receive communion, all likely during the 1743 Narragansett awakenings.[22]

The nascent Narragansett Christian community that Niles joined functioned as a de facto Separate church. Despite admitting approximately sixty Indians into his Westerly church in 1742 and 1743, Joseph Park reported in early 1744 that the Narragansett Christians "have frequent private Meetings amongst themselves for Prayer and Praise, and Conference, particularly stated on Sabbath-day evenings, and Wednesday evenings."[23] Park occasionally met with the Narragansett Christian community during their Wednesday evening meetings, but, aside from attending his services on Sunday mornings, the community was on its own and, according to Park, mostly illiterate.[24] Niles, not content for long to simply receive instruction at the hands of Park, soon began exhorting during the services at Park's church, which Park and the elders at the Westerly church were not about to tolerate. Niles recounted that he was "dealt with" by Park and the Westerly elders; later generations of Narragansetts put it more bluntly, saying that Park "reproved them, in a time of awakening, for becoming noisy, by speaking & praying, in his meeting."[25] Offended at the chastisement, in 1750 Niles and approximately one hundred Indians officially withdrew from Park's church along with a vocal Baptist-minded white elder named Stephen Babcock, who had been similarly reprimanded by Park.[26] This nascent Indian Separate church met for a while in wigwams at Narragansett, in which they held "meetings together whole nights."[27] Babcock and a few other non-Natives joined with some white Separates from Stonington and founded their own Separate church in Westerly on April 5, 1750, with Babcock as their minister.[28] Babcock also provided early leadership for the Indian church at Narragansett, meeting with them in their wigwam services.

Within a year or two, the Narragansett Separates built a new meetinghouse for their own use, still refusing to attend Park's church but continuing their prior practice of meeting separately on Sundays and during the week. The new Narragansett Separate Indian church building was located just north of the center of the Indian town, roughly a half mile from the school building, and was a barebones and crowded twenty-five square feet.[29] Only twenty-five of the original one hundred Natives who withdrew from Park's church ended up covenanting "to walk together" as a church. The other seventy-five either attended the new Indian church sporadically, found other churches to take part in, or perhaps even dropped formal Christian affiliation entirely. In 1752, however, the Indian Separate church also experienced a division, when a Mashantucket Pequot Indian from Connecticut named James Simon contended for the leadership of the Narragansett Indian Church.[30] The Narragansett church was clearly divided over whether Simon or Niles should serve as their pastor, for they wrote to the Separate white church in Canterbury, Connecticut, and requested advice in their decision making. "We have been in Search of a Pastor till many of us is Lost in the Wilderness," the Narragansett Separates explained, "for our Evidences Cross each other, some for James Simon and some for Samll. Niles."[31] Babcock and other Separates laid hands on Simon and ordained him as Elder of the Narragansett Indian Church. When Niles and other Indians protested, James Simon and half a dozen other Natives subsequently left the Narragansett church and met together in a private house, where Simon administered the Lord's Supper and baptism and preached and taught the Indians around him.[32]

Having triumphed over the challenge to his leadership, Niles continued to minister in the Indian meetinghouse, where fifteen of the Indian congregants who had refused James Simon officially called Niles as their minister and requested the Separate elders—including Babcock—to ordain him. When Babcock and the other elders refused to ordain Niles, the audacious and creative response of the Narragansett Indian Church was to appoint three "Indian brethren," including William Cohoize (also Coheis or Coheys), to ordain Niles entirely on their own during a marathon ordination service in their own church that began around noon and ended at sunset. During the lengthy service, Cohoize prayed over Niles and "gave him the charge" over the flock; Niles later recounted that during the charge "such a Spirit was outpoured and fell upon them" that "many others of the Congregation prayed aloud and lift up their hearts with prayers and Tears to God"—all at once—for close to an hour. The cacophonous blending of prayers was too much for the few English colonists who attended the event, and they left long before the end of the meeting, taking this exhibition of spontaneous Indian spirituality as "confusion." The Indians, however, continued into the evening, and finally concluded the meeting with a hymn.[33]

Local ministers, missionaries, and officials now had a problem. The Narragansetts had a church with a Christian Indian minister who preached, baptized, and served communion, which is what missionaries said they wanted. The only problem was that the church was completely outside Euroamerican control and was pastored by an unlicensed, illiterate, uneducated Indian minister with Separate tendencies and rather "unorthodox" theology and religious sensibilities. North Stonington minister Joseph Fish reported in 1765 that although Niles was a "very honest man" and had memorized "a good deal of the Scriptures by heart," he "cannot read a Word." Unable to read the Bible himself, Niles relied "very much upon the *Spirit* to teach him *Doctrine* and *Conduct*," which Fish feared would lead to his "leaving *The Word*, for the Guidance of *Feelings, Impressions, Visions, Appearances* and *Directions* of Angels and of Christ himself in a Visionary Way."[34] No English minister visited or instructed the congregation, Fish lamented, with the exception of an occasional visit by "One of the Separate Stamp."[35] Furthermore, Niles was technically an Anabaptist (another anathema for Congregationalists), since he was baptized a second time, this time by "plunging" or immersion, as he did not view the mode of baptism—sprinkling—he received under Park as legitimate. In his church at large, however, he professed "to hold it indifferent," and the church agreed that disagreements over modes of baptism—even infant baptism versus adult baptism—"should be no Terms of Communion."[36] Accordingly, Niles baptized both infants and adults and allowed the adults to choose whether they preferred sprinkling or immersion.

If the response of Joseph Fish to Niles and his church is any indication of how the colonists viewed Separate Indian congregations, the colonial consensus was that they were not legitimate churches, hardly capable of handling their own ecclesiastical affairs, and generally in need of reform. "The poor people are not fit to be left alone," Fish reported, "Not being Equal to the Important affair of Conducting their Religious and ecclesiastical Matters, agreeable to Gospel Order." The church also displayed numerous "Enthusiastic Notions," and, Fish fumed, "Nor will any of them, (I imagine,) be told, that the Spirit (which They think they have,) is a Safe and Sufficient guide, Without the Scriptures." Most pernicious in Fish's eyes was the absolute intractability of the church; the church members in general "cant bear to be told, Directly that These are Errors," and Niles—or Father Sam, as his congregants called him—refused to be told "that his Ordination twas not according to Gospel Order." Nonetheless, the report was not all negative. Many of the Narragansett Separates, Fish admitted, seemed to "Retain a good Measure of the Serious Impressions of Truth, from the painfull Labours of the Revd. Mr. Park" more than two decades prior. Even under Niles the Indians seemed to sincerely practice their faith, in the eyes of Fish. "They give a Decent and Devout Attention to every Branch of Worship," Fish noted, "Whether at Table, or in public Assembly."[37]

Over time, Niles became a well-respected leader among the Indian communities. In 1765 he was listed among the "council of Indians" that missionary Edward Deake consulted when considering the best course of action for the education of Narragansett children.[38] Niles also regularly served as a minister to the Indian Christians at Groton and Mohegan, particularly in the celebration of communion. By 1772, Ezra Stiles could report that Niles had ninety "Indian Communicants" at his church in Narragansett. With his insatiable curiosity with all things Indian, Stiles thought it "extraordinary" that Niles, who visited him on May 8, 1772, "should be a Pastor," since he "cannot read." Despite this apparent liability, however, Stiles concluded that Niles was "of an unblameable Life as to Morals and Sobriety" and "has very great Influence over the Indians."[39]

Not all Narragansetts were interested in Niles's separatistic, revivalistic practice of Christianity, however. Two very different visions—if not more of a spectrum of visions—of what Christianity might accomplish existed within the Narragansett community that were in fact representative of the diversity of views within Native communities more broadly. Niles used Christianity to position himself against colonial religious and temporal authorities and to carve out a separate space within which Indians could exist and practice their own version of Indian Christianity. The Narragansett sachems, however, including Charles Augustus Ninigret (1723–1735), George Ninigret (1735–1746), and Thomas Ninigret (1746–1769), used Christianity—much as Ben Uncas II had done—to strengthen their bonds to leading Rhode Island figures and to live relatively comfortable lives. The religious divisions within the Narragansett community, however, followed older fault lines that traced their way back to at least the 1710s, and grew stronger under the sachemship of Charles Augustus Ninigret after 1723. Charles Augustus Ninigret firmly allied himself with local and regional magistrates, aggrandized his own position and family within the Narragansett community, surrounded himself with the visible material comforts of English finery, and showed a clear preference for Anglicanism. The controversies heated up when the tribe was divided over who should succeed him in the early 1730s. George Ninigret soon emerged triumphant and quickly exceeded his father's indebtedness and opulent lifestyle. When an English visitor, Dr. Alexander Hamilton, traveled through Narragansett territory in 1744, he was shocked to be hosted by a well-dressed George Ninigret who served him good wine in a spacious stone "palace" surrounded by thousands of acres of prime land that hosted tenants, horses, and cattle. Even George's wife was adorned with "silks, hoops, stays, and dresses like an English woman."[40] The Ninigret family's lifestyle came with a cost, however, and triggered a cycle of indebtedness and land sales that lasted until the dissolution of the sachemship in the 1770s.

There is no indication that Niles and the Indian Separates were ideologically opposed to the Ninigret family in the 1740s, despite their differing levels of participation in the Awakening (the Ninigrets preferred Anglicanism, Niles the New Lights); however, the pattern of land sales by the sachems certainly caused considerable consternation among Natives living on the reserved lands. Samuel Niles seems to have lent his implicit support of sachem Thomas Ninigret even as late as 1759, when Ninigret petitioned the Assembly to remove all restrictions on land sales by him.[41] By the 1760s, however, things had changed, and Niles was a strong opponent—as were many other tribal members—of the profligate, land-selling, colony-supported practices of Thomas Ninigret. In many ways, religious differences became rallying points for Niles and company and created new contexts in which old antagonisms and tribal fault lines could be played out.[42]

Samuel Ashpo

While Niles was leading the Narragansett church in Rhode Island, Samuel Ashpo was operating in a slightly less formal way at Mohegan in Connecticut.[43] Born in 1718 as a member of the "royal family" of the Mohegans, Ashpo served in a variety of important roles within the Mohegan community throughout his long life.[44] Ashpo was part of an important transitional generation in the mid-eighteenth century, having been exposed to Euroamerican religious and cultural offerings in a sustained way. As a young boy in the 1720s, he undoubtedly attended the school that John Mason kept at Mohegan and heard the sermons of the resident minister, Jonathan Barber, in the 1730s. Ashpo's education and involvement in tribal affairs are evident from documents on which he signs his own name, even as early as 1737 (whereas most other Indians merely put their mark).[45] During the protracted contestations over the sachemship between Ben Uncas II and his cousin, John Uncas, Jr., in the 1730s, Ashpo—unlike the Occom family—sided with John Uncas, Jr., as did the majority of the Mohegans.[46]

Like many other Native men in the eighteenth century, Ashpo decided to improve his lot in life by going to sea. Seafaring and whaling were risky but potentially lucrative occupations. Indians and free blacks in New England provided the cheap, backbreaking labor required to keep a whaling ship at sea for months at a time.[47] Sometime between August 2, 1737, and October 5, 1742, Samuel Ashpo spent fourteen months on a whaling ship. When he returned, he realized that it was the "Common Publick Report" that his wife—whom he had married in his late teenage years—had committed herself to another man. After waiting for what Ashpo felt to be a "Considerable time"—only a few months, actually—to see if she would come and ask for forgiveness (she didn't), Ashpo married another Indian woman named Hannah Mamnack of the Wangunk community. The wedding ceremony was conducted distinctly "after the Indian manner," which most likely meant during a small feast that included neighbors and family members and without the presence of an English minister of any sort.[48] But by February 1743, Ashpo was convinced that what he had done was "Evil in the Light of God" and was full of regret for three reasons: first, he had left his first wife "without a trial of the Case"; second, he had not gone "to her & use Endeavours to Convince her of her sin"; and third, he "was married in the old Indian mode & not in a Christian manner." Although little could be done after the fact, Ashpo hoped that by an open confession he might prevent "the dishonour of god & Prejudice of Religion" caused by his actions.[49]

In part because of his long exposure to Christianity, Ashpo was caught up in the religious revivals of the early 1740s. Radical New Light Christianity might have resonated with the increasingly antagonistic stance Ashpo took with regard to authoritarian institutions within colonial culture. He—like Occom—likely professed Christianity at a revival meeting conducted by James Davenport. Early in his religious education, Ashpo came under the influence of the Reverend Eleazar Wheelock of Lebanon, just fifteen miles north of Mohegan, whose church he joined during or after the revivals in the 1740s.[50] Shortly after his public profession of faith he was examined and ordained by "certain lay exhorters of the Separatist school," perhaps New Lights associated with the Separate school in New London. Wheelock later remembered that during this time Ashpo had "imbibed such independent and Brownistic principles"—meaning that Ashpo was a confirmed Separate, possibly even bordering on baptistic principles—but that he was not "one of the most bitter, sensorious, furious and uncharitable sort."[51]

Perhaps because of his education, Ashpo already served as a leader to his people, as had John Mettawan in Farmington more than a decade earlier. His exposure to revivalist Christianity thrust him into the position of teacher, religious leader, and—from the perspective of local Anglo ministers—unlicensed minister. Despite his lack of official ordination, in the early 1740s he began to form around him a group of Mohegans affected by the revivals but also not inclined to walk the seven miles north to Norwich or the three miles to David Jewett's church in the North Parish of New London.[52] Samuel Ashpo might have been increasingly motivated to separate from Anglo churches after the prolonged, public meetings of the royal commission in the summer of 1743 regarding the Mohegan land controversy. Some local ministers generally sided with the colony of Connecticut against the Mohegans, creating a situation that Ashpo and the other John's Town Indians found untenable.[53] Over time, Ashpo's group of Separate Mohegans became "an important seat of power" for John Uncas, Jr., and the other Mohegans who continued to lay claim to Mohegan lands.[54]

In the late 1750s, Ashpo spent some time with his old whaling friends in New London and got drunk. His tender conscience—perhaps primed by a distinctly Christian, Euroamerican sensitivity regarding the sinfulness of drunkenness—soon got the best of him. Knowing his English sponsors would look down upon this indiscretion, Ashpo confessed his drunkenness "with Tears" but resolved to not let it happen again.[55] Perhaps it was shortly after this bout with drunkenness that Ashpo undertook to reform his own community, and even his own household. One day when Samuel and Hannah Ashpo were helping an English neighbor build a mill over the nearby Stony Brook, Hannah occasionally stole a drink of unkupi, or rum, from a flask she had hidden in her dress. When she started sharing the rum with others, Samuel got angry and smashed the flask on a rock, and all the rum spilled out. Hannah was furious and a few moments later retaliated by striking Samuel on the forehead as he was bending over. Samuel fell down, blood gushing from his head. At that moment, there was a deafening thunderclap in the sky, despite the absence of storm clouds. Samuel recovered from his head wound and the lesson was not lost on Hannah, for from that day on she did not drink rum.[56]

In many ways, Ashpo's early career shows that Indian Christianity was not a controlled, calculated product of designing English colonial metropolitans and local ministers. In almost every way, Ashpo subverted colonial conventions.

Instead of training for the ministry, receiving a calling to a church, and being ordained by a local church and board of clergy, Ashpo skipped straight from profession of faith to minister and received his formal training and license later. Although itinerating had been outlawed in May 1742 in the colony of Connecticut, Ashpo continued to preach to official and unofficial congregations among the Niantics, Mohegans, Pequots, and Narragansetts.[57] In the late 1750s and early 1760s, Ashpo began taking trips to Indian communities in New York that shared his Separate and New Light sentiments. A fascinating testimony to Ashpo's popularity as a minister and leader in the Native Christian underground comes from the Moravian records of the mission in Pachgatgoch. On September 7, 1759, Ashpo and sixteen other Indian Separates arrived at Pachgatgoch en route to visit the intertribal Iroquois town of Onaquaga in New York.[58] Ashpo and his entourage returned again on May 29, 1760, on their way back to Connecticut and conducted a two-hour afternoon meeting and an evening meeting that lasted long into the night and attracted "many white people." So popular was Ashpo among Indians and whites alike, in fact, that the mere rumor of his passing through Pachgatgoch in September of 1760 caused a number of white people to show up, only to be turned away by the Moravian missionaries, who said they had not seen him.[59]

Wheelock and other Euroamerican ministers recognized Ashpo's potential as a missionary to the Haudenosaunee in New York but were concerned that he might spread his separatistic principles abroad or possibly even have them reinforced, depending on where he went. Since Ashpo's favor with the New York Indians presented an opportunity too good for the commissioners to pass up, the obvious solution was to attempt to reform Ashpo's Separatism. Wheelock himself took "much Pains" to convince Ashpo of his misguidedness, which included nothing short of a bribe: if Ashpo repudiated his Separatism, the NEC might see fit to fund future trips Ashpo might make to New York. Wheelock suspected that Ashpo would visit New York regardless of whether the commissioners paid him.[60] He was right. But Wheelock was also pleasantly surprised that Ashpo seemed, in part, to reform his ways. On November 1, 1761, David Jewett reported to Wheelock that Ashpo had "returned to his Duty & Priviledge" by joining the New London North Parish Church on Wheelock's recommendation. Even more important, however, Ashpo agreed in the interim to "Desist in Preaching" until local ministers could give their approval.[61] On July 29, 1762, Ashpo was examined by four area ministers—including Jewett and Wheelock— who recommended additional theological training before sending him off as a missionary.[62]

As a result, Ashpo enrolled in Moor's Indian Charity School in Lebanon run by Wheelock. It is a bit puzzling why Ashpo agreed to this, given the relative humiliation it must have been to attend the boarding school as a forty-four-year-old

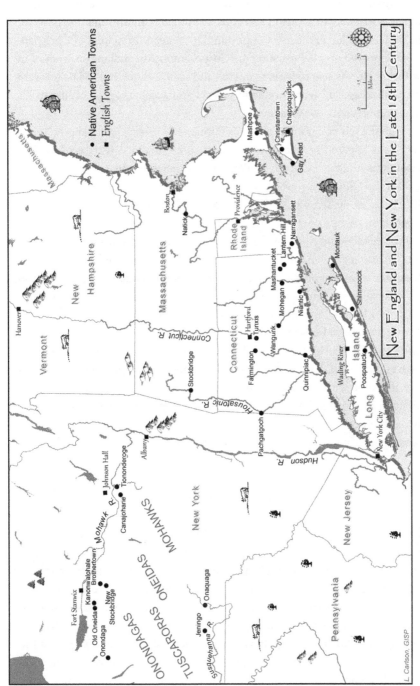

Map 3. New England and New York in the Late Eighteenth Century. Map by Lynn Carlson, Geographic Information System Professional, Brown University.

man next to Wheelock's mostly prepubescent and teenage students. Nonetheless, if formal legitimacy is what Ashpo was after, he got it. A year later, a group of Congregational ministers met in Hartford, examined Ashpo, found him to be "of good Understanding in the most important Doctrines & Principles of Christianity," and approved of "his Preaching the Gospel among the Indians" at Jeningo, in New York.[63] He was sent to Jeningo in 1763 and again in 1766. In 1764 he was sent to the Onondagas, all with moderate success and acceptance, according to his sporadic reports back to Wheelock.

Despite the self-congratulation of his Euroamerican sponsors, Ashpo's "reformation" was apparently incomplete, and his time in actual service of English sponsors was limited.[64] On July 1, 1767, the Connecticut Board of Correspondents (for the SSPCK) reported that since the autumn of 1766, Ashpo had been guilty of "Drinking Strong Drink to Excess, & of Quarrelg, Indecent, unChristian behavior." Ashpo's actions prompted a notice of suspension by the board, which was read publicly by David Jewett in his church and at his weekly "Indian lecture" at Mohegan.[65] Again humiliated, Ashpo likely resolved never again to seek out the approval of white ministers. For the remainder of his life, Ashpo preached and taught among the various Indian communities of southern Connecticut and Rhode Island, often preaching at two services each Sunday, with mid-week lectures in between.[66]

The lives of Ashpo and Niles, while differing in many ways with regard to education and official English endorsement, demonstrate the great fluctuations in Native affiliation with Euroamerican Christian movements, missions, and ideas. As Ashpo's experience illustrates, this was one way in which Natives tried to work out their own ideas and practices in relation to the various circles of Indians and English in which they continued to find themselves.

Samson Occom

Undoubtedly the most famous Indian minister of the eighteenth century was Samson Occom. Despite being heralded as a model Indian convert, over time Occom learned to please his English sponsors while pursuing his own community-centered purposes. In big and small ways, Occom abetted the emergence of Indian Separatism. Occom's churches on Long Island differed in tone but not in function from the more radical Separate Narragansett church led by Samuel Niles. Occom, while receiving funds from the Separate-averse NEC, was at the same time self-consciously providing a Separate Indian alternative for education and church attendance. Occom might not have yet been a self-proclaimed Separate, but from very early on he operated as one and over time influenced dozens of other Indian leaders throughout southern New England.

Figure 5.1. Samson Occom. Courtesy of Dartmouth College Library.

Occom was born in 1723 and raised at Mohegan, Connecticut, the son of Sarah and Joshua Occom. The Occom family lived in Ben's Town, and largely took the side of Ben Uncas II in the ongoing dispute over the sachemship. Occom's eventual "Discovery of the way of Salvation" in the early 1740s thrust him into the position of an evangelist of sorts among the Mohegans, talking "freequently" with them "Concerning Religion." In 1743, his mother arranged for him to be tutored by the Lebanon New Light minister Eleazar Wheelock. Occom's actual time spent at Wheelock's over the ensuing four years was sporadic. His journal reports frequent trips back to Mohegan, Niantic,

Groton, and other neighboring Indian communities to hold meetings and visit friends—an indication of the interconnectedness of the various Native communities in the region and the way Occom effortlessly moved between them. In mid-September 1745, Occom and a group of Mohegans traveled to Montauk on Long Island and held several religious meetings where he reported a small-scale religious revival.[67] By 1747, Occom had quit his course of study. After unsuccessfully attempting to set up schools among the Niantics (who already had one) and the Narragansetts (who did not want one), Occom went on a fishing excursion to Long Island in 1749 and was asked by the Montauketts to serve as their schoolteacher. That November he moved to Montauk and began a formative ten-year phase of his life serving as educator, minister, community leader, and father.

The Montauketts' request for Occom to come serve them could be read in a variety of ways. On the surface, he was invited as a teacher, and indeed, during his first winter of 1749–1750, Occom reported he had approximately thirty students and held school sessions during the day and at night for those otherwise occupied with the hardship of day labor required to meet the exigencies of Indian reservation life.[68] Very quickly, however, Occom's duties began to expand. Even though the Montauketts and Shinnecocks already had a minister—the SSPCK-sponsored Azariah Horton—within a few months Occom began to hold additional church services. His justification for replicating Azariah Horton's ministrations was that Horton was based in Southampton and spent most of his time with the nearby Shinnecocks, whose reserved lands were over thirty miles from Montauk.

There was more to the story, however. Although Azariah Horton spent close to a decade itinerating among the various Long Island Indian communities from 1741 through 1751, and although he founded and served several Indian churches at Montauk, Shinnecock, and Poospatuck, over time he found his authority questioned and challenged by the Indian communities he served.[69] Occom arrived at the height of a longer controversy between some Montauketts, who had been influenced by Separate New Lights in Connecticut and on Long Island, and Horton, who was moderately New Light but decidedly not a Separate. Occom observed that the Montauketts "had Some Prejudices infusd in their minds, by Some Inthusiastical Exhorters from N England, against Mr Horton, and Many of em had left him." In this way, a Separate Indian movement on Long Island was already under way by the time Occom arrived. That Occom so quickly began fulfilling pastoral duties (instead of just keeping a school) seems to indicate that the Montauketts, in their invitation to him, saw him as replacing Horton entirely. Noticing that the Montauketts increasingly did not turn out for his regular lectures and sermons, Horton spared himself the wearisome sixty-mile (round-trip) trek from his house in Southampton to deliver them and instead focused on the nearby Shinnecocks. When the Shinnecocks similarly began looking to Occom and other local Indian ministers for ministrations, Horton became altogether discouraged. In 1751, he requested and received a dismissal from his charge over the Montauketts and Shinnecocks by the SSPCK and left to serve a congregation at South Hanover (Bottle Hill), New Jersey.[70]

Neither Occom nor Horton recorded an outright break, and in Occom's 1768 retrospective narration of the events, he made it clear that he had not supported or encouraged the "Inthusiastical" and Separate leanings of his congregants, a claim Horton himself confirmed to the antirevivalist Goshen minister, Solomon Williams, in early 1750.[71] Occom, being quite familiar with the Anglo and Indian Separate movements in New England (and well aware of the negative perception the NEC commissioners had regarding Separates), said he "took a mild way to reclaim" his Separate-leaning parishioners.[72] Nonetheless, Horton was clearly annoyed with the Indian Separates among the Shinnecocks and Montauketts, as he conveyed in a letter on September 14, 1751, in which he complained of a "defection" of a number of them.[73] What role Occom played in the ongoing separation of the Indian Christian communities among the Montauketts and Shinnecocks is not clear, but it is certain that he was at home in the small world of Separate Indian Christianity.[74] Occom encouraged Separate Native worship and meetings on Long Island by his very presence and had few regrets about the departure of Horton.

After Horton left Long Island in 1751, the frequency of Occom's trips to the Shinnecocks increased. On the Sundays that he led the three services at Shinnecock, he would leave Montauk on Saturday evening after sunset, ride the thirty miles to Shinnecock at night, hold a full day of services and visitations, and then return to his family and community at Montauk on Monday. In addition to all this, he spent time making pastoral rounds, visiting the sick and presiding over funerals.[75]

From the mid-1740s on, Occom established himself as a major intertribal Indian leader in southern New England, traveling frequently back and forth by boat between the Indian communities of mainland New England and Long Island. Over time, he began again to attract the attention of colonial missionaries who were devising plans to utilize his obvious talents. Some proposed various missionary trips for Occom, either to the Delawares in New Jersey or the Cherokees in the Southeast. On July 13, 1757, Occom underwent a rigorous examination as a preliminary test for ordination by the Windham (Connecticut) Association of Congregationalist Ministers. Although Occom passed the examination, his actual ordination was withheld. The Long Island Presbytery did not pass up such an opportunity, however, and on August 29 and 30, 1759, Samson Occom was examined and ordained a Presbyterian minister at the East Hampton church of Samuel Buell.[76]

The colonial ministers seemingly had their model Indian preacher, and Occom had secured the additional spiritual weight and legitimacy of English ordination, something not shared by many Indian ministers. Perhaps more than any other Indian minister, Occom adopted the dress, rhetorical style, and sermonic structure of his English ministerial colleagues.[77] Although he preached without notes, white observers who came to hear him could not detect anything immediately that would distinguish him as a Native—so much so, in fact, that when Occom failed to show up in New Haven for a scheduled preaching visit, Nathan Strong—non-Indian and white, although with a reportedly dark visage—instead got up to preach and was mistaken for Occom by at least one attendee, who sat in the back, muttering, "See how the black dog lays it down."[78] Occom's Separatism, and general contempt for certain aspects of English leadership, became more pronounced in the late 1760s, however, as he inserted himself into the Mohegan land controversy and the sachemship disputes at Mohegan.

"Unofficial" Separate Indian Churches

In 1771, Ezra Stiles reported that in all of New England there were seven official Indian congregations, and only one of these—at Narragansett—was among the Indian communities in Connecticut, Rhode Island, and on Long Island that had professed Christianity for the first time in the 1740s.[79] Unlike some English observers, however, Stiles additionally recognized that "there are a few small Congregations besides which [have] preachg occasionally, but are not Chhs." These smaller, "occasional Congregations" included communities of Christian Indians among the Lantern Hill Pequots, the Mashantucket Pequots, the Mohegans, and the Niantics.[80]

What Stiles observed in 1771 had a thirty-year history in southeastern New England. Not all Indian communities had a resident Indian minister like Ashpo, Occom, or Niles, or even an "official" Indian church. Regardless of their lack of "official" status according to Anglo-Americans, many Indian towns contained subcommunities of Indian Christians who met in private homes and elected or requested other Indians to serve as teachers and preachers among them. Among the Niantics in Lyme, Connecticut, for example, there was no official Indian church or even an NEC-sponsored school in the years immediately following the Great Awakening, and yet from the early 1740s onward a good number of Niantic Christians met regularly in "Gideon's mantion house," a structure built by Gideon Qequawcom in "the middle hundred acres" of Niantic lands.[81] A Niantic Indian minister, Philip Occuish (Cuish), who was later reported as favoring adult baptism over infant baptism (and therefore probably had been influenced by some Baptist Separates), served as minister and teacher to the

Indians under his care from as early as the 1740s.[82] Occuish, like most other unofficial Indian ministers, preached and taught in other Indian communities.
Joseph Johnson reported that Philip Occuish preached at an Indian meeting
held at Mohegan on November 29, 1771.[83] Like Niles, however, Occuish was
unlicensed and illegitimate from the perspective of local Euroamericans.

Similarly, the Lantern Hill Pequots operated without an official Christian
Indian leader. Like the Narragansett and Montaukett Indians, the Lantern Hill
Pequots seem to have been influenced initially by Anglo Separates in the region.
Between 1743 and 1746, North Stonington minister Joseph Fish lost a full two-
thirds of his congregation to Separates and Separate Baptists, including a number
of Indians whose church attendance and baptisms he had labored so hard to procure.[84] Over time, the resultant Christian Indian Pequot community received
pastoral oversight from a variety of Christian Indian leaders without any one in
particular remaining in residence for a significant amount of time. Fish himself
preached to them several times a month in the 1750s.[85] The Indian church at
Mashantucket was similarly serviced by a rotation of Indian leaders, including
Samuel Niles and Philip Occuish.[86]

On Long Island, too, after Occom's permanent departure in 1764, the Indian
churches continued to thrive under a different Native minister, Peter John.[87]
Peter John was born at Hayground, New York, within the town limits of Bridge-
hampton on Long Island between 1712 and 1715.[88] Like some other Natives on
Long Island, he was drawn into the revival services of the Great Awakening and
professed Christianity in 1741, perhaps after hearing James Davenport, as some
accounts suggest.[89] At some point Peter John was commissioned or ordained as
a preacher, perhaps by the Shinnecocks themselves (as Samuel Niles had been
by the Narragansetts), but also possibly by a Separate group in Connecticut.
Although Horton does not mention him by name, Peter John's Separate leanings
and proximity to Horton likely made him one of the Separates who ultimately
drove Horton away in the early 1750s. Peter John was a man of surprisingly independent means, as he eventually purchased land and settled at a place called
George's Manor, on which his descendants lived for at least a century and a half.
In the 1740s and 1750s, Peter John ministered to (and in some cases, founded)
four Indian churches in rather far-flung locations on Long Island, at Wading
River, Poospatuck, Islip, and Canoe Place. Islip was the farthest west, about forty
miles from Canoe Place, which was the easternmost of the four towns. Poospatuck lay roughly midway between Islip and Canoe Place on the south side of
Long Island, with Wading River located thirteen miles due north of Poospatuck.
Peter John also traveled regularly to other Indian congregations, including the
one at Montauk. His home base seems to have been Canoe Place on Shinnecock
reserved lands, although when he passed away in approximately 1800, at the age
of eighty-eight, he was laid to rest at Poospatuck.[90]

In general, there was a cadre of unlicensed Indian ministers who traveled among the various Native communities in Rhode Island, Connecticut, and Long Island between 1750 and 1770, preaching and administering sacraments as needed or desired. Samuel Niles, James Niles, James Simon, Samson Occom, Joseph Johnson, John Nanepome, John Shattock, Sr., Henry Quaquaquid, John Shattock, Jr., Jacob Fowler, David Fowler, John Cooper, Hezekiah Calvin, Peter John, Cyrus (Silas) Charles, Paul Cuffee, Samuel Ashpo, John Ashpo, and others provided a continual alternative on Indian lands to Anglo-led services, sometimes traveling widely to provide their ministrations. The Pequot James Simon, for example, after losing the bid for the Narragansett Indian Church leadership in the early 1750s, continued to serve as an itinerant Indian preacher, even traveling into Massachusetts to preach to Indian communities there. On December 13, 1752, Baptist minister Isaac Backus in Titicut, Massachusetts, welcomed James Simon to his town, where he preached twice, first at the house of another Indian, James Thomas, and in the evening at Backus's own house, where "a great number of all Sorts of people came in, and seemed to be something affected with his discourse."[91]

Most Indian communities also had a few lay ministers, exhorters, and educators; some of them were approved by colonial ministers; some were not. In early 1742, Azariah Horton reported hearing an unlicensed, uneducated Montaukett Christian Indian preaching to some Indians in his own language. Horton, who himself could not speak Montauk, had to rely on local bilingual colonists to provide a rough translation.[92] Another unnamed Indian on Long Island served as an unofficial exhorter for the seven months prior to his death: "He made it his business, at every feasible Opportunity, to exhort his Fellow Indians, old and young, to put them in Mind of their great Concerns, earnestly pleading with them to come and taste of the inexpressible Sweetness of the Lord Jesus Christ."[93] In the 1760s, John Shattock, Sr., served as a lay minister among the Narragansetts, and his son, John Shattock, Jr., kept a school among the Pequots in Stonington.[94] On Long Island, the Montaukett Cyrus Charles was said to be serving as an "Indian teacher" in 1773, and David McClure reported that the Montauketts were "serious and devout, and spend considerable part of their time in religious exercises."[95] An unknown number of these Native preachers and exhorters never appeared in written colonial records, however, at least not while they were alive. The Narragansett "Jo: Potter" served as Indian exhorter among the New Lights in Rhode Island and was only mentioned by the Anglican minister James McSparran when Potter passed away in 1751.[96]

Meetings of Christian Indians took place on a fairly regular basis throughout the 1750s and 1760s. These gatherings included regular, weekly church services, mid-week singing services, and annual, biannual, and impromptu intertribal meetings with regional Christian Natives. Since most of these gatherings happened in Indian houses or wigwams, they remained largely invisible to colonial observers. On Friday, September 5, 1760, for example, Occom traveled from Mohegan to Farmington and was surprised to find his friends from Mohegan, Niantic, and Groton all assembled in the house of Adams Solomon, where he preached to them that night and then again on Sunday, September 5.[97] On October 28, 1761, the Narragansett minister Samuel Niles preached to a large gathering of Narragansett, Mohegan, and Niantic Indians (including the Mohegan sachem, Benjamin Uncas III), who assembled at Niantic in a sizable "House of Two Rooms" roughly the size of two and a half wigwams.[98]

In almost every instance, Natives in various towns preferred these Indian itinerants and ministers over settled, paid Euroamerican ones. On October 14, 1770, for example, the Mohegan John Cooper preached at Narragansett to two hundred Indians assembled from various communities. The very next day, Joseph Fish held a service for the Indians at the home of Edward Deake, the Narragansett schoolmaster, and only four Indians showed up. The unavoidable conclusion for Fish was that the Narragansetts "seem determined to discourage me from coming to preach to them." It was not just that the Narragansetts rejected Fish, however; it was that they actually preferred Indian preachers like Samuel Niles and John Cooper over Fish. "They had rather follow that Ignorant, proud, conceited, Obstinate Teacher, poor Sam Niles," Fish fumed, "than Attend regular preaching of Sound Gospel Doctrine."[99] At Stockbridge, too, the Mohicans began to push for their own Separate church in the 1760s, although, ironically, the whites in the biracial church at Stockbridge resented such a separation in part because their minister, Stephen West, was paid directly by the NEC as a missionary. If the Indians left, so would West's funding, and Stockbridge residents—wealthy as they were—did not wish to ante up for their own minister.[100]

Native Christian Practice

Although some aspects of this emerging Indian Separatism were unremarkable and "orthodox," in many ways the Separate Indians refashioned various Christian practices to serve their own needs. Glimpses of the contours of Indian Christian practices as well as beliefs and spiritualities can be found in the various sermons, diary entries, and other reports written between 1750 and 1775. Joseph Johnson recorded a variety of Christian practices in his journals, including reading passages from the Bible and devotional works like Richard Baxter's *The Saints' Everlasting Rest* (1680), praying, meditating, and composing hymns, along with corporate practices such as attending worship services and singing.[101] As with Christian Wampanoags on Martha's Vineyard in the early eighteenth century, Bible reading was a central devotional practice for some Indians.[102]

Jacob Johnson reported in 1755 that John Ashpo, who served in the 1750s as a schoolmaster to Indian children in Groton, "reads much in his Bible, both to himself, to his Schollars, & to the other Indians, till he Has very much defaced, & obliterated his Bible; and is hardly able to buy him another."[103] By the time the NEC sent a large replacement Bible, however, John Ashpo had joined the colonial forces during the French and Indian War (1754–1760), and the Bible was placed for general use in the school instead.[104]

The Bible was only one source of revelation and inspiration for Indian Separates. The almost universal assessment of Native Christianity in this time period was that it gave great weight to traditional modes of revelation and insight, including dreams, visions, and trances. Most radically, perhaps, Niles—who could not read the Bible—was reported to rely on the Spirit "to teach him Doctrine and Conduct," and to look to the "Guidance of Feelings, Impressions, Visions, Appearances, and Directions of Angels and of Christ himself in a Visionary Way."[105] Samuel Niles and the Narragansett Separates were perhaps the most notorious example of this, but they were not the only ones. When David McClure visited the Montauketts in September 1773, he noted in his journal that "their religious services are, chiefly, remarkable impulses and mental visions." It wasn't simply that Native Separates believed their indigenized Christianity was equally as good as their colonial counterparts; they actually viewed it as superior. Lamenting to the NEC commissioners in October 1769, Joseph Fish said the Separates told him that "because we depend upon what the Bible Says, & not upon what the Spirit teaches—that they have their Teaching directly from the Fountain, So [it is] above ours."[106] Other ministers felt less threatened, however. For McClure, the Montauketts' visionary spirituality prompted speculation about the possibility of God working in a different way to speak to the Natives. "Perhaps God is pleased," mused McClure, "to bring them to the knowledge of the Saviour, in a way and manner different from that which we experience who have the advantages of knowledge & the instituted means of light and grace."[107]

Like their Euroamerican New Light counterparts, Indian Christians inhabited a "world of wonders," drawn jointly from European Christian supernaturalism and Native ideas about the supernatural world.[108] Joseph Johnson noted that on December 22, 1771, all those in his uncle's house heard an "Uncommon noise, as if one Struck with all his might upon the housetop," once in the evening, and twice more at daybreak. Just the day before, a large black spot "about the bigness of an half Copper" appeared on the palm of the hand of Johnson's aunt, which stayed for a while, then vanished, but left her with "a strange sort of feeling after Some time." "What can be the meaning of these," Johnson pondered, "we must leave to time to determine."[109] The question was not whether there was meaning in such events, but what that meaning was. On December 20, 1772, Johnson recorded an early morning drowsy vision, in which he saw "the likeness

of a lamb that had been Slain, Standin at the foot of my Couch." According to
Johnson, the sight of the lamb caused him to wake up; but the lamb ("Jesus
Christ") was still there. "No sooner I awoke but got directly up," Johnson wrote,
"and followed the Blessed Lamb out, and there I worshipped him."[110] Johnson,
Niles, and other New Light Indian Christians viewed dreams as important and
worthy of parsing for meaning. Samson Occom also recorded a "remarkable
dream" on April 2, 1786, in which the famed evangelist George Whitefield—
dead for sixteen years—appeared to him and affirmed Occom's life and ministry.
Such dreams were believed by Algonquians to be messages from ancestors,
which illustrates not only the close affinity Occom imagined with Whitefield,
but also the ways in which traditional Native interpretations of dreams overlapped and co-existed with New Light understandings of the same.[111]

In other ways, too, Native Separatism blended elements of Christian and traditional practices. In some cases, traditional rituals aimed at effective control
over the natural world were replaced (or at least supplemented) by Christian
ones. The Narragansett Christians, for example, gathered in their Separate
church during an intense drought and prayed for rain. No sooner had they
started praying than a cloud appeared in the southwest and, when it arrived,
drenched the entire area. One Indian in attendance reported that they "went
home dripping, and praising God."[112] Natives performed rituals and prayed for
rain long before they professed Christianity, however. In this particular case, it is
clear that the desired effect remained the same; the only change was the being to
whom the petition was addressed. More often than the records indicate, Indian
ministers undoubtedly infused long-standing Indian meetings and rituals with
Christian significance. Niles incorporated traditional Narragansett festivals into
the Christian calendar, including an annual church-sponsored harvest festival
(the August meeting), in which Natives from surrounding communities would
come together to "dance, feast, renew acquaintances, and hold religious services."[113] Similarly, at Montauk, Occom regularly participated in the Montaukett
Green Corn Festival and befriended a Montaukett herbalist, from whom he
learned the widely sought arts of Native herbal medicine, which on Long Island
drew from over fifty varieties of herbs and roots.[114]

The more formalized Indian Separate churches, like the one at Narragansett,
largely adopted features and practices of English Congregational churches such
as covenants, family worship, singing and prayer times, baptisms, and the celebration of the Lord's Supper. A variety of worship, prayer, and singing services
punctuated the rhythms of weekly affairs on Native lands. There were the usual
Sunday morning and Sunday afternoon services, like the two sermons Samuel
Ashpo preached in the forenoon and afternoon at Mohegan on November 3,
1771. The Narragansett Indian Church held services on Tuesday, Thursday, and
Saturday evenings, in addition to the normal Sunday services. Communion was

often celebrated monthly, with the Thursday before the celebration set aside as a time of preparation.[115] On Long Island, Occom held three worship services each Sunday, at 10 A.M., in the afternoon, and again in the evening, and also on Wednesday evening. Each of the four weekly services followed roughly the same format. The meeting opened with singing, some collective prayer, and more singing. Occom would then read a passage from the Bible, expound upon it, and conclude with prayer and singing.[116] Throughout, Occom reported that he exhorted and preached to the Montauketts and Shinnecocks in his native Mohe-gan-Pequot language, which was closely related to Montauk.[117] Preaching in any Indian language at all was something local white ministers simply could not do and was undoubtedly one of the many attractive elements of Occom's services. Non-Indian listeners who heard him in both Indian and English contexts agreed that "when he preaches to the *Indians,* is vastly more natural and free, clear and eloquent, quick and powerful, than 'tis wont to be, when he preaches to others."[118] By some reports, these Indian-led services and exhortations were interactive. When David McClure preached to the Montauketts in September 1773, he observed that the congregants—and especially the older ones—often would "break out in exclamation, saying, Amen—or that's true—that's right."[119] Native corporate prayers, too, reflected a collective sensibility, with everyone praying out loud at once, "some in English and some in Indian." White observers often concluded it "was indeed a confused noise."[120]

Lots of robust, group singing seems to have been one central and widespread feature of Native services. Hymn singing had a long history with Native Chris-tians, dating back to the 1650s and the evangelization efforts of John Eliot. Singing hymns was part of the educational and evangelistic efforts in southern New England in the eighteenth century and was seemingly one of the first things that resonated with Natives who attended revival services during the Awak-ening.[121] For Occom, it was important that his congregants understood what they were singing, so he would first read a hymn to them, "give the Meaning of it," and then proceed to sing it.[122] Hymnody and singing became yet another way in which Native Separate Christians adopted Euroamerican Christian practice and made it distinctly their own. The Narragansett Indians, for example, held their own separate singing meetings on Tuesday, Thursday, and Saturday even-ings and often sang English hymns "in their Way," according to Joseph Fish.[123] When existing hymnals failed to satisfy his musical preferences, Samson Occom took it upon himself to publish a lengthy and eclectic collection of 109 hymns titled *A Choice Collection of Hymns and Spiritual Songs; Intended for the edification of sincere Christians* (1774) and drawn from more than a century of European hymnody and a surprisingly wide swath of denominations.[124] Occom's hymnal contained some of his own hymns, including "Throughout the Savior's Life We Trace." At least one of Occom's hymns, "Awaked by Sinai's Awful Sound," was still well known almost one hundred years later in some regional nineteenth-century evangelical circles.[125]

Another unique and defining feature of Native group worship services was the sharedness of religious exhortation. Such practices likely had roots in both pre-Awakening traditional Native customs at tribal meetings and the emphasis on democratic sharing of experiences by radical New Lights in the Awakening. Such freedom in worship also paralleled religious expression among black Christians in this time period, enslaved and free. The Euroamerican model of *a* preacher and *one* sermon seems to have been replaced by a multiplicity of voices in the form of several individuals—notably both men and women—sharing their life experiences and offering comments and challenges to the gathered group. One service David McClure attended in the summer of 1768 at Narragansett involved the Mohegan Indian minister Samuel Ashpo and four or five other individuals exhorting over the course of the evening.[126] The exhorters "attempted generally to describe the Christian life" by talking about "their own religious experiences, which were mostly visions, dreams, impulses & similitudes." Far from a simple rationalistic exposition, however, these exhortations played heavily on the emotions. "They were all very earnest in voice & gesture," McClure observed, "so much so that some of them foamed at the mouth & seemed transported with a kind of enthusiasm."[127]

Similarly, on Tuesday, November 5, 1771, Henry Quaquaquid, John Nanepome, and Samuel Ashpo all took turns preaching at Mohegan in a tag-team extravaganza.[128] In these sermons, several recurring themes stand out. The first is the immediacy of spiritual temptations. Nanepome's sermon described the Christian life as dotted with potential pitfalls and dangers in which "the Devil is always with us ready to tempt us into sin, and ready to snatch us away every moment." A second and related theme is the importance of individual choices in the Christian life. In the same sermon, Nanepome emphasized that Christ is interceding for individuals and yet individuals are ultimately responsible for their own fate and potential "eternal damnation." A third major theme is the impending "latter Day," and in particular, the final judgment before God when, as Ashpo warned, "we must give an account of all our actions, whether good or evil, and so be rewarded according to our behavior." Fourth is the promise of a future paradise. The exhorters reminded the assembled "to set their mind heavenward, and . . . spoke of the glories of heaven, as sat forth in the Holy Bible." A fifth and final recurring theme is that of the necessity of the rising generation to not spurn the offer of grace.[129] Henry Quaquaquid especially addressed "the young folks" present, lamenting that they "chose rather the pleasures of flesh and sense before the service of God." Nanepome later warned the youth, "though you contradict us, you can't contradict God, who takes an account of all your actions."[130]

Overall, these Indian churches practiced their own versions of Christianity that built on the experience of the revivals of the 1740s and yet were firmly shaped by Indian religious sensibilities. The Narragansett church used the older and more basic Apostles' Creed as their doctrinal basis, not the Calvinistic Westminster Confession of Faith as the surrounding Congregational churches would have undoubtedly done. In terms of membership, the bar was set rather high. Samuel Drake reported that "they are not fond of receiving any into church fellowship, but such as can give some good account of their being born again, renounce their heathenish practices, subject themselves to the ordinance of baptism, and embrace the above articles of faith."[131] For those church members who returned to their "sinful practices," the other members would "mourn over them as if their heart would break." If there was satisfactory repentance on the part of the offending members, the church would welcome them back with rejoicing that was "equal to their former mourning." If, however, after several meetings, the fallen individual persisted in his or her ways, "they bid the offender farewell, as though they were going to part to meet no more, and with such a mourning as resembles a funeral."[132]

In all of this, Native Separates were defiantly protective of their right to work out the details of their own practices of Christianity. In the summer of 1768, McClure attended Niles's Narragansett Indian Church and found it to be unlike anything he was accustomed to. During the service, one of the exhorters stopped and addressed McClure and his friend, Chester Bingham (who were unavoidably outsiders), saying, "this is the way that we Indians have to get to heaven. You white people have another way. I don't know but your way will bring *you* there, but I know that our way will bring *us* there."[133] Such sentiments surfaced repeatedly throughout the colonial period and were essentially a Christianized version of a Native critique in which Natives defended their own way of viewing the world or worshiping the Creator and declared them just as valid as the ways of the colonists.[134]

It is important to stress that not all—likely not even the majority of—Indians were Christians, and not all Christian Indians were Separates. Indian Separate Christian practices became a feature of reservation life, but they were not universally participated in, shared, or agreed upon. Despite the vibrant Christian Separate church at Narragansett, for example, Fish noted that some Indians remained aloof and would "rather follow, Some their work, other their pleasures, Idleness, Drunkenness, or any Way of Serving the Devil and their Lusts, than to Spend An hour or Two in hearing the precious Truths of the Gospel."[135] Nonetheless, for those who did take part, the Separatist impulse had a long life in many Indian communities throughout the eighteenth century. Many Indians who identified with Christianity even into the 1770s were typically identified—or self identified—as Separates. Tobias

Shattock, a Narragansett leader, schoolteacher, and attendee at Wheelock's Indian school, was eulogized in 1771 by Joseph Fish as having religious sentiments which were "Something of the *Separate* way."[136] Similarly, when Joseph Johnson experienced a second conversion of sorts in early 1772, he recounted that "I *was called by them a Separate, a New light*," an epithet he embraced.[137] Although Johnson attended the local Congregational church led by Timothy Pitkin while serving as a schoolteacher in Farmington in the early 1770s, he also functioned as a Separate Indian minister to the local Farmington Indians, organizing singing meetings on Tuesday and Friday evenings and holding a Sunday evening full worship service complete with a sermon and exhortations, all of which were conducted outside of white churches and homes.[138]

Well into the late eighteenth century and beyond, Indian Separatism thrived. The ways in which the basic ideas of autonomy and separatism took root in Indian communities over the course of the eighteenth century can also be seen in Native responses to and rejection of ongoing Anglo-European attempts to reform them through education, long after the events of the Great Awakening.

‖ 6 ‖

Educating

The Lantern Hill Pequots insisted on a female schoolteacher. And not just a woman, but an Indian woman. Joseph Fish, the North Stonington minister, was trying to fulfill the Pequots' wishes and a mandate from the New England Company to hire a schoolmaster for the Lantern Hill Pequot children in 1757. Believing the Pequots were "naturally a very jealous people & hard to please"—Fish had seen several dozen Lantern Hill Pequots join and then depart from his North Stonington church during the Awakening—he decided to let them propose their own candidates for schoolmaster. From the start, the Pequots expressed a strong desire for a female Indian teacher if at all possible, since most of their school-age children were girls. Although Fish was worried that the NEC commissioners might not approve, he allowed the Pequots to move ahead in selecting a female teacher. Several Indian women were proposed, although there was little agreement about which one should be chosen; Fish found each candidate unfit for the task. He finally convinced the Natives to open their search to include Indian men, and "several again were propos'd, but either objected against, or unqualifyd, or both." Fish himself inquired into possible Indian male schoolteachers in the region but came up empty-handed. Frustrated, Fish hired an English male schoolteacher, but the teacher insisted that he needed £10 to do the task—£5 more than the NEC was willing to pay. To make up the difference, Fish proposed that the Indian school be opened up to English children, whose parents could afford to pay for their children to attend. Local English parents agreed, and so did some of the Pequots—at first, at least. Before the school actually got under way, the Lantern Hill Pequot parents grew so disaffected with the idea that Fish was forced to abandon that plan, too, since the Pequots "refused to have any thing to do with the English, in the affair of a school: being possessed with this notion, that the English had a Design upon their mony." Fish was defeated for the moment: three months of negotiating, and nothing to show for it. Nonetheless, the Pequots told him they were going to prepare a building over the winter in which to house the school in the hope that it would open in the spring. Fish pleaded with the Boston commissioners to help him find a female teacher—Indian or English—who would be willing to keep school at Lantern Hill.[1]

As this story illustrates, the post–Great Awakening period (1750–1775) was marked by another upsurge in educational efforts orchestrated by English missionaries and ministers and mostly welcomed by Natives—with some distinct qualifications. This was the third such wave of educational and evangelistic efforts, following those in the 1660s and then again between the 1710s and the 1740s. From the colonists' perspective, these efforts were an attempt to further reform Indian communities and either supplement or undercut tribal leadership that was uncomfortable or "unorthodox." As they did with most English offerings in the eighteenth century, the Indians of southern New England responded to educational opportunities in ways that partially went along with colonial designs but also shaped these designs for their own purposes. Natives increasingly channeled educational opportunities to serve their own communities. The literacy skills learned in schools were used to write petitions to ministers, local magistrates, colonial governors, and even the British king, and, over time, to create far-flung networks of literate Indians with shared concerns. Through the written word, reputations were defended, English institutions and decisions were questioned, white morality was challenged, old friends were greeted, and loving letters were passed between husbands and wives, parents and children.

One of the main differences between pre- and post-Awakening Indian schools was that the ones that followed the Awakening were often led by Indians. Although at one level this can be explained as a practical outcome of Natives themselves receiving education over the course of the eighteenth century, there is more to the story. Starting in the 1750s, Natives increasingly took an active interest in and—when possible—control of the educational opportunities in their midst in ways that resonated with but were not the same as the Separatist impulse in Indian churches. Many Native communities, who initially looked to ministers and missionaries to aid them in their struggles against colonial governments and warring parties within Indian communities, over time became disillusioned with the motives of English involvement and often took educational matters into their own hands—by refusing to send their children to Anglo schools, deposing Anglo schoolteachers, or supporting unofficial Native teachers and ministers. In some cases, Indian parents simply insisted on the right to their own school, separate from white children and taught by an Indian.[2] It was not just at Lantern Hill. There were schools on tribal lands at Stockbridge, Niantic, Farmington, Mashantucket, Narragansett, Montauk, and Shinnecock—all in addition to the much publicized educational efforts at Moor's Indian Charity School run by Eleazar Wheelock in Lebanon.

In these locales, the struggle for the shape and meaning of education was part of the much larger tumult in the 1760s to continually define Native communities, defend land rights, and, above all, to protect what remained of Native cultural and religious sovereignty and autonomy. Native schools became important not only in terms of the number of students who attended, but also as sites for asserting Native sovereignty. In this way they should be considered central to the many ways in which Natives sought to creatively address ongoing issues of dispossession, economic disparity, and racial injustice in the post-Awakening period.

Post-Awakening Indian Education

Most English missionaries and ministers stepped up their educational efforts in the years following the season of increased Indian affiliations in 1741–1743, particularly in the 1750s. In some ways, this was in keeping with Protestant views of spiritual formation as ongoing and necessarily renewable, but in other ways it was more closely linked to colonists' disdainful views of Indian cultural practices and suspicions that Christianity had not really taken root—or at least not in the totalizing, life-changing ways that were desired by many English clergy and missionaries. Euroamerican ministers and missionaries recognized that even some Indians who had professed Christianity and joined local churches were "backsliding" into old cultural patterns, "sins" of drunkenness and not keeping the Sabbath, and, in some cases, simple nonpractice of Christianity. For some Indians, it was as if the Awakening had never happened. Additionally, so many Native Christians and leaders continued to prefer New Light modes of worship and to demonstrate Separate tendencies that more moderate ministers were motivated to provide ongoing education in hopes of tempering such enthusiasms.[3]

Ongoing educational efforts targeted three overlapping and yet distinct groups of Natives largely separated by age and experience. The first group was Natives who were born in the 1710s, 1720s, and 1730s, who experienced the Great Awakening firsthand (like Occom, Niles, and Ashpo) and emerged post-Awakening with a spectrum of religious affiliations and religious practices (and nonpractices), most of which English ministers found disappointingly insufficient. Educational efforts also focused, second, on Natives who were born during or after the Awakening and who were often children of current, former, or lapsed Indian members of white churches—or, worse yet (from the Anglo ministers' perspective), children of Indian Separates. Third, Anglo ministers, educators, and officials also sought to reach subsections of the Native populations from both generations who had been fairly unaffected by Christianity in the first place. The ongoing educational efforts, then, were an attempt to win the younger generation while simultaneously reforming their elders. As before the Awakening, missionaries often found more success among the younger generations. John Sergeant, serving at Stockbridge, noted of the older generation with exasperation that "nothing but the extraordinary power that attended Christianity in its first propagation will be sufficient to reform them."[4]

Starting in the late 1740s and early 1750s, a more permanent school was reopened, continued, or founded among every major Indian community in southeastern New England. In most cases, this was a continuation of previous educational attempts (sometimes even the same schoolhouse was used that had been built before the Awakening). In other cases, this was a new effort on Native lands. Several overlapping models for Indian education existed in southeastern New England. The first was the reservation school, usually funded by local towns, colonies, and/or British missionary societies and run by English schoolteachers. This was clearly the model preferred by whites in the eighteenth century and had roots back to the 1720s and 1730s. The second model was a slight variation of the first, namely, a school on Indian lands, taught by a Native but still often receiving varying levels of support from local white organizations, whether governments or missionary societies. This, too, had precedent in the decade prior to the Awakening but grew increasingly common afterward.

In the aftermath of the Awakening and what was widely considered to be the failure of evangelization and education to reshape Native cultural sensibilities, a third, somewhat newer, model emerged, namely, that of the boarding school. The idea had been floated occasionally over the course of a few decades—and some earlier schools, like Mason's at Mohegan in the 1720s and 1730s, operated as functional boarding schools—but in the decade following the Awakening, two different Indian schools were founded based on this model. The first, in Stockbridge, Massachusetts, was founded by John Sergeant and funded by the Massachusetts colony, the NEC, and a wealthy British patron, Isaac Hollis. The other, in Lebanon, Connecticut, was founded by Eleazar Wheelock and funded by a wide swath of evangelistically minded people and institutions in the colonies and abroad, including the NEC and the SSPCK.[5] The boarding school model was especially despised by Natives over time, as it fairly effectively cut off Indian children from their parents' and community's oversight. But that was precisely the point. In the face of prior failure (through evangelism and education), English educators like Sergeant and Wheelock were not simply seeking to hand out the rudiments of literacy; they sought nothing less than a totalizing, civilizing transformation, which they felt was best done away from the interference of Native families and communities.

Some of the earliest and most important post-Awakening educational efforts were centered in Stockbridge, Massachusetts. Although an Indian school was established at Stockbridge before the Awakening, in the early 1740s Sergeant concocted a more ambitious boarding school plan for Indian boys and girls. Part of the proposed plan included carving two hundred acres out of the ten square miles that comprised the town of Stockbridge on which to build the boarding schoolhouse. The Indian students—ideally between the ages of ten and twenty—would be placed under two "Masters," one to watch over them during their hours of study and one during their hours of labor. The boys would work on clearing the land, raising crops, and tending cattle, sheep, and hogs, all in the hope of earning enough through surplus production to make the school—and, later, the Indian boys—self-sustaining. From the beginning, however, Sergeant proposed "to take in Girls, as well as Boys, to be educated in a Manner Suitable to the Condition of their Sex," which would involve the production of wool, flax, and dairy products, as well as typical English domestic skills like spinning, knitting, and sewing.[6] One final component of Sergeant's plan was to take in Native children from the more distant River Indians to the west but also—more important—children from the Six Nations in New York with the idea that they might "open the way for the Propagation of Christianity to the remotest Tribes."[7] By removing children from their parents, this plan had the overall goal of nothing less than a total cultural transformation of Native students and eventually communities: to "change their whole Habit of thinking and acting; and raise them, as far as possible into the Condition of a civil industrious and polish'd People."[8]

Sergeant's proposals reached a surprisingly wide and initially receptive English audience, in part because they were pitched as a way to more effectively keep the Natives living in New England (and eventually the Six Nations) firmly within the "British interest."[9] Despite the quick and sufficient support for Sergeant's design, the precarious position of Stockbridge between the English and French empires made it almost impossible to implement the proposals until after the tumult of renewed war with the French (in King George's War, 1744–1748). Sergeant opted to instead select twelve Mohican boys and send them to Captain Martin Kellogg in Newington, Connecticut, southwest of Hartford, to begin the first implementation of his boarding school design. On May 23, 1748, the twelve hand-selected boys traveled the seventy miles to Kellogg's house to be instructed "both in Learning & in hard Labour."[10] The following spring the twelve boys and Kellogg moved back to Stockbridge, first to a private house, and later into the newly constructed Indian school house that measured thirty-eight feet long and thirty-six feet wide, with several large rooms with fireplaces and a spacious cellar below.[11] Sergeant also extended to the Mohawks in the late 1740s an offer of sending their children to his school.[12]

Sergeant quickly learned that he had far less control of the boys under his guidance than he desired. In 1743, he confessed to Isaac Hollis, the English benefactor who later sponsored the initial twelve Indian boys in the boarding school, that three or four of the older male students "could not be prevail'd with to keep from marrying." Likewise, it was difficult to keep the students at school during the hunting and sugar-making seasons, so Sergeant refused to continue their various means of support from Hollis's fund until he could "see the Success of your

Bounty." Moreover, from the beginning he was painfully aware of the "Jealousies and Suspicions" the Indians had regarding the mission and school, particularly displaying "their great Aversions to such Restraints, looking upon them as Infringements of their Liberties." Sergeant and the schoolmaster Timothy Woodbridge were "forc'd in Compliance with their Weakness and silly Prejudices to deal only in the gentle Methods of Persuasion."[13]

Sergeant passed away on July 27, 1749, at the age of thirty-nine, before all of his proposals could be implemented. By then, Stockbridge boasted a thriving school of fifty-five students under Woodbridge, in addition to the twelve initial students at the boarding school.[14] In 1751, Elisha Williams revived Sergeant's desire to include Native girls in his educational program by proposing a school for Indian girls "where they might be taught the Arts in use among the English women (as well as reading &c.)."[15] The NEC offered £30 per year to John Sergeant's widow, Abigail (Williams) Sergeant, who agreed to serve as a teacher in 1752.[16] A separately funded school for Indian girls was necessary because Isaac Hollis had restricted his funds to be used for the education of Indian boys only.[17]

The Stockbridge boarding school also became a short-lived center for the education of Haudenosaunee children from New York. In February 1750, the NEC granted £200 to be used for a meeting house and schoolhouse to facilitate the settlement of Iroquois children at Stockbridge and to pay for a schoolmaster to instruct the Indians "in Reading and Writing and in the Principles of the Christian Religion."[18] By spring of 1751, a few Mohawks were in residence, and in July 1751, the famed New Light revivalist Jonathan Edwards, who had fled to Stockbridge to fill Sergeant's empty position after an uncomfortable ousting in Northampton, traveled to Albany, New York, to meet with representatives from the Mohawks and Oneidas in an attempt to recruit additional children to study at Stockbridge. More Mohawk children arrived in the fall of 1751, and in December a group of Oneidas came from Onaquaga. In February 1752, the white missionary Gideon Hawley was hired on NEC funds as a schoolteacher for the Oneida, Mohawk, and Tuscarora children.[19] The experiment did not last long, however. The dissension and divisiveness at Stockbridge, largely between the Williams family and Kellogg on the one side and Edwards, Woodbridge, and Hawley on the other, eventually was part of the reason that the Mohawk parents removed most of their children by July 1752.[20] The Oneidas followed suit in February 1753, after the schoolhouse burned down under suspicious circumstances.[21] Hawley—himself reviled by Kellogg—subsequently moved to the Iroquois town of Onaquaga, where he served as a minister to the nascent Protestant Iroquois community.[22]

In other locales, Indian education had more success in the post-Awakening years. The same year Sergeant passed away in Stockbridge, Samson Occom moved to Long Island, where he founded one of the most creative and influential

Indian schools in southeastern New England. Occom's school became an important starting point for several key Montauketts who later attended Wheelock's school and became leaders and educators in various Indian communities in the 1760s and 1770s. Occom's school also served as an occasional boarding school; from time to time he personally housed some Shinnecock children as well as a Mohegan "young Man" for half a year and a Niantic youth for a whole year. Occom's pedagogical methods were straightforward and effectively tailored to his Indian students. His most important innovation was an alphabet game in which he glued each letter of the alphabet onto a separate small cedar wood chip. This allowed him to teach the individual letters to beginners (by having them bring requested letters or to rearrange the chips in alphabetical order) and, as they improved, to have them spell words—a method that was "a Pleasure" to his students.[23] In many ways, however, Occom's school demonstrates the degree to which he believed a specifically Christian education was important for his Indian pupils. He started and ended the day with prayer and catechized his students three or four times per week, usually from the Shorter Catechism of the Westminster Assembly, the standard Calvinist Presbyterian and Congregational catechism dating back to 1647. Occom was not merely tied to the words and forms of the catechism; he reported that he often "Proposd Questions of my own, and in my own Tongue."[24] By 1757, there was also a Native school with an Indian schoolmaster among the Shinnecocks.[25]

Among other communities, Indian education often fell by the wayside during the decade immediately following the Awakening. Such was likely the case with the Indian school at Mohegan, one of the oldest such schools in Connecticut or Rhode Island. The schoolhouse seems to have fallen into disuse during the early 1740s, but by the 1750s there was a renewed attempt to repair it and return it to its intended use. Robert Clelland, an English teacher employed by the NEC, kept a school at Mohegan for more than a decade beginning in 1752, continuing the work of John Mason, Jonathan Barber, and Ben Uncas III in the 1720s and 1730s.[26] In May 1752, the Connecticut General Assembly set aside £150, in response to a petition from Eliphalet Adams and David Jewett, to repair the Mohegan schoolhouse since it was "in a shattered condition, and not suitable for the schoolmaster and his family to live in."[27] Clelland's school was jointly supported by the colony of Connecticut and the New England Company; the colony provided emergency help for the students, like bread for dinner when the parents were too poor to provide it, while the NEC paid Clelland's salary.[28]

Other schools also maintained an important educational presence among Native communities across southern New England. Jacob Johnson, the minister of the North Groton Congregational Church, took immediate interest in the Mashantucket Pequots after assuming Andrew Croswell's former post in 1749. In 1753 John Ashpo—possibly the son of the Mohegan Separate minister,

Samuel Ashpo—began to serve as a schoolmaster to the Mashantuckets. By 1755, Johnson reported that twenty-nine Indians were in regular attendance under Ashpo, with an additional ten who planned to join for the winter months when their agricultural labors were less vital. This listing of Mashantucket students is surprising not only because of the number but also because of the gender of most of the students. Of the twenty-nine students Johnson listed in 1755, nineteen were females. A full fifteen of these Indian girls were among the most advanced in the school and were reading from the primers, a level reached by only three of the Indian boys.[29] Indian sachems and English observers often noted the small number of males in Indian communities—absences resulting from service in colonial wars and from seeking employment off the reservations, particularly in the whaling and seafaring industries—and Johnson's listing certainly confirms this reality. Ashpo kept this thriving school until 1759, when he enlisted to serve during the French and Indian War (1754–1760).[30] Hugh Sweetingham took his place until at least 1767, but the school clearly suffered during the war years, with Indian parents not sending their children as regularly.[31] The school was at times supported financially by the colony, as in 1766, when the General Assembly set aside £20 to provide food and clothing for the children of poor Indian parents, particularly those who had lost family members in the French and Indian War.[32]

Among the Lantern Hill Pequots near North Stonington, Joseph Fish worked to provide lectures and keep a schoolmaster employed to instruct the Eastern Pequot children. Following the long and frustrating attempt to find a female Indian schoolteacher for the Lantern Hill Pequots, the Indian Edward Nedson began holding a school at his own house beginning February 22, 1758, which he continued until September 1769, when he passed away.[33] Fish reported in 1769 that he was again trying to find an Indian schoolmaster for twenty-five school-age Pequot children. The Narragansett John Shattock, Jr., soon filled the position, followed briefly by Jacob Fowler.[34] In 1771, however, Edward Nedson's widow, Mary, refused to allow the school to continue in her house, so Fish and the Eastern Pequots made plans to build a schoolhouse and secured a promise of lumber from Stonington resident Cyrus Wheeler.[35]

Although the Narragansetts had a small school led by an Indian woman on reservation lands during the 1740s, it apparently came to a close a few years later, for when Occom offered to hold a school among them, the Narragansetts told him they did not want one (perhaps no surprise, given the illiteracy of their Separate Indian minister, Samuel Niles).[36] By the mid-1750s, however, some of the Narragansetts had changed their minds. In September 1757, Joseph Park reported to the NEC that there seemed to be a "full inclination" of at least a portion of the Narragansetts toward having a school among them. The primary impetus, as Park reported it, came from the sachem, Thomas Ninigret, who himself had been educated at an English school at Newport and "can read and write, and encourages it amongst his tribe," and who told Park that "he wish'd, he had the offer of a free school as the Indians had before his times."[37] Nonetheless, Ninigret's desire for a school did not come to fruition until the mid-1760s.

Schooling among the Niantics started before the Awakening and continued rather steadily through the mid-1770s. The school was initially founded in 1736, and in 1742 Reuben Ely became the schoolmaster. In 1749, David Latham began his long tenure as the Niantics' schoolmaster, serving until the American Revolution.[38] In 1757, Joseph and Hannah Piancho sold to the NEC the large and somewhat decrepit house formerly owned by Gideon Quequawcom for use as a schoolhouse.[39] From this point on the schoolhouse served the double purpose of housing students and serving as a meeting place for the Niantic Christian Indians, where Philip Cuish, the Baptist minister, regularly served, and where Ashpo and Occom often preached.[40]

The French and Indian War brought hard times to every Native school in southeastern New England. At Mohegan, the fathers of so many children had died in the war that the schoolmaster, Robert Clelland, was moved to intervene on their behalf; in 1761 and 1763, he petitioned and received from the General Assembly money to help feed the children of especially destitute families.[41] In difficult economic times, practical aid, as always, was welcomed by Native communities. In September 1766, Jacob Johnson reported that, due to a recent distribution of blankets, Mashantucket Pequot Indian youths had been "more Steady, & Cheerful in attending" the Indian school there.[42] More broadly, the French and Indian War and its aftermath strengthened preexisting ties between Native communities in New England and the Iroquois and Sir William Johnson, the British superintendent for Northern Indian Affairs, in New York. New England Natives joined colonial troops in the 1750s and camped with and fought beside members of the Six Nations in New York and elsewhere. Mohegan and Stockbridge Indians served together under a "Capt. Jacob" in 1758.[43] The Stockbridge Indians also offered sixty (and eventually sent thirty) of their warriors to Sir William Johnson in 1763 in an attempt to squelch the unrest among the Delawares and the Shawnees to the west.[44]

The ongoing colonial interest in Indian education and evangelization after the French and Indian War is in part demonstrated by a failed attempt of New England Congregationalist ministers to form their own missionary society to evangelize the Indians. In 1762, a petition was submitted to the Massachusetts legislature requesting the incorporation of a "society for propagating the Gospel among the Indians in North America." The Massachusetts Assembly passed an act of incorporation in late January 1762, and Governor Francis Bernard officially approved the legislation on February 9, 1762. The creation of this society came as an unpleasant surprise to Anglican leaders in London and the colonies, however. The correspondence between Archbishop Thomas Secker in London and Samuel Johnson in New York reveals concerns that such a society, promoted entirely by "zealous dissenters" would be "to the disadvantage of our Society [i.e., the SPG], and the strengthening of the Dissenting interest."[45] Under pressure from the archbishop and—eventually—the king, the Lords of Trade declared the incorporated society void in March 1763.[46] This heavy-handed imperial rejection prompted enough outrage that Jonathan Mayhew—the liberal minister of Boston's West Church and son of Experience Mayhew, the long-time missionary on Martha's Vineyard—quickly fired off a screed against the SPG and its irritating pro-Anglican activities in New England, thereby adding even greater fuel to the growing resentment in the colonies against both the Anglican Church and the British crown.[47] However, the attempt to create a New England–based missionary society indicated that, more than ever before, colonists were willing to financially support efforts to educate, evangelize, and civilize regional Native groups.[48]

Moor's Indian Charity School

Eleazar Wheelock was a relative latecomer to Indian education. His school was like other Indian schools run by whites in that he, too, took great interest in shaping post–Great Awakening Native spirituality in particular ways. Like Sergeant, Wheelock wanted his students to be removed from their families and communities. Given the array of educational opportunities on Native lands all around southern New England, it is not surprising that Wheelock's school— despite its striking attractiveness to fund-raisers and later historians—was a relative numerical failure as far as New England Indians are concerned, particularly because his model, methods, and outcomes were often at odds with Native communities' own concerns and desires.

Wheelock graduated from Yale in 1733, within a year of James Davenport, Benjamin Pomeroy, and others who would later be leaders in the New Light revivalism of the early 1740s. He was inspired to educate Natives partially through his successes with Occom and partly through the vision and implementation of Indian education of John Sergeant, whose 1743 proposals for an Indian boarding school made ripples in humanitarian circles in both Old and New England. In 1747 the Lebanon Congregational Church not far from Wheelock's own church raised £49 for Stockbridge's boarding school, a request Wheelock himself must have also received—and apparently ignored.[49] After Occom left Lebanon in 1747, Wheelock began scheming about a "grand Design" to open a boarding school to educate Natives by the dozens and send them back into their home communities—undoubtedly inspired by the twelve Stockbridge youth who were sent to neighboring Newington in 1748.[50]

Wheelock's school, when it finally opened in 1754, was only modestly oriented toward local Native groups. His real interest was in the powerful Six Nations of the Iroquois Confederacy. Accordingly, most of Wheelock's pupils were recruited from tribes in New Jersey and New York. His first official Native students were two Delaware boys (from New Jersey), John Pumshire (14 years old) and Jacob Woolley (11), who the SSPCK missionary John Brainerd sent at Wheelock's request on December 18, 1754.[51] Pumshire fell ill and was sent back to his hometown on November 14, 1756, where he soon died. More students eventually trickled in. On February 8, 1757, the Pequot Simon Wauby entered the school, and on April 9, 1757, two additional Delaware boys, Joseph Woolley and Hezekiah Calvin, arrived.[52] Within a few short years, Wheelock was actively recruiting students from the Oneidas and Mohawks in New York. It is likely that the parents of some New England Algonquian youth saw no need to send their children away to a boarding school when they had more local, tribally based options available.

Life in Moor's Indian Charity School—far more than at the local reservation schools—was a jarringly regulated environment governed by English cultural norms and the unbending regimen of clocks, as reported by Wheelock:

The Method of conducting this School has been, and is designed to be after this Manner, viz. they are obliged to be clean, and decently dressed, and be ready to attend Prayers, before Sun-rise in the Fall and Winter, and at 6 o'Clock in the Summer. A Portion of Scripture is read by several of the Seniors of them: And those who are able answer a Question in the Assembly's Catechism, and have some Questions asked them upon it, and an Answer expounded to them. After Prayers, and a short Time for Diversion, the School begins with Prayer about 9, and ends at 12, and again at 2, and ends at 5 o-Clock with Prayer. Evening Prayer is attended before the Day-light is gone. Afterwards they apply to their Studies. &c.[53]

On Sundays, Wheelock's students filed into his Lebanon Crank Congregational Church, where they worshipped with their English neighbors. The Indian boys sat in "a Pew devoted to their Use," located in the gallery of the church over the west stairs, as per vote of the church, while the Native girls sat on the ground floor in the rear of the women's side.[54] According to Wheelock, between the morning and afternoon public worship services in Lebanon, and sometimes following the afternoon service, he or another local minister "inspects their Behaviour, hears them read, catechises them, discourses to them." Other occasional weekly lectures "upon the most important and interesting Subjects" delivered by Wheelock or another interested party and "calculated to their Capacities" punctuated the rhythms of their educational lives.[55]

It is difficult to sufficiently register the deep levels of cultural shock experienced by many of Wheelock's preteen and teenage students. Even though numerous Native families had increasingly adopted various elements of Euroamerican culture over the course of the eighteenth century such as clothing and housing styles, Wheelock reported his frustration with getting some of his students to comply with what he considered to be basic elements of civilized colonial life, such as wearing English-style clothes and sitting on chairs. "They are used to set upon the Ground, and it is as natural for them as a seat to our Children," Wheelock complained. Additionally, the students did not want "to have any Cloaths but what they wear, nor will they without much Pains be brot to take care of any." Wheelock perceived his Indian students to not be "used to any regular Government" or have any training in planning for the future, remaining content instead to live "from Hand to Mouth."[56]

Like Sergeant, Wheelock demonstrated an interest in the education of Indian girls. Four of the twenty-five students under Wheelock's care in 1763 were girls, who received a distinctly English and gendered education while in Lebanon. Wheelock's female students were permitted to spend only one day each week in their studies. The other days were spent with white women Wheelock hired from the neighboring towns "to instruct in all the Arts of good Housewifery . . . till they shall be fit for an Apprenticeship, to be taught to make Men's and Women's Apparel."[57] Less often discussed by Wheelock was the surprisingly large population of non-Indian students at Wheelock's school from the beginning. Long before he opened the Indian Charity School in 1754, Wheelock had been tutoring local English boys either in preparation for or in conjunction with a college education. When Wheelock's Indian school got under way, he seemed to have included large percentages of non-Indians, perhaps to bolster the school's finances. Wheelock's report in 1763, for example, that the school had twenty-two Indian students and only three white ones (published in a promotional pamphlet) seems sharply at odds with David McClure's count just a year later. When McClure arrived in late June 1764 at the young age of fifteen, he counted thirty students total, half of whom were Indians. The other half were white English students either preparing to be missionaries (like Samuel Kirkland, then in residence) or to attend college (McClure went from there to Yale).[58]

New England Indians in Iroquoia

Wheelock's ultimate "Grand Design" for his school was to educate and send out Natives to evangelize the Haudenosaunee, or Six Nations of the Iroquois Confederacy, in New York. With this vision, Wheelock joined a long-standing fixation on the part of New England ministers and missionary societies in the British Isles (NEC, SPG, and SSPCK) regarding the Iroquois. By the time Wheelock's missionaries showed up in Mohawk and Oneida territory, the Six Nations had endured a century and a half of evangelization, first by the French, then the Dutch, and finally, the English, and were more than a little wary of English (and even Indian) missionary motivations. In 1761, however, the Haudenosaunee were in a position that was less secure than they had been even a decade prior. For most of the colonial period the Iroquois successfully played the French and English empires to their advantage, making alliances, securing gifts, and using missionaries in ways that solidified their control over the Great Lakes region and beyond. The French and Indian War (1754–1760; part of the Seven Years' War in Europe) changed much of this, however. The effective removal of the French empire from the Northeast at the close of the Seven Years' War meant that the Iroquois could no longer creatively use French influence, presence, and power against the British. In 1754, a British officer wryly noted, "To preserve the balance of power between us and the French is the great ruling principle of the modern Indian politics."[59] A decade later, without this balance of imperial power and without the military need for Indians by the British Empire (as allies against the French), the Haudenosaunee began to fear—rightly, as it turned out—that dispossession was sure to follow.

The first missionary venture associated with Wheelock's school to the Six Nations in 1761 was merely one more attempt by New England missionaries funded by charitable societies in England. It was a continuation of what the NEC had started in the late seventeenth century, what the SPG had done a bit more successfully in the eighteenth century, and the efforts made by Sergeant and Edwards a decade earlier. The missionary trip from Wheelock's school also built upon the already established lines of communication and networks of intertribal relations between the Oneidas and New England Natives that some Indians like the Mohegan Samuel Ashpo seemed to navigate fluidly. So it was, on Wednesday, June 10, 1761, that Samson Occom and his Montaukett brother-in-law, David Fowler, set out from Lebanon for New York under the auspices of the SSPCK. Occom and Fowler spent most of their nine weeks at Old Oneida, where, after an initially cold reception, the Oneidas seemed willing to entertain the idea of resident missionaries. The reasons for such acceptance, however, were laid out clearly by the old Oneida chief, Connoquies, at a large gathering of Oneidas and Tuscaroras just prior to the missionaries' departure, on September 18, 1761. Although the chiefs voiced their intentions—perhaps overly optimistically—to "repent of all our sins and all our heathenish ways & customs" and support the effort to "set up a School," they also saw themselves as entering a reciprocal relationship with the New England Indians and their sponsors. In short, they had something concrete they wanted out of the deal, too. First, Connoquies, speaking for the group, stated the desire that "strong Drink may be prohibited, that it may not be brought among us for we find it kills our Bodies and Souls." The second concern was equally as practical: "We desire to be protected on our Lands, that none may molest or encroach upon us."[60] To confirm these ideas and agreements, Connoquies gave Occom and Fowler a wampum belt, a traditional way to conclude a treaty or series of negotiations.

In the 1760s, Wheelock and his English sponsors sent well over a dozen Indian and white missionaries to the towns of the Six Nations in New York. Some of the missionaries were Mohawk boys who had been trained at Wheelock's school and then sent back to their own communities. Others were young Natives from New England and mid-Atlantic communities, for whom life in New York among the Six Nations was a culturally and linguistically disruptive and disorienting experience.

Unraveling of Education and the Missionary Program

Despite these various attempts by the English to reform Native religious sensibilities in the 1750s and 1760s, at almost every level and in almost every educational context, Indians in southeastern New England began to assert control over their own education and direction in ways that paralleled and overlaid broader areas of conflict, including ongoing land controversies and internal divisions over tribal leadership. At Mohegan, the decades-old community divisions again boiled to the surface in the late 1750s and early 1760s. For one, the Mohegan land controversy, which started in 1704 and periodically resurfaced in the late 1710s, late 1730s, and early 1740s, was by the late 1750s once again a highly contentious issue that continued to deeply divide the Mohegan community and pitted the Mason party/John's Town Mohegans against the sachem's party (Ben Uncas III) and most of the local English ministers, schoolteachers, and officials. Although colonial officials dismissed the Mohegan land controversy as merely a way for the Mason family to pursue their own private interests, it is clear that the land case continued to animate and divide the various factions on Mohegan land in a way that cannot simply be reduced to the instigation of the Masons.[61] According to Ben Uncas III, the rival John's Town faction in late 1758 or early 1759 invited "a party of Indians most of them not Mohegan's but by marriage" to live on Mohegan lands—perhaps to defy the sachem, who opposed the move, or perhaps to numerically bolster their own numbers. Either way, shortly thereafter the John's Town Mohegans also "Sett up another Sechem"—mostly likely Henry Quaquaquid—and withdrew their allegiance from Ben Uncas III.[62]

In an attempt to reopen the land case, Henry Quaquaquid appealed directly to the most powerful British authority figure in the Northeast, Sir William Johnson—a move that was just slightly less forceful than appealing directly to the crown. Quaquaquid showed up in person at Johnson Hall in Johnstown, New York, in the spring of 1760 with the whole history of their predicament and land losses and a request for Johnson's personal intervention.[63] Johnson apparently did support this rival faction and suggested sending Quaquaquid and Samuel Ashpo to London dressed as "Moyhacks" [Mohawks] in an attempt to bolster their case. It is not clear how Samuel Ashpo got involved, but it is obvious that over time he used his Wheelock-sponsored trips to the Six Nations as a venue for drumming up support for this movement against Ben Uncas III and the colony of Connecticut. More generally, Ben Uncas III reported that the anti-sachem party refused to attend the preaching of David Jewett at Mohegan or attend the school of Robert Clelland and discouraged others from attending as well.[64]

The John's Town/anti-sachem Mohegans received a boost in the spring of 1764 when Occom returned from several missionary journeys in New York and moved his growing family into a house on Mohegan lands. The John's Town Mohegans asserted themselves against local colonial leadership in two specific areas. First, Occom and the anti-sachem party critiqued the educational efforts of the English among the Mohegans. The main focus of their ire was Robert Clelland, who in 1752 was hired by the NEC to hold a school among the Mohegans.[65] On April 26, 1764, a newly constituted tribal council headed (or at least heavily influenced) by Occom listed six reasons that the Mohegans desired to have Clelland removed from their lands and his post as schoolteacher. First on the list was that Clelland "takes a great Number of English Children, and they take Room from Indian Children, and keep them from the Fire in the Coldest Seasons." The other five reasons all relate to Clelland's neglect of the Indians, including not hearing his students carefully, not praying in school, not teaching the Indian children English manners, not providing dinner for his students as he promised, absenting himself from the school for long periods of time, and frequently using the horses of local Indians "without the leave of the owners."[66] The NEC was convinced and fired Clelland, who complained bitterly, "I am forc't away to make way for an Indian master."[67] Within a year and a half, Jewett and the NEC found a non-Indian replacement for Clelland—William Hubbard—who the Mohegans seemingly tolerated because he was willing to keep the school within their houses and wigwams during the cold winter months and then move it back to the schoolhouse for the other seasons.[68] Not only had the Mohegans forced the removal of an unwanted schoolmaster, but they made sure his replacement was willing to teach their youngsters on their terms. This contrasted sharply with the relative inflexibility of Wheelock's boarding school model.

Second, the John's Town Mohegans asserted themselves by speaking strongly against the colony of Connecticut and, by extension, against Clelland and David Jewett, minister of the New London North Parish Congregational Church, both of whom supported the colony of Connecticut in the ongoing land controversies with the Mohegans. It is a testament to the persistence of the John's Town Mohegans that the decades-old land case at Mohegan was reopened at all. When the committee in London for hearing appeals in the colonies granted the Mohegans' appeal to the 1743 decision on July 8, 1766, the colony of Connecticut was forced to throw an enormous amount of resources behind the legal case in an effort to stave off Mohegan claims, even as they protested that it was unfair to hold a hearing about North American land in England.[69] The reopening of the Mohegan land case tended to prejudice Connecticut magistrates, leaders, and affected landowners against the Mohegans who were pressing for their land rights. The increasing acrimony between Britain and her North American colonies following the Stamp Act (1765), the resultant riots, and the repeal of the Stamp Act (1766) made some colonists certain that the British crown would side with the Mohegans as a way of reining in the unruly colonies. Connecticut governor William Pitkin confided to Richard Jackson in late 1766, "This Affair spreads a new Gloom over us, that so many Thousand Inhabitants should be turned off, from their lands."[70]

The tensions between the John's Town Mohegans and Jewett and local magistrates also played out over the allegiance of the Mohegan Christians. Apparently English and Indian Separates who long enjoyed the ministrations of Samuel Ashpo were incensed when Ashpo was convinced to make a public confession of his sins of drunkenness and Separatism and join Jewett's North Parish church in 1761. Even before Occom returned to Mohegan in 1764, Jewett found his position, congregation, and authority constantly challenged. In the early 1760s, these white and Indian Separates were in the process of trying to draw off Mohegans and whites alike from attending Jewett's church and regular lectures to the Mohegans. When Occom arrived, he supported the Mohegan Separates by holding his own services among the Mohegans and at Niantic, services which were, Wheelock reported, "much crowded with English as well as Indians."[71] This only further frustrated Jewett, who had hoped Occom could calm what he saw as the unreasonable demands of the Separate Indians. In a July 9, 1764, letter to NEC commissioner Andrew Oliver—another stern critic of Separates of all stripes—Jewett confessed that he hoped Occom would "remove the Prejudices which the Indians have imbib'd not only against me, but all who take Money for Preaching, wear white Wigs, etc."[72] Instead, Occom turned even more Mohegans against Jewett. By August 11, 1764, Nathaniel Whitaker reported that Occom had successfully drawn off the Mohegan Christians so that only three or four attended Jewett's lectures, as most preferred Occom's sermons.[73]

By early 1765, Jewett had had enough. In a searing letter written to the Boston commissioners on January 21, 1765, Jewett accused Occom of many things, but in particular, he claimed that Occom's arrival at Mohegan had thrown the entire tribe into "the greatest Contention, and confusion" that Jewett had ever witnessed in his twenty-six years in the area.[74] Jewett's letter had its intended effect. Shortly after it was made public, Wheelock reported that "Clamours spread through the Government, and almost every one cryed out against Mr. Occom as a very bad, michevious, and designing man." Occom's purported misbehavior negatively affected both him and Wheelock. The commissioners quickly suspended Occom's meager salary (with additional prompting from Jewett), and the Connecticut General Assembly turned down Wheelock's application to incorporate his Indian charity school.[75]

With his plans for enlarging his school (and its fund-raising capacities) in jeopardy, Wheelock could stand by no longer. He arranged a meeting to resolve the disputes on March 12, 1765, at his own house, which was attended by members of the Connecticut Board of Correspondents (a local board of the SSPCK), Jewett, Occom, and other local ministers. The accusations against Occom were wide ranging and included siding with the Separates at Mohegan; "ill Conduct" toward the Mohegan overseers regarding the leasing of lands; threatening to turn Anglican; questioning infant baptism; disrespecting David Jewett; instituting "illegal proceedings" against Robert Clelland, the ousted schoolmaster; and "engaging in the Mason Controversy." Despite Jewett's repeated accusations during this meeting, in the end those present found Occom guilty only for his involvement in the Mohegan land controversy. Consequently, Occom was forced to submit a formal apology in which he admitted that it was not right for him to get so involved with "temporal affairs" and that he would in the future steer clear of the land controversy at Mohegan "unless called thereto and obligated by lawful authority."[76]

While controversies were brewing at Mohegan, the Narragansetts were in the process of grudgingly accepting the presence of an English missionary and schoolteacher and were increasingly embroiled in a struggle against their own sachem over land. From the beginning of his time among the Narragansetts in 1765, Joseph Fish believed that educating Indian children was essential to changing the culture of the Narragansetts (even as he labored to the same end among the Lantern Hill Pequots). During one of his first official visits to the Narragansetts in late 1765, Fish started making plans to set up a school on their reservation—the second part of his two-pronged approach (the first being monthly lectures). Fish received approval from the Narragansett tribal council, which met at John Shattock, Sr.'s, house on November 26, 1765, and "unanimously Agreed" to aid in the erection of a schoolhouse by supporting the schoolmaster and providing labor. Fish hired the white teacher Edward Deake to teach the Narragansett children "to read English, write and Cypher," all for £24 per year, plus space to live in the schoolhouse with his wife and the possibility of an increased salary should Deake have more than one hundred students.[77]

Plans for the schoolhouse quickly moved forward, although it took a few years to actually construct it. It was to be forty feet in length, sixteen feet wide, and only one story high "with a Strait Roof," and a chimney in the middle. It had to be sizable in order to hold the children; Deake reported in late 1765 that the Narragansett leaders told him there were 151 "Children that is fit for Instruction," although clearly not all of the parents could be persuaded to send every child.[78] The proposed curriculum of the Narragansett school mirrored the standard educational tools and literature used in Anglo and Indian schools (at least those run by Euroamericans) in New England. Fish ordered eight dozen spelling books, three dozen New Testaments, several copies of the Westminster Confession of Faith (1643–1647), and a number of "Spelling Books" by Thomas Dilworth, titled *A New Guide to the English Tongue.*[79]

At first, things seemed to go well. By December 13, 1765, Deake could report that one-third of these school-age children—fifty-three—had enrolled in his school, and he thought he could "Expect many more."[80] Within six months, however, Deake and Fish ran into problems. First, the Narragansetts became suspicious about the purpose and motivations of the school. Disagreements arose when the Boston commissioners for the NEC voiced their intentions of "Appropriating the House, and the Land to use of a School." Although some of the tribal leaders agreed, Deake reported to Fish that "the grater part of the tribe opposed it, through fear of being led into a Snare by the Commissioners."[81]

Fish was able to smooth things over, but many of the Indians continued to question the benefit of Deake's presence and the education of their children if the most pressing thing on their minds—the loss of their lands—was not being addressed. One year later, on June 29, 1767, after Fish's monthly lecture, Samuel Niles, John Shattock, and James Niles queried Fish "about the Danger they are in, of loosing their Lands; and What Method to take to prevent it." The Narragansett leaders wanted to know "To What purpose do we build Schoolhouse, Set up preaching, And lay ourselves out for Public Benefit here, When All Our Lands are like to be Sold under us, and We turnd off, we dont know where?"[82] In other words, what were the tangible benefits of Fish, Deake, education, and their English versions of Christianity?

These questions had taken on increasing urgency in the 1760s, since the Narragansetts were also in the middle of their own prolonged land controversy—in this case the struggle was with their own sachem, Thomas Ninigret, who had been selling tracts of the Narragansetts' land to pay off his own personal debts. Frustrated with the inconsistent policies of the Rhode Island legislature (which tended to favor the sachem), the anti-sachem party broadened their circle of appeals to include Eleazar Wheelock and Sir William Johnson. In August 1767,

Wheelock aptly summed up the irony of the situation to Johnson: "just as they have got well engaged in cultivating their Lands, and begin to know the worth of them, by tasting the sweets of a civilized life, their best farms are slipping from under them, one after another."[83] Just one month later, on September 19, 1767, Sir William Johnson replied that from the many reports he heard about the Narragansetts, he too, was inclined to think "they are much injured," and promised to "recommend their case to his Majesty's Ministers."[84] Johnson's influence wound its way back to the Rhode Island General Assembly; by October 2, Tobias Shattock reported to Wheelock that Andrew Oliver, the treasurer of the NEC, had put pressure on the Assembly to halt the sale of Narragansett lands by the sachem Thomas Ninigret, which they did, at least temporarily.[85]

Two months later, however, a committee formed by the Assembly to deal with the Narragansett land complaints recommended making a one-time sale of Narragansett lands to pay off completely the large debts racked up by the sachem.[86] Incensed and disillusioned, the Narragansetts mapped out their own plan that included the ultimate appeal: to King George III. First—if they could raise sufficient funds—they planned to send John Shattock, Jr., to England to present the Narragansett case. If that failed, Shattock indicated they would take up Wheelock's prior offer to send the case to the Earl of Dartmouth to see if he could influence people in London to help. If all of these appeals failed, however, the Sam Niles (anti-sachem) portion of the Narragansetts agreed they would try to get free and clear titles to their lands, sell them, and move elsewhere.[87]

Meanwhile, many Narragansetts were increasingly unconvinced that the English educational investment was worth the payoff. In just under two years, Fish lamented that "but Very few Children Attended the School Steadily, not above 12 or 13 at most Since I was here last."[88] The building of the schoolhouse proceeded slowly and Deake's school suffered from diminished attendance.

Appeals to England

Despite the obvious tension created between Occom and Wheelock over the Jewett affair, Wheelock desperately needed Occom's participation in a fund-raising scheme that had been in the works for several years. The basic idea was, as Wheelock's schoolmaster Charles Jeffrey Smith put it, to send an Indian minister to England to "get a Bushel of Money for the School."[89] By late 1764, as the controversies between Occom and Jewett reached their peak in Mohegan, concrete plans were put into place for the proposed trip to England. Occom was the first choice of Wheelock and others, and when the elderly George Whitefield declined to serve as Occom's traveling companion, the Chelsea (Norwich) minister Nathaniel Whitaker was voted by the Connecticut Board of Correspondents to go to England with Occom.[90] Whitefield agreed to meet them in England and to personally make as many connections as possible.

On December 23, 1765, wielding recommendations from Sir William Johnson, Wheelock, Whitefield, and other leading evangelistically minded ministers, Samson Occom and Nathaniel Whitaker departed Boston for the arduous trip to England. During the more than two years between their arrival in England on February 3, 1766, and their departure for Boston in late spring of 1768, Occom and Whitaker crisscrossed their way all over England, Ireland, and Scotland, meeting with dignitaries, preaching in churches and before large audiences, and continually making pleas for funds on behalf of Wheelock's Indian Charity School. The trip narrowly escaped a tragic and early ending when Occom contracted smallpox in March of 1766—a month after arriving—but he quickly recovered.[91] Occom rapidly became the focus of national attention and preached in the pulpits of George Whitefield, John Wesley, and countless other ministers throughout Great Britain. Occom, like his Mohegan predecessor Mahomet II, wondered at the vastness and busyness of London and took in the famous tourist attractions of the city such as the Tower of London, Parliament, and Westminster Abbey. So widely known was Occom's presence in England that he was parodied on London's stages and in penny-papers.[92] Everywhere they went, people gave money. Most—if not all—of the financial success of the trip was due to Occom. He was a gentleman and a gifted orator. His surviving sermons are rich and yet straightforward; elegant and yet direct; relevant and yet staunchly scriptural. Perhaps the most gratifying portion of the trip for Occom was their two-month tour of Scotland, during which time he was able to meet the members of the Scottish Society for the Propagation of Christian Knowledge (SSPCK)—the organization that had first supported his ordination and had funded his various missionary activities. By the time Nathaniel Whitaker sailed for Boston in the spring of 1768, more than £12,000 sterling had been raised to support the training of American Indians to evangelize other Natives.[93] The amount was simply staggering and far exceeded even Wheelock's expectations.

Occom's presence in London, however, is best understood within the broader context of other American Indians who traveled to the British Isles in the 1760s, mostly to petition for the rights of their Native communities. Occom's actions were far more in line with these other Native delegations—as well as Mahomet II and Cato in 1736—than appears on the surface. The Mohegan Indian Reuben Cognehew traveled to London in 1760 to represent the Mashpee with land grievances; the Cherokee warrior Osteneco traveled with two fellow Indians in 1762 to obtain redress for personal and tribal issues; in 1766, a Stockbridge Indian delegation toured England and sought and received an audience before the king regarding Wappinger and Mohican land claims; and in 1772 Simon Porridge (Wampanoag) showed up in London to speak for Chappaquiddick Island land claims.[94]

More important, the Narragansett brothers Tobias and John Shattock departed for London in early January 1768, just as Occom was finishing up his tour of Great Britain. They were undoubtedly encouraged by the previous successes of the Stockbridge delegation in 1766 and Occom's own grand reception in 1766–1768.[95] The Shattocks had the support of the same important individuals: Wheelock, Whitefield, and Sir William Johnson, among others. Within a few weeks of their arrival in Scotland, however, both Narragansett men contracted smallpox, the disease that had ended the Mohegan Mahomet II's life in 1736 when he was in London.[96] A rather vigorous attempt to save them ensued, led in part by Benjamin Rush, who at the time was a medical student and later became a world-famous physician. John survived; Tobias, at the age of twenty-six, passed away on May 6, 1768, and was buried as "the first Christian Indian" in the church graveyard in Edinburgh. John Shattock continued on to London but was ultimately unsuccessful before the Privy Council and was forced to return to New England empty-handed.[97] Within a year and a half, the twenty-four-year-old John Shattock became sick and died on December 21, 1770. John Shattock, Sr.'s, heart-wrenching letter to Joseph Fish regarding the loss of nine of twelve of his children over the course of his life reveals the great and incalculable costs of colonialism and the attempts of his sons to defend Indian land and sovereignty.[98]

Although Occom's trip seemingly was serving different ends from those of other Natives who traveled across the Atlantic, he almost certainly did not see things this way. Promoting and securing funds for the education of Natives in New England was merely the flip side of seeking redress for injustices related to land. Both contributed to the well-being of Native communities and ensured sovereignty for future generations. Occom's independent actions in Great Britain demonstrate how he always kept the interests of his own home community of Mohegans in mind. Probably much to Wheelock's chagrin, Occom did not immediately return to New England with Whitaker in the spring of 1768. Once again, he maximized the position and contacts gained through Wheelock in an attempt to benefit his own people. While Occom was in England, the final hearings of the Mohegan land controversy opened in London, and all of New England watched with great interest.[99] Connecticut had already sent its own agent, William Samuel Johnson, as a representative to London; Samuel Mason was there to represent the interests of the Mohegans. Although Occom had promised in his March 1765 confession before the Connecticut Correspondents for the SSPCK that he would "not for the future act in that Affair," and despite the stern warning Wheelock gave to Occom not to get involved in the controversy while in England, Occom could simply not pass up the chance to possibly influence the ruling.[100] Occom not only met with Mason but lent him some money and personally testified before the royal council regarding the long history of infringement on Mohegan lands.[101] Occom's participation in the land controversies continued when he returned to

New England as well. In late 1768, a half a dozen of John's Town Mohegans, including Occom, sent a petition to King George III proposing that, should the Mohegan land controversy be settled in their favor, they would turn the lands over to the Crown and pay annual quitrent fees for their use. "They have a very strong hint of the disaffection of the Coloneys in general," Henry Babcock of Stonington complained to Connecticut governor William Pitkin in January 1769 and called the petition and promise of annual payment a "Notable Bribe."[102]

When Occom returned from England in June 1768, he found that his popularity among the Native communities had greatly increased, and he was in even more demand as a preacher, mentor, advisor, and community leader. Despite his popularity, all was not well. Occom also returned to a series of longer-term personal and tribal disappointments. Contrary to promises made by Wheelock, Occom discovered that his family had been ill-cared for in his absence, and none of his debts had been discharged or reduced. His financial hardship and continual unemployment was especially difficult given his success in raising so much money for Wheelock's school.

Ironically, this pinnacle of fund-raising success for Wheelock coincided with the almost total collapse of the Indian Charity School itself in terms of New England Native participation and Wheelock's design for evangelizing the Iroquois. Although Wheelock's vision was to send his newly educated New England Indian pupils to the Haudenosaunee, this was not necessarily the plan or the desire of his students. Many of them were very young when they entered Wheelock's school, and while they might have recognized the benefit of education, most did not wish to travel hundreds of miles away from family and friends to serve in a seemingly hostile and foreign environment. In response, many of the New England Natives under Wheelock's care and authority dragged their feet, wrote complaining letters to Wheelock, abandoned their mission posts, got drunk, and even reverted to a more promiscuous Native sexual ethic while serving as schoolteachers among the Six Nations. Wheelock misread these Native acts of resistance as signs of the weakness of Indians themselves and the impossibility of educating and "civilizing" them.[103] But it was no secret among Wheelock's students as to why they abandoned his plan for them. They were underpaid as missionaries, despised being away from home, chafed under the strict moral guidelines placed upon them, resented the disciplinary measures (including corporal punishment) taken against them, and did not appreciate the "civilizing" aspects of Wheelock's school and program that also included copious amounts of hard physical labor in the fields and elsewhere. By the 1770s, virtually every New England Native had abandoned Wheelock's Grand Design in favor of their own home communities.

Perhaps in part due to his miscalculations regarding Native education and evangelization and the mishandling of funds and other resources, Wheelock had been planning a radical redirection for Moor's Indian Charity School. After much deliberation as to location, Wheelock successfully moved his educational operations 180 miles up the Connecticut River to Hanover, New Hampshire, in 1770, where he founded an entirely new educational institution, Dartmouth College, once again named after a prominent donor. The fact that he at least officially kept Moor's Indian Charity School as a separate, adjoining institution meant little to donors, magistrates, and—especially—Natives like Occom.[104] In a heart-wrenching letter to Wheelock in July 1771, Occom accused Wheelock of a change of heart:

> I am very Jealous that instead of your Semenary Becoming alma Mater, she will be too alba mater ["white mother"] to Suckle the Tawnees, for She is already aDorn'd up too much like the Popish Virgin Mary . . . I think your College has too much Worldly Grandure for the Poor Indians they never have much benefit of it.[105]

Occom was right. Of the twenty-four students at Dartmouth College/Moor's Indian Charity School in 1771, only five were Indian and one was of mixed ethnicity.[106] Wheelock continued to recruit Indians from the Six Nations and Native communities in Canada, but most New England Natives and even some whites felt—understandably—that Wheelock's primary focus had shifted to non-Indian students. The ethnic ratios at Wheelock's school had been completely reversed in less than a decade, and Wheelock could provide no explanation that satisfied his critics.[107]

Native disaffection with Wheelock reverberated throughout Indian country, even as far west as the Haudenosaunees. In many ways, however, it had been building for quite some time. In 1763, realizing that Wheelock and others were not upholding their end of the agreement they had reached in the summer of 1761, the Oneidas had requested the tangible symbol of that agreement—the wampum belt—to be returned.[108] No New England Indian or Iroquois child enrolled at Wheelock's school after 1768, and, in fact, in early 1769 some Oneida parents and chiefs showed up in person in Lebanon to withdraw their children from Moor's Indian Charity School.[109]

Narragansett Rejection of Euroamerican Supervision and Education

The disillusionment of Wheelock's students coincided with a larger, growing dissatisfaction with and rejection of white Christian educational and ministerial oversight among Indian communities in the late 1760s and early 1770s. Over

Figure 6.1. Founding of Dartmouth College. Courtesy of Dartmouth College Library.

time, more issues surfaced in the Narragansett community that encompassed a broader critique of Euroamerican educational and ministerial practices. The growing list of Narragansett complaints was long and far-reaching. Joseph Fish—undoubtedly still fuming from the substantial losses suffered by his own North Stonington church because of Separates—preached and published against Separatism, which the Narragansetts under Niles greatly resented.[110] The Narragansetts also disliked Fish because he was a paid minister, "And therefore cant be a true Minister of Jesus Christ." Additionally, the Narragansett Separates couldn't be bothered by Fish's insistence on the Bible as a foundation for faith and life, and instead claimed that they were "taught by the Spirit, immediately from Heaven," which was better than the Bible. They also suspected that Deake and Fish were "Seeking the Dominion Over Them, in Some Form or Other; And Are Afraid of Their Liberties."[111] John Shattock, Sr., told Fish plainly in December 1770, after a lecture to five Indians and three whites, that the Indians were fed up with Deake, in part for making some structural changes to the schoolhouse, but also "For not keeping School Steadily." Shattock later informed Fish that while he didn't entirely disagree with Fish's "Doctrine or performances" he and others were greatly upset by how he was "Taking the Government out of the Indians hands" and chipping away at the right of the Narragansetts to govern themselves.[112]

Although Deake and Fish tried to keep their educational mission to the Narragansett alive even with the realities of virtual nonattendance at religious lectures and the school, within a few years they, too, had given up. In light of the virtually unanimous opposition to his presence, Edward Deake requested to be dismissed from his position on January 2, 1776, with permission to occupy the schoolhouse until warmer weather in the spring when he could better manage to move. Even then, James Niles, Jr., asked Fish to tell him precisely "What Month twas expected Mr. Deake would go out of the house."[113] The Narragansetts wanted him gone immediately.

With Deake removed from his position, and the Narragansetts in virtual nonattendance at the monthly church lectures, Fish, too, decided to close shop: "And seeing no prospect of my own further Serviceableness to These Indians, Ether as Preacher or Inspector of their School Affairs, I took my leave of them." For Fish, Narragansett rejection of his spiritual input opened up the door to their total spiritual loss. In his farewell speech, he gave the Narragansetts "a Solemn admonition for neglecting and practically despising a preached Gospel, and Bible Truths, and warning of Satans recovering his Kingdom among them, as in the days of their heathenism." The final entry in Fish's journal registers his deep regret and pessimism: "Thus Ends a Ten Years mission, promising as the rising Sun, in the Beginning, but Setting, in a Cloud."[114] The sun, however, was hardly setting on the Narragansetts. Times were tough, but they were continuing to create their own solutions.

Similarly, at Stockbridge, by the 1760s, three decades of blatant misuse at the hands of white Stockbridgers had taken its toll on the Mohicans. From the very beginning, the intentional design (by the English, not the Indians) of including English families in the town turned out to be completely at odds with Indian interest and well-being. Although only a few English families moved there initially, by the early 1760s there were thirty-two non-Indian families in the town, crowding out the Indians, taking the best land available, squandering valuable resources, and edging the Natives out of the Indian church.[115] From the Mohicans' perspective, there was no such thing as an indifferently benevolent English person. Even those sent to "help" them greedily and illegally snatched up hundreds of acres of land in a twisted version of a retirement scheme: in 1739, Stephen Williams, Samuel Hopkins, John Sergeant, and Jonathan Edwards each received 480 acres of prime land within Stockbridge in exchange for "equivalent" lands outside the town limits.[116] This was not enough for Edwards, however, who, shortly after his arrival in 1751, petitioned the Massachusetts legislature to purchase 150 acres for him, and when they declined, he set about buying small quantities of land from the Mohicans.[117] By the 1760s, the Stockbridge Indians were demanding solutions, part of which involved their delegation to London. By 1772, Stephen West, who had been serving as minister to Indians and whites in Stockbridge since 1757, was reported to be "tired of Indian Service."[118] In 1773, West excommunicated the final remaining Indian from his church and turned the whole missionary project over to his successor, John Sergeant, Jr.[119]

In the light of such widespread disappointment and disillusionment, it is interesting how Native individuals redirected the education they received for their own purposes. Some returned to their own communities as schoolteachers; others used their literacy to become community leaders and petition colonial officials for Native land rights. Even Native individuals who served among the Iroquois often made connections with Iroquois and English leaders, most notably Sir William Johnson, to aid their home communities. Virtually every major Native group in southeastern New England successfully petitioned Johnson to act on their behalf during the late 1760s and early 1770s.[120]

Additionally, by the late 1760s—and in a few places, before—many of the Indian schools in southeastern New England had Indian schoolmasters. In some cases, the Indian teachers were disillusioned former students of Wheelock's school who chose educating their home communities rather than serving in culturally foreign Indian communities hundreds of miles away. In December 1767, David Fowler left his position at Oneida and returned home to Montauk, where he filled Samson Occom's vacant position as schoolmaster. Although his salary was a measly £15 per year, Fowler likely decided that proximity to his home community was worth it. When Fowler lost his teaching post at Montauk in 1770 (due to other distractions, such as taking care of his aging parents and his parents' wigwam burning down that same year), fellow Montaukett David Hannibal took his place.[121]

At Mashantucket, David Fowler's brother Jacob took up the schoolmaster post in the winter of 1770 and continued to late 1774, at which time he accepted an offer to become a tutor at Dartmouth College.[122] The Narragansett (and Wheelock-trained teacher) Abraham Simon took Jacob Fowler's place for a year in 1775, until he decided to enlist to serve in what became the American Revolution.[123] At Stonington, after John Shattock, Jr.'s, death in December 1770, first Jacob Fowler and then the Narragansett Charles Daniel were subsequently hired by the NEC to serve as the Indian schoolmaster. Daniel first served for a few months in 1771, and then for a longer stint starting in January 1772. By September of that same year, twenty children were enrolled in his school and a few of the students could "read handsomely" in their Bibles and Psalters.[124] In November 1773, however, Fish confronted Daniel because of rumors that he was behaving badly and drinking. When Fish demanded a "reformation," Daniel retorted that he "did not care Much" about the school. William Pendleton was hired to keep the school instead, but Fish soon reported that the Indians were "not Zealous to send their children" to the school any longer.[125]

Table 6.1. **Wheelock Student Tribal Affiliations**

Tribal/Geographic Distribution of Indians Educated at Moor's Indian Charity School, 1754–1770

Mohawk	19
Narragansett	15
Mohegan	8
Delaware	7
Oneida	5
Pequot	2
Montaukett	2
Farmington	1
Niantic	1
Wampanoag	1
Total:	61

Source: Adapted from James Dow McCallum, *The Letters of Eleazar Wheelock's Indians,* 297.

By a simply numerical measurement, Wheelock's school had surprisingly little influence on New England Native communities. Of the hundreds of school-age Native youth in southeastern New England between 1754 and 1770—there were 88 youth under the age of sixteen among the Mashantucket Pequots alone in 1766, and 151 at Narragansett—only 29 *total* from New England ever attended Wheelock's school over a sixteen-year period, and some for only a few months.[126] This number is especially stark in comparison to other schools in the same period. Stockbridge had fifty-five Mohican students in 1749; John Ashpo had thirty Indians at his school at Mashantucket in 1755; and Deake had fifty-three at Narragansett in 1765. When looking at the impact of education on Indian girls, too, Wheelock's school pales in importance to local tribal schools. In 1763, for example, Wheelock had four Indian girls in his school; Ashpo's Indian school at Mashantucket boasted nineteen in 1755.[127]

These discrepancies can partly be explained by Wheelock's primary fixation on the Six Nations. According to the records that have survived, a grand total of approximately sixty-one Natives from a dozen Indian communities in the mid-Atlantic, New England, and New York attended Wheelock's school between 1754 and 1770.[128] In keeping with Wheelock's focus on the Six Nations and his philosophy of educating Indians to reach their own people, the greatest single concentration of Indians came from the Mohawks, at nineteen. Of the sixty-one Natives who attended Wheelock's school before its removal from Connecticut to New Hampshire, none of them continued on to a four-year college.[129] Native youth (and their parents) got what they wanted out of Wheelock and moved on or, in some cases, did not like what they got and refused to return to his school. Although approximately twenty-four Indian youth from the Six Nations attended during this time period, recruiting youth from the Six Nations was far more difficult than expected. The abrupt withdrawal of all Iroquois children from the school in the late 1760s combined with the refusal of New England Indians to send any more children meant that by 1770, Wheelock's Grand Design was in shambles, and it is unclear whether he actually cared that much, apart from the loss of fund-raising leverage.

Of far more importance for the everyday lives of Native communities were the local Indian schools on Native lands, often taught by Indians themselves. Taken as a whole, the educational efforts in each Native community did provide a surprisingly robust educational opportunity for Indian youth in the post-Awakening period. American Indians put this education to good use, often in the service of their home communities. As scholars have demonstrated, by the mid- to late eighteenth century, abundant evidence of the increasing literacy among New England Natives can be literally traced in the form of independently written petitions, letters, wills, sermons, articles, poems, and hymns, all in the service of Native land rights, cultural sovereignty, diplomacy, and religiosity.[130] But even this increased education and literacy could not solve the growing divisions on tribal lands.

Migrating

The room was crowded. A number of Christian Indians from various communities in southeastern New England had gathered at Mohegan on March 13, 1773. Led by regional Christian Indian leaders such as Joseph Johnson and Samson Occom, the group deliberated for several days about the various solutions to the shared scourges of colonialism: land dispossession, alcoholism, internal divisions, poverty, and racism. Part of the purpose of this meeting was to explore the possibility of a joint settlement elsewhere—a relocation project that would remove them from their ancestral homelands but also away from their severely diminished land holdings and penurious existence eked out at the mercy of English masters and creditors. For those in favor of such a relocation, the list of possible destinations was short but contested. "Some were of a Mind to go southward as far as to Ohio, and some not so far that way," Joseph Johnson recalled. Others suggested that "it would not do to live so far from the English."[1] Pro-removal Indians wanted distance, but not too much of it. After several days of deliberations, the tribal representatives parted ways, vowing to send a delegation after the late summer harvest to investigate lands farther westward that they could possibly call home.[2]

This intertribal meeting at Mohegan in 1773 represented a crossroads for Natives in southeastern New England. The problems were shared and agreed upon; the solutions were not. One proposed solution that resulted from this meeting— that of an intertribal migration—was taken seriously by a small, active, and literate core of Native Christians who participated in an underground network of reformed Indian Protestantism and worked hard to bring the migration into being. From the beginning, however, the idea of migration was really just a radical notion that had many seemingly insurmountable obstacles. The idea had to be sold to various constituents including other New England Natives, the Indian hosts of the proposed location for migration, and several important colonial leaders who could assist with the negotiations necessary to broker whatever deals might take place. So difficult was this task that the first effort, orchestrated primarily by Joseph Johnson and a small core of Christian Indians between 1773 and 1775, failed. The Revolutionary War disrupted the lives of Indians in New England and New York and brought to a close the first migration effort. Starting in 1783 and 1784, a slightly broader, multigenerational coalition of Christian leaders led the second—and more successful—attempt of this planned migration, which also paralleled a similar migration by the Stockbridge Indians in western Massachusetts.

These collective migrations and the founding of two new towns in Oneida country in New York—Brothertown and New Stockbridge, respectively—constitute an important piece of New England Native history, although the ideas about migration were contested and only feebly pursued by the larger Native population.[3] Even at that initial meeting in 1773, some Natives present certainly must have disagreed with the migration proposal—as their later actions (or inaction) showed—and, although such proposals are not recorded, they must have favored other strategies for cultural preservation and cohesion, such as continuing legal actions to prosecute land loss and asserting the right of self-governance. The reality is that most Native Americans from southern New England did not move to Brothertown. The Native Christians who left were usually the most literate, so their stories echo the loudest through the halls of history. But, in fact, there was not one unified response to the particular problems Natives faced in the 1770s or even widespread agreement that Christianity or a Christian migration was the best way to revitalize Indian communities.

The early 1770s presented a series of opportunities and challenges to Native communities in southeastern New England, even as it was a time of intense crisis between the colonies and Great Britain. Some of the problems, such as land loss and internal tribal turmoil, had plagued these Native communities for years. Others, however, had only recently become matters of serious tribal consideration, such as increasing intermarriage with Africans and other outsiders. For the more explicitly Christian subset of Natives, the 1760s had been a time of increasing disillusionment with English ministers, missionaries, and educators, such as Joseph Fish and Eleazar Wheelock. These Native Christians still leaned on their English sponsors when necessary to accomplish their own goals, but the increasing divide was magnified in the late 1760s when almost all of the Christian Indians educated by Wheelock "fell" in some fashion or another—often a rejection of Wheelock's schemes for their lives.[4]

Disillusionment came in other forms as well. Land continued to be a sticking point, and the reluctance of the British crown to intervene proved immensely disappointing for Native communities. The Mohegan land controversy, for example, received its final hearing on June 11, 1771, in London.[5] The final ruling came more than a year and a half later, in late 1772 and early 1773, when the Privy Council decided—and then affirmed that decision—in favor of the colony of

Connecticut.[6] It was an unsurprising and yet extremely disheartening ending to a series of legal cases that had been ongoing since 1704. Occom's stolid reporting of the decision in a letter to East Hampton, Long Island, minister Samuel Buell in early 1773 masked the emotional intensity the issue held with many Indian families and communities: "the grand Controversy, Which has Subsisted between the Colony of Connecticut and the Mohegan Indians above 70 years we hear is finally Decided, and it is in Favour of the Colony."[7] John and Tobias Shattock had similarly been unable to procure action from the crown on behalf of the anti-sachem Narragansetts in the late 1760s.

Things were bad, but there were still signs of hope. Although Native communities tended to be sharply divided over issues of land and cooperation with English officials, in at least a few locales, tangible progress was evident in the struggle against the internal structural factors—most notably the sachemship—that had abetted dispossession for decades. In many Indian communities, the sachems served as the gatekeepers of lands, often renting, granting, and selling lands without the permission of the Native community as a whole. This was especially true at Mohegan and Narragansett, where decades of heavy-handed abuse by sachems had reduced the land base and divided the community. At Narragansett, the anti-sachem party's struggle against Thomas Ninigret ended with his death in 1770, and although first Esther Ninigret and later George Ninigret replaced him, the tribe had already won the effective right to negotiate through the Indian tribal council with the town of Charlestown regarding the most pressing issue—land sales.[8]

Similarly, at Mohegan, through the late 1760s a good portion of the Mohegan land was leased out to white farmers and other settlers, who accordingly paid rent to the sachem through the Mohegan overseers (who also took a cut). When Ben Uncas III passed away in May 1769, the Mohegan supporters of John Uncas and those who favored Benjamin Uncas III's family were sharply divided over whether they needed or wanted another sachem.[9] So deep was the division, in fact, that during the widely attended funeral ceremony of Ben Uncas III, Samson Occom led a large number of Mohegans out of the service in protest.[10] This disagreement followed the same fault line that had existed among the Mohegans since the 1720s, between the Ben's Town/pro-colony Mohegans and the John's Town/anti-sachem Mohegans. The small Ben's Town faction made Isaiah Uncas their sachem and asked the colony of Connecticut to approve this appointment, which it did. The anti-sachem Mohegans, however, refused to recognize Isaiah.[11] When Isaiah Uncas passed away in 1770, the tribe made the bold decision not to name a successor, in part to break up this colony-sachem alliance that had slowly sapped money, land, and other resources out of the community.[12] Instead, as at Narragansett, a tribal council headed by Zachary Johnson became the primary point of negotiation with local magistrates.

The Mashantucket Pequots—who, along with the Shinnecocks, showed perhaps the least interest in the idea of migration—were actually making modest gains in their land claims at precisely the same time the relocation conversation began. They successfully petitioned the Connecticut General Assembly in May 1773 to have 989 acres of land laid out for them, land that had been promised to them by the Assembly in 1761. This redrawing of Mashantucket boundaries seems to have satisfied them for a short while.[13] The Montauketts, too, were literally gaining some ground. They had appealed directly to Sir William Johnson in 1772 regarding their long and frustrating struggle with blatant land dispossession and discrimination on the eastern tip of Long Island and were graced by a personal visit in 1773, when Johnson stayed in Samson Occom's old house as he listened to the complaints outlined by David Fowler and Cyrus Charles.[14]

The absence of a sachem at Mohegan after 1770 gave the community a chance to rethink land ownership afresh. In May 1773 the Mohegans petitioned the General Assembly to divide up their lands among the remaining families—in part to give more control of the land to individuals instead of tribal leaders and in part to settle ongoing disputes about how the rental income of much of the land should be distributed. Christian Indian leaders like Joseph Johnson fully supported such allotments and made their case in writing to the Connecticut governor in October 1773.[15] Although some adjustments were made in October 1774, it was not until 1790—well after some of the Mohegans had already left for New York—that this request was actually granted in full.[16] Such an approach was widely shared on other reservations, and by the 1770s, most tribes began to see individual ownership as the new ideal. Indian land at Farmington, Connecticut, was allotted by the General Assembly in May 1777, with the lot sizes ranging from one to ten acres, but presumably the process had been under way for a while prior to this.[17] At Stockbridge, Indian lands had been allotted to individual families as early as 1739.[18]

Another issue New England Natives faced was intermarriage between tribal members and "strangers" of various stripes, including Africans, outside Indians, or—in a very few cases—whites. The problem of "racial purity" was one that emerged slowly over the course of the eighteenth century. Early in that century, individuals of mixed ethnicities (white-black, white-Indian, black-Indian) seem not to have been looked down on very strongly within Indian communities.[19] This was, in part, because of the relative isolation of many Indian communities, the small numbers of blacks in New England, and the relative infrequency of intermarriage between Africans and Indians. As Indian labor and patterns of settlement changed over time, and as more blacks served in English households and worked on farms, intermixing, cultural exchange, and intermarriage became more common. Indian-black marriages became more frequent as Indian males joined colonial militias and never returned from battle, particularly during the

French and Indian War (1754–1760). Widows and younger females searching for spouses or replacement partners often looked to the growing enslaved and free African populations in the neighboring urban centers like New London, Stonington, Lyme, and Norwich in Connecticut, and Charlestown in Rhode Island. Although Indian communities were not initially inclined to look unfavorably upon such marriages, over time they created internal problems in individual communities, as local Indian lands became a place of refuge for a variety of persons of color, often those who were unemployed.[20]

In some situations, however, racial separation and segregation were imposed from the outside, at least initially. As early as 1719 the East Hampton town trustees met with a delegation of fourteen Montauketts and required them to agree that they would not "let nor take any strange Indians in nor suffer any such to be on Montauk to use or improve any part of said land directly or indirectly by taking of a squaw or squaws."[21] In 1754, this agreement was confirmed and enlarged when, mostly at the trustees' urging but perhaps also somewhat proactively desired by the Montauketts, they agreed that if any Montaukett would marry an outside or "strange" Indian, the offending Montaukett and his or her children would forfeit all rights to land and membership at Montauk. The town of East Hampton similarly reserved the right to prosecute any "mustee, molato, or strangers, or foreign Indians" who settled on Montauk lands.[22]

Within each Native community, then, tension arose over how to handle these perceived intrusions. Adding more people to the increasingly shrinking quantities of Indian lands was bound to cause problems, even aside from racial considerations. Indian leaders differed greatly over how to respond. In 1765, for example, the Mohegan sachem Ben Uncas III and Samson Occom disagreed about whether to allow "mullatoes" onto Mohegan lands (Occom favored it in this case, although by the 1780s he had changed his mind).[23] A similar situation existed among the Narragansetts. When Edward Deake first arrived in Charlestown, Rhode Island, in 1765 as their schoolteacher, he noted the presence of "a considerable Number of mixtures as melatoes and mustees which the tribe Disowns, and Sundry families of Indians which properly Belongs to other tribes."[24] This presence of outsider Indians and Indians of mixed ethnicities caused considerable consternation among the Mohegans as well. In 1774 Zachary Johnson complained to the General Assembly that "many Interlopers from other tribes & Straggling Indians and Mulattoes have crowded in upon said Lands, whereby many Difficulties and Disputes have arisen."[25] In response, the General Assembly formed a committee and set up specific laws governing the occupancy and sale of lands.[26] Individual Native communities did not always wait for colonial laws, however; Rebecca Boham, a "Negro woman," had a hut on Mohegan land that was torn down by Mohegan Indians for reasons that are not entirely clear but were undoubtedly related to her ethnicity.[27]

The problem escalated considerably when local colonial governments threat-ened to (and in some cases did) stop recognizing individuals of mixed ethnic-ities as "authentic" Indians. Individuals who were not "pure" Indians were often not counted in colonial tallies of the Indian populations. Joseph Johnson, very aware of the contestation of authentic Indian identity in the late eighteenth cen-tury, referred to himself in several letters to whites as a "True Mohegan."[28] In a letter to Governor Trumbull regarding land allotments, Johnson suggested that any income from land rental should be distributed equally among the Mohegans, but with one major caveat: that only those who are "True Mohegan Indian[s]" should receive the disbursements.[29]

Migration and Christian Revival

It is within these various contexts—dispossession, internal discord, and the dif-ficulty of racial identity, all of which impinged on Native political and cultural autonomy—that discussions of a joint, intertribal migration first arose as a se-rious solution. Nonetheless, the idea had been floated prior to 1773 in overlap-ping contexts. At one level, the idea of migration seemed to have emerged from within some Natives communities themselves. For some of the leaders, the idea grew organically out of New England Natives' interactions with the Oneidas on missionary trips coordinated by Wheelock and sponsored by the New England Company, for as early as 1761 David Fowler discussed a possible relocation of Montauketts to Oneida country.[30] The Narragansett Tobias Shattock mentioned a similar possibility on October 2, 1767, in a letter to Eleazar Wheelock.[31]

Some Natives, however, certainly must have suspected that this scheme—no matter how sincerely promoted by other Natives—resonated too suspiciously with broader white desires and plans for dispossession. And for good reason. By 1767, some English religious and political leaders on both sides of the Atlantic Ocean saw the relocation of New England Indians (couched in the language of being given new lands elsewhere) as the only long-term solution to a seemingly impossible disagreement over land in New England.[32] Wheelock in particular thought such a solution would happily feed into his fantasies about evangelizing the Six Nations.[33] High-ranking members of the British government in London, however, were interested in such schemes as a simple way of reducing what many saw as unnecessary expenditures on Indian affairs in the colonies. In 1767, the Privy Council was considering mass relocation of New England Natives to Illi-nois country or along the Ohio River as a way to "ease the Crown of the immense expenses attending the present management of Indian affairs . . . with the inten-tion to devolve the care of Indian affairs upon the Colonies, and leave it to them."[34] No matter what the source and motivation, by 1770 such ideas of relocation were largely abandoned, perhaps in part because of the growing tension between Britain and her rebellious North American colonies.

When the idea of a joint, multitribal migration to New York resurfaced within Native communities during the next few years, it emerged almost exclusively within a tightly knit coalition of young, educated, Christian Indians who had spent considerable time under the influence of Eleazar Wheelock. Most members of the pro-migration group, including Elijah Wimpey, David and Jacob Fowler, Joseph Johnson, James Cusk, Andrew Corcomp, and John Adams, were part of the generation who had been born and raised in Indian communities shaped by the long processes of English education and evangelization.[35] More immediately, the early 1770s was a time of sustained Christian revival among the Native Christian communities of southern New England; this activity provided an additional opportunity for Christian Indians to cement their mutual commitments and reignite their Indian Christianity. The life of Joseph Johnson weaves together these various strands that culminated in a deep interest in a joint migration.

Joseph Johnson (Jr.) was born in 1751 in Mohegan, Connecticut, the son of Joseph and Betty (Garrett) Johnson.[36] The community of his birth contained at least a fairly Christianized subsegment of the population, given their individual and collective experiences of education, lectures, and church services from the 1730s onward. His own family had also been distinctly shaped by the Indian Great Awakening.[37] Johnson's mother Elizabeth (Betty) Garrett joined the First Congregational Church of New London, Connecticut, on May 1, 1743, during the Awakening. Joseph Johnson, Sr., and Betty's first two children, however, were baptized "at Mohegan" by Eliphalet Adams: Hannah, in April 1748, was brought forward by Elizabeth, and Joseph, Jr., on June 3, 1751, was brought forward as an infant by his nonmember father (whose request for his son's baptism was honored "by right of his wife").[38] In December 1758, just a few months after his father's death in September, the seven-year-old Joseph Johnson was sent to Eleazar Wheelock's Indian Charity School. A fascinating handwriting sample by Joseph Johnson just eleven months after entering Wheelock's school indicates his academic aptitude, like that of John Mettawan, Samson Occom, and dozens of other bright Indian youth who had come before him. Dated November 6, 1759, Johnson produced the following lines in neat handwriting:

> Obedience to Superiors, a dutiful Submissive
> Deportment to all Men a high Esteem of and Love
> For his Teachers, with a thankful Heart to all his
> Benefactors are peculiarly ornamental to an indigent
> Pupil[39]

Johnson's eight years under Wheelock's tutelage were perhaps not entirely continuous given the close proximity to his family but were nonetheless formative—especially given his young age. In November 1766, fifteen-year-old Johnson was sent on his first mission to act as an assistant teacher at the Oneida village of Kanonwalohale. He served in various roles among the Oneidas until late 1768; among these were holding school for Oneida youth and otherwise trying to integrate into Oneida community life. During 1768, Johnson became disillusioned with his missionary assignment and behaved in ways that irritated the Oneidas and disappointed Wheelock. By December 1768, Johnson had fled his post in Oneida and gone to Providence, Rhode Island, where he felt too "ashamed"—and too unhappy—to return to Wheelock's service.[40]

Johnson's choices and activities during the subsequent years hint at the alternatives Natives—and especially Native young men—had and often chose as a result of the various colonial pressures on Indian families and communities. Although the Christian Indian subgroups are the best documented, a substantial number of Native young people chose to seek their fortunes off the reservation, far from the influence of the English and even Christian Indians. Johnson spent the next several years first as a schoolteacher in Providence and later on a whaling ship, during which time he sailed as far east as the Azores and to many islands in the West Indies, including Antigua, Grenada, the Virgin Islands, and Puerto Rico.[41] From the perspective of a sailor on the high seas of the Atlantic, Wheelock's Indian Charity School and the Oneida mission must have seemed like a distant memory. After a few years, however, Johnson decided to return to his home and relatives at Mohegan. In October 1771, at the age of twenty-one, Johnson returned from his whaling expeditions and took up residence at Mohegan working on his uncle's farm; here he helped with the various agricultural tasks and filled his days making utensils such as ladles, spoons, and brooms, and learning how to cane the seats of chairs.[42]

When Johnson returned to Mohegan, he entered into a small but fervent Christian Indian revival that drew together Native Separate Christians from Connecticut, Long Island, and Rhode Island.[43] Within a month of returning from whaling, Johnson seems to have been especially moved during a prolonged illness while listening to several sermons preached by the Mohegan minister Samuel Ashpo in early November 1771. After several months of emotional turmoil regarding his lost state, spiritual release finally came for Johnson on Sunday, March 1, 1772, when during two "very powerful" meetings, Johnson stood up and committed himself to "henceforward no more to live to my Self but to him who has dyed and rose again for me."[44]

For a subset of New England Algonquians, and particularly for some of the younger generation who felt disillusioned with colonial treatment, this renewed Christianity served as a revitalizing force that created a new framework of meaning and fostered intertribal connections. On Saturday, February 1, 1772, for example, Johnson traveled to Groton to spend time with friends and family— in particular, his uncle Benjamin Garrett and close friend Sampson Paukanop.[45] In the early evening, the "Indians of Narragansett arrived and held a conference" there. After the service, James Niles, Jr. (the nephew of the Narragansett Separate minister Sam Niles), spent the night with Johnson, and they stayed up almost the whole night talking. The next day, Sunday, this intertribal group of Mohegans, Pequots, and Narragansetts held another lengthy meeting, in which there was "Exhorting, Singing, Praying," until the evening, when they took part in the "Lords supper."[46] In November 1772, Johnson moved fifty-five miles northwest of Mohegan to Farmington, Connecticut (west of Hartford), to serve as an NEC-funded schoolteacher among the Indians there.[47] At Farmington, Johnson joined a close Christian Indian community, and he quickly found himself serving not just as teacher but also as preacher, song leader, and community leader. The rhythms of the weekly communal life at Farmington included community worship, prayer, and exhortation on Sunday evenings; and singing meetings on Tuesday and Friday evenings.[48] Even while he was at Farmington, Johnson recorded that his Indian friends made the fifty-five-mile trip from Groton and Mohegan to visit him and that they joined in the collective meetings.[49]

It was in this context of Christianity-enhanced intertribal relations that Johnson and his young fellow Christian visionaries called the meeting on March 13, 1773, at Mohegan to discuss the possibility of moving elsewhere. As Johnson quickly learned, however, several important pieces had to come together before such a migration could take place. Securing the support of Sir William Johnson and the permission of the Oneidas turned out to be relatively easy. Convincing the majority of Natives from their own home communities to participate, however, was far more difficult. Johnson tried without success to get each of the main Indian communities in Connecticut, Rhode Island, and on Long Island to send representatives to meet with Sir William Johnson and the Oneidas in 1773 and again in January 1774. Each time, however, he showed up in New York with only one or two traveling companions.[50]

With the help of Sir William Johnson, Joseph Johnson was able to successfully negotiate a tract of land from the Oneida chiefs in a lengthy series of meetings in January 1774. By mid-1774, however, only a handful of New England Natives were taking decisive action regarding the migration. On May 19, the Farmington Indians Elijah Wimpey, Solomon Mossuck, and Samuel Adams (not the Boston politician and patriot) petitioned the Connecticut General Assembly for permission to sell their lands near Hartford in anticipation of their planned migration westward.[51] The General Assembly accordingly appointed a committee to oversee and authorize the sale of Farmington lands.[52] A small core of anti-sachem Narragansetts showed enough interest in relocation to at least take a look at the newly acquired lands in New York. On August 22, 1774, Joseph Fish recorded in his journal that he preached at the Indian schoolhouse in Charlestown to only five "Indian Hearers" since "Many of the Heads of the Tribe (and *Sam Niles* for one,) are gone off, with a view to Settle beyond Albany."[53]

On the whole, things progressed rather slowly. On October 4, 1774, the Oneidas finally sent a deed for land in Oneida country—drawn up by Guy Johnson, Sir William Johnson's nephew and successor—to Joseph Johnson and any interested New England Indians.[54] By early 1775, the small core of pro-migration Natives had concrete plans for the move, with a staged strategy for settlement. The first step was to send a group of younger men to plant fields and build temporary huts. After this initial stage, when rudimentary shelters were in place and crops planted, the "families" and the "aged Men and Women" could then move to the new town.[55] In February 1775, Johnson reported that a group of fifty-eight "young men" planned to depart for their new lands on March 13, 1775. These individuals came from Indian towns throughout southeastern New England: ten from Mohegan, twenty from Narragansett, ten from Farmington, five from Niantic, and thirteen from Montauk. No representatives were sent from the Mashantucket and Lantern Hill Pequots, Shinnecocks, or Mohicans in Stockbridge.[56]

Divided over Migration

At first glance, a voluntary mass migration must have at least sounded attractive to many New England Natives. After all, the migration purported to solve many of the shared problems faced by Native communities. Especially the promise of land—and lots of it, according to Joseph Johnson, free from external control and protected by the Oneidas from colonists—must have had some draw for dispossessed individuals and communities that had fought for decades and generations for land rights against individual colonists, local town and colony officials, and even their own Indian sachems. However, some of the most critical land situations actually improved slightly by 1773, which undoubtedly made the migration less appealing for some. Despite the rhetoric of the pro-migration leaders (which appeared especially weighty since their letters were convincing and plentiful), the migration simply did not interest the core populations on each reservation. The activities of the pro-relocation groups versus groups who were indifferent are telling. In January 1774, for example, Mohegan councillor Zachary Johnson and schoolteacher Willard Hubbard petitioned the General Assembly for funds to repair the aging and decrepit Mohegan schoolhouse. Zachary Johnson had no intention of going to New York and was making long-term plans for continuing education at Mohegan. Joseph Johnson, on the other hand, just four months later petitioned the General Assembly for aid in the

"Considerable Expence in making the Necessary preparations for the Removal of Sundry tribes of Indians out of this Colony."[57]

Two other intertwined "solutions" proposed by the migration actually served to turn Native individuals and families away from it: first, the "racial purity" principle behind the movement, and second, the explicitly Christian nature of the new proposed community. The new community in Oneida country was designed to circumvent entirely the problem of racial mixing by creating a place for racially "pure" Indians. The 1774 deed to Oneida lands granted to the New England Indians stated in no uncertain terms the concerns of some Indians in this time period. The deed gave the New England Indians a large tract of land (approximately 10,000 acres) that was granted "to the New England Indians, & their Posterity, without Power of Alienation," with no restrictions on the land itself except one: "that the same shall not be possessed by any Persons deemed of the said Tribes who are descended from, or have intermixed with Negroes, or Mulatoes."[58] All of the hundreds of racially intermarried folks on Indian lands around New England—Christian or not—need not apply.

It is likely that this racial exclusion clause reflected concerns shared by the Oneidas and the New England Indians. The language and restrictions seem to reflect those of the 1754 agreement signed between the Montauketts (and mediated by Samson Occom, then serving as minister and schoolmaster at Montauk) and the East Hampton trustees. Similarly, petitions filed by other Native communities in May 1773 and September 1778 sought to exclude the presence of blacks. In the 1778 petition filed by Nathan Bradford, the Mohegan overseer, the Mohegans clearly stated to the Connecticut Assembly that "they do not want Negroes nor Mollatoes to inhabit their Lands" and that they "wish them to be kept out of our Tribe."[59] Yet the Iroquois had their own reasons to resent black presence. In the eighteenth century, Africans were widely used as slaves on farms in the New York backcountry surrounding Iroquois land, often performing fieldwork that the Six Nations considered to be reserved for women. On several occasions in 1765, Seneca chiefs, in response to Samuel Kirkland's evangelistic overtures, declared that if they should "change or renounce" their religion for that of the "white people," they would "soon lose all their martial spirit & be no better than dutch negroes who stooped down to milk cows & went to hoe in the corn fields, an employment proper only for women."[60] Blacks—who made up 10 percent of the non-Indian population in the vast region surrounding Albany, New York, by 1771—represented the opposite of the very sovereignty the Six Nations were working so hard to retain.[61]

In this way, using racial concerns to determine membership of the proposed new settlement naturally cut across other possible ways of deciding who was in and who was out. Limiting membership to Christians, for example, might have been another possible way to determine membership—one that would have included blacks and all people of mixed ethnicities. By enforcing a "racial purity" principle, those who migrated automatically excluded or designated as second-class residents their Christian relatives and friends who might have intermarried with non-Indians. By the 1770s, in most communities intermarriage was common enough that a rule barring individuals involved in mixed marriages would have certainly excluded up to half the reservation populations and caused an immense offense in the process. Such decisions must have driven deep wedges in Native communities and virtually guaranteed that the migration would be an exclusive and divisive—rather than inclusive and unifying—event.

Even if some Native individuals and families agreed with the racial exclusion principle, they might have felt more ambivalent about the explicitly Christian and even evangelistic nature of the migration and proposed settlement. Although the majority of New England Natives had been exposed to Christian ideas over time, they did not all share the visionary, passionate evangelistic Reformed Christianity of Occom, Johnson, Elijah Wimpey, and the Fowler brothers. And the evangelistic component played a key part in the migration leaders' rhetoric. Several Indian leaders from the Farmington community, for example, explained to Governor Trumbull their motivation for selling their lands and heading west, listing the reasons as twofold: to do what would be best for themselves and "to extend & advance the kingdom of Christ among the heathen Nations."[62] Similarly, Occom explained to the overseers of the Indian Charity School trust (namely, the funds he had helped raise in the 1760s) that the "Main View" of the migration was to "Introduce the Religion of Jesus Christ by their example—among the benighted Indians in the Wilderness."[63]

The curious thing about such rhetoric is that a subset of the Oneidas was clearly Christianized by 1774—particularly at Kanonwalohale—in part because of more than four decades of evangelization and education from various quarters of New England and New York. Equally as important, the English missionary Samuel Kirkland had served in the principal Oneida town of Kanonwalohale since 1764. Even after the other New England Indian missionaries and school-teachers abandoned the mission (like Johnson) or went home burned out and homesick (like David Fowler), Kirkland continued to receive generous support from the NEC (which had also partnered with the Harvard Corporation and the SSPCK in a time of financial crisis). Additionally, English missionary presence was steadily felt in the intertribal Oneida town of Onaquaga. In 1773, the English missionary Aaron Crosby was ordained in a large service in New York over which at least four ministers and missionaries from New York and Connecticut presided, including Samuel Kirkland from Kanonwalohale. Approximately sixty Oneidas and other Indians attended as well, both from Onaquaga and Kanonwalohale; they sang hymns in three parts for the assembled crowd at the beginning and end of the service as well as "an Anthem in Indian" composed by

Kirkland for the event. The ministerial charge was given by Kirkland in both "English and Indian for the benefit of the promiscuous Multitude," as was the sermon Kirkland later delivered that evening.[64]

Given this history, it is less surprising that in a speech to Joseph Johnson the Oneidas asserted their own spiritual sensibilities. "Brethren, two things, we six united Nations do follow," the Oneidas declared. "The first, and Chief is Religion, or to follow the directions given to us in Gods Word. The second is to concur with the Unchristianized Nations, so far as will promote Peace, and Tranquility in our Land." In other words, New England Indians, don't come here and rock the boat. Within the wider Six Nations, each group and town handled the issue of Christian practice and missionary presence differently. Kirkland reported that while the Onondagas seemed interested in moving closer to Kanonwalohale (to be nearer to Christian worship services, in Kirkland's reading), the Tuscaroras seemed less inclined to embrace missionary presence. One Tuscarora sachem in particular, Kirkland lamented, "continues to oppose & reproach the work of god with all his might, & uses every Artifice to dissuade his people from attending divine worship within here."[65] And the Senecas, as Kirkland painfully remembered, resoundingly rejected his presence as a missionary in the spring of 1765. Nonetheless, it is clear that, despite the pretensions of some New England Indians to view a move among the Oneidas as an evangelistic move, the Oneidas themselves saw it as the joining of two communities with equal religious aspirations. If anything, the New England Indians were coming in as distinct inferiors within the larger context of the Six Nations.

Natives and the Revolutionary War

The growing tensions between Britain and the North American colonies soon stalled whatever migration efforts Johnson and his co-religionists had started. Although some Native individuals and communities seemed to have a studied indifference to the controversies over taxation and colonial sovereignty in the late 1760s and even early 1770s, by 1775 they found it increasingly difficult to remain completely aloof. Rumors of sharp political disagreements and debates that started in urban centers and emanated outward into the colonial countryside caused Natives to pay attention, as did rumors of impending actual military conflict. As the colonial populace became increasingly politically polarized, Native nations found their allegiances torn and solicited from both sides. Allegiances to one side or another had consequences, as they quickly learned. For example, several Oneida chiefs asked Samuel Kirkland to explain what the First Continental Congress was debating in 1775. When Guy Johnson learned that the Oneidas favored the "dissenting cause," he blamed Kirkland and chased him out of Oneida and New York.[66]

In this new political environment, the New England Indians' associations with the Six Nations took on far greater significance, since most New England colonists saw the Six Nations as firmly under British political authority. Before long the Native Christian leaders who favored migration found their very loyalties and motives questioned by anti-British colonists. In the early planning stages, many colonial leaders, like Sir William Johnson and Connecticut governor Jonathan Trumbull, clearly supported the idea of migration. With the outbreak of actual hostilities imminent, however, things changed, and quickly. In March 1775, for example, Governor Trumbull denied Joseph Johnson a pass (for safe travel) and instead told him that it was better for the Indians "to stay at home."[67] A month later, the Montauketts reported that "they had often been threatened by different persons, even to the taking away their Lives if they pretended to come away" to New York. Colonists in the towns close to the Montauketts reportedly agreed that "it would be best to knock all the Indians in the head rather than that they Should go to the Mohawk Country."[68] Such threats came mostly from a pernicious suspicion that the New England Indians and the much more numerous and feared Haudenosaunees had "held a private Correspondence together in these difficult times & were united to join his Majesties Troops."[69] New England Indians had repeatedly proved their fealty in colonial wars in the eighteenth century, but the prospect of hundreds of New England Indians joining with the nations of the Iroquois Confederacy (many of whom had strong ties to England via Sir William Johnson and Guy Johnson) was downright alarming.

Although by April 14, 1775, Johnson and the first group had reached Oneida to clear some land, plant corn and potatoes, and build temporary housing, Johnson at least did not remain there for long. In light of whites' suspicions about his British allegiances—fueled, he was shocked to learn, by his close Farmington friend and co-migration leader Elijah Wimpey—Johnson increasingly seemed determined to prove himself faithful to patriot officials.[70] In late June—just a few short weeks after the Battle of Bunker Hill in Boston—Johnson made the dangerous journey back to New England, stopping at New York City and Hartford en route to deliver lengthy letters to the assemblies in each city in which he defended his allegiances and actions against circulating rumors.[71] As Revolutionary rhetoric increasingly turned into armed resistance, the fifty-eight Natives who had moved to New York in the spring of 1775 were forced back to either Stockbridge, Massachusetts, or—more embarrassingly—their home communities in New England before the year was out.

Native communities in New England and New York experienced the onset of the war of American independence in different ways.[72] The Six Nations were sizable enough that both the British imperial representatives and the patriot colonists desired their allegiance (or, at first, simply their neutrality). The Revolutionary War presented the Six Nations with a series of very difficult decisions that had to be deliberated at a variety of local and intertribal levels; ultimately, it led to divisions between the various nations in the confederacy, with only the Tuscaroras and the Oneidas siding with the colonists.[73] For Natives in southeastern New England, by the 1770s the population was sufficiently dispersed and decentralized (with the clear exceptions of the reservation communities) that discussions about the war took place at the local, community, and even family levels. Furthermore, in southeastern New England, the allure of quick cash in the form of enlistment bonuses and the promise of regular pay for service were enough for some Indian males to quickly side with the patriots. In some areas, ironically enough, local Anglo officials at first did not want Indians to enlist in local militias. When the posters, newspaper announcements, and broadsides were posted in Connecticut announcing voluntary and mandatory enlistments, some of the Indians who tried to enlist were turned away. Some English colonists, thinking even a year of military service beneath them, tried to pay some Indians to go in their stead, which seemed workable until the militia agents discovered the scheme and "turn'd them back again."[74]

Over time, however, neutrality and noninvolvement ceased to be an option as colonial officials and military leaders increasingly viewed Indian nations as untapped reserves for more specialized kinds of warfare. Aspirations of neutrality vaporized for the Six Nations when fighting erupted in their own backyard, first in several battles in the mid-1770s and later with the devastating Sullivan-Clinton Expedition into the heart of Haudenosaunee lands in 1779, during which the Continental Army destroyed towns, farmlands, houses, and food supplies of loyalist Iroquois.[75] Similarly, despite his original professed neutrality, by late 1775 Johnson had committed himself to the rebel cause—or at least as much as necessary to secure the ongoing support of the colonial legislatures. In January 1776, Johnson was commended by the colony of New Hampshire as "a Friend to the Cause of American Liberty."[76] On February 20, 1776, the self-styled "Chief Warrior" of the United Colonies, George Washington himself, wrote to Joseph Johnson, thanking him for continuing to convince the Six Nations not to "take up the hatchett" for or against the colonies, despite the impossibility of such a task.[77] Many of the literate, Christian Indians, like Wimpey and Johnson, threw their lot in with the patriots and served as negotiators and messengers between New England and New York, even as they lamented the war, its meaning, and their own involvement.[78] "I feel Sorrow in this once Savage heart of mine," Johnson mourned, "when I Behold in my mind, not only a civilized, but a Christianized People Bleeding. . . . O Britain! O North America! Can the heathens Say, Behold and See how those Christians love one another?"[79]

Nonetheless, hundreds of New England Indians made it onto the official militia rolls as times grew more desperate. Reuben Cognehew, a Mohegan schoolteacher who spent time at Mashpee, went with Wimpey on a diplomatic trip to New York and then promptly enlisted in the Connecticut army, which had changed its policy toward Indians.[80] Jonathan Occom (Samson's younger brother) served in General Putnam's regiment during the war. Two of Samson Occom's nephews, John Tantaquidgeon and David, also served; David died doing so. Joseph Johnson served in more unofficial roles as a liaison to various Indian communities for the Continental Army.[81] All four of Samuel Ashpo's sons fought—and died—in the Revolutionary War, including Samuel, Jr., who was killed during the Battle of Bunker Hill.[82] More than seventy-five Indian men from Connecticut served as soldiers, crewmen, and privateers, and the war claimed the lives of dozens, if not well over a hundred, of New England Natives. Each community lost some of its men, although how many is unclear. The Mohegans lost at least seventeen males, and the Pequots at least eighteen.[83] The Stockbridge Indians served—and lost—the most out of the New England nations.[84] The war also stole away the twenty-five-year-old promoter of the migration movement, Joseph Johnson, who passed away sometime between mid-1776 and May 1777.[85]

Despite this devastating loss of husbands, fathers, and sons, most Native reservations in southern New England were physically untouched by the war itself, and life—even with the absence of younger males who went off to war and did not return—seemed to continue on as usual, with internal dissent and pressing land claims. But times were hard, and a general scarcity of resources, jobs, and food, combined with a general economic inflation, was felt by all, Indian or not. "The Times are Extreamly Distressing in this part of the World," Occom lamented to a benefactor in London in 1776, "these Unnatural Wars have effected and Distrest everyone, especially the Poor, I have never had such a Burden, I have had much Sickness in my Family lately, and every thing extreamly Dear [i.e., costly], especially Cloathing."[86] In such an environment, even more was at stake in Indian communities regarding land claims and efforts to gain the upper hand in the ongoing internal disputes within various communities. At Narragansett, on December 13, 1777, the Indian Council petitioned the State of Rhode Island Council of War to request the removal of an Irish tenant on the land of recently deceased James Niles; the tenant had first rented the land without the approval of the tribal council and now refused to leave.[87] On Long Island, the Montauketts sided with the British partly because of the British occupation of the area and partly out of pure disgust for colonial mistreatment. As a result, many Montaukett leaders on Long Island continued to appeal to the British authorities during the war regarding their land loss and mistreatment. A complaint from the Montauketts in 1778 elicited a strong reprimand from British superintendent of

Indian Affairs Guy Johnson to non-Indian "Inhabitants near Montok," in which he admonished them to, for the king's sake and for their loyalty, "Afford these Poor People such Liberty and Indulgence as they have reasonably required."[88]

From the perspective of some of the Christian Indian leaders, the war had destroyed most of what they had worked to build. On many Indian lands, the schools were gone, the missionaries had left, sources of funding had dried up, and the Indians had been robbed of whatever little "Spiritual and Temporal Injoyments" they had in the first place.[89] Even so, migration was not pursued as a near-universal option. The war seemed to strengthen the resolve of the pro-migration faction in some communities, and—as in the case of the Stockbridge Indians—made such a migration a real option in others, but otherwise it did not convince the numerous Natives who had not been previously interested to join the movement. The experience of the war did convince Occom, who had been somewhat reluctant to move in the early 1770s, and perhaps for good reason. After all, despite his complaints to the contrary, he did have a relatively good life at Mohegan that included a respectable two-story English-style house—surely an anomaly on the Mohegan reservation—with "papered & painted" rooms, comfortable feather beds, and a separate library room consisting of "a handsome collection, brought by him, principally from Great Britain."[90] Nonetheless, a decade and a punishing revolution later, things looked different. This was in part because his presence at Mohegan was being challenged even more forcefully by Zachary Johnson. In May 1781, Johnson complained to the state of Connecticut on behalf of "the True Mohegan Indians" regarding "spoils and devestations committed by strange Indians and disorderly white People, on the Mohegan Lands." In particular, Johnson was concerned about "the Strange Indians headed and assisted by a Certain Indian Minister" who laid claim to Mohegan land by the "sanction of the British King." Johnson and the Mohegans, however, "entirely disown[ed]" these Indians and pleaded for an intervention from the General Assembly, particularly because these "strange Indians" were settling on Mohegan land merely "to avoid paying Taxes to the State."[91]

In spring 1784, just half a year after the Treaty of Paris brought an official end to the Revolutionary War, Occom, Wimpey, and the Fowlers renewed the call to move to New York. Like Joseph Johnson had done a decade earlier, they had to rally the reluctant individual communities, ensure that relations were still open with the Oneidas, and, most important, find a way to secure funds for what was for many Indians an expensive move. One strategy to pay for the move was to sell land. In some cases, a deal was negotiated directly with local magistrates. In 1784, Occom wrote to the trustees of Easthampton, encouraging them to "buy of Indians their Rights of Montauk" for a "Very handsome" amount. In this case, one of the émigrés was Occom's own aged mother-in-law, Mrs. Fowler. "She is an old Woman," Occom explained, "and She is going With us and I believe it will be doing good to help her, She Will Want something to pay her passage to Oneida, and She Will need Provisions by the way."[92] In this way, for the Indians that remained, the migration contributed to the very dispossession that they had fought so hard to prevent.

On May 8, 1784, twenty Indian families from southern New England sailed from New London, along the Long Island Sound and up the Hudson River to Albany, where they most likely transferred their belongings to horses and wagons and made their way westward to the tract of land given to them by the Oneidas.[93] After another series of migrations the next year, for the first time, in November 1785, this small cluster of Christian New England Indians organized themselves into a "Body Politick" and officially gave a name to their settlement: Eeyawquittoowauconnuck, or simply "Brotherton" in English.[94] A few miles across the rolling hills of central New York the Mohicans from Stockbridge, Massachusetts, formed a town at the same time. The devastating experience of the war, combined with increasingly tense relationships with whites in town during and after the war, had made remaining at Stockbridge entirely undesirable for some Indian families. When the New England Indians who had taken refuge at Stockbridge during the Revolutionary War once again made their way to Oneida country in 1783, many of the Stockbridge Indians decided to relocate as well.[95] The Oneidas granted the Stockbridge Indians a tract of land six miles square just southwest of Brothertown, which the Stockbridge Natives promptly named "New Stockbridge."[96]

Reassessing Involvement in Brothertown

Although the Brothertown migration was an important moment in New England Native history, it was also a socially divisive movement and involved far fewer people than contemporary observers and later historians have assumed. The collective migration to Brothertown has been the focus of writing about the history of Natives in Connecticut, Rhode Island, and on Long Island, in part, due to a century-long interest in the Christian Indians in southeastern New England.[97] In this reading of events, the largely Christian Brothertown migration becomes a fascinating "end" to 150 years of colonization, and the action moves westward, leaving the remnant New England Indians numerically crippled, socially marginalized, and doomed to an even quicker disappearance.[98] This, however, was simply not the case; at every turn, the migration movement was treated with relative apathy by the majority of New England Natives, and in most cases Native communities continued on as they had before the migration.

As small, pro-removal clusters from many Native communities were gearing up for the relocation, the other nonmigrating members of the same communities were redoubling their efforts to assert their own cultural vitality and political sovereignty. On October 24, 1784—just five months after the first group of New England migrants sailed for New York—the Mohegans and Niantics submitted a joint complaint to the Connecticut General Assembly, placing the relatively short span of colonialism within the much longer time frame of creation and the period in which their Native ancestors had populated and enjoyed the earth "the Supreme Spirit" had given them. The problem was that local whites were attempting to prohibit the Niantics and Mohegans from fishing on and along the Connecticut River, something they had done as far back as they could remember and an activity they regarded as a God-given right. The Natives asserted their own rights to the waters and asked for the protection of the General Assembly so that they "may not be molested or be deprived of these our Priveledges by any Contentious People."[99] Similarly, just four months later, in February 1785, thirty-one Narragansetts petitioned the Rhode Island General Assembly to appoint a committee of judicious non-Indians who would be given "full Power of hearing & determining all Disputes and controversies that may arise between any of the Indians of the Narragansett Tribe, among themselves, or with any of the Citizens of this State."[100]

The relative reluctance of most New England Natives to take part in the migration is clear from a later census taken at Brothertown. In 1795 only 135 individuals were listed as residents, drawn from almost every major Native community in southeastern New England: Farmington, Mashantucket, Mohegan, Montauk, Narragansett, and a handful whose tribal identity was not listed.[101] Although it is difficult to get precise numbers for New England Indians on reserved lands in the 1780s (and, indeed, even the first official US federal census in 1790 does not separate out Indians as a distinct group), there are a few possible points of comparison. A 1783 census in Rhode Island, for example, lists 280 Indians in Charlestown, where the Narragansett reservation was located.[102] The 1795 Brothertown census, however, lists only nineteen Narragansetts, most of whom were adults (an unspecified but small number of children under ten years of age were present), which suggests that approximately 7 percent to 10 percent of the total Narragansett population participated in the Brothertown movement up through 1795. But the Narragansett reservation contained only a third of Rhode Island's Indian population in 1774 (528 out of 1,482). Taking the state as a whole, then, the Rhode Island Natives who participated in Brothertown represented approximately 2 percent to 5 percent of the state's Indian population. Similarly, in Connecticut, the 1774 Indian census recorded a total population of 1,363 Indians, over half of whom were in New London County. Even if one hundred Connecticut Indians had migrated to Brothertown by 1795, they still made up only approximately 7 percent of the state's Native population.[103] Overall, then, it is likely that the Brothertown migration involved less than 10 percent of the Native population in and near the Indian reservation communities in Rhode Island, Connecticut, and the eastern end of Long Island.

One way of accounting for this lack of unanimity is to recognize the depth of internal divisions in Indian communities that had existed in increasing measure during the eighteenth century; these divisions had arisen over issues of land, tribal citizenship, English overseers, religion, and (later) migration. Sometimes the dividing line between those who stayed and those who left followed older tribal fault lines over contestations for the sachemship and how to deal with the sale and leasing of lands. This was especially the case with at least the Mohegans and the Narragansetts. In other tribes, the line was more clearly drawn along other points of division, such as adherence to Christian ideas or European culture more generally, or even issues of race and intermarriage. The Mashantucket Pequot community, for example, was split into two groups; only the more Christianized Pequot community at Indiantown participated in the Brothertown migration.[104] Similarly, the Montaukett community on Long Island experienced a rift over the question of migration, with the more traditional Montauketts preferring to find alternate solutions and remain on their lands while Christian Montauketts were drawn to the idea of Brothertown.[105]

Furthermore, a move to Oneida country represented a distinctive commitment to Euroamerican-style agrarian subsistence and economy versus other options, including hunting, fishing, making crafts, whaling, and leasing out land for income. For many coastal New England Natives—particularly the Narragansetts, Montauketts, and Shinnecocks—the loss of the rich maritime waterways for clamming, fishing, and whaling meant a severe restriction in options, from subsistence to vocational pursuits. Only thirty-five Montauketts had moved to Brothertown by the mid-1780s, and in 1789 three Montauketts visited Oneida country and told Samuel Kirkland that they were afraid that "they would suffer and come to poverty if they should move as a body into this part of the world, where there were no oysters and clams."[106]

The way in which the Brothertown migration served as a major point of social division—not unification—for Native communities as a whole is evident in a host of ways. Sometimes major decisions—such as relocation, accommodation to European culture, and Christianization—were split along generational lines. With regard to Brothertown, most of the leaders were young (Occom excepted) and had been born after the Awakening. Joseph Johnson, for example, was born in 1751, almost a full decade after the initial involvement of many New England Natives in the Awakening. Similarly, most of the Brothertown leaders had attended Wheelock's school and had been shaped by a particular New Light, evangelistically oriented Christianity. Is it possible that this younger generation saw things differently? James Niles, Jr., the nephew of the New Light Narragansett minister, had a falling out with his uncle Sam and publicly criticized the

Narragansett Separates for "their Want of Discipline and Rule of Conduct," for which he was censured.[107] For James Niles, Jr., the move to Oneida represented an escape from a kind of Indian Christian practice that he did not fully agree with (as well as a way to escape the potentially awkward censure at the hands of his uncle). Generational considerations also played into the decision-making process at Stockbridge. The first generation that welcomed Sergeant and Wood-bridge onto their lands at Stockbridge in the 1730s viewed proximity to English resources and religious offerings as a concrete way to deal with a changing world, but by the 1780s, the second—and even third—generations felt differently about such associations. The rising generation often preferred a "cultural sepa-rateness," which, when they were feeling crowded out of Stockbridge, made moving elsewhere a much-desired option.[108]

The decisions surrounding possible migrations also divided families, even the families of the leaders themselves, sometimes in acrimonious ways. In 1787, two Narragansett brothers, John and Daniel Skesuck, requested and received permis-sion from the state committee to oversee Narragansett affairs to sell their land in order to fund their relocation to Brothertown. Their plan was broken up when two members of the Indian council, Joseph Cuzzens and James Wampy, reported that the Skesucks did not have the title to the land they were trying to sell, and, even worse, they were attempting to sell land right out from under their own flesh and blood—several sisters who lived on the same tract of land and who, in their poverty, would have become a financial burden to the tribe or wards of the state had the sale gone through.[109] In other, less dramatic, ways however, the re-location scheme divided New England Indian families. Although Occom moved to Brothertown in the late 1780s with Mary and some of their younger children, Tabitha, Occom's third child, who had married Joseph Johnson, remained at Mohegan. Benoni Occom, Samson Occom's seventh child, born in 1763, remained in Mohegan, where he passed away in January 1829.[110] Several others of Occom's children died in various communities around New England prior to 1800 and never moved to Brothertown, though some, including Andrew and Sally, did make the move with their parents.[111] Similarly, the Niantic Baptist Sep-arate minister Philip Occuish and his wife, Sarah, finished out their lives on land they owned in Lyme; Sarah passed away on April 16, 1787, and Philip died two years later, on March 20, 1789. Philip Occuish, Jr., however, moved to Brother-town in approximately 1799, as did two other sons or grandsons, Joshua and Abraham, although the parents' land at Niantic remained in the family for an-other twenty-five years. Some of the land was eventually passed down to Philip and Sarah's granddaughters, both of whom had moved to Brothertown.[112]

Despite the explicitly Christian nature of the Brothertown migration, it did not attract the interest of all Christian Indians or even some of the most prominent Christian Indian leaders in southeastern New England. Joseph Johnson told the

Oneidas that it was "the great drinkers, & Lazy Persons" who were hesitant to move to New York, but this certainly does not adequately describe the situation, particularly in 1784 and beyond.[113] Nonetheless, the perception that the Brothertown migration dealt a deathblow to Native Christianity in southeastern New England was proclaimed by contemporaries and was often repeated thereafter. The Baptist minister Isaac Backus rather dismissively mentioned the Narragansetts in the second volume of his massive *A History of New-England* (1784) when he noted that Samuel Niles's Separate (and Baptist) Indian church in Charlestown, Rhode Island, at one time "had many valuable Christians therein; but most of them are since dead, and the church is dissolved. The chief of the Indians who are living have removed into the State of New York."[114] Such a pronouncement was wildly inaccurate, however, since Samuel Niles was still, in fact, residing in Charlestown in 1784 and had not moved to New York, nor would he ever do so. Likewise, the Separate Mohegan minister Samuel Ashpo did not move to New York. It is certainly possible that Ashpo was intrigued by the new settlement, for he made several visits there in the decade before his death.[115] In December 1793, the seventy-five-year-old Ashpo visited Brothertown and gave a sermon to an expectant crowd of assembled Indians, who were visibly disappointed that the enfeebled Ashpo delivered his address with "great deliberation" and in a "low voice" instead of the "flame and zeal and an elevated voice" for which he was renowned.[116] Nonetheless, his primary commitment remained with the Mohegans in Connecticut. Ashpo died on November 7, 1795, at the age of seventy-seven and was buried in a Mohegan burial ground about a half-mile from the Mohegan church. His short obituary printed in the *Norwich Packet* stated that he was the "Pastor of a Church in Mohegan" and also served on a "Committee in behalf of the tribe of Mohegan Indians."[117] Even his wife, Hannah, was listed on a tribal census in 1799 and passed away on July 10, 1801, also at Mohegan.[118] Similarly, Deacon Henry Quaquaquid—a major Mohegan tribal leader, rival sachem, and Christian Indian leader—remained in Mohegan, and seemingly none of his immediate family members moved to Brothertown.[119] Most surprising, perhaps, Joseph Johnson's widow, Tabitha, remained in Connecticut the rest of her life. Tabitha later married the Mohegan Joshua Cooper and had another son.[120] Other members of the prominent Cooper family likewise stayed, including the Mohegan Christian leader, John Cooper.[121] The descendants of Edward Nedson, the longtime Indian schoolmaster at Lantern Hill (1757–1769) remained in Connecticut as well.[122]

Even a place like Farmington, which had perhaps the highest percentage of participants in the migration, did not become completely devoid of Native presence and leadership. Most prominent among those who stayed in Farmington was the Mossuck family. Solomon Mossuck, who joined Timothy Pitkin's Farmington Congregational Church in June 1763 (and his wife in September 1765), passed away in Farmington on January 25, 1802, and was buried in the old Indian graveyard close to where John Mettawan's schoolhouse stood.[123] The Mossucks and other Tunxis continued to live on land on Indian Neck and in the surrounding neighborhood well into the early nineteenth century; the "last" Mossuck family member in Farmington did not pass away until 1883.[124] These examples show that many Christian Natives and leaders opted to remain in New England.

Another factor that might have prevented a larger drain of New England Indians to Brothertown was that, although the new community got off to a good start, within a few short years it and New Stockbridge were wracked by factionalism, internal religious discord, and racial tension. Such developments were not lost on New England Natives who remained on their homelands, and for whom, a decade after the war, life had largely returned to normal. Although a house of worship was designated at David Fowler's house in Brothertown and at the home of Hendrick Aupaumut in New Stockbridge, the communities were less than unified, even over questions of Christian doctrine and practice. Initially both communities jointly desired Occom's ongoing ministerial services when he finally moved there in 1787, but Brothertown residents were soon so divided that Occom moved to New Stockbridge and attended to the church there. Even in New Stockbridge there were divisions, with some of the Natives preferring John Sergeant, Jr., over Occom.[125] Within five years, however, Occom passed away, in July 1792 in New Stockbridge. More than three hundred Indians from Brothertown, New Stockbridge, Oneida, and the surrounding towns attended the funeral sermon given by Samuel Kirkland on July 15.[126]

Moving to New York hardly solved the problems of land and dispossession, as New England Natives also noticed. History merely repeated itself in their new location, with more land loss, intermarriage, and settler encroachment. Soon after arriving in Oneida country, the Brothertown Indians (as they soon were called) found their original land grant contested by the Oneidas themselves and, in a few short years, their lands were once again slipping into the hands of local white settlers through long-term leases, rentals, and purchases. As early as 1791, the Brothertown Natives complained to the New York Assembly that "the White People have Come in amongst" with their "Children, Horses, Cattle, Hogs, and Dogs . . . and they bring Rum," creating a "Deplorable situation"—so deplorable, in fact, that already in 1791 some people talked of moving elsewhere.[127] The Brothertown and New Stockbridge Indians also found they still had to fight for equal rights with local and state governments and at times used their self-proclaimed identity as Christian and civilized to make their cases as strong as possible. In February 1792, the Brothertown leaders sent a petition to the state legislature asking to "be put on the footing of free white citizens" with the major exception being that "they do not wish the privilege of selling their land." As to why they should be allowed to become free citizens, the Brothertown Natives stated that "they have been brought up in a civilized life, and that they profess the Christian religion."[128]

Despite the goal of the migration to secure land and eliminate the intrusions of local colonists and other non-Indians onto their lands, less than four decades after the migration to New York, the Brothertown and New Stockbridge Indians were once again at a breaking point of frustration. In 1818, in another attempt to escape ongoing land loss and increasingly onerous white settlement, many Brothertown and New Stockbridge Indians tried to move west again, first to southern Indiana, along the White River. When that did not work out, however, they ultimately moved to Wisconsin, settling on the shores of Lake Winnebago, in the 1830s.[129]

When the Cambridge, Massachusetts, minister Abiel Holmes was traveling through Mohegan in approximately 1800, he happened upon a Mohegan Indian with a fiddle on his back traveling on foot between Norwich and New London. Holmes proceeded to ask the Native directly "Whether a great part of the tribe did not go to Oneida with Mr. Occom." Likely to Holmes's surprise, the unnamed Mohegan replied, "No, there didn't hardly any go—Mr. Occom and a few more." Holmes then asked why the Indian himself did not "accept the offer of the Oneidas," to which the Mohegan replied, "Oh, live well enough here—land enough—and good fishing!"[130] Holmes's encounter at Mohegan highlights the different choices Natives in New England made in response to the shared and real problems they faced together. Despite the attraction that migration might have posed for some, most New England Natives weathered the various land controversies of the eighteenth century, either by waiting out or participating in the Revolutionary War. By the opening years of the nineteenth century, they had settled back into prewar and pre-migration patterns that had sustained them for centuries: subsistence farming and fishing. The Brothertown migration did bring about one specific change to the New England Native landscape in that it effectively broadened the geographical breadth of Native kinship networks and mobility patterns. But such networks and pathways still stretched out from the same core reservations in New England that had remained continuous throughout the colonial period.

8

Remaining

On a sultry August day in 1809, the Narragansetts found yet another white out-sider on their reservation. Arriving on horseback, the elderly man said he was sent from a society in Boston that wanted to help the Narragansetts by providing a preacher and setting up a school for their children. Some of the older members of the Indian tribal council must have looked knowingly at each other. This all sounded too familiar. Just three decades earlier, the Narragansetts had forced Joseph Fish and Edward Deake to abandon their New England Company funded efforts in the mid-1770s, and there had not been any serious attempts by whites to challenge their religious authority and reshape their practices since that time. Plus, their reservation already had a church that held weekly Christian services and other community meetings, and its independence was among the most jeal-ously guarded element of their reservation traditions. A school for their chil-dren, however, sounded more appealing, especially since their schoolhouse had recently blown down in a storm.

The would-be missionary was Curtis Coe, a Brown University alumnus and retired Congregational minister who had been sent by the Society for Propa-gating the Gospel among the Indians and Others in North America (SPGNA), with the support of the Rhode Island Domestic Missionary Society (RIDMS). This was his initial missionary journey to visit and preach to the residents of Rhode Island and to evangelize the Narragansetts. After spending a few weeks itinerating through much of southern Rhode Island, Coe showed up in Charles-town in search of the Narragansetts. What he found, however, completely sur-prised him. Three miles outside of Charlestown, set back from the road in the woods, centered in a cluster of one-story wood frame houses and a church building situated on approximately two thousand acres of Narragansett land, Coe found a thriving, relatively indigent, and yet fiercely independent commu-nity of "140, or 150 souls" that served as a gathering point and crossroads for a surprisingly interracial population of Indians, blacks, and local whites. Their church building—apparently the same one built in the 1750s, although with var-ious repairs and upgrades—was the only one in the entire town of Charlestown

(Coe noted with disapproval), and on Sunday mornings it attracted a mélange of whites, Indians, and blacks for a lengthy, egalitarian, participatory service usually led by an itinerant Baptist Indian or black preacher.

The Narragansetts exhibited a robust sense of their own history and involvement with Euroamerican dealings that both positively and negatively shaped their interactions in the early nineteenth century with missionaries and local magistrates. Over time, the Narragansetts told Coe stories that stretched back almost a century. They recalled the missionary and educational efforts of Joseph Park in the 1730s, the evangelistic sermons of "Revd Messrs Whitefield, Davenport, & others" during the Awakening and the Indian church that gathered under Park in the 1740s, the separation from Park's church that took place when he "reproved" the Narragansett Christians for being too noisy in church, and how they met in a wigwam until their own church was built. They recounted Samuel Niles's eventual leadership and the coming of Joseph Fish and Edward Deake to preach to and teach them.[1] One older (unnamed) Narragansett woman had actually attended Wheelock's Indian Charity School forty years earlier.[2] But land and dispossession were part of the story, too. Several of the Narragansetts seemed particularly upset about the misuse of some lands granted to Charlestown—stretching back to 1727—including one grant intended for a church building. One Narragansett individual bitterly recounted how "our fore fathers has given a lot of forty acres of land to the whites, for the purpose of Erecting a church on. They have not Erected any church but still hold our land."[3]

Nonetheless, Coe found the Narragansetts' Christianity peculiar and—by his own standards—woefully inadequate, particularly with regard to basic biblical knowledge and instruction. There was not one Bible in the entire church, and the Natives' religious education was so deficient that the Indian children he talked to had no knowledge of the Ten Commandments.[4] Coe conducted several visits over the course of a week and handed out dozens of books including Bibles, New Testaments, copies of the hymns of Isaac Watts, and other devotional works—all well intended, except, as he learned later, none of the Narragansett men knew how to read.[5]

Curtis Coe's initial visit in 1809 turned into a two-and-a-half-decade-long attempt by the SPGNA to evangelize and educate the Narragansetts. As a manifestation of the fourth wave of attempted evangelization between the 1670s and the 1810s, the SPGNA's mission to the Narragansetts reveals the cyclical nature of the attempts made by English colonists and—eventually—Americans over the course of a century to reshape the religious sensibilities of the Native communities in southeastern New England in ways deemed acceptable to whites. And, indeed, the religious state of the Narragansetts in 1809 also revealed the degree to which Natives continued to define and defend their particular versions of religious practice (and nonpractice), no matter how partial and incomplete their

Christianization might have seemed from the outside and despite generations of evangelization at the hands of whites. Nonetheless, Coe—who was vaguely aware of this longer history—optimistically reported back to the SPGNA in late 1809 that the Narragansetts were eager for a school (which they were) and that they were also willing to hear a preacher from time to time. Before leaving, he told them that he could return next year, provide them with consistent preaching, hold a school for them, and—perhaps most important—procure funding for a new school building on their reservation. A few months after his departure, the Narragansett Indian council sent Abiel Holmes, the president of the SPGNA, a letter thanking him for sending Coe, since they had "for a long time been left in an illiterate irregular state." In particular, the Narragansetts seemed especially grateful for the combined total of $350 pledged from the SPGNA and the RIDMS "to build a schoolhouse," and they vowed to start initial work on it that very winter.[6] And so the process began all over again.

The experiences of the Narragansetts paralleled that of other Native communities in southeastern New England after the American Revolution with regard to ongoing cultural persistence, land, religion, kinship, and regional mobility during the critical early decades of the new American republic. Despite the rapidly changing world around them and the struggles they faced—poverty, dispossession, and struggles for identity—Natives across southeastern New England continued to implement strategies of selective religious engagement while nurturing tribal customs that gave life, vitality, and cultural sovereignty to their communities. Along the way, Indian individuals and communities accepted white support when proffered, particularly when education, books, clothing, and food were part of the package. But as the case of the Narragansetts makes clear, even after a century of evangelization and education, Native cultures were still as dynamic and engaged in 1810 as they had been in 1710.

When John Lyon Gardiner sat down to write a few "notes and observations" regarding the town of East Hampton on Long Island in 1798 (much like Thomas Jefferson's *Notes on the State of Virginia*), he devoted only a precious few paragraphs to the Montauketts. Clustered on the eastern tip of the lower fork of Long Island, Gardiner noted that most of the Montaukett males "get their living by whaling at sea, or from the shore at Montock." The Montauketts enjoyed a thousand acres that, in Gardiner's assessment, was more than they were able to "improve." Gardiner gave a predictably non-Indian spin to the long-standing controversies over land when he noted that though the Montauketts "sold their lands to the English 130 or 140 years ago in the most incontestable manner, they are not satisfied with the bargain that was made & the pay they received." Despite an ongoing, thriving Native presence, like most other late eighteenth-century Americans, Gardiner had an outlook regarding the Natives that was dour indeed: "Rum has reduced them from a very powerful tribe to a few persons," he stated; "they are continually disappearing."[7]

Gardiner's descriptions illuminate the various problems New England Natives still faced in the years following the Revolutionary War, when Americans were hammering out the contours of an Indian policy that—for the first time—was free from the restrictions of the British crown. Although it varied slightly from state to state in New England, elements of this policy included an amplified paternalism combined with relative indifference, all framed by an increasingly romanticized view of these "noble" tribes as disappearing.[8] Life for Natives in this period was not easy, to be sure. Contributing to the overall social and economic difficulties for reservation individuals and communities, however, was alcoholism and the resulting social problems—in the worst cases, indebtedness, poverty, imprisonment, and dispossession. Indian tribal councils and individuals repeatedly appealed to their overseers and state assemblies to restrict the sale of alcohol on reservations.[9] In some cases, Indian churches took the lead. In March 1787, the Narragansetts complained to the Rhode Island General Assembly that their church—"chiefly Indians of the Denomination of Separates"—was plagued by some enterprising nearby individuals who "make a practice of selling strong Drink on those days appointed for Worship." As a result, during the middle of the worship services drunken individuals who were "loose, disorderly, vain & thoughtless, sally upon the Meeting, replete with Language horrid to the Ear, and Behaviours disagreeable to behold," to the general disruption of the congregation. The General Assembly responded immediately, passing a law that prohibited both the drinking and the selling of "any strong liquors" within one mile of the meetinghouse.[10]

More than ever, Natives left the reservation to pursue a wide variety of day labor opportunities. Women often produced crafts—baskets, spoons, brooms—to sell in local urban centers. Of particular interest to some of the males in the seaboard communities were fishing, whaling, and seafaring. Such menial day labor often went unnoticed, except for the occasional reference to deaths of Indians while at work that appeared in the local newspapers. For example, on Monday evening, August 21, 1797, Joshua Ashbow (Ashpo) fell "between a vessel and a wharf" in New London and drowned.[11] Natives also continued to labor as indentured servants, sometimes thrust into such situations by their parents, but at other times voluntarily entering into agreements as teenagers. Such was the case with William Apess, a Pequot youth who was essentially orphaned at a young age, beaten by his grandmother, became a ward of the town of Colchester, and was eventually bound out as an indentured servant and passed around from family to family over the course of several years.[12] Once again, such servitude was so common as to be unnoticed except for cases when the servant rebelled and ran away. On November 22, 1804, a nineteen-year-old indentured Indian boy named Richard Ned ran away from Stephen Billings in Groton, prompting Billings to advertise a measly four cents as a reward for his return.[13]

Native families and communities also received help from local town governments, who occasionally voted to provide monetary or material aid for Native families and individuals who needed it. In 1788, the Shinnecocks petitioned the state of New York for aid, noting that all of their land that formerly allowed "Hunting, Fishing, and Fowling" was gone, and they were poorer now than their forefathers had been when the English first arrived.[14] In 1793, the Stonington magistrates paid for several coffins for the family of Benjamin Garrett, and a year later the town also provided money for Garrett's rent and firewood.[15]

In the face of difficulties, however, Natives pursued various strategies to secure their land base and protect their cultural sovereignty. Most Native communities continued to seek legal recourse to either retain or recover their lands. Other Indian individuals—usually males, and often unmarried ones—opted to leave the reservations in favor of pursuing better fortunes elsewhere. A few Indian towns became even more protective of their own communities and stridently policed tribal membership. Despite the forlorn pronouncements that Indians were a disappearing race, doomed to extinction, at every turn Native communities proved them wrong. In many ways, life continued on much as it had done before, often with an intensification of trends that were well in motion by the mid-eighteenth century, if not before, especially with regard to land rights, migration, and labor.[16]

Communal Land Use and Controversies

In the postwar years, the most visible representation of Native presence remained the reservation communities located around nodes of social life that had existed throughout the eighteenth century. Although reservations were not usually the numerical center of Native populations in New England by 1800, they nonetheless still served as the social and political anchor for a wide swath of Native families, even those who moved away for work or marriage.[17] Local power dynamics between the reservation communities and the states remained largely unchanged after the Revolution, with most Indian communities remaining under the jurisdiction of the state and mediated by local overseers. The one major change in the postwar years was that the powerful and often-used recourse to the British crown and regional royal representatives was effectively removed. Native nations felt this absence immediately after the war's end in 1783, as the Mohegans and Niantics stated plainly in 1785 when, in response to restrictions on their fishing rights imposed by the state, they sharply reminded the Connecticut Assembly that "Whilst the King of England had authority over here they order no such things upon us."[18] The US federal government was hardly an equal replacement, and although Natives sometimes appealed to Congress and the president, the political leverage was rarely the same.

As a result, negotiation with local towns and states became even more critical. Indian communities continued to seek legal recourse to defend their land rights and presence, took active roles in selecting their state overseers, and petitioned the state general assemblies for relief. Local governments, however, were just as often the problem as they were the solution. In 1797 the East Hampton trustees required the Montauketts' numerous hogs that were roaming the local forests and swamps in large numbers to be fitted with a nose ring or risk being captured and impounded. They then proceeded to round up the pigs before the Montauketts had time to install the newly required rings.[19] The Montauketts petitioned the New York state government for aid in 1800, 1807, and 1818, each time describing the systematic destruction of timber and crops on Montaukett lands and, in extreme cases, the burning down of wigwams as a way to frighten the remaining Montauketts into submission.[20] At Lantern Hill, thirty Pequots—twenty-two of whom were women—petitioned the Connecticut General Assembly in May 1788 to reappoint competent overseers who would protect them from their neighbors who wanted to "to strip us of everything we posses."[21] Governmental efforts helped, but were often ineffective.

Overall, however, most reservation communities developed an even stronger ethic of land usage in the 1780s and beyond, in part because of the shifting demographics on the reservations (older and infirm) and the ongoing need to care for an even larger population of people who could not support themselves. One recurring issue was that of leasing individual lands. Of particular interest to the Indian tribal councils were Natives who, when they desired to move off of the reservation, found what amounted to be a lifelong tenant for their lands and made the terms of the lease twenty, thirty, and even one hundred years, thus guaranteeing the landlord a trickle of stable income over time. Generally, Indian councils and state representatives resented such arrangements because they bypassed the internal charity structure common to late eighteenth-century Native communities, in which a portion of the rental income (or, in some cases, the entire rental income of common lands) went to assisting the poorer and older members of the reservation community.[22]

In this context, the Brothertown migration proved to be yet another point of division and contention. On almost every major reservation, the Indian councils complained of individuals who leased their lands to fund the move to New York but never contributed to the overall financial care and well-being of the tribes. Natives who moved to Brothertown wanted it both ways; they desired a new life in New York but still wanted to make a claim on common or sequestered lands on specific reservations back in New England. Tribal councils would have none of it. In May 1811, representatives from Mashantucket complained to the General Assembly about Pequots who had "Remov'd to the Oneida Country" and yet continued to lay claim to some of the common land at Mashantucket based on their ancestral connections to the tribe. Such claims, the white overseer Samuel Mott explained, undermined the intention of the overseers and tribe that the common land should be "Improv'd for the Benefit of the Tribe."[23] The solution most tribes adopted was to restrict access to hereditary lands for those who left, and, for those who already owned such land, to restrict the length of the leases to tenants. The Narragansetts in 1792 limited the term of such leases to six years, with the land reverting to the heirs of the original Native deed holder or, in the absence of heirs, the tribe as a whole.[24] Similarly, the Mohegan tribal council decreed that land allotments should stay in a particular family only "as long as any of said Family remain" and should otherwise "revert back to the Tribe at large."[25]

In some cases dispossession still occurred from within. At Narragansett in particular, despite having effectively replaced the sachemship with an Indian council in the 1770s, in the 1780s and beyond Natives remained suspicious that they had merely traded one kind of irresponsible form of governance for another. Like the sachem Thomas Ninigret three decades earlier, the Indian council found itself in debt and was forced to sell lands to pay off those debts. Some Narragansetts were convinced that "the Monies arising from the Sales and Rents of the Lands, were not appropriated towards the Discharge of the Debts of the Tribe."[26] Two decades later, after a particularly heavy round of land sales to alleviate debts, forty Narragansetts petitioned the Rhode Island General Assembly, asking that all land sales be halted at Narragansett until the Indian Council could give an accounting of which lands were being sold and what was being done with the money. "We have good Reasons to believe," the petitioners asserted in 1813, that the money is "taken up and Spent in Spirituous Liquors to the Benefit of the Council only."[27]

More generally, New England Natives retained surprisingly "traditional" notions of land usage, despite the burgeoning market economy flourishing around them in the early nineteenth century. In 1809 one white observer reported that although the Narragansetts had what he considered to be a sizable amount of land at their disposal—an irregularly shaped three miles square of land, or approximately 1,900 acres—the Natives were not actively farming much of it. Some of the better portions of land was leased to local white farmers; a large wooded portion was reserved to provide timber for firewood and building materials; a small section was used for modest garden plots; and the rest was of "indifferent quality." The Narragansetts still practiced seasonal patterns of hunting and fishing, supplementing when necessary with a few cultivated crops and produce traded with local farmers and merchants.[28] This contrasted sharply with the

Brothertown community, which at the same time boasted two thousand acres that had been put into agricultural production, producing in 1812 approximately 11,300 bushels of grain and 3,400 bushels of potatoes.[29] This merely confirms that many of the Brothertown migrants from New England were among the most Anglicized and industrialized of the New England Natives, having embraced Euroamerican-style farming and cattle raising.

Mobility, Demographics, and the Struggle for Identity

In the years following the Revolutionary War, even during these broader patterns of population shifting and loss, the primary centers of Native population concentration in southeastern New England remained in 1800 where they had been for the prior century: at Shinnecock and Montauk on Long Island; Mohegan, Mashantucket, Lantern Hill, Farmington, and Niantic in Connecticut; and Narragansett in Rhode Island. At least two dozen or more nodes of social gathering on and off reservations served as centers and crossroads for an increasingly multiracial population.[30] Other smaller communities gathered at locales in all three states, including western Connecticut (especially at Pachgatgoch), northeastern/eastern Connecticut (Colchester), and southeastern Rhode Island.

Native communities both benefited and suffered from an increased Indian mobility in a variety of directions. Although such mobility and population dispersal had been unfolding slowly through much of the eighteenth century, the years between 1770 and 1820 were a more concentrated time of such movement in southern New England, which often led—at least initially—to a slight decline in observable reservation populations. Individuals and families migrated regionally within New England to pool resources and to be nearer to jobs and sales markets. A few Indians from Mohegan, Narragansett, and Long Island, for example, moved to Mashpee.[31] Some Tunxis, instead of migrating west, moved east, joining larger Indian reserves in the southeastern part of Connecticut.[32] An extended Pequot family, according to tribal oral tradition, moved from Connecticut to just outside Providence around 1800 in an attempt to be closer to employment and fishing opportunities.[33] Individual Indian lives wound their way over a surprisingly wide geographical terrain, particularly during their teen years. Although William Apess might have been somewhat exceptional, his journeys included Colchester, New London, New York, Montreal, Vermont, Quebec, and then, finally, in 1812, back home to Colchester in Eastern Connecticut (although he didn't stay there for long, either).[34] Brothertown was one small part of this broader pattern of mobility and reservation decline, but trends in other locales confirm that Native New England as a whole was experiencing mobility and population dispersal in far greater ways.

Over time, these other locations simply became an extension of New England Indian networks of community and kinship, as well as one more possible destination for Indian individuals and families who increasingly sought better fortunes off the reservation. As such, the connections between the New England Native reservation communities and those who left remained surprisingly strong. Many New England Indians felt a close connection to the land near the reservations as a place where their ancestors had lived and died, where family members were buried, and where they themselves had been born and raised. Although the majority of the Farmingtons left for New York in the 1780s, groups of Natives often returned from Brothertown to Farmington to visit friends and relatives and "hold dances at the old burying place, and evening powwows, and give splendid exhibitions of their agility and strength."[35] Timothy Woodbridge, the grandson of Jonathan Edwards who was born in Stockbridge the same year the Stockbridge Indians left for New York, recalled that every year a group of Mohicans would return from New Stockbridge to Stockbridge—thirty to forty per year—in order to "rekindle the fire upon the old hearthstones," spend time in the old Indian burial grounds at the west end of town, build wigwams for the winter on the sides of nearby mountains, and "occup[y] themselves in making baskets and brooms for a subsistence." Woodbridge was especially struck by the "wild Indian costume" the Indians wore as they strolled through the town, peddling their wares.[36] Such a return was likely a means of maintaining ties with Mohican relatives and friends who never removed in the first place and lived in the hills outside town.[37] In at least one instance, a whole group of New England Indians gave up on the Brothertown project altogether. In the early 1830s—precisely when the Brothertown and New Stockbridge Indians decided to move to Wisconsin from New York—twenty or so Natives returned to Mohegan and "resumed their rights there."[38]

Despite these various departures and migrations, in a few cases the reservation populations either remained stable or even increased between 1800 and 1820. Although the Narragansetts reported only 150 individuals on their lands in 1809, by 1820 they easily counted 400.[39] Such gains could have been due to consolidation of other smaller Native communities but was also likely due to intermarriage with local African and white populations. A number of whites lived with or near the Narragansetts, some of whom had married Narragansett women. Such was the case with Frederick Bosemsdes, a Swiss Protestant immigrant who married the Narragansett Fanny Daniels. Bosemsdes also served as a functional go-between—in an ironic reversal of the cultural intermediary role that Natives often played—typically translating documents and writing letters for the Narragansett community.[40] The Narragansetts were not alone. At Mashantucket, the Pequots were known to be "extremely hospitable to all vagabonds; receiving, without hesitation, all that come to them, whether white, mulatto, Indian or negro."[41]

In addition to ongoing intermarriage and an increased presence of blacks, reservation populations also grew when states and local towns tried to force indigent Natives back onto the reservations to avoid the cost of supporting them. In February 1816, for example, a law passed in Rhode Island permitted individual towns to physically send to the Narragansett reservation indigent Indians who were unable to take care of themselves. Such heavy-handed moves saved local towns a load of money by protecting them from having to take on the financial burden of supporting Natives as wards of the town. The Narragansetts, however, did not appreciate this new policy and tried to fight it. In February 1817, the Narragansett Indian council wrote to the General Assembly complaining that the town of South Kingstown had recently forced them to take in Hannah Fowler Jack based on the new law passed a year earlier. Hannah's husband and son had both passed away, leaving Hannah in the unfortunate—but common—position of having no further political or legal identity. The town took her land and—now unable to support herself—declared her a ward of the town and promptly shipped her to the Narragansett reservation. When the Narragansetts protested—claiming Hannah's land was wrongfully taken from her—and sent her back to South Kingstown, the town returned her once again to the reservation, threatening to prosecute the Indian council if they sent her back again.[42]

Although racial concerns surfaced periodically in the New England Native communities in southern New England, most Native communities there exhibited less of the racial anxiety regarding blacks that was demonstrated by the Brothertown Indians. The Narragansett Indian church in 1809 boasted between thirty and forty members, and the actual worship service included a small number of white people and a sizable proportion of "colored" individuals. At the SPGNA-funded Narragansett school, Indian, black, and white children all sat together in classes, although the tribe had at first voted not to allow any white children to attend.[43] Despite the relative inclusivity of Native communities, the presence of "strange" Indians and intermarried blacks did cause real problems and tensions, often through black men marrying Indian women.[44] In response, reservation residents at times actively policed their own communities. In 1788 the Mohegans drove off two members of the George family, Pompey George and the widow of Tom George.[45] Just a year later, in 1789, when the state of Connecticut put together an official tribal roll, the Mohegans challenged one family in particular, the Moses Muzzeens family, first on the basis that no one could testify to Moses's lineage, and additionally because "he is Blacker than our Indians, and we think he is from Guinny partly." Either way, the Mohegans reasoned, "the whole Tribe objects against him," not just because he would then have access to their land, but, perhaps more important, since he fathered "Guinney" and "European" children, the Mohegans were afraid that he was setting a bad example for their own daughters.[46]

On most reservations, Natives and blacks who were deemed outsiders were given second-class status. With the Narragansetts, in 1792 the Rhode Island Assembly limited annual votes cast for tribal council members to males older than twenty-one and born of either an Indian woman or an Indian man and non-Negro woman (apparently in this case the son of an Indian-white marriage was allowed to vote).[47] Such laws were intended to limit who could vote, but they did not restrict who could live on the land or take part in other community activities. In practice, however, the Narragansett community was surprisingly interracial. Inheritance practices were still maintained by the traditional matrilineal calculus (following the mother's bloodline), which meant that far more people lived on the land than were actually considered to properly belong to the tribe. Since the Narragansetts had been intermarrying with blacks and even a few whites for half a century or more, Coe observed—rather subjectively—that "very few clear Indians are now on the land."[48]

Similarly, leaders at Brothertown claimed that their racial concerns and policies, while perhaps more stringent than in the New England Indian communities, grew organically out of their home communities back east. In practice, at least after the mid-1780s, when the settlement actually got under way, people of mixed ethnicities (and even white people) certainly lived on the land, either as renters, leasers, squatters, or relatives of "pure" Indians. But the leadership of Brothertown was rather uncompromising about who could *own* the land. In the mid-1790s, for example, Sarah Pendleton (formerly Potteogue), a Narragansett Indian, and her "negro" husband, James Pendleton, moved to Brothertown and requested a plot of land—as they would have been allowed to do given their affiliation with the Narragansetts. When James's mixed ethnicity was found out, however, Sarah's request for land was flatly denied. "It has been an immemorial custom among all the nations as well Narragansetts as others from whom the Brothertown Indians descended," the Brothertown leaders asserted, "that if any indian woman or girl married a negro man, or any one who had a mixture of negro blood, she forfeited all her rights and privileges as an individual of the Nation from [which] she and they descended and particularly all right and title to lands belonging to the Tribe or Tribes to whom they belonged."[49]

But racial policing ultimately failed at Brothertown, too. In other instances Indians who married whites—a rather rare occurrence—were not similarly penalized. William Coheis (Coyhis) married a white woman named Mary and moved to Brothertown in 1800. William briefly served as the town clerk before passing away in 1804, but that same year his sons were assigned a plot of land with the stipulation that they take care of their white mother.[50] By 1855, Thomas Commuck, a Narragansett-turned-Brothertown Indian reported to the Wisconsin Historical Society that "Already has inter-marriage with the whites so changed the Brothertowns, in complexion, that three-quarters of them would be

readily considered as white, where they were not known, and in another generation our Indian blood will probably become so intermixed with the general mass
of mankind."[51]

Native Christianity and Renewed Evangelism

All of these textured features of New England Native American communities in
the early nineteenth century largely went unnoticed by a group of individuals
and institutions who had invested—for good or for ill—quite a bit in Native
Americans during the colonial period: ministers, missionaries, and missionary
societies. The tangible absence of missionary societies on Native lands was a noticeable change that stemmed directly from the Revolutionary War. This was
particularly true with regard to the New England Company. As a London-based
British organization, the NEC leaders voted to discontinue funding for any missionaries working within the United States after the war's end (funding was
largely directed to Canada instead). This absence of NEC resources did not
always affect Native churches in southeastern New England (which often operated without the support of the NEC), but it did reduce the educational offerings for which Natives had worked so hard to maintain control. The loss was
tangible, especially because the SPGNA, the Boston-based missionary society
that was formed to take the NEC's place in 1787 (and in part revived from the
failed 1762 society), preferred to focus on the more remote missionary efforts in
New York and Maine as well as a few established missions in Massachusetts
instead of the Native groups in Connecticut and Rhode Island.[52] This focus was
in part because the SPGNA's mission—much like that of the Anglican SPG
founded in 1701—was aimed at relatively unchurched whites in rural parts of
the country. The new SPGNA did, however, fund a few white missionaries to
Indians in Massachusetts, Maine, and New York starting in 1790 with Zechariah
Mayhew (Martha's Vineyard), John Sergeant, Jr. (New Stockbridge), and Gideon
Hawley (Mashpee). The SPGNA also flooded Native American and remote
white communities with an astonishing supply of books, a bit ironically, since
literacy levels were still surprisingly low, especially among the older generations.
By 1804, the SPGNA had purchased and distributed 607 Bibles, 1,151 New Tes-
taments, 1,649 spelling books, 801 Psalters, 2,310 primers, 140 copies of Isaac
Watts' *Psalms and Hymns*, 768 copies of Doddridge's *Rise and Progress of Religion
in the Soul*, and an additional 9,898 pamphlets, books, and treatises.[53]

More broadly, the early national period marked the beginning of a surge in
new state and national missionary societies, which had as their focus the spread
and support of Christian practice, morals, and values to all populations, whether
white or Indian. Such societies were merely the beginning of a torrent of

reformist-minded societies that proliferated throughout the country between 1800 and 1860, focusing on prison reform, keeping the Sabbath, temperance, and a host of other cultural reforms and changes. These societies were often, but not always, extensions of the vibrant evangelicalism that emerged out of the Second Great Awakening (1820s and 1830s in the northeast).[54] The New York Missionary Society, for example, was founded in 1796 to "send the Gospel to the frontier settlements and among Indian tribes in the United States."[55] The Connecticut Missionary Society was founded in 1798 to "Christianize the heathen in North America, and to support and promote Christian knowledge in the new settlements within the United States."[56] Similar societies were founded in New Hampshire (1801), Rhode Island (1803), Maine (1807), and Vermont (1818).[57] In some cases, at least, the SPGNA worked in tandem with state missionary societies (that also received funding from state governments) to sponsor local missionary and educational efforts.[58] Evangelically motivated Protestants also formed missionary societies whose primary focus was outside the geopolitical boundary of the United States, such as the American Board of Commissioners for Foreign Missions (ABCFM, chartered in 1812), the Congregational society that sent missionaries to East Asia (including Hawaii), Central Europe, and Africa, as well as to the Cherokees in the American southeast.[59] Ironically, internationally minded groups like the ABCFM articulated a vision for world evangelization based on the labors of the seventeenth-century "Apostle to the Indians," John Eliot, even as they overlooked Eliot's relatively unfinished business among the hundreds of Natives still in New England.[60]

The SPGNA and individual state missionary societies in New England were up front and mostly unapologetic for their inattention to New England's Natives.[61] "Where is the field of our labours?" Abiel Holmes queried the members of the SPGNA at the annual meeting in 1808. His answer was immediate and telling: "Not in our backyard, but in a distant wilderness."[62] No missionaries were sent to Rhode Island Indians until twenty years after the founding of the SPGNA, and no missionaries were sent specifically to Connecticut's Natives through 1840, although, in the case of the Mohegans, educational and evangelistic input came at a more local level in the 1820s and 1830s.[63] The SPGNA also exhibited very little initial interest in funding Native missionaries and schoolteachers, which represented a fairly abrupt change in policy from long-standing NEC practice.[64] It is tempting to speculate that the Wheelock educational debacle of the late 1760s, along with the clear and decisive statements and demonstrations of Native autonomy in Connecticut and Rhode Island, effectively warned those involved in the founding of the SPGNA that local Indian nations were not worth additional time and effort. More likely, however, was the deep-seated belief that Natives were not numerically significant enough to warrant attention. Abiel Holmes, president of the SPGNA, lamented of the New

England Natives that "most of them are extinct" and that there "can scarcely be found a collection of Indians sufficiently numerous to be denominated a tribe." Such rhetoric belied reality, as he well knew, for even as he lamented Natives' extinction, he laid out a plan to "meliorate the condition" of these same Indians, which included instituting schools for their children, giving them tools and utensils necessary for agricultural pursuits, and offering them—once again— the "knowledge of CHRIST."[65]

Perhaps the most comprehensive insight into the ongoing Christian engagement and practice—or nonpractice, as the case may have been—comes from the Narragansett reservation, thanks to the meticulous journals kept by SPGNA missionaries and schoolteachers between 1809 and 1820.[66] They reveal that in the opening decade of the nineteenth century, the Narragansett Indian Church was still going strong in surprising continuity with eighteenth-century practices. In part, this continuity was aided by an unbroken succession of Christian Indian leadership. Upon Niles's death in 1785, the semi-literate Narragansett leader John Sekatur was selected as minister, serving in that capacity until his death in 1808.[67] Although an Indian minister had not yet been identified to replace Sekatur a year later, on many Sundays the church was supplied with a variety of itinerate Indian Baptist preachers from nearby Connecticut. On Sunday, June 29, 1811, for example, Coe noted the involvement of two preachers: "A Molatto who is a professed preacher," and an "illiterate Baptist preacher."[68] In 1812, the Narragansetts reported they had a "stated publick religious instructor" who was a "mulatto man" and did not belong to the tribe. He, like Niles before him, was illiterate, but this didn't stop the Massachusetts Bible Society from sending "a large handsome copy" of the Bible, along with several other Bibles to be distributed to the adults.[69]

The Narragansett congregation met each Sunday in their own church building for vigorous five-hour services. The hallmark of Narragansett church services was free-exhortation and sharing that represented the possibility of genuinely democratic participation—regardless of gender—that most New England churches born in the excitement of the Great Awakening had long abandoned.[70] As in eighteenth-century Separate Indian churches, it was highly unusual for only one preacher to share in each service. Instead, perhaps one or two designated preachers would speak, followed by or even intermingled with most of the people present taking turns sharing "their feelings" and giving examples from their lives intended to instill faith in others present. Throughout, other congregants would chime in, saying, "Hold on brother J. Hold on brother G, Hold on sister S. &c.," or "Be strong, one & all be strong."[71] Such collective exhortation and prayer took up most of the time and to outsiders could seem like a loud and confusing jumble of voices. Throughout, various hymns were interspersed between the prayers and exhortations, sung in unison and completely from memory. Such hymns had been passed down in the Narragansett Christian community for seventy years and included hymns from Isaac Watts, the famous British eighteenth-century composer whose hymns aided the Great Awakening. While singing such hymns, the congregation often "took hold of one another's hands & reeled back & forth."[72] The Narragansett church was hardly unique; such practices were observed in other Native Christian churches in southeastern New England as well. At Lantern Hill, a visitor reported in 1820 that during the monthly meetings of the small group of Christian Pequots, the most notable feature was the time when each person present spoke in turn.[73]

Even more than when Niles was their minister, the Narragansett Indian Church had moved firmly into a partisan Baptist belief while seemingly relaxing a bit of the moral policing that the congregation had exhibited at times. The Narragansett Christians practiced adult baptism only, although they did hold an open communion, meaning that all were welcomed to take part in the Lord's Supper.[74] Narragansett religious life still intertwined more traditional elements with religious ecstatic belief, including a heavy emphasis on personal revelation and the experience of dreams. Having spent many long months worshipping with the Narragansetts over the course of three years, Coe concluded that "they often tell of things extraordinary, & the most marvelous accounts appear most to please."[75] On Sunday, July 21, 1811, during the normal worship service that was held in a private house "for the benefit of an aged infirm woman," one of the elderly Indian woman present recounted an experience from her youth. As a young girl she was walking in the woods when suddenly "she was taken to heaven, while her body lay, like a lump of clay, on the earth—and that her spirit returned to one end of it, & it again rose to life."[76] Coe seems to have been the only person present who thought such experiences to be exceptional.

Some Narragansetts also continued to participate in a regional Native Christian network that included Pequots, Mohegans, Montauketts, and, occasionally, a few Brothertown Indians. These meetings were "common"—perhaps every month or two—and "many attend," according to Coe. The content of such meetings was not strictly "religious," but they often occurred over the weekends (perhaps for other practical reasons). On June 9, 1811, for example, when Coe showed up to preach at the Narragansett church, he found that their "principal leaders were absent to hold a meeting out of town." Similarly, on August 11, 1811, the Narragansett leaders traveled to the Mashantucket reservation, where they met with natives from Connecticut, Long Island, and New York, including some Brothertown Indians, to whom the Narragansetts "sent their love."[77] The activities of such meetings were often reported at the next church service at Narragansett to inform those who had not attended of the various developments in other Native communities. Coe blamed these regional meetings for the ongoing attachment of Native Christians to "their own modes" of church services.[78]

Nonetheless, despite the seeming vitality of the Narragansett Indian Church and the ways that it functioned for some individuals as a social and cultural anchor for the reservation, it was not in fact a central part of the weekly routine for the majority of the Narragansett community. Although many of the Narragansett adults were members—approximately forty—on most Sundays far fewer than that actually attended the church. Near the end of his second stint among the Narragansetts in 1810, Coe lamented that the "Lord's day & public worship are little regarded by most of the Tribe," and he often reported Indians at work or play on Sundays instead of attending the church.[79] One Sunday morning when Coe set out to preach to the white Charlestown residents at the schoolhouse, he passed a local store where he saw three members of the Indian council drunk and acting disorderly, along with "other black people."[80] Even more than in the eighteenth century, far more women than men were involved in the church at Narragansett and—seemingly—elsewhere. Fifteen of the twenty congregants present on Saturday, June 29, were women, for example.[81] Even complete outsiders observed a similarly low level of involvement by Indian males. When a visitor passed through Charlestown in 1812, he stopped at the Narragansett Indian Church and "found a few of the female members of the church still living and active in religious affairs," while most of the male members of the church were "absent on a fishing voyage."[82]

Overall, the Narragansetts still retained the vibrant sense of autonomy that drove the formation of their Separate church in the first place in the 1740s and motivated them to chase Fish and Deake off their lands in the 1770s. When Coe arrived, the Narragansetts initially seemed welcoming—so much so that they wrote a letter to the SPGNA expressing their "sincere & grateful acknowledgement for the privilege of a Missionary."[83] He was therefore surprised at the deeply ingrained suspicion of him during his successive trips in 1810 and 1811. When he returned in September 1810, in both the church service on September 2 and the tribal council meeting the following day (to which he had been invited), he found his presence and motivations strongly challenged by a few individuals. During the church service, several individuals made speeches that suggested that Coe and the SPGNA had "evil designs" in mind. At the tribal council the next day, a few leaders were more explicit. Some feared that Coe planned to "take the government of the church," even though they "wished to carry on their own worship." Another mixed-ethnicity man who had married into the Narragansett community suggested that Coe and the SPGNA "wished to get their land."[84] A few months later after a worship service, some of the Narragansetts publicly asked Coe again why he had come among them. When Coe patiently explained his mission and the nature of the SPGNA, the Narragansetts present seemed uncomfortable with the idea that Coe might be getting paid by the SPGNA for being among them. This was likely because—as in the eighteenth century—they thought ministers should not be paid, but it was also partly because they believed Coe's salary might be taking away money that they might otherwise be receiving directly from the SPGNA.[85]

A year later, Coe was still unable to shake the suspicions of him and called a meeting to ask what their main concerns were. The objections came fast and furious. One person asserted that the Narragansetts had the sole right to the meetinghouse, and Coe should preach in a different location if he insisted on preaching at all. Others objected yet again to the fact that he was paid by the SPGNA. More important, however, was the Narragansetts' resentment that Coe's preaching "prevented their speaking, when they felt the spirit"—a direct echo of their similar resentment toward Joseph Park for reproving the Narragansetts in the 1740s when they spoke out during the service. Coe's Congregationalism was also an issue, since the Indians were Baptists. The overall sense was one of a studied protectiveness of their modes of worship and autonomy. The Narragansett Christians feared that if they "gave way" to Coe, they might "lose their government," which was something "former Elders" had specifically charged them not to do. Other examples warned them as well: one individual told a story of a "tribe which had in that way lost their house of worship."[86]

Despite these objections, the Narragansetts grudgingly tolerated Coe's presence, in part because of the connections and services he represented. Coe lamented that they had a clear preference for Indian Baptist preachers and flatly refused to receive regular preaching from Coe or any Congregationalist, Presbyterian, or Anglican minister. They did, however, consent to let him preach on Sundays when they were unable to get a regional Baptist Indian itinerant to come preach to them. Even then, however, Coe's sermons seemed more a necessary inconvenience to sit through than an important part of the service. On the Sundays when Coe was allowed to preach, the Narragansetts sat somewhat impatiently through his lengthy, hour-long sermon and then proceeded to spend the next four hours conducting the church service in "their mode"—with vigorous hymn-singing and collaborative exhortation—while a disgruntled and likely bored Coe looked on. Indeed, so fearful was Coe of imposing on the Narragansetts that he made a concerted effort to leave the area on the weekends when another Indian minister was preaching at the Narragansett church. On Saturday, September 22, 1810, for example, Coe recorded in his journal that he "rode about 15 miles to Towerhill, as the Indians expected two preachers," where he visited two white families instead.[87]

With education, however, things were vastly different. Even before Coe showed up on Narragansett lands, Indian parents were seeking education for their children. The school that the NEC funded and the Narragansetts built in the late 1760s had fallen into disuse (likely after Deake left in the mid-1770s), and at some point in the opening years of the nineteenth century, it weakened structurally and blew down. By 1809, there was no school or school building on Narragansett lands, although a few families who could afford to do so sent their children to a local white public school. In the winter of 1807–1808 (before Coe arrived), a white schoolmaster held classes two miles from the Narragansett reservation, and fifteen Indian children attended. Some of the Narragansett parents also learned through local magistrates that the SPGNA might be sending a missionary their way, and they "took a great interest in the subject, and made inquiries in Newport [to the RIDMS], from time to time, respecting it."[88]

Despite their misgivings about Coe's presence after 1809, the tribal leadership usually affirmed the overall plan of educating their children, and between 1809 and 1811 wrote three letters to the SPGNA leadership, thanking them for Coe's presence and the schoolhouse that was planned.[89] "It was evident that they had the greater regard for the school," Coe noted dryly, than for his sermons.[90] When Coe arrived for a second short-term stay among the Narragansetts (September–November 1810), he continued to preach to them but also—at the Indians' request—held a school for Narragansett children, which attracted an average of twenty or so students for several months.[91] This school, which increasingly occupied the majority of Coe's time in 1810 and 1811, eventually became the primary point of successful collaboration between the SPGNA and the Narragansetts.

Despite the Narragansetts' embrace of education, the Natives were clearly the ones in control of the situation and decided which parts of what Coe was offering they wanted to accept. Consequently, a deflated Coe wrote to Abiel Holmes in 1811 and reported that "extreme fondness of the church of their own modes & the indifference of others to all religion" made his prospects among them very bleak indeed. Instead, Coe recommended that the SPGNA hire an English schoolteacher, who could, under the cover of education—which the Narragansetts desired for their children—"instruct them in the doctrines & duties of our holy religion."[92] Coe made two more trips to Rhode Island, in 1812 and in 1814. During the 1812 trip he spent precious few days at Narragansett, stopping by mainly to check on the school. On his final SPGNA missionary journey across Rhode Island in 1814, he did not even bother to visit the Narragansetts at all.[93]

Based in part on the Coe's recommendation, the SPGNA, the Narragansetts, and the RIDMS collaborated to build a schoolhouse on Narragansett lands. The SPGNA contributed $100; the RIDMS gave $80; and the Narragansetts provided the lumber and some of the labor. On July 20, 1812, Jeremiah Niles, a non-Indian SPGNA missionary, opened up the Narragansett school in the new building. Niles kept school from July 20 through October 22 in 1812, and then again between late November 1812 and early April 1813. Niles was replaced after April 1813 by Silas Shores, another SPGNA missionary, who kept school fairly continuously through at least 1815. As in the colonial period, this proffered education was heavily and intentionally intertwined with Christian doctrine, teaching, and morality. Jeremiah Niles described his educational curriculum in 1812 as being almost entirely based upon learning to read out of the Bible. Niles opened the school each day with prayers and then led the class through a reading of a chapter in the Bible, after which he gave them his interpretation of it. He then assigned a different Bible chapter to the different age groups in the school, and a new chapter or two after lunch. A portion of the afternoon was also set aside to teach them how "to Spell," and then he closed the school day around 5 P.M. with prayer.[94] Silas Shores reported in 1814 that his "general practice has been twice a week, & frequently 5 times" to teach the catechism to every student, even those who had not yet learned the alphabet. Additionally, he gave them "moral & religious council" and always observed morning and evening prayers."[95]

Both Niles and Shores kept meticulously detailed attendance charts for their schools. These charts reveal that a large number of children attended the school for at least a few days in each session, but that only a small core attended a large percentage of the possible school days. Niles and Shores both learned that certain times of the year—late summer for harvest, and midwinter—were not productive times to hold school. For the late November 1812 through early April 1813 session of school, for example, Niles recorded that forty-four (unique) children attended the school. The most who attended on one day was twenty-four on December 30; the low was a string of days around March 25, when only one student showed up.[96]

Actual progress in education was slow, perhaps hindered by the sporadic attendance of Native children. By 1816, Shores—having grown increasingly disillusioned with the prospect of effecting any long-term change, even through education—declined to be reappointed as the Narragansett schoolmaster. "I cannot think of any means to recommend to you for the benefit of those poor Natives," Shores wrote to Holmes dismissively, and instead recommended that the SPGNA's money would be better used to have a missionary serve the surrounding non-Indian communities, who also lacked regular church services. Still believing in the importance of education, however, the SPGNA hired—for the first time at Narragansett in the nineteenth century—an Indian schoolmaster, Mr. Paul, to keep school.[97] Starting in 1819, the SPGNA also hired the white missionary Frederick Baylies to oversee education at the Narragansett community, which he continued into the mid-1830s.[98]

Such educational efforts, as in the eighteenth century, produced results that disappointed the schoolteachers and missionaries but gave individual children a vital boost in literacy. One such youth was Tobias Ross, who was given a basic education in the early 1810s at the SPGNA school and later became a Narragansett secretary, scribe, and leader. Similarly, in 1811, a six-year-old Narragansett boy named Thomas Commuck began attending the SPGNA-sponsored school and continued sporadically through 1814. In 1825, Thomas Commuck moved to New York to join the Brothertowns, and in the early 1830s, he made the migration to the new settlement in Wisconsin. Commuck's 1855 report to the Wisconsin Historical Society contains one of the most-cited narratives of the Brothertown movement and is a direct product of the literacy training he received as a young boy in the SPGNA school at Narragansett.[99]

One of Commuck's lesser-known publications illustrates the fascinating uses to which some Native leaders put their education and Christianity. In 1845, Commuck published an eclectic collection of 121 hymns, titled *Indian Melodies*.[100] Commuck's hymnal—printed in New York with the explicit aim of making money—was a complicated text that accomplished several things at once. Far more than a simple collection of Christian hymns, Commuck designed it as a repository for—and a shaper of—collective Native memory and history, simultaneously serving a wide Indian audience as well as a non-Native American readership whose romantic appetite for Indians of yore was reaching an all-time high (Henry Wadsworth Longfellow's *Song of Hiawatha*, for example, was published a decade later). The title of each hymn had nothing to do with the theological content of the lyrics. Instead, Commuck assigned to each hymn "the names of Indian chiefs, Indian females, Indian names of places, &c.," and in other cases tribal names as a tribute to the "memory of some tribes that are now nearly if not quite extinct" or even simply as a "mark of courtesy" for other tribes that Commuck knew or had heard of. The result is that titles of hymns like "Pequot," "Mohegan," "Groton," "Niantick," and "Mohawk" served to remind Natives—particularly those whose roots lay in New England, like the Brothertowns—of their past histories and homelands. Hymns named after famous Indians invoked the long history of Natives' struggle with colonization, such as "Powhatan," "Massasoit," "Uncas," "Philip" (King Philip), "Sassamon," "Apes," "Pocahontas," "Occom," and, rather brashly, "Commuck." The hymn titles also created a mostly fictive Christian connection with other Indian nations in North America whose members had likely never heard of the hymns that bore their name, such as "Sioux," "Seminole," "Tallahassee," "Cummanche," "Huron," and "Shoshonee."

The one hymn that had an explicit historic tribal affiliation, however, was simply titled "Old Indian Hymn." It contained a legend that required some unpacking by Commuck. The Narragansetts, as Commuck explained in a footnote, "have a tradition that the following tune was heard in the air by them, and other tribes bordering on the Atlantic coast, many years before the arrival of whites in America." When the Narragansetts went to visit the recently arrived English colonists at Plymouth in 1620, they were shocked to hear the same tune sung during the course of the English church service. The tune was preserved among the Narragansetts "to this day," Commuck reported, and so merited inclusion in his book.[101] The implicit moral of the hymn was that Natives, too, had received independent revelation regarding God that Euroamerican Christianity could only supplement, not supplant.

Other Native communities throughout southeastern New England maintained churches and, in some cases, schools. On Long Island, an Indian minister named Paul Cuffee and his two sons provided leadership to a collection of churches that had been founded by Azariah Horton in the 1740s and then had received Christian Indian leadership from Samson Occom, Peter John, Cyrus Charles, and the Fowler brothers, among others, over the course of the eighteenth century. Paul Cuffee was born on March 4, 1757, near Wading River on Long Island. Cuffee's mother was a member of the Indian Separate church in Wading River (founded by her father, the Indian minister Peter John) and was a servant of a local wealthy white person, Major Frederick Hudson.[102] At a young age, Paul Cuffee was bound out to Hudson, for whom he labored as a farmer until the age of twenty-one.[103] During his indentured years, Cuffee became locally notorious as the leader of a "thoughtless band" of roving Indian and black youth. This all changed during a series of revivals on Long Island in the late 1770s, and by 1779—after a dramatic and public commitment to Christianity— Cuffee followed the footsteps of his grandfather (Peter John) and even Occom by providing local and regional religious leadership. Like Samuel Niles, Paul Cuffee had little formal education but quickly became well known for his rhetorical flourishes in the pulpit. Cuffee and his wife, Hannah, had several children, two of whom later became ministers of Indian congregations: Obadiah served at Poospatuck, and Vincent served at Shinnecock.[104] By 1789 Paul Cuffee had moved ten miles south to Moriches, where he continued his itinerate ministry to various congregations. Like Occom and Ashpo, Cuffee sought the greater legitimacy that official ordination brought. In 1790 he was ordained by the Separate Connecticut Convention to minister to several Indian congregations on Long Island, and in 1792 he was admitted to the Strict Congregational Convention of Long Island (organized in 1791 in conjunction with the Separate Connecticut Convention). Connections with external, white organizations increased his reach and effectiveness, and the small salary he received after 1798 when he was placed on the payroll of the New York Missionary Society (NYMS) helped support his large family.[105]

All extant reports indicate that Cuffee served a geographically far-flung collection of churches on central and eastern Long Island. Based on a report he sent to the NYMS in 1811, he was actively servicing four churches at Islip, Poospatuck, Coldspring, and Montauk with a total of sixty-three communicants: twenty at Islip, sixteen at Poospatuck, fifteen at Coldspring, and twelve at Montauk.[106] Later reports of Cuffee indicate that he was widely revered as a talented preacher who attracted white, black, and Indian audiences and was often in high demand as a guest preacher.[107] One of Cuffee's contributions to the religious culture of Long Island Indian churches was a yearly corporate ritual called "June Meeting" or "June Sunday," which was an annual meeting of the church designed to celebrate communion and to set aside time to renew and rededicate one's self as well as make peace with those in the immediate church community. In the weeks preceding the June Meeting, Cuffee advised his congregants that "no one should come to the communion if he had any unsettled difficulty with any member of the church."[108] Over time it morphed into an "Indian Fair," combining elements of religious festival and cultural celebration with indigenous wares, activities, and food in abundance.[109] Later in his life, Cuffee struggled with "consumption," grew weaker, and eventually died in March 1812. He was buried at the Shinnecock Indian church at Canoe Place, marked with a gravestone and a short epitaph summarizing his life:

> ERECTED by the New York Missionary Society in memory of the REV. PAUL CUFFEE, an Indian of the Shinnecock Tribe, who was employed by that society, for the last thirteen years of his life on the eastern part of Long Island, where he labored with fidelity and success.
>
> Humble, pious, and indefatigable in testifying the Gospel of the Grace of God, he finished his course with joy, on the 7th of March, 1812, aged 55 years and 3 days.[110]

Almost every other major Indian reservation in southern New England had some sort of Christian Indian presence and practice in the early nineteenth century, although it usually occupied only a minority of local Natives. The Mohegan John Cooper served as a preacher at large for the Mohegan Christians after the death of Samuel Ashpo in 1795. He, along with Deacon Henry Quaquaquid, provided community leadership and exhortation, and—continuing prior patterns of intertribal preaching and sharing—likely served the nearby communities at Niantic and Groton as well. Cooper in particular was noted as possibly the wealthiest man in the small reservation community at Mohegan, owning two cows and a yolk of oxen, in addition to some land.[111] Among the Lantern Hill Pequots, Timothy Dwight reported with considerable surprise that when he passed through Stonington in 1807 he found "an aged Indian" who for a long time served as their preacher. Dwight described him as a man who possessed a "considerable share of understanding" and commanded respect from the other Eastern Pequots, who "very generally assemble" to hear his sermons and exhortations.[112] But spiritual leadership was not limited to men. Among the Mashantucket Pequots, Sally George served as a strong tribal and Christian leader for the immediate Mashantucket community, providing direction for and preaching at the larger intertribal meetings that occurred bimonthly in the early nineteenth century. Sally George also itinerated to other, smaller Indian communities, sometimes making an arduous twenty-mile trip to provide exhortation and, in many cases, serve as a doctor to the sick and needy.[113]

Sally George played a formative part in the life of her nephew, William Apess, undoubtedly one of the most famous nineteenth-century New England Natives. Apess was born in Colrain, Massachusetts, and was sent to live with his grandmother in Colchester, Connecticut—twenty-five miles northwest of Mashantucket—at the age of three. During his horrific childhood of being orphaned at a young age and serving under several masters (who flogged him regularly), he attended the various white churches of his masters, including Baptist and Congregationalist. None of these churches felt right to him, however, and in the 1810s he was drawn to the *"noisy Methodists"* who were leading revival services in the region, much like James Davenport had done seventy-five years earlier. It was through the Methodists and the revivals of the Second Great Awakening (1800–1830s), more than any Native Christian influence or practice connected with the Mashantucket Pequots, that Apess experienced the conviction of Christ as his savior. After largely abandoning his newly professed evangelicalism (like Joseph Johnson), Apess returned to Methodism seven years later and eventually also to his home community at Mashantucket, where he came under the influence of his aunt, Sally George, with whom he stayed for at least one winter (1817–1818).[114] It was likely through her mentorship and that of other regional Native Christian leaders—all shaped by eighteenth-century educational processes and the Indian Great Awakening—that Apess was able to reconcile his Native and Christian identities and direct his gifts to the benefit of the wider regional Native population. Apess's service included a relatively prolific writing career, ministry as a Methodist Indian preacher, and leadership in the infamous Mashpee Indian revolt of 1833, which stood as a definitive push for Mashpee (and, by implication, Indian) self-governance. Nonetheless, Apess was a complicated figure, who was rightfully bitter about the treatment he had received at the hands of Christian whites, and used his own Indian Christian morality (which he saw as superior to that of the white Christians around him) along with the language of republican egalitarianism as a stringent critique of the dominant white American culture.[115]

Like Apess, other Natives who moved off the reservation often joined mixed ethnicity religious communities wherever they found them, particularly in urban centers. Charles Plato and Lewis Cuffee, both Montauketts who moved to Sag Harbor on Long Island, helped to found St. David's African Methodist Episcopal (AME) Zion Church. The same was true of George Fowler, another Montaukett who was involved in the Bethel AME Church in North Amityville in south-central Long Island.[116] Even as late as the 1890s a few Shinnecocks and Montauketts who had moved to Brooklyn attended the Bridge Street African Methodist Episcopal Church.[117]

In many ways, the varying paths of the Native individuals and communities that made up the New England Indian landscape in the early nineteenth century represent the diversity of decisions that Indians had been making for two centuries. Although local whites and state and federal officials often viewed Native communities with disdain, Indians took pride in their communities as exemplary and self-sufficient. In July of 1820, Tobias Ross—himself a student under Jeremiah Niles in 1813—addressed a letter to SPGNA missionary Frederick Baylies, partially in response to Baylies's inquiries on a variety of issues. However, the letter was mostly a defense of the vitality, contentment, and independence of the Narragansett communities. "Our Morals is I Believe in our tribe as Sivel [civil] as you will Generally find in any tribe whatever," Ross explained; "we have laws to go by among ourselves and council men to over see the tribes affairs and a clerk, to Do the Business." Baylies and others had inquired about the Narragansetts' interest in relocating—perhaps to New York or, by the 1820s, perhaps even to Indiana, Wisconsin, or elsewhere. Ross and the Narragansetts, however, were firm: "As to Being Removed we wish not to Remove in a wild country we have farms and houses-here our charter is good. & those that will work may get a comfortable liveing here. and those that will not work here it is not likely they would Do much in a wild wilderness. we have land Enough, and wood Enough, and gain the salt water, own Boats for [f]ishing &c. &c."[118] Despite having relatives and friends in far-flung places like Massachusetts, Connecticut, and New York (and soon, even farther west, in Wisconsin), the four hundred or so Narragansetts in 1820 were ostensibly pleased with their lives. They had found a way to continually and creatively adapt to varying forms of white encroachment and, like members of other New England Indian communities, were still standing strong.

Epilogue

Feathers and Crosses

From the outside, the Mohegan Church looks like the hundreds of other Congregational churches that dot the contemporary New England landscape, with its pristine, white clapboards; squat, modest belfry; and arched sanctuary windows. Set back from the Norwich-New London Turnpike that was carved through Mohegan land in the eighteenth century (today Route 32), the clean and crisply painted church building and carefully manicured grounds seem somewhat out of place on the Mohegan reservation, visually at odds with both the far smaller, modest building across the street that houses the Tantaquidgeon Indian Museum and the gleaming towers of the Mohegan Sun Casino down the road. Even the interior of the church offers few clues as to the church's dual Congregational and Native affiliation, with its orderly rows of high-backed white hardwood pews, unadorned white walls and ceiling, and elevated pulpit in the front center.

Upon closer inspection, however, one thing stands out to a careful observer: a solitary eagle feather, hanging in the front of the church. It is "only" a feather, at least to an outsider. Nonetheless, the eagle feather is full of tribal symbolism, pregnant with meaning, history, and possibilities, historically representing sacred power, as well as—from the late-nineteenth century on—a visible emblem of pan-Indian identity. Equally important is where the feather is placed: above the smooth, wooden, empty cross in the arch behind the pulpit. A feather and a cross. Two symbols. Two histories. Two sets of meanings. Purposefully juxtaposed and yet so intertwined that the removal of one would completely change the meaning of the sacred space they both inhabit. The last minister—a non-Native—who tried to remove this feather was physically hustled out into the parking lot and fired on the spot.[1]

The Mohegan feather and cross are reminiscent of the seventeenth-century Pequot medicine bundle. These objects—Bible page, bear paw, feather, and cross—span a full three hundred years and speak of decisions made, paths taken,

Figure 9.1. The Mohegan Church. Photograph by the author.

compromises embraced, things simultaneously imposed and owned, and meanings borrowed and refashioned. As this book has shown, the story of New England Native religious engagement between 1700 and 1820 and beyond is far more complex and nuanced than the framework of "religious conversion" can effectively or accurately capture. Native Americans did participate in the Indian Great Awakening for a variety of reasons, but the effects of such participation and the slow and uneven changes over time defy simple description or analysis.

Native individuals responded to the religious and cultural options before them in vastly divergent ways over the course of multiple generations, always shaping and reshaping their involvement according to their own perceived religious and communal needs. Of course, it was hardly the Awakening alone that led to the relative Christianization of Native cultures in New England; rather, it was the long educational processes combined with the more episodic and short-lived Indian Great Awakening (or awakenings if we consider the local Native revivals in the early 1770s) and the cyclical nature of the evangelization process at the hands of whites. Nonetheless, over time evangelism and education produced—however incompletely—a diffuse and diverse indigenized Native Christian sub-culture that persisted on almost every Indian reservation in southeastern New England and served as a means of cultural influence and renewal for at least a subsegment of the population. Still, even within this Christianized subculture, Natives applied Christian ideas, affiliations, and cultural forms in surprising ways.

The Mohegan Church and its eagle feather are reminders that these stories do not end in nineteenth-century Rhode Island, Connecticut, New York, or even Wisconsin. Contrary to our deficient—at times, willfully deficient—national memory regarding American Indians, the story has never ended. Although the national drama of ongoing Indian policy in the nineteenth century quickly shifted to the west with each successive expansion of the western frontier, Native nations in the northeast fought to maintain cultural identity, physical land, and legal status through the long and hard nineteenth and twentieth centuries and continue to do so.

Distinct echoes of all of these various threads of Christianization, affiliation, and the appropriation of Christian forms in surprising and nominal ways can be found on three present-day Native reservations in southeastern New England in the form of Indian church buildings at Mohegan, Narragansett, and Shinnecock. Each one is part of a visible and enduring religious and cultural legacy of the colonial period. All three church *buildings* (or, with the Shinnecock church, por-tions of it) date back to the nineteenth century, but the roots of the *congregations* date back to the eighteenth century and to the era of the Indian Great Awak-ening. These Native churches represent the ways in which Christianity in its vis-ibly Western, Euroamerican forms (steeples, pews, pulpits) have been subtly indigenized. These Native churches also illustrate the ways in which the physical church buildings operate conceptually on the reservations in terms of cultural memory and identity, even as they attract only a small minority of Native reli-gious practitioners today.

According to the Mohegan Medicine Woman Melissa Zobel, the history of the Mohegan Church building has become the primary lens through which the Mohegan Nation views most historical encounters with Christianity, including the profession of faith by Ben Uncas II in 1736 and subsequent Mohegan involvement in the Great Awakening.[2] Like the Narragansetts before 1809, in the early nineteenth century the Mohegans had been largely overlooked by state, regional, and national missionary societies. They soon became the personal missionary field of Sarah L. Huntington, a young girl living in Norwich six miles from the reservation, who in the late 1820s was swept up in a series of revivals and became enamored with the prodigious efforts of the American Board of Commissioners for Foreign Missions in far-flung regions of the world. By 1829, Huntington had opened a school at Mohegan in the house belonging to the Occom family and also spent most Sundays on the reservation holding a Sunday School.[3] The 1820s were also a time when the removal of Indian tribes to remote western reserves was seen by an increasing number of state and federal legislators as the answer to the "Indian problem." Some congressmen suggested that the much smaller tribes of the northeast—including the Mohegans—should also be moved west of the Mississippi, particularly if they were not civilized or Christianized.[4] Working with several elderly Mohegan women, including Cynthia Teecomwas Hoscott, Lucy Tantaquidgeon Teecomwas, and Lucy Occom Tantaquidgeon (Samson Occom's sister), Huntington devised a plan to avoid removal: constructing a church on Mohegan lands.[5] Through a year of tireless correspondence with the ABCFM, the secretary of the federal Department of War, and a host of personal friends and relatives, Huntington secured local funding for a church building and federal money for a resident minister, Anson Gleason, who had previously served as a missionary among the Cherokees.[6] The opening of the Mohegan Church in 1831, according to some accounts, averted the forcible removal of the Mohegans. The early years of the Mohegan Church also coincided with the revivals and reforms of the Second Great Awakening. Huntington reported on April 4 of that year that a "powerful revival" was under way in nearby Montville, and an "increasing attention to the means of grace" was occurring among the Mohegans as well.[7] By 1843 the reservation once again hosted a separate schoolhouse not far from the church building.[8]

The only problem was that not many Indians attended the church. In fact, in 1845 there were only thirteen Mohegans—ten of whom were women—among the forty members in the church, and through the early twentieth century perhaps little more than half of the members were Indian. Additionally, by 1845 one Indian woman had already been excommunicated.[9] But the lack of many official Indian members obscures the cultural role the church played in community life, as well as the ways in which the Mohegans have used it in ways unintended, perhaps, by its evangelistically minded, non-Indian sponsors. Every year, for example, for well over a century the spacious church lawn became the site of the

annual Green Corn and—later—Wigwam festivals, perhaps the most important community events for the Mohegans. Later, when the Mohegan Nation officially received federal recognition on March 7, 1994, the Mohegan Church was
once again crucial to their ongoing existence, this time in proving—through the
land on which the church had been built—that the tribe had maintained a continual presence in Connecticut since the early nineteenth century. And with federal recognition, of course, comes the right to build gaming facilities, so ironically
enough, the Mohegan Church is largely responsible for the towering Mohegan
Sun Casino right down the road. Today the church also serves as a partial repository of Mohegan history and culture via a small collection of artifacts, including
a mortar and pestle, a ritual mask, and a wooden basket. The Annual Wigwam
Powwow—no longer a fund-raiser for the church—celebrates the cultural continuity of the Mohegan community and fosters intertribal relations in the region.

The point here is that according to Zobel, both "conversion" to Christianity in
the eighteenth century and the building of the church in the nineteenth century
are indicative of the rather practical, political relationship many Mohegans have
had with Christianity since they discovered Europeans on their shores. Yes, they
have had their Samuel Ashpos and their Samson Occoms, both dedicated Christian ministers and missionaries, but for some Mohegans, Christianity was incorporated into tribal life only to the extent it was necessary to allow the Mohegans
to continue living undisturbed by non-Indians, or to the extent that Christianity
created a space within which the tribe could ensure their ongoing survival. For
many Mohegans, life continued on largely as usual after encounters with Christianity, whether through the evangelistic attempts of James Fitch in the 1660s,
the Great Awakening of the 1740s, or the building of the Mohegan Church in the
1830s. The Mohegan Church has never had a Mohegan or even an Indian minister, and yet the building and grounds are meticulously maintained by the Mohegan Nation using revenue from the casino.[10]

The present-day Narragansett Indian Church has played a somewhat similar
role, although with some significant differences. The modest granite one-story
church building located on Narragansett lands just outside of Charlestown,
Rhode Island, dates back to 1859; the congregation, however, traces its founding
to the 1740s. The church sits at one corner of a large field and powwow grounds
and has an Indian burial ground behind it that contains the final resting place of
its founding minister, Samuel Niles. For several centuries, the church grounds—
much like those at the Mohegan Church—have hosted an annual regional
powwow in August that corresponds with an even older harvest festival.[11] In the
mid-nineteenth century, these "Indian Meetings" took place on the second
Sunday in August and were a regional spectacle, drawing Indians, blacks, and
whites from Rhode Island, eastern Connecticut, and Long Island for a multiday
series of meetings, powwows, and celebrations. Some local whites and blacks

Figure 9.2. The Narragansett Indian Church. Photograph by the author.

came explicitly to sell crafts, food, and drinks to the hundreds of people who came and pitched tents and other temporary dwellings next to the church for the duration of the festival.[12]

Nonetheless, not even the annual powwow and physical church building could sufficiently mitigate against larger anti-Indian assimilationist biases during the last half of the nineteenth century. Even as New England whites prematurely lamented the passing of the "last" members of various tribes (most popularly represented by James Fenimore Cooper's *The Last of the Mohicans* [1826]), in some cases states approved legislation that tried to make it official.[13] In January 1880, the Rhode Island legislature passed a bill titled "An Act to Abolish the Tribal Authority and Relations of the Narragansett Tribe of Indians." Almost two years later, on December 26, 1881, state representatives and Narragansett tribal leaders signed an agreement that transferred the entirety of Narragansett lands to the state in exchange for an offer of full US citizenship and $5,000, to be divided among those who could legitimately claim to be Narragansetts, as determined by the tribal council.[14] After months of contentious debates over who qualified, 302 Narragansett individuals out of the 572 who applied received their shares of $16.56.[15] Nonetheless, during the relative cultural nadir of Narragansett tribal life in the late nineteenth and early twentieth centuries, present-day tribal members recount stories they heard from their great-grandparents who used the church—and its

Figure 9.3. The Shinnecock Presbyterian Church. Photograph by the author.

land—as a base from which to maintain a physical tribal presence and to plan for future land claims and cultural revitalization. While the women sat inside the church and sang, the Narragansett elders met outside at the council rocks and deliberated over tribal matters. "They claimed to be receiving the message of Christianity, but they were holding tribal meetings," recalls Lloyd Wilcox, the Narragansett Medicine Man.[16] And once again, the Indian church was part of a petition for federal recognition (again by virtue of the land it was on), which the Narragansetts received in 1983. The annual Narragansett powwow and Green Corn celebration is still held on the grounds directly in front of the church, a celebration that the tribe claims, as of August 2011, to be in its 336th year.

The Shinnecock Presbyterian Church, originally located on Shinnecock lands just west of Canoe Place on Long Island, New York (on the west side of Shinnecock Bay), is one of the oldest continuous Indian churches in the region. The congregation was unofficially founded by Azariah Horton in the early 1740s and was through the 1810s successively attended to by Native ministers, including Samson Occom, Peter John, and Paul Cuffee. Sometime between 1780 and 1813, the first Shinnecock Indian church building was constructed at Canoe Place. In the nineteenth century, as the Shinnecock land holdings were slowly reduced, the church was moved across the Shinnecock Bay (five or six miles east by land) to its present location on the Shinnecock reservation.[17] After Cuffee's death in 1812, however, official Indian leadership seems to have languished, with the New York Missionary Society occasionally providing non-Native ministers through the end of the nineteenth century.[18]

Today the Shinnecock Presbyterian Church, like the Narragansett church, reflects the relative embrace and indigenization of a particular kind of Christianity on the Shinnecock reservation. The church sits next to the reservation community center, and when I visited in 2010, the parking lot between the two buildings served as a hangout for a dozen Shinnecock teenagers. Like the Mohegan Church, the brown and aged cedar-shingle building shows no indication of its Native connection and long history. Similarly, the small sanctuary inside is inviting and somewhat informal, although the high-back pews retain the feel of a distant colonial past. Once again, at the front is an empty wooden cross, formed by two rough-hewn pieces of timber. In this case, however, the actual cross has been refashioned to reflect its indigenous context. Carved into the top of the vertical piece of wood is an eagle's head, with the impression of an eagle's feather carved into the neck as it descends and then blends into the rest of the uncarved piece of wood. As at Mohegan and Narragansett, the nation's traditional powwow is interwoven with the existence of the church: in 1946 the Shinnecocks recovered their past tradition of an annual powwow as a fund-raising activity for the church, which now draws thousands of visitors each fall.[19] The Shinnecocks have also found recent success—as of October 2010—in gaining federal recognition.

The long history of native religious engagement has taken on different and less visible forms on reservations of other Native nations, however. The Mashantucket Pequots, for example, do not have a church building that dates back to the nineteenth century. There was one, but it was burned to the ground by local whites because its late nineteenth-century Native minister, Ephraim Williams, led a controversial but racially embracing congregation of Natives, blacks, whites, and intermarried families. Despite the brazen arson, Williams and his congregation continued to meet near a pond on the reservation so they could baptize people as needed.[20] But as Mashantucket Cultural Director and tribal member Wayne Reels explained to me, the lack of a historic church building is a nonissue for many present-day Pequot Christians, since he believes "the history of the church is within you."[21] One of the main Native Christian congregations presently at Mashantucket, All Nations Christian Fellowship, was founded in the early 1990s by the granddaughter of Ephraim Williams, Laughing Woman— who serves as the Mashantucket Spiritual Leader—and her husband. The group began in their home and in the mid-2000s gathered the resources to build a tribal Spiritual Center, which serves as the meeting place for All Nations but is also open to any religious group and for other tribal activities on the reservation, such as weddings and funerals.[22]

In each of these cases, the official church buildings at Narragansett, Mohegan, Shinnecock, and even at Mashantucket obscure the diversity and reality of contemporary Native religious practice. In each place, general Christianization forms the religious backdrop for the vast majority of tribal members. Most members can recount growing up in a Protestant church or going to mass, and Christianity is generally as much a part of their Native cultures as it is the wider US culture. Nonetheless, there are ongoing deep divisions about Christianity itself and, given its long and contested history in Native groups, there is wide divergence in present-day practices and affiliations. Among the Narragansetts, according to Tall Oak Weeden, a Native of both Narragansett and Mashantucket Pequot ancestry who currently lives in Charlestown, approximately half of the Narragansetts have clear Christian affiliation with either the Native-led Peace Dale First Church of God or the Jehovah's Witnesses. A quarter or so of the Narragansett population pursues a recovery of traditional Native spirituality that draws on sources and prophecies from across Native North America and even, in some cases, from Mayan prophecies about the end of the world. The rest of the Narragansetts vacillate between various modes and beliefs, remaining conversant with traditional Native spirituality while sometimes participating in an explicitly Christian congregation. "Native religious association is difficult to pin down," Weeden warns, "because it is very fluid."[23]

In a somewhat similar breakdown, by some estimations the "majority" of the present-day Shinnecocks are Christians of various stripes. Some Natives on the reservation attend the Shinnecock Presbyterian Church, others attend Protestant and Catholic churches off the reservation, and a small core of tribal members prefer instead to practice "traditional worship."[24] And the Mohegans, according to Zobel, are diverse in their religious practices, ranging from New Age to traditional Native spiritual practices to evangelical Christianity. In all three of these locales, religious affiliation is contested, with evangelical Native Christians often attempting to actively evangelize other Natives, including their own family members who prefer traditional worship and beliefs.

At Mashantucket, religious practices are equally diverse and fluid, although perhaps a bit less contested. Plenty of nonbelievers and traditionalists can be found on the reservation (one such individual I spoke with briefly mistakenly assumed her nonbeliefs would be of no interest to me). They co-exist alongside Pequots whose religious affiliations include Mormonism, Catholicism, Seventh Day Adventism, Jehovah's Witnesses, Pentecostalism, and even Islam. There is no "center" even to Pequot Christianity (as if such a monolithic entity existed) in the rhythms of ongoing tribal life. In addition to the All Nations church, the Tree of Life Ministries serves the Mashantucket reservation community under the leadership of Patricia Sebastian, an ordained Pentecostal minister. Other Pequot Christians, like Sebastian's daughter, Tribal Councilor Fatima Dames, attend Tree of Life Ministries as well as other local churches such as Rescue Mission Church in New London. Additional Native ministers serve in various capacities on and off the reservation, and Pequot Christians attend a wide variety of churches on Sunday mornings. In general, the Natives at Mashantucket who spoke with me exhibited very little anxiety about the religious practices and affiliations of other subgroups, denominations, or individuals. One of the Pequot Muslims also attends a Pentecostal church in New London, Connecticut, and All Nations recently had a shofar-blowing Jewish rabbi as a guest.[25]

In many ways, contemporary Mashantucket Pequot Christians seem to profess Christianity *despite* the long history of evangelization and education, not because of it. Councilor Dames, for example, views her own religious beliefs as "separate" from the "infiltration of the Christian indoctrination" that happened long ago. The sordid history of colonialism—as passed down through oral traditions—serves for many nonbelievers as the only reason they need to eschew the religion of the whites. Laughing Woman, herself an ordained minister, says that when, over the course of her lifetime, she has pressed her nonbelieving or traditionalist friends about their rejection of the Bible, one thing has always repeatedly come up: "The Ten Commandments: 'Thou shall not murder'—and yet they massacred us. 'Thou shall not steal'—and yet they stole our land. Whites broke all of them; this is why the word of God was hard to accept by the Indians."[26]

Nonetheless, many Pequots who profess Christianity do so in a way that complements Native lifeways. Laughing Woman, for example, declares: "I believe in one God; I believe that Jesus was born to the Virgin Mary; I believe he lived and was crucified; I believe he rose again from the dead; and I believe he is coming back again, and very soon." In the same breath, however, Laughing Woman affirms that the Pequots "always knew about the Creator." The main elements of Christian doctrine—good, evil, morality, even punishment in the afterlife—were all basically known in rough form long before the coming of the Europeans. "Take the eagle feather, for example," she explained. "It contains two colors, light and dark, which our people have for centuries understood to represent the two forces of good and evil in the world." Such histories and interpretations resonate with the documentary record as well, as when Experience Mayhew held a joint meeting with the Eastern and Mashantucket Pequots in 1713 and told them about the great God who had made the world; the Pequots listened patiently but eventually informed him that his speeches were in vain, for they knew about all of that as much as he did.[27] For herself, Laughing Woman has found "a balance between being a Native woman and respecting the sacred elements of our tribe and my beliefs in Christianity." It is her ability to keep these two elements in creative tension that allowed her to be elected to the "Hallelujah Indians," a fascinating but little-known group of traditionalists who, tribal oral tradition recounts, were present at least as far back as the Pequot War in 1636–1638. Some Pequots, in fact, escaped harm in the war by telling the English troops, "Me Hallelujah Indians; me know Roger Williams." Still, Laughing Woman affirms that this Christian traditionalism is her choice, and others "have to find their own way."[28]

Wayne Reels also lives out a dynamic intertwining of traditional and Christian practices. "I believe in Jesus, but I still smoke the [peace] pipe," Reels explains. In Reels's experience, Christianity enhances traditional religious practices. The smoke of the pipe becomes symbolic of his prayers rising to Jesus. It is the same with sweating, another traditional practice that has long been the target of missionary campaigns in Native history. "We'll sweat traditionally," says Reels, "but I'll use the name of Jesus." Similarly, Reels still maintains "traditional beliefs about nature," but some elements of traditional Native oral tradition and practice—like traditional creation stories (the retelling of which, Laughing Woman tells me, takes three full days)—are "replaced with the Bible and the stories of Genesis and Jesus."[29]

In this way, Native religious engagement is ongoing, as we might expect it to be. The line between the eighteenth century and the present, however, is not so direct or strong as one might expect. The church buildings provide the primary point of continuity, but many present-day members of these Native nations construct meaning and their religious lifeworlds with merely a sideways glance at the overlapping and broader contexts surrounding the Indian Great Awakening that this book has illuminated—all of which feels like part of a longer, painfully negotiated history. Missionaries, I was told by one Native individual, had the most devastating effects on Native communities in the colonial period and beyond, with alcohol coming in as a close second.[30] Nonetheless, amid the mistreatment and dispossession is a story of resilience—of American Indians working within and against larger structures of power to create options and pursue goals meaningful to individuals and communities that were otherwise hemmed in by colonists. Evangelization at the hands of non-Indians is an ongoing reality for the vast majority of Native groups today. A simple survey of religious groups who target present-day Native nations and reservations reveals an astonishing fixation on providing humanitarian aid, educational services, and Christian instruction to the farthest reaches of Native North America.[31] Narratives about Natives having converted in the past are incongruous with the missionary activity that exists in the present. However, it's not that Native communities are not Christianized; it's that they aren't *sufficiently* Christianized, at least in the eyes of missionaries. Such perceived insufficiency has a very long history, as this book has shown. Although missionaries in the present still offer education and emphasize cultural change, many Natives in New England and elsewhere continue to find methods of incorporating Christian and "traditional" modes of spirituality in meaningful ways, much like Laughing Woman's "Christian traditionalism," Samson Occom's "traditionary religion," and even the Pequot medicine bundle.

And, indeed, the long-term religious engagement by Native Americans and their affiliations with various forms of evangelization and education, along with the wider anti-Indian currents in colonial and US culture, did partially and gradually reshape Native communities during the colonial period and beyond. Native mourning and burial rituals, traditional ways of dealing with illness, modes of subsistence, styles of housing, methods of communicating, ways of dressing, and the kinds of livestock kept all intermingled with Euroamerican ways of doing and thinking about these things without ever disappearing completely. It is not possible or historically accurate to pin all of these larger changes in Native lifeways on the Indian Great Awakening. Nonetheless, religion was often at the center of the ways in which at least some subsets of these Native groups increasingly began to think of themselves. Even as early as the mid-eighteenth century, the physical presence of a church building on Native lands became a complicated symbol of their Christianization. But such change was never complete, and in other ways, Natives in 1820 operated with pragmatic, community-centered frames of reference similar to those of their ancestors in 1700 or even 1600. Native understandings of the world ran deep, so deep, in fact, that two hundred years of colonization could only reshape, not obliterate, their communities and cultures, as is evidenced by the religious and cultural diversity and the vitality exhibited by these same Native groups today.

ABBREVIATIONS

BCP — Benjamin Colman Papers, Massachusetts Historical Society.
CCHS — *Collections of the Connecticut Historical Society.*
CHS — Connecticut Historical Society.
CMHS — *Collections of the Massachusetts Historical Society.*
CSL — Connecticut State Library.
CWSO — Occom, Samson. *The Collected Writings of Samson Occom, Mohegan.* Joanna Brooks, ed. New York: Oxford University Press, 2006.
GCC — Connecticut, Uncas, and John Mason. *Governor and Company of Connecticut, and Moheagan Indians.* London, UK: W. and J. Richardson, 1769.
IPCSL — Indian Papers, Connecticut State Library.
LEWI — McCallum, James Dow. *The Letters of Eleazar Wheelock's Indians.* Hanover, NH: Dartmouth College Publications, 1932.
MHS — Massachusetts Historical Society.
MPMRC — Mashantucket Pequot Museum and Research Center.
MSA — Massachusetts State Archives.
NEC LMA — Manuscript Records of the New England Company, London Metropolitan Archives.
NEC NEHGS — Manuscript Records of the Company for the Propagation of the Gospel in New England, New England Historic Genealogical Society. Boston, Mass.
PAAS — *Proceedings of the American Antiquarian Society.*
PCRN — Paul Campbell Research Notes. Rhode Island Historical Society. Providence, Rhode Island.
PRCC — *Public Records of the Colony of Connecticut.*
PRSC — *Public Records of the State of Connecticut.*

RCRI   *Records of the Colony of Rhode Island.*

SPGNA MHS   The Society for Propagating the Gospel Among the Indians and Others in North America Records. Massachusetts Historical Society. Boston, Mass.

SPGNA PEM   Society for Propagating the Gospel among the Indians and Others in North America Records, 1791–1875. Phillips Library, Peabody Essex Museum. Salem, Mass.

WJJ   Johnson, Joseph. *To Do Good to My Indian Brethren: The Writings of Joseph Johnson, 1751–1776.* Laura Murray, ed. Amherst: University of Massachusetts Press, 1998.

WP   Wheelock Papers, microfilm edition.

NOTES

For the full bibliographic information of the references in the notes below, please consult the Bibliography.

Introduction

1. As scholars have noted, the etymology of "conversion" implies a turning. Rambo, *Understanding Religious Conversion*, 3.
2. Hindmarsh, *The Evangelical Conversion Narrative*, 328–29.
3. McBride, "Bundles, Bears, and Bibles," 132–41. See also Amory and Hall, *Bibliography and the Book Trades*, ch. 1. The circumstances surrounding the uncovering of the Pequot graves at Long Pond were tragic and unfortunate. Nonetheless, the Mashantucket tribe made the best of the situation and were able to work with archaeologists to carefully remove and rebury the human remains and funerary objects. Although much was learned in the process, the disruption of Native graves is always horrific and should be avoided at all costs.
4. Psalm 98:1–2. *The Holy Bible, King James Version.*
5. McBride, "Bundles, Bears, and Bibles," 141.
6. Morrison, *The Solidarity of Kin*, ch. 1.
7. Gow, "Forgetting Conversion," 235.
8. The literature on Euro-Indian cultural and religious encounters in North America is large, but a few of the enduring and more recent notable works include Richter, *Facing East from Indian Country*; Jennings, *The Invasion of America*; Axtell, *The Invasion Within*; Bowden, *American Indians and Christian Missions*; Berkhofer, *Salvation and the Savage*; Griffiths and Cervantes, *Spiritual Encounters*; Silverman, "Indians, Missionaries, and Religious Translation"; Martin and Nicholas, *Native Americans, Christianity, and the Reshaping of the American Religious Landscape*; Wheeler, *To Live upon Hope*; Griffiths, *Sacred Dialogues*; Greer, *Mohawk Saint*; Anderson, *The Betrayal of Faith*; Calloway and Salisbury, *Reinterpreting New England Indians and the Colonial Experience*; Brooks, *Captives and Cousins*; Wyss, *Writing Indians*; Kupperman, *Indians and English*; Cogley, *John Eliot's Mission*; Lepore, *The Name of War*; Calloway, *After King Philip's War*; Gutiérrez, *When Jesus Came, the Corn Mothers Went Away*; Richter, *Before the Revolution*; and Salisbury, *Manitou and Providence*.
9. Griffiths, "Introduction," 2.
10. In many ways this book is indebted to the very old and yet informative work of William DeLoss Love from the late nineteenth century. Nonetheless, *The Indian Great Awakening* is different at many points in its outlook and scope, and at almost every turn I have gone back to the primary sources as much as possible and even tapped into new sources Love did not utilize. The result is, I hope, a significant reframing of the religious and cultural negotiations of New England Natives in this time period. See Love, *Samson Occom*.
11. Hall, *Lived Religion in America*; Orsi, "Everyday Miracles: The Study of Lived Religion."
12. For a broader context, see, for example, the two volumes edited by Kenneth Mills and Anthony Grafton on conversion throughout the history of Christianity. Mills and Grafton, *Conversion in Late Antiquity and the Early Middle Ages*; Mills and Grafton, *Conversion: Old*

Worlds and New. Also Viswanathan, *Outside the Fold.* Other classic discussions of conversion among American Indians include Simmons, "Conversion from Indian to Puritan"; Axtell, "Were Indian Conversions *Bona Fide*?" More recent discussions include Cohen, "Conversion among Puritans and Amerindians"; McCarthy, "Conversion, Identity, and the Indian Missionary"; Simmons, "Red Yankees: Narragansett Conversion in the Great Awakening." On Native Christianity, see Martin and Nicholas, *Native Americans, Christianity, and the Reshaping of the American Religious Landscape*; Silverman, *Red Brethren*; Wheeler, *To Live upon Hope*; Fisher, "'In the practice and profession of the Christian Religion'"; Wyss, "Things that Do Accompany Salvation"; Van Lonkhuyzen, "A Reappraisal of the Praying Indians"; Conkling, "Legitimacy and Conversion in Social Change"; and Morrison, *The Solidarity of Kin.*

13. Although scholars have begun to reimagine religious conversion among Anglo-European populations as more fluid and dynamic, there is still a widespread and general presumption about the totality of conversion. See, for example, Hindmarsh, *The Evangelical Conversion Narrative*; Sweet, *Bodies Politic*, 132–33.

14. Kenneth Morrison takes on the ethnocentrism of historians with regard to the concepts of "religion" and "conversion" in Morrison, *The Solidarity of Kin*, ch. 1. See also Salisbury, "Embracing Ambiguity."

15. Studies of New England Natives tend to focus on either American Indians in seventeenth-century Massachusetts and Plymouth or well-known, literate Mohegans such as Samson Occom and Joseph Johnson in the mid-late eighteenth century. The best study of seventeenth-century evangelization efforts in New England is Cogley, *John Eliot's Mission.* For Martha's Vineyard, see Silverman, *Faith and Boundaries.* For an analysis of southeastern New England Natives in the eighteenth century through the lens of race, see Silverman, *Red Brethren.*

16. Szasz, *Indian Education in the American Colonies, 1607–1783*; Axtell, *The Invasion Within*; Monaghan, *Learning to Read and Write in Early America.*

17. In many of these efforts, funding from England-based missionary societies was critical. The best study of the New England Company is Kellaway, *The New England Company, 1649–1776.* For the Scottish Society for the Propagation of Christian Knowledge, see Szasz, *Scottish Highlanders and Native Americans.*

18. On dispossession in colonial New England, see O'Brien, *Dispossession by Degrees*; Conroy, "The Defense of Indian Land Rights"; Weinstein-Farson, "Land, Politics, Power"; Den Ouden, *Beyond Conquest.* For a more broad-ranging view, see Banner, *How the Indians Lost Their Land.* Also Cronon, *Changes in the Land.*

19. The question of whether or not there even was a Great Awakening has been debated by scholars during the past twenty-five years. Butler, "Enthusiasm Described and Decried"; Kidd, *The Great Awakening*; Lambert, *Inventing the "Great Awakening."*

20. For the view that Indians converted suddenly and completely in the Awakening, see Simmons, "The Great Awakening and Indian Conversion in Southern New England," 25. Also Cogley, *John Eliot's Mission*, 186, and Mandell, *Behind the Frontier*, 127.

21. C. C. Goen mentions the Narragansett church briefly in Goen, *Revivalism and Separatism in New England, 1740–1800*, 90–92. More recent scholars have referenced the presence of a Separate Indian network but have not done the legwork to reveal its contours. For example, see Brooks, *American Lazarus*, 61. Also Sweet, *Bodies Politic*, 136–37.

22. Two recent books on this are Silverman, *Red Brethren*; Jarvis, *The Brothertown Nation of Indians.*

23. The most thorough recent book on New England Natives in the post-Revolutionary period is Mandell, *Tribe, Race, History.*

24. Dowd uses the phrase "The Indians' Great Awakening" to refer to these nativist movements. Dowd, *A Spirited Resistance.* See also Cave, *Prophets of the Great Spirit.*

25. At many points in this project I was tempted to make this a study of Indians and Africans in southeastern New England. Although Indians' and Africans' religious experiences overlapped and intersected at times in interesting ways, I became increasingly convinced that the actual social context of each group was sufficiently different to warrant a separate study. The primary difference was land. The fact that most Native communities owned large amounts of land put them in a very different place socially, culturally, and politically. Other factors, too, were important—populations, levels of "freeness," and military potential—but the ownership of land placed them at the political and religious forefront in a much different

way when compared with Africans—even free ones—in this time period. This changed slowly over time during the eighteenth century as the two groups began to intermarry.

Chapter 1

1. Renamed the Thames River by the English, this river runs south past the Mohegan reservation and New London and then empties into the Long Island Sound.
2. Hubbard, *The History of the Indian Wars in New England*, 289–90.
3. Young and Fowler, *Cahokia, the Great Native American Metropolis*.
4. Fagan, *Chaco Canyon*.
5. Abrams and Freter, *The Emergence of the Moundbuilders*.
6. "Algonquian" is a linguistic descriptor and is used to reference most of the northeastern Native tribes who spoke dialects that were linguistically related. One of the best summaries of New England Algonquian lifeways is Simmons, *Spirit of the New England Tribes*, ch. 3. For examples of Native disillusionment with their own practices, see Hopkins, *Historical Memoirs*, 10.
7. For an excellent essay on Indian perceptions of Europeans in the seventeenth century, see Axtell, "Through Another Glass Darkly." On disease, see Salisbury, *Manitou and Providence*, 23ff; Cook, *Born to Die*, 5, 12.
8. James Axtell's provocative counterfactual essay highlights how central Natives were to the success of European settlements in the New World. Axtell, "Colonial America without the Indians."
9. De Forest, *History of the Indians of Connecticut*, 346.
10. Albanese, *America, Religions and Religion*, 26.
11. Hopkins, *Historical Memoirs*, 12.
12. Martin, *The Land Looks after Us*, 5.
13. Mentioned in Williams, "To my Deare and Welbeloved Friends and Countrey-men."
14. Williams, *A Key into the Language of America*, 127.
15. Williams, "To my Deare and Welbeloved Friends and Countrey-men."
16. Williams, *A Key into the Language of America*, 116. Quote is taken from Occom, "Account of the Montauk Indians, on Long Island," 49.
17. Occom, "Account of the Montauk Indians, on Long Island," 49.
18. Salisbury, *Manitou and Providence*, 37–38. Williams, *A Key into the Language of America*, 118.
19. Occom, "Account of the Montauk Indians, on Long Island," 49. Williams, *A Key into the Language of America*, 67, 119. Simmons, "Southern New England Shamanism."
20. Williams, *A Key Into the Language of America*, 119, 190.
21. Occom, "Account of the Montauk Indians, on Long Island," 49. Occom, writing as a Christian Indian minister, attributed such revelations to the devil and demonic influences.
22. See, for example, Mavor and Dix, *Manitou: The Sacred Landscape of New England's Native Civilization*, 172–73. For the Latin American context, see Mills, *Idolatry and Its Enemies*.
23. *New England's First Fruits*, 16.
24. Stiles, *The Literary Diary of Ezra Stiles*, 1:386. The exact date is unclear. Writing in 1773, Stiles says it occurred forty to fifty years prior.
25. Personal interview with Laughing Woman, May 5, 2011, Mashantucket, Connecticut.
26. Hopkins, *Historical Memoirs*, 24.
27. Occom, "Account of the Montauk Indians, on Long Island," 49. Richard Cogley, in his discussion of John Eliot's view of Indian powwows and medicinal practices, says that Eliot was not opposed to Indian traditional herbal practices. Cogley, *John Eliot's Mission*, 175.
28. Occom, "Account of the Montauk Indians, on Long Island," 50.
29. Edward Winslow, as quoted in Simmons, *Spirit of the New England Tribes*, 39.
30. Stiles and Dexter, *Extracts from the Itineraries and Other Miscellanies of Ezra Stiles*, 409.
31. Hopkins, *Historical Memoirs*, 38.
32. Simmons, *Spirit of the New England Tribes*, 64.
33. Talcott, *The Talcott Papers*, 2:483–84.
34. Taylor, *The Divided Ground*, 35.
35. Hopkins, *Historical Memoirs*, 11.
36. The best description of these various physical evidences is Mavor and Dix, *Manitou: The Sacred Landscape of New England's Native Civilization*.

37. Hopkins, *Historical Memoirs*, 34.
38. Baker, *History of Montville, Connecticut*, 5–6.
39. Seed, *Ceremonies of Possession*, 18–19.
40. Recent transnational studies of indigenous land loss in international colonial European contexts up through the twentieth century reveal parallels in terms of dispossession and the use of local court systems. See, for example, Olson, *The Struggle for the Land*.
41. Williams, *A Key into the Language of America*, 93 [97]. For a concise discussion of differences between European and Native understandings about use of land, see Cronon, *Changes in the Land*, 58–68. See also Brooks, "The Common Pot," 76–77.
42. Cronon, *Changes in the Land*, 58–59.
43. In addition to Cronon, for more on the use of livestock, see Anderson, "King Philip's Herds."
44. For more on the ways in which Euroamerican land use was connected to ideologies of colonialism, see Cronon, *Changes in the Land*; Seed, *Ceremonies of Possession*.
45. Winslow, *Master Roger Williams*, 104–6. The same question had been raised more than twenty years earlier in Virginia in a sermon by William Crashaw in February 1609. Crashaw argued that the colonists did not have the right to take land from the "heathen." Banner, *How the Indians Lost Their Land*, 13–14.
46. Salisbury, *Manitou and Providence*, 48.
47. Stuart Banner documents some of these instances and insists that, in general, English land purchases were made at or above fair market value. Banner, *How the Indians Lost Their Land*, 10, 12, 26, 84. For more on land speculation (that directly affected Native communities) see Martin, *Profits in the Wilderness*.
48. See, for example, Cañizares-Esguerra, *Puritan Conquistadors*, 28.
49. Richard Cogley has called this the "affective model" of early English colonial evangelism. Cogley, *John Eliot's Mission*, 21–22.
50. Wequash is one possible example. See Williams, "To my Deare and Welbeloved Friends and Countrey-men."
51. Cave, *The Pequot War*; Karr, "'Why Should You Be So Furious?'"
52. Cogley, *John Eliot's Mission*, 187.
53. Ronda, "Generations of Faith." Kristina Bross has argued that with the successful Puritan takeover in London, New England colonists needed an ongoing raison d'être. Evangelism of New England Natives for a time at least served as this justification. Bross, *Dry Bones and Indian Sermons*, ch. 2.
54. Kellaway, *The New England Company*, 85, 87. O'Brien, *Dispossession by Degrees*, 42.
55. For the longer story of Natick and dispossession, see O'Brien, *Dispossession by Degrees*.
56. For a recent critical edition of the Eliot tracts, see Clark, *The Eliot Tracts*.
57. Several missions agencies during the seventeenth and eighteenth centuries are understandably conflated and confused by historians because they overlapped in name, chronology, and purpose: the Society for the Propagation of the Gospel in New England (1649–1660; Puritan/Independent), which was rechartered in 1662 as the Company for the Propagation of the Gospel in New England and Parts Adjacent (normally referred to as the New England Company, or the NEC; also Puritan/Independent); the Society for the Propagation of Christian Knowledge (SPCK; 1698; Anglican); the Society for the Propagation of the Gospel in Foreign Parts (SPG; 1701; Anglican); and the Scottish Society for the Propagation of Christian Knowledge (SSPCK; 1709; Presbyterian). To make things even more complicated, in 1762 the Massachusetts Congregationalists attempted to create a "Society for Propagating Christian Knowledge among the Indians of North America"; it was affirmed by the Massachusetts Legislature but Parliament refused to acknowledge it, so it disbanded. In 1787, the Society for Propagating the Gospel among the Indians and Others in North America (SPGNA) was formed and incorporated by the General Court in Massachusetts as a replacement of the NEC since the NEC cut off support during the American Revolution. Many of the papers for the SPGNA are at the Massachusetts Historical Society and the Philips Library of the Peabody Essex Museum. See McCallum, *The Letters of Eleazar Wheelock's Indians*, Appendix B, 299ff; Weis, "The New England Company of 1649 and Its Missionary Enterprises," 152; Love, *Samson Occom*, 12–13, n.15.
58. Kellaway, *The New England Company*, 15, 18.

59. Cogley, *John Eliot's Mission*, 208. Kellaway, *The New England Company*, 45–46.

60. Tooker, *John Eliot's First Indian Teacher and Interpreter, Cockenoe-de-Long-Island*, 16–17.

61. Wheeler, *History of the First Congregational Church, Stonington, Conn.*, 90.

62. James Fitch to Daniel Gookin, November 20, 1674, in Gookin, "Historical Collections," 209. More on Fitch can be found in Fitch, *Puritan in the Wilderness*.

63. James Fitch to Daniel Gookin, November 20, 1674, in Gookin, "Historical Collections," 209.

64. *PRCC*, 1:575–76.

65. Correspondence between Governors and Treasurers of New England, 1657–1712. New England Company Collection, 1649–1775, American Antiquarian Society.

66. As quoted in Stone, *The History and Archaeology of the Montauk*, 161.

67. Silverman, *Faith and Boundaries*, 157. For older estimates, see "An Account of Indian Churches in New-England [1673]," in *CMHS*, ser. 1, vol. 10, 124.

68. Drake, *King Philip's War*.

69. Lepore, *The Name of War*; Silverman, *Faith and Boundaries*, 112.

70. For a full account of Sassamon, see Lepore, "Dead Men Tell No Tales"; Kawashima, *Igniting King Philip's War*; See also LaFantasie, "Introduction," in *The Correspondence of Roger Williams*, xxxii, xliii; Sainsbury, "Indian Labor in Early Rhode Island," 260–63.

71. Lepore, *The Name of War*, 7.

72. As just one example, this is the basic interpretive line of Bross, *Dry Bones and Indian Sermons*. See also, Clark, *The Eliot Tracts*, 23. Similarly, most studies of New England Indian missions in the seventeenth century end with King Philip's War. See, for example, Cogley, *John Eliot's Mission*. The obvious exception in the field is Axtell, *The Invasion Within*.

73. Rowlandson and Harrington, *A Narrative of the Captivity, Sufferings, and Removes, of Mrs. Mary Rowlandson*, 9.

74. For a concise summary of these series of events, see Lepore, "When Deer Island Was Turned into Devil's Island."

75. New England Company Collection, 1649–1775, American Antiquarian Society, Folder 3. Taken from the *Long Island Historical Society Collections*, vol. 1.

76. Letter from John Eliot to Robert Boyle, November 4, 1680, *CMHS*, ser. 1, vol. 3, 181. For a description of the church service, see Eliot to Boyle, April 22, 1684, *CMHS*, ser. 1, vol. 3, 183.

77. John Eliot to Robert Boyle, August 29, 1686, "in the third month of our overthrow." *CMHS*, ser. 1, vol. 3, 187.

78. Mayhew, *Indian Converts*, xvii.

79. The most comprehensive study of the development of Wampanoag Christianity pre- and postwar is Silverman, *Faith and Boundaries*.

80. "Books and Tracts in the Indian Language or Designed for the Use of Indians, Printed at Cambridge and Boston, 1653–1721," *PAAS* (October 1873).

81. Kellaway, *The New England Company*, 147.

82. "Queries Relating to the Colony of Connecticut, From the Board of Trade and Plantations, With the Answers Thereto, 1729–1730," *PRCC*, 7:584. The Board of Trade and Plantation didn't ask—and the colony didn't provide—the number of nonenslaved Indians in Connecticut, but five years earlier Talcott had estimated 1,500–1,600 Indians in the colony. In 1730, a Rhode Island census found 15,302 Englishmen, 985 Indians, and 1,648 "negroes." Callender, *An Historical Discourse*, 94.

83. For more on the murky lines between early Congregationalism and Presbyterianism, see Foster, *The Long Argument*.

84. The diary of Joshua Hempstead illustrates the interconnectedness of Long Island with Connecticut. Hempstead, *Diary of Joshua Hempstead*.

85. In at least a few cases, "Congregationalist" and "Presbyterian" were seen as roughly synonymous, as in the case of the Westerly Congregational Church, founded in 1742. Letter from Joseph Park, August 1, 1743, *The Christian History*, no. 26, 27. See also Love, *Samson Occom*, 192.

86. For more on the Connecticut River valley, see Sweeney, "River Gods and Related Minor Deities."

87. Jean M. O'Brien's assessment that they became "effectively 'detribalized'" is perhaps a bit too strong in some cases, but certainly the times had changed. O'Brien, "Divorced from the Land," 145.
88. Several good studies of servitude and slavery in colonial New England are available, including Newell, "The Changing Nature of Slavery in New England, 1670–1720"; Herndon and Sekatau, "Colonizing the Children"; and Newell, "Indian Slavery in Colonial New England."
89. IPCSL, ser. I, vol. II:15, 16.
90. Several boxes containing hundreds of lawsuits by and against Connecticut Indians at the Connecticut State Archives testify to this. See New London County Court Records, Native Americans Collections, Connecticut State Library (Hartford, Conn.).
91. *East Hampton Trustees Journal, 1725–1772,* 1:46, 95.
92. Dally-Starna and Starna, *Gideon's People,* 1:233, 337, 497.
93. Tucker, *Historical Sketch of the Town of Charlestown,* 16.
94. "Account of an Indian Visitation, A.D. 1698," in *CMHS,* 129–30.

Chapter 2

1. Jonathan Barber to Benjamin Colman, October 2, 1733, BCP.
2. Gookin, "An Historical Account," 435.
3. Stiles and Dexter, *Extracts from the Itineraries and Other Miscellanies of Ezra Stiles,* 405.
4. Hopkins, *Historical Memoirs,* 48.
5. *Documents Relative to the Colonial History of the State of New York,* 4:230.
6. On the Deerfield raid, see Haefeli and Sweeney, *Captors and Captives.*
7. Kellaway, *The New England Company,* 259.
8. For a concise summary of the events leading up to Father Rale's War, see Kidd, *The Protestant Interest,* ch. 4. An older but worthwhile analysis is Eckstorm, "The Attack on Norridgewock 1724."
9. Kellaway, *The New England Company,* 263.
10. As quoted in Kellaway, *The New England Company,* 263.
11. Kellaway, *The New England Company,* 261–64.
12. Thompson, *Into All Lands,* 12.
13. Kellaway, *The New England Company,* 257.
14. Stoddard, *Question: Whether God Is Not Angry,* 10.
15. Lovelace, *The American Pietism of Cotton Mather.*
16. Several letters, composed entirely in Latin, between Mather and Francke are among the Curwen Family Papers at the American Antiquarian Society. See box 2, folders 1 and 2.
17. October 2, 1696. Mather, *Diary of Cotton Mather, 1681–1724,* 1:206.
18. *CMHS,* ser. 6, vol. 3, 347–48. Kellaway, *The New England Company,* 251. Also see the Minutes of the Meeting of the NEC Commissioners for September 30, 1706, NEC LMA, Ms.7953.
19. Apparently not everyone shared Mather's enthusiasm. Mather, *Diary of Cotton Mather, 1681–1724,* 2:133.
20. Stone, *The History and Archaeology of the Montauk Indians,* 102.
21. Stone, *The History and Archaeology of the Montauk Indians,* 166.
22. Minutes of the Meeting of the NEC Commissioners, November 21, 1705, NEC LMA, Ms. 7953; Kellaway, *The New England Company,* 240.
23. Mayhew, "1713 Journal," 101, 110.
24. Mayhew, "1714 Journal," 119.
25. Mayhew, "1714 Journal," 125.
26. Mayhew, "1714 Journal," 120.
27. Mayhew, "1714 Journal," 114. The Mashantuckets submitted a petition regarding the case in May of 1713. IPCSL, ser. 1, vol. 1, 75. See also Den Ouden, *Beyond Conquest,* 148–53.
28. IPCSL, ser. 1, vol. 1(A), 87. Transcriptions by the MPMRC.
29. *PRCC,* 6:15, 31, 32. See also IPCSL, 1:86. Love, *Samson Occom,* 27.
30. IPCSL, ser. 1, vol. 1(A), 88. Transcriptions provided by the MPMRC.

31. Samuel Sewall to Robert Ashurst, September 9, 1720, NEC LMA. 7955/vol. 1, 1677–1761, 59.

32. *PRCC*, 7:491. See also IPCSL, 1:167b. The same was true in other colonies. See Brainerd and Edwards, *An Account of the Life of the Late Reverend Mr. David Brainerd*, 65.

33. NEC LMA, Ms. 7957, 5, p. 14. Transcription by Faith Davison.

34. Talcott references Mason's June 18 letter in his response to Mason on June 22, 1725. Talcott, *The Talcott Papers*, 2:395ff. Love, *Samson Occom*, 253.

35. As quoted in Kellaway, *The New England Company*, 254.

36. Minutes of the Meetings of the NEC Commissioners, August 19, 1726, NEC LMA. Ms. 7953.

37. NEC LMA, Ms. 7955 vol. 2, item 1, 79a.

38. Barber was dismissed by the NEC on June 22, 1738, largely because he sided with John Mason and against Ben Uncas II and the colony of Connecticut in the ongoing land case. For Barber's career after this dismissal, see Love, *Samson Occom*, 29, n. 17; Kidd, *The Great Awakening*, 62.

39. Love, *Samson Occom*, 32.

40. *RCRI*, 4:397.

41. For a concise summary of McSparran's life, and in particular, the protracted controversy over the glebe lands in the 1740s, see Bilder, *The Transatlantic Constitution*, ch. 7.

42. Lawrence, *The Old Narragansett Church (St. Paul's)*, 7–8. In 1800, the church building was moved from North Kingstown to Wickford. Updike, *A History of the Episcopal Church in Narragansett*, 144.

43. Denison, *Westerly (Rhode Island) and Its Witnesses*, 78. McSparran, writing in 1752, stated that the church on Narragansett lands was no longer under his control. McSparran, "America Dissected [1752]," 512.

44. Letter from Joseph Park, August 1, 1743, *The Christian History*, no. 26, 27.

45. Minutes of the Meetings of the NEC Commissioners, May 23, 1737, NEC LMA. Ms. 7953.

46. Letter from Joseph Park, August 1, 1743, *The Christian History*, no. 26, 27. See also Love, *Samson Occom*, 192.

47. Adam Winthrop to Joseph Williams, November 5 [8th?], 1734, NEC LMA, 7955, vol. 2, 101a.

48. Adam Winthrop to Robert Clarke, March 7, 1734, NEC LMA, 7955, vol. 2, 104.

49. Talcott, *The Talcott Papers*, 1:314–15. May 23, 1737, Minutes of the meetings of the NEC Boston Commissioners, NEC LMA. Ms. 7953.

50. Hopkins, *Historical Memoirs*, 2.

51. Hopkins, *Historical Memoirs*, 3–4.

52. Hopkins, *Historical Memoirs*, 6, 8, 14.

53. "Deerfield, September 1, 1735," *New England Weekly Journal* (Boston, Mass.), issue 440, p. 442.

54. Hopkins, *Historical Memoirs*, 42.

55. Hopkins, *Historical Memoirs*, 38.

56. Hopkins, *Historical Memoirs*, 55.

57. Hopkins, *Historical Memoirs*, 65.

58. Hopkins, *Historical Memoirs*, 59.

59. Hopkins, *Historical Memoirs*, 44.

60. Hopkins, *Historical Memoirs*, 58.

61. Hopkins, *Historical Memoirs*, 71.

62. Hopkins, *Historical Memoirs*, 71.

63. "Norwich, (in Connecticut) May 8th," *New England Weekly Journal*, May 28, 1734.

64. Wheeler, *History of the First Congregational Church, Stonington, Conn.*, 39.

65. Manuscript Records of the North Groton (Ledyard) Congregational Church, CSL, 1:31.

66. Love, *Samson Occom*, 198.

67. Kevin McBride, "'Desirous to Improve after the European Manner,'" 5. See also Fisher, "'Traditionary Religion,'" 161.

68. *PRCC*, 8:38.

69. Love, *Samson Occom*, 199.

70. Hopkins, *Historical Memoirs*, 87, 89.

71. Hopkins, *Historical Memoirs*, 90.
72. Hopkins, *Historical Memoirs*, 91.
73. Axtell, *The Invasion Within*, 188.
74. *The New-England Primer, Enlarged*.
75. Mayhew and Cotton, *The Indian Primer*, 13.
76. Kellaway, *The New England Company*, 150.
77. *The First Annual Report of the American Society for Promoting the Civilization and General Improvement of the Indian Tribes in the United States*, 54.
78. Talcott, *The Talcott Papers*, 1:107.
79. Talcott, *The Talcott Papers*, 1:110.
80. Governor Talcott to Adam Winthrop, September 20, 1725, Talcott, *The Talcott Papers*, 2:397–99
81. *PRCC*, 7:102–3.
82. Colonists gave other reasons, too, of course. Hutchinson, *A Collection of Original Papers Relative to the History of the Colony of Massachusetts-Bay*, 490.
83. Adam Winthrop to Robert Clarke, March 7, 1734, NEC LMA, 7955, vol. 2, 104.
84. Winthrop mentions four in the 1730s: two under Joseph Bourne at Mashpee, John Robbin under Reverend Thatcher in Middletown, and John Mettawan under Whitman at Farmington. Adam Winthrop to Robert Clarke, July 2, 1736, NEC LMA, 7955, vol. 1., Item 1, 111.
85. Ottery and Ottery, *A Man Called Sampson*, 42.
86. As quoted in Love, *Samson Occom*, 201. Adam Winthrop to Robert Clarke, July 2, 1736, NEC LMA, 7955, vol. 2, 111. See also Kellaway, *The New England Company*, 230.
87. Adam Winthrop to Robert Clarke, July 2, 1736, NEC LMA, 7955, vol. 2, 111.
88. Adam Winthrop to Robert Clarke, March 7, 1734, NEC LMA, Ms. 7955/2, 109. Original in Latin. Translation by Amy Remensnyder. See also Peyer, *The Tutor'd Mind*, 51.
89. January 23, 1737, NEC LMA, Ms. 7955/2, 128.
90. Samuel Whitman to Governor Talcott, November 14, 1737, Talcott, *The Talcott Papers*, 2:33. See also a letter written by Whitman on January 23, 1737, NEC LMA, Ms. 7955/2, 128.
91. Samuel Whitman to Governor Talcott, November 14, 1737, Talcott, *The Talcott Papers*, 2:33.
92. Mettawan was still serving at Farmington in 1743, as attested by a report on him from the New England Company commissioners. Andrew Oliver to Joseph Williams, July 4, 1743, NEC LMA, Ms. 7955/2, 145.
93. Wheeler, *To Live upon Hope*, 48.
94. Gookin, "Historical Collections," 209.
95. Mayhew, "1713 Journal," 101, 110.
96. November 18, 1711, Mather, *Diary of Cotton Mather, 1681–1724*, 2:133.
97. As quoted in Kellaway, *The New England Company*, 268.
98. Talcott, *The Talcott Papers*, 1:284.
99. Talcott, *The Talcott Papers*, 2:480, note.
100. *CWSO*, 52.
101. Mayhew, "1714 Journal," 116.
102. IPCSL, 1:227. Also printed in Talcott, *The Talcott Papers*, 319–21.
103. Caulkins, *Memoir of the Rev. William Adams*, 35.
104. Hopkins, *Historical Memoirs*, 22–24.
105. December 2, 1734, *New England Weekly Journal*, 2.
106. The most recent and comprehensive study of the Mohegan land controversy to date is Den Ouden, *Beyond Conquest*.
107. "Deposition of Thomas Waterman and William Hide." Not dated but listed with other depositions dated May 30, 1738. See *GCC*. For a map of the two settlements, see Stiles and Dexter, *Extracts from the Itineraries and Other Miscellanies of Ezra Stiles*, 1:359.
108. Hempstead, *Diary of Joshua Hempstead*, 153.
109. Love, *Samson Occom*, 28.
110. October 26, 1731, meeting of the Boston Commissioners for the New England Company, NEC NEHGS, Box 3, Correspondence, Ms. B C40.

111. Love, *Samson Occom*, 28. Kellaway, *The New England Company*, 230. "Ben Uncas, his indenture," November 14, 1734, IPCSL, ser. 1, vol. 1, 236, 237.
112. Love, *Samson Occom*, 31.
113. Talcott, *The Talcott Papers*, 1:107.
114. IPCSL, 1:162. Transcription by the MPMRC.
115. "Norwich, (in Connecticut,) May 8th," *New England Weekly Journal*, May 28, 1734.
116. *PRCC*, 7:472.
117. Jonathan Barber (Mohegan) to Benjamin Colman, October 2, 1733, BCP.
118. Hopkins, *Historical Memoirs*, 19.
119. *PRCC*, 8:72–73.
120. For a broader background on the transatlantic legal appeals process in the colonial period, particularly on the various and complicated power dynamics they represented, see Bilder, *The Transatlantic Constitution*, ch. 4.
121. Saltonstall, *A Memorial*.
122. *GCC*, 29.
123. Beardsley, "The Mohegan Land Controversy," 212.
124. Ann was the daughter of Caesar and was the same woman who would marry Ben Uncas III just one or two years later, *GCC*, 235.
125. "Deposition of Joseph Tracy, Jr, and Jabez Crocker, May 29, 1738," *GCC*, 235. Beardsley, "The Mohegan Land Controversy," 215. Davison, "Sachem Mahomet /Weyonomon: Mohegan Hero or Mason Tool?" 3. For more on the black dance, see *GCC*, 204, 208. See also Den Ouden, *Beyond Conquest*, ch. 4.
126. For details of their trip, see Thomas Coram to Benjamin Colman, September 21, 1738, BCP. Regarding Mahomet II's death, see *The Daily Journal*, no. 5761, Wednesday, August 11, 1736. Another shorter notice was printed in the *Gentlemen's Magazine*, VI, 487. See also Talcott, *The Talcott Papers*, I:374. And 270 years later, on November 22, 2006, Queen Elizabeth II, the Duke of Edinburgh, Mohegan tribal leader Bruce "Two Dogs" Bozsum, and other Mohegans held a ceremony at Southwark Cathedral in which a carved granite stone was taken to London to commemorate Mahomet's death in 1736. "Native American Honoured by Queen," November 22, 2006. BBC News online edition. http://news.bbc.co.uk/1/hi/england/london/6172062.stm. Accessed November 23, 2006.
127. *PRCC*, 8:166.
128. Caulkins, *Memoir of the Rev. William Adams*, 35–36.
129. *PRCC*, 8:245; Love, *Samson Occom*, 32.
130. Kellaway, *The New England Company*, 218.
131. Simmons, "The Great Awakening and Indian Conversion in Southern New England," 31.
132. IPCSL, ser. 1, vol. 1(A), 88. Transcriptions provided by the MPMRC.

Chapter 3

1. *CWSO*, 53.
2. Hempstead, *Diary of Joshua Hempstead*, 379. Caulkins, *History of New London*, 454. Stout and Onuf, "James Davenport and the Great Awakening in New London," 569.
3. For a discussion of carnival and social reversals in an early modern European context, see Bakhtin, *Rabelais and His World*, 81.
4. *CWSO*, 53. See also Love, *Samson Occom*, 30.
5. For just one example, see Calloway, "Introduction," in Colin G. Calloway, *After King Philip's War*, 9. See also Simmons, "Red Yankees: Narragansett Conversion in the Great Awakening"; Simmons, "The Great Awakening and Indian Conversion in Southern New England."
6. Occom, "Autobiographical Narrative, Second Draft (September 17, 1768)," in *CWSO*, 52–53.
7. See, for example, Brooks, *American Lazarus*, 56.
8. Benjamin Uncas II to Governor Talcott, May 11, 1736, Talcott, *The Talcott Papers*, 1:354.
9. The fact that there are two drafts of his autobiographical narrative (varying quite a bit in content and length) should also remind us of the importance of considering this 1760s

context. In the second draft, Occom used variations on the word "heathen" four times in the first three sentences to get his point across. See *CWSO*, 51–57.

10. John Thornton persuasively argues for a similar process among African slaves in the Atlantic world. Thornton, *Africa and Africans in the Making of the Atlantic World*, 254. For both Africans and Indians, the idioms and rituals of English Protestantism were first and foremost learned over time, with multiple exposures required to "learn the language of Canaan," as Christine Heyrman has suggested of evangelicals in the antebellum South. Heyrman, *Southern Cross*, 4–5.

11. For the Awakening in the British Atlantic world, see Hindmarsh, *The Evangelical Conversion Narrative*; Sensbach, *Rebecca's Revival*; Schmidt, *Holy Fairs*. For the American colonies, see Kidd, *The Great Awakening*; Lambert, *Inventing the "Great Awakening"*; Crawford, *Seasons of Grace*; Gaustad, *The Great Awakening in New England*; Butler, "Enthusiasm Described and Decried"; Winiarski, "Jonathan Edwards, Enthusiast?"; Stout and Onuf, "James Davenport and the Great Awakening in New London"; Bushman, *From Puritan to Yankee*; Goen, *Revivalism and Separatism in New England*; Merritt, "Dreaming of the Savior's Blood"; Westerkamp, *Triumph of the Laity*; Seeman, *Pious Persuasions*.

12. For more on this, see Lambert, *Inventing the "Great Awakening."*

13. Whitefield, *A Continuation of the Reverend Mr. Whitefield's Journal*, 52, 65, 66, 96. Tracy, *The Great Awakening*, 88, note.

14. See, for example, "London, March 29," *New-York Weekly Journal* (New York, N.Y.). Jonathan Parsons, "Account of the Revival at Lyme," in Tracy, *The Great Awakening*, 37. Whitefield even won over Benjamin Franklin in Philadelphia. Franklin, *The Autobiography and Other Writings*, 106.

15. See Onuf, "New Lights in New London."

16. Winiarski, "Jonathan Edwards, Enthusiast?" Edwards took a more conservative stance on the revivals just two years later. Hempstead, *Diary*, 407.

17. For a concise description of the spectrum of responses, see Kidd, *The Great Awakening*, xiv.

18. The most comprehensive study of eighteenth-century Separatism is Goen, *Revivalism and Separatism in New England, 1740–1800*.

19. Goen, *Revivalism and Separatism in New England, 1740–1800*, 69.

20. For a fairly comprehensive listing, see Goen, *Revivalism and Separatism in New England, 1740–1800*, ch. 3 and Appendix.

21. Browning, "The Preston Separate Church," in *Records and Papers of the New London County Historical Society*, part 2, vol. 2, 153ff. Not all Separate churches became Baptist, however.

22. For more on the political effects of the Awakening, see Bushman, *From Puritan to Yankee*, chs. 15 and 16. On itinerancy, see Hall, *Contested Boundaries*.

23. On New England Indians in the Great Awakening, see Sweet, *Bodies Politic*; Simmons, "Red Yankees: Narragansett Conversion in the Great Awakening"; Simmons, "The Great Awakening and Indian Conversion in Southern New England." Sections of other books deal with this topic, but usually with regard to one particular Native community. See, for example, Brooks, *American Lazarus*; Brooks, "Introduction," in *CWSO*; Peyer, *The Tutor'd Mind*; Murray, *WJJ*; Kidd, *The Great Awakening*, ch. 13. For the mid-Atlantic region, see Merritt, "Dreaming of the Savior's Blood."

24. Saturday, July 14, 1744. *The Christian History*, no. 72, 154. See also Eleazar Wheelock to Daniel Rogers, January 18, 1742, WP, 742118.

25. Hempstead, *Diary*, 342.

26. Tracy, *The Great Awakening*, 234. In the summer of 1740, Davenport publicly predicted the precise date a reportedly insane and mute woman living near Southold would be fully recovered; he prayed and fasted to that end. When the woman died on that exact day, Davenport proclaimed it as an answer to his prayer, because she was now in heaven.

27. For Tennent's call for this sort of practice, see Tennent, *The Danger of an Unconverted Ministry*.

28. Stout and Onuf, "James Davenport and the Great Awakening in New London," 567.

29. Josiah Cotton, *Memoirs*, 314–15, as quoted in Shipton, *Sibley's Harvard Graduates*, 390.

30. *Boston Evening-Post*, April 11, 1743. See also "Extract of a Letter from Rhode-Island, Dated March 11," in *The Pennsylvania Gazette*, April 4, 1743; see also the *Boston-Evening Post*, March 14, 1743.

31. "Extract of a Letter from Rhode-Island, Dated March 11," in *The Pennsylvania Gazette*. April 4, 1743. For another account of the story, see Stout and Onuf, "James Davenport and the Great Awakening in New London," 556–57. See also Tracy, *The Great Awakening*, 230–55. Hamilton and Bridenbaugh, *Gentleman's Progress*, 161.

32. See Fish, *The Church of Christ a Firm and Durable House*, 125ff.

33. Davenport's great uncle, Abraham Pierson, published a 1659 tract in the Quinnipiac language titled "Some Helps for the Indians Shewing them How to improve their natural Reason, to know the True God, and the true Christian Religion." See "Books and Tracts in the Indian Language or Designed for the Use of Indians, Printed at Cambridge and Boston, 1653–1721," *PAAS* (October 1873).

34. "An Account of the Revival of Religion at LYME," Saturday, June 2, 1744, *The Christian History*, no. 66, 106.

35. IPCSL, ser. 1, vol. 2, 238.

36. Hempstead, *Diary*, 380.

37. Regarding eighteenth-century New England Congregational Church architecture, see Benes, *New England Meeting House and Church: 1630–1850*.

38. Park, "An Account of the late Propagation of Religion at Westerly and Charlestown in Rhode-Island Colony," August 27, 1743, *The Christian History*, no. 26, 205.

39. Hempstead, *Diary*, 380.

40. Hempstead, *Diary*, 380.

41. Hempstead, *Diary*, 380.

42. *Boston Post Boy*, October 10, 1741.

43. IPCSL, ser. 1, vol. 2, 238. Transcriptions provided by the MPMRC.

44. IPCSL, ser. 1, vol. 2, 239. Transcriptions provided by the MPMRC.

45. IPCSL, ser. 1, vol. 2, 238, 239. See also Law, *The Law Papers*, I:36.

46. J. Lee to Eleazar Wheelock, April 20, 1741. WP, 741270. See also Jonathan Parsons to Eleazar Wheelock, April 20, 1741. WP, 741271.

47. "An Account of the Revival of Religion at LYME," Saturday, June 2, 1744, *The Christian History*, no. 66, 109.

48. Tracy, *The Great Awakening*, 138.

49. "An Account of the Revival of Religion at LYME," Saturday, June 2, 1744, *The Christian History*, no. 66, 105–8.

50. "Account of the Revival of Religion at LYME East Parish, in Connecticut, finished." June 9, 1744, *The Christian History*, no. 67, 113ff. See also De Forest, *History of the Indians of Connecticut*, 384.

51. George Griswold, "An Account of the Beginning of the Revival of Religion at New London, North Parish," April 9, 1744, *The Christian History*, no. 67, 115.

52. Occom, "Autobiographical Narrative, Second Draft (September 17, 1768)," in *CWSO*, 52–53.

53. Caulkins, *History of Norwich, Connecticut*, 321; Hempstead, *Diary*, 446.

54. Regarding Horton's salary, see Records of the Society in Scotland for the Propagation of Christian Knowledge, National Archives of Scotland. RG GD95/1/4 Minutes of Gen'l Meetings, January 1, 1736–November 15, 1759, p. 328. Transcriptions by John Grigg.

55. Horton, "Journal," 195.

56. Horton, "Journal," 196.

57. Horton, "Journal," 195.

58. Horton, "Journal," 196.

59. Horton, "Journal," 197.

60. Horton, "Journal," 197.

61. Horton, "Journal," 198.

62. Horton, "Journal," 198.

63. McClure and Dexter, *Diary of David McClure*, 138.

64. Horton, "Journal," 196.

65. *The Christian Monthly History*, 32.

66. Horton, "Journal," 202–3.

67. Horton, "Journal," 209.

68. Death had provoked a similar interest in religion and revival at Northampton, Massachusetts, under Jonathan Edwards in 1735.
69. Horton, "Journal," 203.
70. Occom, "An Account of the Montauk Indians, on Long-Island" in *CMHS*, ser. 1, vol. 10, 110.
71. Horton, "Journal," 208–9.
72. Brainerd and Edwards, *An Account of the Life of the Late Reverend Mr. David Brainerd,* 63. Brainerd was providing a six-week long pulpit supply at the East Hampton church (something Horton could not do since he was commissioned specifically to the Indians). See John A. Grigg, "'How This Shall Be Brought About,'" 55.
73. Park, "An Account of the late Propagation of Religion at Westerly," August 27, 1743, *The Christian History*, no. 26, 208; 27, 1.
74. Park, "An Account of the late Propagation of Religion at Westerly," August 27, 1743, *The Christian History*, 26, 208.
75. "The Remainder of Mr. Park's Account." September 3, 1743, *The Christian History*, no. 27, 1ff.
76. "The Rev. Mr Park's Account of the Progress of Religion at Westerly, &c. finished." March 24, 1744, *The Christian History*, no. 56, 19–22.
77. "The Rev. Mr Park's Account of the Progress of Religion at Westerly, &c. finished." March 24, 1744, *The Christian History*, no. 56, 19, 21.
78. IPCSL, ser. 1, vol. 1, 240.
79. Brainerd and Edwards, *An Account of the Life of the Late Reverend Mr. David Brainerd,* 40.
80. For details of this trial and the surrounding events, see Fisher, "'I believe they are Papists!'"
81. July 16, 1743,. *The Christian History*, no. 20, 153.
82. For an excellent translation of the Pachgatgoch diaries, see Dally-Starna and Starna, *Gideon's People*.
83. Cothren, *History of Ancient Woodbury, Connecticut,* 2:103. See also *PRCC*, 8:372.
84. Andrew Oliver to Joseph Williams, July 4, 1743, NEC LMA, Ms. 7955/2, 145.
85. This reality also serves as a reminder of how influential Edwards's publication about—rather than the experiences of—the revivals were for a wider audience outside of Northampton.
86. July 16, 1743, *The Christian History*, no. 20, 153.
87. Hopkins, *Historical Memoirs,* 103.
88. Brainerd and Edwards, *An Account of the Life of the Late Reverend Mr. David Brainerd,* 40.
89. Horton, "Journal," 220.
90. Report of Joseph Park, March 24, 1744, *The Christian History*, no. 56.

Chapter 4

1. North Stonington Church Records, CSL, 1:9.
2. As early as the 1660s New Englanders commonly utilized the English practice of asking a woman during labor to name the father of her illegitimate child, with the assumption that she would not—or could not—lie. Nonetheless, this was likely offensive to Native sensibilities and practices. Ulrich, *A Midwife's Tale,* 149. My thanks to Daniel Mandell for clarifying this point.
3. North Stonington Church Records, CSL, 1:132.
4. Although in the church records "partial" members are not listed as such (usually they were adults who had not been baptized as children), their not-full status is implied by the contrasting status of being "in full communion" given to those who gave a profession of faith.
5. Other options apart from churches were available to colonial men and women who wanted to get married (such as before magistrates in a nonchurch setting). Choosing to do so in a church—then as now—required a specific choice. I am thankful to David Hall for pointing this out. Additionally, in some towns, marriage seems to have been primarily a function of the magistrates, not the clergy. Or so it seems in East Hampton, New York. See *East Hampton Trustees Journal,* 1:260.
6. Anderson, *The Betrayal of Faith*; Barbour, *Versions of Deconversion*.

7. Goen, *Revivalism and Separatism in New England, 1740–1800*, 12–18. Goen is summarizing the process described in Jonathan Edwards's 1737 *Narrative of Surprising Conversions*. *Revivalism and Separatism in New England, 1740–1800*, 13–14. See also Richter, *Facing East from Indian Country*, 119–21.

8. Horton, "Journal," 196. A similar morphology—and tentativeness about people being saved—was also used for non-Indian participants in the revivals.

9. Goen, *Revivalism and Separatism in New England, 1740–1800*, 12–18.

10. The proliferation of scholarship on Occom demonstrates this point. All of it draws heavily on his autobiographical accounts to describe his conversion. See Occom, "Autobiographical Narrative, Second Draft (September 17, 1768)," *CWSO*, 52–53.

11. "Books and Tracts in the Indian Language or Designed for the Use of Indians, Printed at Cambridge and Boston, 1653–1721," *PAAS*, 45ff. This was Eliot's last translation before his death in 1690.

12. The Moravians in western Connecticut reported similar difficulties translating words like grace, blessing, and redemption. Dally-Starna and Starna, *Gideon's People*, 1:533.

13. Gookin, *Historical Collections of the Indians in New England*, 76.

14. Sprague, *Annals of the American Pulpit*, 3:195. Also quoted in Allen, *Memoirs of Samson Occom* (unpublished ms., William Allen Papers, Rauner Special Collections, Dartmouth College, 1859), ser. 1, box 1, folder 8, p. 153. Also in *CWSO*, 161, and Brooks, *American Lazarus*, 62–63. Oxford English Dictionary Online, "traditionary": www.oed.com. Accessed April 17, 2007.

15. One recent example of this is John Wood Sweet, whose otherwise lucid analysis uses this totalizing view of conversion. Sweet, *Bodies Politic*, 133. A more thoughtful analysis of this is Morrison, *The Solidarity of Kin*, 161ff.

16. Axtell, *The Invasion Within*, 330.

17. Williams, *A Key into the Language of America*, 115.

18. Axtell, "Were Indian Conversions Bona Fide?" For a thoroughgoing, critical engagement with Axtell's essay, see Morrison, *The Solidarity of Kin*, ch. 8.

19. Seeman, *Pious Persuasions*, 80.

20. The following analysis is based upon my examination of the manuscript records of these three churches, all available at the Connecticut State Library: the First/West Stonington Congregational Church, the East Stonington Congregational Church, and the North Stonington Church. The records of the First (West) Stonington Congregational Church were also printed in Wheeler, *History of the First Congregational Church, Stonington, Conn., 1674–1874*.

21. With regard to partial membership, the various classifications of people who affiliated—whether white, African, or Indian—makes clear that such a partial membership existed. See, for example, Blake, *The Later History of the First Church of Christ*, 31. Also a heading in the East Church Records: "The Names of Them Who Own Covenant, But Don't Joyn In Full Communion," Wheeler, *History of the First Congregational Church, Stonington, Conn., 1674–1874*, 236, 240.

22. Porterfield, "Women's Attraction to Puritanism," 196. Porterfield is drawing upon older studies, however, including Moran, "Sisters in Christ," and Pope, *The Half-Way Covenant*. See also Ulrich, *Good Wives*, 216.

23. Pequot petition to the General Assembly, May 5, 1742, IPCSL, ser. 1, vol. 1, 239.

24. Mather, *Pray for the Rising Generation*, 12.

25. Personal interview with Melissa Zobel, Mohegan Nation Medicine Woman, January 2007.

26. Simmons and Simmons, *Old Light on Separate Ways*, 43, 44.

27. For broader trends regarding sexual norms see Godbeer, *Sexual Revolution in Early America*.

28. North Stonington Church Records, CSL, 1:126.

29. Brown and Rose, *Black Roots*, 519.

30. First Baptist Church of Groton Church Records, CSL, 1:24, 28, 29.

31. North Groton (Ledyard) Congregational Church Records, CSL, 75ff.

32. Stiles, *The Literary Diary of Ezra Stiles*, 1:413.

33. Wheelock, *A Plain and Faithful Narrative*, 36; Sweet, *Bodies Politic*; Stone, *The History and Archaeology of the Montauk*, 166. Also *East Hampton Trustees Journal, 1725–1772*, 66. See the Manuscript Records of the First Presbyterian Church of East Hampton.

34. Hempstead, *Diary of Joshua Hempstead*, 400.
35. The Indian Separate movement in New England is discussed in detail in chapter 5.
36. "The Remainder of Mr. Park's Account," September 3, 1743, *The Christian History*, no. 27, 1ff. See also Griswold, "Account of the Revival Religion of LYME East Parish, in Connecticut, finished," June 9, 1744, *The Christian History*, no. 67, 114.
37. Talcott's numbers are the most complete for this general period, and other population estimates from the late 1730s do not indicate a major change in the intervening years. Regarding omissions, Ezra Stiles, for example, in 1761 placed the total number of people (adults and children) on the Narragansett reservation in Charlestown, R.I., at 248; just a year later, however, the Narragansetts themselves took a count and came up with over double that number, a full six hundred, not counting other Indians on the reservation. Stiles and Dexter, *Extracts from the Itineraries and Other Miscellanies of Ezra Stiles*, 54, 115. See also Mayhew, "1713 Journal," 110.
38. Although I initially hoped to find more evidence of Native affiliations during the Great Awakening, the combination of poor record keeping, lost or missing records, and the lack of consistent ethnic designation made this difficult. Overall, however, I was surprised at how few Natives affiliated. I was able to look at the records of the following churches: First, Second, and East Congregational Churches in Stonington; New London, North Parish Congregational Church; Christ Church, New London; Columbia (Lebanon Crank) Congregational Church; First Congregational Church of Norwich; East Lyme Baptist Church; First Baptist Church of Groton; Groton First Congregational Church; North Groton (Ledyard) Congregational Church; St. Paul's Episcopal Church (Kingstown, Rhode Island); Shinnecock Presbyterian Church; First Presbyterian Church of Southampton; First Presbyterian Church of East Hampton; and the First Presbyterian Church of Southold. There are no eighteenth-century records for any of the Indian Separate churches, including the one at Narragansett. The same is true with the church in Westerly founded by Joseph Park. Nonetheless, the trends from the extant church records all seem to point in the same direction.
39. Saturday, June 2, 1744, *The Christian History*, no. 66, 109–10. Griswold reported two on March 7, 1742; five on July 18; one on September 5; one on November 7; two on March 13, 1743; one on March 27; and one on May 8, 1743. Interestingly enough, however, he counted an additional seven Indians as having been "hopefully converted," despite their lack of full membership in his church, bringing the total number to twenty. Since I do not know the affiliation levels (if any) of these additional seven, I have not used them in the calculations. Saturday, June 9, 1744, *The Christian History*, no. 57, 113–14.
40. March 17, 1744,. *The Christian History*, no. 55, 22, 24. The affiliations happened over time. Park reported that by September 1743, seven months after the February meeting with the Pequots, eight Narragansetts had been baptized. On October 9, 1743, nine more Narragansetts "were baptized and received to full Communion; who gave very hopeful Evidence of a Work of saving Grace wrought in them." Park baptized and received into full membership twenty-six more on January 15, 1744, and on February 5 of the same year he reported that "fifteen came under the Bonds of the Gospel." Such an ambiguous phrase would not necessarily mean full membership, but either way Park took them as signs of conversion. The records of Park's church have been lost; a few fragments from the early 1750s were printed in "Extracts from Westerly Church Records," in *New England Historical and Genealogical Register* 26, 326.
41. Caner, *A Candid Examination of Dr. Mayhew's Observations*, 45.
42. Because Park's descriptions of affiliations are not very precise, it is not entirely clear if these sixty-four affiliations were all full memberships or not.
43. Taken from the author's tally of the St. Paul's records, found in Updike, *A History of the Episcopal Church in Narragansett*, vol. 2. For just one example of a non-Indian affiliation, see Updike, 2:513–14.
44. The Native affiliations chronologically closest to the Awakening appear on February 19, 1727, and January 10, 1751. See the Manuscript Records of the First Presbyterian Church of East Hampton. Also printed in the *Records of the Town of East Hampton*, 5:456–571. Thanks to Erin Calfee for compiling the data from the printed records. I reviewed the manuscript records at the East Hampton Library (Long Island Room) but did not see any major differences.

45. When the minister who replaced Sylvanus White sat down in 1785 to write a short history of the Presbyterian Church in Southampton, he lamented that "all former records are not at hand and therefore a journal of this Church from its first planting here is impossible." See *Journal Book of Proceedings of the First Church of Christ* (Southampton, New York: Unpublished Manuscript, First Presbyterian Church of Southampton Archives).

46. These journals were originally sent to the SSPCK and published serially in *The Christian History Monthly*. They have also been collected, transcribed and published in Stone, *The History and Archaeology of the Montauk*. There are no records of the Shinnecock Presbyterian Church prior to the nineteenth century.

47. The numbers are taken from an analysis of Azariah Horton's journal by myself and Erin Calfee. Deciphering Horton's creative (and, of course, highly subjective) evaluation of Natives' religious experiences is tricky, to say the least. Other tabulations by contemporary chroniclers, however, do not differ substantially from our results. See, for example, Gillies, *Historical Collections*, 2:408.

48. Hopkins, *Historical Memoirs*, 42.

49. Hopkins, *Historical Memoirs*, 128.

50. These numbers come from a report by Timothy Woodbridge in 1749. See Hopkins, *Historical Memoirs*, 143.

51. One way to account for this seeming reticence to join as full members is possible scrupulosity, or the fear of incurring damnation for being ill-prepared. I have not found any Indians who give this as a reason for not joining as full members, but such a scenario is nonetheless plausible.

52. "The Remainder of Mr. Park's Account," September 3, 1743, *The Christian History*, no. 27, 1ff. George Griswold, "Account of the Revival Religion of LYME East Parish, in Connecticut, finished," June 9, 1744, *The Christian History*, no. 67, 114.

53. Hopkins, *Historical Memoirs*, 128.

54. Jacob Johnson to Boston Commissioners, June 20, 1755, NEC LMA, Ms. 8011a.

55. See, for example, *WJJ* and *CWSO*.

56. George Griswold, "Account of the Revival Religion of LYME East Parish, in Connecticut, finished," June 9, 1744, *The Christian History*, no. 67, 114.

57. Gillies, *Historical Collections*, 2:448. Another short summary of his frustrations with the Long Island Natives can be found on Gillies, 2:409.

58. Occom, "Account of the Montauk Indians, on Long Island," in *CWSO*, 50.

59. Jacob Johnson to Boston Commissioners, June 20, 1755, NEC LMA, Ms. 8011a.

60. Silverman, "Indians, Missionaries, and Religious Translation." On Native "popular religion" in this time period, see Winiarski, "Native American Popular Religion in New England's Old Colony, 1670–1770." Some of these issues are also taken up in Fisher, "'In the practice and profession of the Christian Religion.'"

61. McClure and Dexter, *Diary of David McClure Doctor of Divinity, 1748–1820*, 192; Occom, *CWSO*, 22; Szasz, "Introduction," in Love, *Samson Occom*, xxix.

62. McClure and Dexter, *Diary of David McClure Doctor of Divinity, 1748–1820*, 192.

63. Horton, "First Journal," 197.

64. Dally-Starna and Starna, "American Indians and Moravians in Southern New England," 92.

65. Stiles and Dexter, *Extracts from the Itineraries and other Miscellanies of Ezra Stiles*, 160–61.

66. Cooper, *The Diary of Mary Cooper*, 17.

67. Sweet, *Bodies Politic*; Simmons, "The Great Awakening and Indian Conversion in Southern New England."

68. Simmons, "The Great Awakening and Indian Conversion in Southern New England," 32–33.

69. While it is true that non-Indian affiliations with local English churches similarly dropped off in the mid- to late-1740s, the social, political, and religious consequences of Indian deaffiliation were vastly different. Indians who left churches or abandoned Christianity were seen as slipping back into paganism and devil worship, and this perceived failure of the Awakening prompted a whole new spate of evangelism on the part of colonists, which was directed at Natives. Similarly, Native deaffiliation was more dramatic and wide ranging than

among whites. A substantial core of colonists remained in local churches post-Awakening, while in the Stonington churches, Indian infant baptisms ceased completely after 1750.

70. See Brown and Hall, "Family Strategies and Religious Practice," 55ff.
71. *Connecticut Church Records, State Library Index, New London First Congregational Church, 1670–1888*, 452.
72. *Connecticut Church Records, State Library Index, New London First Congregational Church, 1670–1888*, 452.
73. Seeman, *Pious Persuasions*, 89.
74. See the Manuscript Records of the First Church of Christ in New London, CSL, 1:33. Also listed in *Connecticut Church Records, State Library Index, New London First Congregational Church, 1670–1888*, 1:33–34, 33:41–42. Hempstead, *Diary*, 400.
75. The order to make clothing for Ben Uncas II and III can be found in several places: IPCSL, ser. 1, vol. 1, 212a, 213, 215, 216.
76. For later proceedings in the Mohegan case, see ch. 7, and Conroy, "The Defense of Indian Land Rights."
77. IPCSL, ser. 1, vol. 2, 251 and 252.
78. IPCSL, ser. 1, vol. 1, 231a.
79. IPCSL, ser. 1, vol. 2, 239. Transcriptions provided by the MPMRC.
80. McBride, "Transformation by Degree," 39–40.
81. John Eliot, "A further Account of the Progress of the Gospel," in *The Eliot Tracts*, ed. Michael Clark, 387.
82. IPCSL, ser. 1, vol. 2, 12a. Transcriptions by the MPMRC. When the Pequots continued to plant their crops on these same lands, the colonists "Cut up & destroyed" the Indians' crops, thereby denying the Pequots "the use of the Grates Parte of the said Reserved Lands."
83. IPCSL, ser. 1, vol. 2, 17. Transcriptions by the MPMRC. The Niantics requested of the Assembly "a Committee of Wise, Disinterested men" to "set up and fix the bounds Thereof Accordingly: that to our Interest may be wholly Severed from theirs."
84. Brooks, *American Lazarus*, 55. Although this is undeniably true for some Indian leaders, it is difficult to know just how widespread and self-conscious this sort of corporate redefinition might have been among nonliterate "people in the pew" type Indians.

Chapter 5

1. Dally-Starna and Starna, *Gideon's People*, 2:216. The Moravians typically conflated Congregationalism and Presbyterianism.
2. The Separate Indian Christian practices and networks are similar to the ones that emerged in southeastern Massachusetts in the seventeenth and early eighteenth centuries, although I have not found many, if any, points of direct influence on Native communities in Rhode Island and Connecticut until the mid-eighteenth century. For a full discussion of these networks in Massachusetts, see Mandell, *Behind the Frontier*, especially ch. 3.
3. RCRI, 4:425–26.
4. Orcutt, *History of the Towns of New Milford and Bridgewater, Connecticut, 1703–1882*, 127.
5. The depositions of individuals during the 1738 and 1743 Mohegan land hearings show the presence of more than a few local colonists, some of who seem to have been sent by the government to keep tabs on the proceedings. See, for example, GCC, 235.
6. Stiles and Dexter, *Extracts from the Itineraries and Other Miscellanies of Ezra Stiles*, 130.
7. Talcott, *The Talcott Papers*, 2:482–83.
8. New London Association Records, 1708–1788, Connecticut Conference Archives, United Church of Christ (Hartford, Conn.), 99–100. I am grateful to Doug Winiarski for kindly providing copies of some of these records.
9. Jacob Johnson to Boston Commissioners, June 20, 1755, NEC LMA, Ms. 8011a.
10. Jacob Johnson to Boston Commissioners, June 20, 1755, NEC LMA, Ms. 8011a. Johnson claimed that this changed over time, however, and that Skuttaub later was "very Steady" at his lectures.
11. North Stonington Congregational Church Records, CSL, 120.

12. Brown and Rose, *Black Roots*, 324.
13. Manuscript Records of the First Baptist Church of Groton, CSL, 16, 17, 21, 23.
14. Jacob Johnson to Boston Commissioners, June 20, 1755, NEC LMA, Ms. 8011a.
15. Jacob Johnson to Boston Commissioners, June 20, 1755, NEC LMA, Ms. 8011a.
16. Manuscript Records of the East Lyme Baptist Church, CSL.
17. Joseph Fish to Andrew Oliver, November 15, 1762. Miscellaneous Bound Manuscripts, MHS. The lines of influence had run in the opposite direction just two decades prior, however, when the Lantern Hill Pequots visited the Narragansetts in February 1743 and facilitated an awakening of sorts. See chapter 3 of this book.
18. Cogley, *John Eliot's Mission*, 243. Silverman, "Indians, Missionaries, and Religious Translation," 145ff. Cohen, "Conversion among Puritans and Amerindians," 250, 255.
19. David Silverman has noted a similar phenomenon in Indian churches on Cape Cod and Martha's Vineyard. See Silverman, "The Church in New England Indian Community Life: A View from the Islands and Cape Cod."
20. The events surrounding the founding of the Separate Indian church in Narragansett are pieced together from a variety of sources, including Simmons and Simmons, *Old Light on Separate Ways*, and Stiles, *The Literary Diary of Ezra Stiles*, vol. 1.
21. Love reports that in the 1761 census Samuel Niles's age was given as sixty years. Love, *Samson Occom*, 194.
22. Stiles, *The Literary Diary of Ezra Stiles*, 1:232.
23. March 17, 1744, *The Christian History*, no. 55, 22, 24. See also Love, *Samson Occom*, 192.
24. Joseph Park Report, March 24, 1744, *The Christian History*, no. 56.
25. August 18, 1811, Curtis Coe, Third Journal, 1811, SPGNA PEM, box 1, folder 21.
26. Dates for this series of events are unclear. I have followed Joseph Fish's rendering of the events narrated to the NEC commissioners in the 1760s after he began spending time among the Narragansetts. Simmons and Simmons, *Old Light on Separate Ways*, 4. See also "Extracts from Westerly Church Records," in *New England Historical and Genealogical Register* 26, 326. For the 1750 date, see Denison, *Westerly (Rhode Island) and Its Witnesses*, 79. William McLouglin, however, asserts the schism took place in 1745. Backus and McLoughlin, *The Diary of Isaac Backus*, 1:260, n. 1.
27. August 18, 1811, Curtis Coe, Third Journal, 1811, SPGNA PEM, box 1, folder 21.
28. The church consisted of congregants from Westerly and Stonington and was called the Church of Christ in Westerly and Stonington in Union. Denison, *Westerly (Rhode Island) and Its Witnesses*, 100, 102. Goen, *Revivalism and Separatism in New England, 1740–1800*, 92.
29. Tucker, *Historical Sketch of the Town of Charlestown*, 65.
30. Simon's tribal identity was identified by Ezra Stiles, who received the story from Samuel Niles two decades later. Stiles, *The Literary Diary of Ezra Stiles*, 1:232–33. See also Goen, *Revivalism and Separatism in New England, 1740–1800*, 91; Simmons and Simmons, *Old Light on Separate Ways*, 9, n. 4.
31. Walker, *Some Aspects of the Religious Life of New England*, 119. See also Simmons and Simmons, *Old Light on Separate Ways*, 10.
32. Stiles, *The Literary Diary of Ezra Stiles*, 1:232.
33. Stiles, *The Literary Diary of Ezra Stiles*, 1:232–33.
34. Joseph Fish to Joseph Sewall, c. September 18, 1765, Simmons and Simmons, *Old Light on Separate Ways*, 5.
35. Joseph Fish to Joseph Sewall, c. September 18, 1765, Simmons and Simmons, *Old Light on Separate Ways*, 5.
36. Stiles, *The Literary Diary of Ezra Stiles*, 1:233.
37. Joseph Fish to Joseph Sewall, c. September 18, 1765, Simmons and Simmons, *Old Light on Separate Ways*, 3–4, 7.
38. Edward Deake to Joseph Fish, December 18, 1765, Indians—Collected Papers (Manuscripts; Microfilm), CHS, 0053.
39. Entry for May 8, 1772, Stiles, *The Literary Diary of Ezra Stiles*, 1:234.
40. Hamilton and Bridenbaugh, *Gentleman's Progress*, 98. See also Sweet, *Bodies Politic*, 15.
41. Simmons, "Red Yankees: Narragansett Conversion in the Great Awakening," 259.

42. For more on the Narragansett intratribal land factions and disputes, see Sweet, *Bodies Politic*, ch. 1.

43. Spellings for his last name vary greatly, including Ashbow, Ashpo, and Ashpow. I have chosen to use Ashpo as it appears in this form most frequently in the records.

44. Love, *Samson Occom*, 78.

45. *GCC*, 223–25. As a later example of this, see Ashpo's letter of confession he wrote on February 12, 1743, WP, 742162.1.

46. *GCC*, 210–11, 218–19, 223–25.

47. On Indians and seafaring, see Little, *The Indian Contribution to Along-Shore Whaling at Nantucket*; Vickers, "The First Whalemen of Nantucket."

48. Occom, "Account of the Montauk Indians, on Long Island (1761)," in *CWSO*, 48–49.

49. "The Confession of Samll Ashbo of Mohegan," February 12, 1743, WP, 742162.1.

50. Many historians assume that Ashpo joined David Jewett's New London North Parish church right away—probably due to the ambiguous church baptismal records, which record that Samuel Ashpo joined sometime after 1739. However, Wheelock states in a letter to Gideon Hawley on June 10, 1761, that Wheelock first admitted Ashpo into his Lebanon church, presumably during the revivals. It is only on November 1, 1761, that Jewett reports to Wheelock that Ashpo was received (as a transfer membership) into the North Parish church upon Wheelock's recommendation. Eleazar Wheelock to Gideon Hawley, Lebanon, June 10, 1761, and David Jewett to Eleazar Wheelock, November 1, 1761, *LEWI*, 37. Additionally, Ashpo's name is the last of the twenty-one or so listed (all undated, but seemingly in order of joining) by Jewett in the North Parish church records. Manuscript Records of New London, North Parish, Congregational Church, CSL, vol. 3, 30.

51. Love, *Samson Occom*, 75.

52. Allen, *Memoirs of Samson Occom*, 4.

53. Brooks, "'This Indian World,'" *CWSO*, 13.

54. Brooks, *American Lazarus*, 58; Love, *Samson Occom*, 74–75.

55. Eleazar Wheelock to Gideon Hawley, Lebanon, June 10, 1761, *LEWI*, 35.

56. Fawcett, *Medicine Trail*, 23. See also Simmons, *Spirit of the New England Tribes*, 84.

57. "An Act for Regulating Abuses and Correcting Disorders in Ecclesiastical Affairs," May 1742, *RCC*, 8:454.

58. On Onaquaga, see Calloway, *The American Revolution in Indian Country*, 112–14.

59. Dally-Starna and Starna, *Gideon's People*, 2:215, 216, 247, 266.

60. Eleazar Wheelock to Gideon Hawley, Lebanon, June 10, 1761, *LEWI*, 36.

61. David Jewett to Eleazar Wheelock, November 1, 1761, *LEWI*, 37. The date of his joining comes from this letter, since no specific date is given in the church records. Manuscript Records of New London, North Parish, Congregational Church, CSL, vol. 3, 30.

62. Recommendation of Samuel Ashpo, July 29, 1762, *LEWI*, 37.

63. "License for Samuel Ashpo to Preach among the Indians," *LEWI*, 40.

64. On self-congratulations, see McCallum, *The Letters of Eleazar Wheelock's Indians*, 44.

65. Suspension of Samuel Ashpo by the Connecticut Board of Correspondents, July 1, 1767, *LEWI*, 45.

66. Love, *Samson Occom*, 74–77. See, for example, Johnson's entry for November 3, 1771 (Sunday), *WJJ*, 100.

67. *CWSO*, 249.

68. Occom, "Autobiographical Narrative, Second Draft (September 17, 1768)," in *CWSO*, 55.

69. Eells, "Indian Missions on Long Island," 178.

70. Occom, "Autobiographical Narrative, Second Draft (September 17, 1768)," in *CWSO*, 56. See also Eells, "Indian Missions on Long Island," 178.

71. Solomon Williams to Andrew Oliver, April 16, 1750, WP, 750266. See also Kidd, *The Great Awakening*, 192.

72. Occom, "Autobiographical Narrative, Second Draft (September 17, 1768)," in *CWSO*, 56.

73. Whitaker, *History of Southold, L.I.*, 268. For a summary and snippet of Horton's letter, see Gillies, *Historical Collections*, 2:409, 448.

74. While visiting Narragansett in 1750, for example, Occom stayed with James Simon, the Pequot Separate minister who opposed the Narragansett Separate minister Samuel Niles. *CWSO*, 252.

75. Occom, "Autobiographical Narrative, Second Draft (September 17, 1768)," in *CWSO*, 55.
76. For the ordination sermon, see Buell, *The Excellence and Importance of the Saving Knowledge of the Lord Jesus Christ in the Gospel-Preacher*.
77. On the relatively formulaic nature of his sermons, see *CWSO*, 161.
78. Sprague, *Annals of the American Pulpit: Trinitarian Congregational*, 2:40.
79. For controversies over Indian Separates even in Massachusetts, on Cape Cod, and on Martha's Vineyard, where there was a long-standing tradition of Native ministers, see Hankins, "Solomon Briant and Joseph Johnson," as cited in Kidd, *The Great Awakening*, 206, 356, n. 244.
80. Stiles, *The Literary Diary of Ezra Stiles*, 1:101.
81. Love, *Samson Occom*, 199. Also Ottery and Ottery, *A Man Called Sampson*, 42.
82. Brown and Rose, *Black Roots*, 276.
83. Journal entry for November 29, 1771, *WJJ*, 112.
84. Fish, *The Church of Christ a Firm and Durable House*, iii.
85. Indians—Collected Papers, CHS, 0041.
86. Stiles, *The Literary Diary of Ezra Stiles*, 1:233.
87. "Early Ministers of Long Island," March 10, 1864, *New York Observer and Chronicle*, 1.
88. The following summary of Peter John's life is (unless otherwise noted) drawn from a remarkable nineteenth-century manuscript history of the Shinnecock Presbyterian Church that I happily discovered in a filing cabinet at the First Presbyterian Church of Southampton in the summer of 2010. *History of the Shinnecock Church* (Southampton, N.Y.: Unpublished Manuscript, First Presbyterian Church of Southampton Archives, n.d.).
89. *History of the Shinnecock Church*, 19.
90. *History of the Shinnecock Church*, 20.
91. Backus and McLoughlin, *The Diary of Isaac Backus*, 1:260.
92. The Horton story is given in Kidd, *The Great Awakening*, 191.
93. Horton, "Journal," 203.
94. Simmons and Simmons, *Old Light on Separate Ways*, 70, n. 71.
95. McClure and Dexter, *Diary of David McClure*, 138.
96. McSparran, *A Letter Book and Abstract of Out Services Written during the Years 1743–1751*, 58.
97. *CWSO*, 258.
98. Stiles and Dexter, *Extracts from the Itineraries and Other Miscellanies of Ezra Stiles*, 151.
99. Simmons and Simmons, *Old Light on Separate Ways*, 79–80.
100. Letter from Stephen West, October 17, 1767, Miscellaneous Bound Manuscripts, MHS.
101. See, for example, *WJJ*, 103–04.
102. For a discussion of devotional Bible reading and the accompanying marginalia in the various Indian Bibles from the late seventeenth and early eighteenth centuries, see Fisher, "'In the practice and profession of the Christian Religion.'"
103. Jacob Johnson to Andrew Oliver, June 20, 1755, NEC LMA, Ms. 8011a. Following the lead of William DeLoss Love, most scholars think this refers to Samuel Ashpo, and Johnson just wrote down the wrong name (Love, *Samson Occom*, 75). Given Johnson's close proximity to Mashantucket and his monthly visits in the 1750s, it seems unlikely that he would have made this mistake not once, but twice (in 1755 and 1759). Additionally, the same year (1759) Jacob Johnson mentioned the recent departure of John Ashpo to fight in the French and Indian War, Samuel Ashpo showed up at Pachgatgoch with a group of Native Separates on their way to Iroquois territory in New York. Although most scholars understand the John Ashpo who does appear elsewhere in New England to be Samuel Ashpo's son (see Brooks, *CWSO*, 251), there were at least two John Ashpos at Mohegan, a junior and a senior, whose marks/names are written on petitions and documents in the 1730s and 1740s (see, for example, *GCC*, 229). It is not clear what the relationship of these two individuals was to Samuel Ashpo. Even if the John Ashpo who served at Mashantucket was Samuel Ashpo's son (whose birth Joanna Brooks places in 1740; *CWSO, 413*), serving as a schoolmaster at the age of thirteen was not out of the question; less than a decade later Joseph Johnson was sent as a missionary to the Iroquois at the age of fifteen.
104. Jacob Johnson to Thomas Foxcroft, June 29, 1759, Miscellaneous Bound Manuscripts, MHS.

105. Joseph Fish to Joseph Sewall, c. September 18th, 1765, Simmons and Simmons, *Old Light on Separate Ways*, 5.

106. Joseph Fish to Andrew Oliver, October 25, 1769, Indians—Collected Papers, CHS, 0063.

107. McClure and Dexter, *Diary of David McClure*, 138.

108. For a discussion of the Anglo-European belief in wonders, see Hall, *Worlds of Wonder, Days of Judgment*. See also Winiarski, "Native American Popular Religion."

109. December 22, 1771, *WJJ*, 123.

110. December 20, 1772, *WJJ*, 161–62.

111. *CWSO*, 334. Peyer, *The Tutor'd Mind*, 97.

112. Denison, *Westerly (Rhode Island) and Its Witnesses*, 80.

113. Quote is from Simmons, "Red Yankees: Narragansett Conversion in the Great Awakening," 263. See also Brooks, *American Lazarus*, 58.

114. *CWSO*, 42.

115. Simmons and Simmons, *Old Light on Separate Ways*, 8, n. 3.

116. Occom, "Autobiographical Narrative, Second Draft (September 17, 1768)," in *CWSO*, 56.

117. Occom, "Autobiographical Narrative, Second Draft (September 17, 1768)," in *CWSO*, 55.

118. Buell, *The Excellence and Importance of the Saving Knowledge of the Lord Jesus Christ in the Gospel-Preacher*, ix.

119. McClure and Dexter, *Diary of David McClure*, 138.

120. McClure and Dexter, *Diary of David McClure*, 189–90.

121. Horton, "Journal," 196.

122. Occom, "Autobiographical Narrative, Second Draft (September 17, 1768)," in Occom, *CWSO*, 56.

123. Simmons and Simmons, *Old Light on Separate Ways*, 31.

124. Joanna Brooks's analysis of Occom's hymnal is insightful. Brooks, *American Lazarus*, 70–84.

125. "Early Ministers of Long Island," March 10, 1864, *New York Observer and Chronicle*, 1.

126. McClure and Dexter, *Diary of David McClure*, 189–90.

127. McClure and Dexter, *Diary of David McClure*, 189–90.

128. Johnson, "An Account of Certain Exhortations," in *LEWI*, 142.

129. This theme, ironically, was one that second-generation Puritans similarly had hammered home in their sermons one hundred years prior.

130. Johnson, "An Account of Certain Exhortations," in *LEWI*, 142–43. See also *WJJ*, 100–101.

131. As quoted in Simmons and Simmons, *Old Light on Separate Ways*, 8, n. 3.

132. Beatty, *The Journal of a Two Months Tour*, 107–8. Joanna Brooks extrapolates from this a fully defined "funeral service" for members guilty of backsliding, but this seems to be an overstatement of Beatty's observations. Brooks, *American Lazarus*, 58.

133. McClure and Dexter, *Diary of David McClure, 1748–1820*, 189–90.

134. Experience Mayhew, "1714 Journal," 119. See also Williams, *A Key into the Language of America*, 115.

135. Simmons and Simmons, *Old Light on Separate Ways*, 79–80.

136. McCallum, *The Letters of Eleazar Wheelock's Indians*, 215.

137. "Joseph Johnson to All Enquiring Friends" [1772 or 1773], *WJJ*, 178. Italics his. See also *LEWI*, 146–47.

138. Bickford, *Farmington in Connecticut*, 160–61.

Chapter 6

1. Joseph Fish to Andrew Oliver, November 4, 1757. Miscellaneous Bound Manuscripts, MHS.

2. For the seventeenth-century dearth of English teachers, see Lepore, "Dead Men Tell No Tales," 491.

3. Joseph Fish's attempts to reeducate and reshape Samuel Niles and the New Light Narragansetts are a good example of this. See Simmons and Simmons, *Old Light on Separate Ways*.

4. As quoted in Frazier, *The Mohicans of Stockbridge*, 51.

5. Even so, the distinctions between these schools were not so simple. Local tribal schools often attracted a few students from other Indian communities who were usually housed with the teacher or a local Indian or—sometimes—a white family.

6. Hopkins includes a summary of Sergeant's plan for the girls. Hopkins, *Historical Memoirs*, 141.

7. John Sergeant to Benjamin Colman, May 18, 1743, BCP. See also Hopkins, *Historical Memoirs*, 97–102; Colman, *A Letter from the Revd Mr. Sergeant of Stockbridge*; John Sergeant to Thomas Coram, January 22, 1747, Hopkins, *Historical Memoirs*, 129.

8. John Sergeant to Benjamin Colman, May 18, 1743, BCP. See also Hopkins, *Historical Memoirs*, 97–102; Colman, *A Letter from the Revd Mr. Sergeant*.

9. Hopkins, *Historical Memoirs*, 124, 139.

10. Hopkins, *Historical Memoirs*, 136.

11. Hopkins, *Historical Memoirs*, 144.

12. Wheeler, *To Live upon Hope*, 211.

13. July 9, 1743, no. 19, *The Christian History*, 150.

14. When Jonathan Edwards arrived in 1751, he noted that there were two Indian schools at Stockbridge: one under Kellogg, and another under Woodbridge. Jonathan Edwards to Isaac Hollis, Summer 1751, draft, *Works of Jonathan Edwards Online*. Accessed November 8, 2010.

15. NEC LMA, Ms. 7927, 267.

16. See a report of Joseph Dwight and John Ashley, December 26, 1752, Indian Affairs, MSA, vol. 32, 324.

17. Hopkins, *Historical Memoirs*, 115.

18. Indian Affairs, MSA, vol. 32, 100.

19. "A Letter from Gideon Hawley," in *CMHS*, ser. 1, vol. 4:51.

20. Wheeler, *To Live upon Hope*, 211.

21. "A Letter from Gideon Hawley," in *CMHS*, ser. 1, vol. 4:54–55.

22. Daniel Mandell, "'Turned Their Minds to Religion': Oquaga and the First Iroquois Protestant Church, 1748–1776." Under review, *William and Mary Quarterly*, 10. Hawley was forced back to Stockbridge in 1756 during the French and Indian War, as his correspondence indicates. See SPGNA MHS, box 1, folder 3.

23. *CWSO*, 57.

24. *CWSO*, 57.

25. *Records of the Town of Southampton*, vol. 5, Appendix, 8.

26. For more on Clelland, see Love, *Samson Occom*, 123. Regarding his starting date, see *PRSC*, 11:383.

27. *PRCC*, 10:115. A similar petition was made again in 1757, Ecclesiastical Affairs, CSL, 1:125.

28. Petition of Benjamin Uncas III to the General Assembly, May 8, 1755. IPCSL, ser. I, vol. 2:94, 95.

29. Jacob Johnson to Boston Commissioners (NEC), June 20, 1755, NEC LMA, Ms. 8011a.

30. Jacob Johnson to Thomas Foxcroft, June 29, 1759, Miscellaneous Bound Manuscripts, MHS.

31. Jacob Johnson to Thomas Foxcroft, June 29, 1759, Miscellaneous Bound Manuscripts, MHS.

32. *PRCC*, 12:525.

33. Love, *Samson Occom*, 198–99.

34. Joseph Fish to Andrew Oliver, October 25, 1769, Indians—Collected Papers, CHS, 0063. See also "Rev. Joseph Fish Diary 1765–1776" (transcriptions), MPMRC.

35. Love, *Samson Occom*, 199.

36. Love, *Samson Occom*, 192.

37. Joseph Park to Andrew Oliver, September 17, 1757, Miscellaneous Bound Manuscripts, MHS.

38. Love, *Samson Occom*, 199.

39. George Griswold to Andrew Oliver, March 8, 1757, Miscellaneous Bound Manuscripts, MHS.

40. Love, *Samson Occom*, 200.

41. *PRCC*, 11:517; 12:169.

42. Jacob Johnson to Jabez Huntington, September 17, 1766, Connecticut Historical Society, Ms. 89378. Transcription provided by the MPMRC.

43. March 12, 1759, *Boston-Evening Post*.

44. Frazier, *The Mohicans of Stockbridge*, 144–45.

45. SPGNA MHS, box 1, folder 1.

46. SPGNA MHS, box 1, folder 1. See also *The Society for Propagating the Gospel among the Indians and Others in North America*, 17. Samuel Dexter to Peter Thacher, June 14, 1788, SPGNA MHS, box 2, Correspondence, August 5, 1782–October 18, 1788.

47. Mayhew, *Observations on the Charter and the Conduct of the Society for the Propagation of the Gospel in Foreign Parts*. See also Stevens, *The Poor Indians*, 115.

48. The financial ledgers for Wheelock's Indian School in the 1760s reveal the vast contributions from colonists, which itself indicated a growing shift in the source of funding (previously the majority had come from England). Moor's Indian Charity School, Records, 1760–1915, Rauner Special Collections Library, Dartmouth College.

49. Hopkins, *Historical Memoirs*, 137.

50. Wheelock used this phrase, "Grand Design," in a variety of forms when talking about his plan to educate Indians to evangelize the Six Nations in New York. For one such usage, see Eleazar Wheelock to David Fowler, August 26, 1766, *LEWI*, 104.

51. Wheelock, *A Plain and Faithful Narrative*, 29–30.

52. Love, *Samson Occom*, 58, 63, 64.

53. Wheelock, *A Plain and Faithful Narrative*, 36.

54. Wheelock, *A Plain and Faithful Narrative*, 36. The short quote is from Wheelock; the exact locations of the pews come from Manuscript Records of the Columbia (Lebanon Crank) Congregational Church, CSL, 3:45, 53. See also Love, *Samson Occom*, 61.

55. Wheelock, *A Plain and Faithful Narrative*, 36.

56. Eleazar Wheelock to George Whitefield, July 4, 1761, *WP*, 761404.

57. Wheelock, *A Plain and Faithful Narrative*, 34. Miss Elizabeth Huntington to Eleazar Wheelock, February 21, 1766, *LEWI*, 78.

58. McClure and Dexter, *Diary of David McClure*, 7.

59. Taylor, *The Divided Ground*, 7.

60. Love, *Samson Occom*, 93.

61. Richard Partridge to King George II, February 26, 1751, Indians—Collected Papers, CHS, 0328.

62. Ben Uncas III also accused this rival faction of illegally cutting, selling, and otherwise squandering precious timber on Mohegan land, something a committee set up by the Assembly confirmed. IPCSL, ser. I, vol. 2:103, 104.

63. Ben Uncas III's petition to the Connecticut General Assembly, May 20, 1760, IPCSL, ser. I, vol. 2:103.

64. Ben Uncas III's petition to the Connecticut General Assembly, May 20, 1760, IPCSL, ser. I, vol. 2:103.

65. College and Schools Manuscript Series, CSL, vol. 1, 125, 147.

66. "Mohegan Tribe against Robert Clelland," April 26, 1764, *CWSO*, 145. Robert Clelland to Andrew Oliver, September 19, 1764, Miscellaneous Bound Manuscripts, MHS.

67. Robert McClelland to Andrew Oliver, September 19, 1764, Miscellaneous Bound Manuscripts, MHS.

68. David Jewett to Andrew Oliver, February 28, 1766, Miscellaneous Bound Manuscripts, MHS. It is also possible that Hubbard was hired to teach the Ben's Town Mohegans only.

69. *William Pitkin Papers*, CCHS, 19:11, 46.

70. *William Pitkin Papers*, CCHS, 19:47.

71. As quoted in Blodgett, *Samson Occom*, 70.

72. David Jewett to Andrew Oliver, July 9, 1764, Miscellaneous Bound Manuscripts, MHS. Shipton, *Sibley's Harvard Graduates*, 10:43–50.

73. Nathaniel Whitaker to Eleazar Wheelock, August 11, 1764, WP.

74. As quoted in Shipton, *Sibley's Harvard Graduates*, 10:48.

75. Eleazar Wheelock to George Whitefield, May 4, 1765, Richardson, *An Indian Preacher in England*, 30.

76. Richardson, *An Indian Preacher in England*, 28–29.
77. Simmons and Simmons, *Old Light on Separate Ways*, 13.
78. Edward Deake to Joseph Fish, December 5, 1765, Simmons and Simmons, *Old Light on Separate Ways*, 22.
79. Edward Deake to Joseph Fish, December 5, 1765, Simmons and Simmons, *Old Light on Separate Ways*, 22.
80. Edward Deake to Joseph Fish, December 13, 1765, Simmons and Simmons, *Old Light on Separate Ways*, 23.
81. Edward Deake to Joseph Fish, June 7, 1766, Simmons and Simmons, *Old Light on Separate Ways*, 26.
82. Fish, Entry for June 29, 1767, Simmons and Simmons, *Old Light on Separate Ways*, 34.
83. Eleazar Wheelock to Sir William Johnson, August 19, 1767, WP, 767469.2.
84. Sir William Johnson to Eleazar Wheelock, September 19, 1767, WP, 767519.
85. Tobias Shattock to Eleazar Wheelock. October 2, 1767, WP, 767552.
86. Tobias Shattock to Eleazar Wheelock, November 30, 1767, WP, 767630.2.
87. Tobias Shattock to Eleazar Wheelock, November 30, 1767, WP, 767630.2.
88. Simmons and Simmons, *Old Light on Separate Ways*.
89. Charles Jeffrey Smith to Eleazar Wheelock, March 30, 1764, Richardson, *An Indian Preacher in England*, 20. Raising money in England, in fact, had long been associated with Indian evangelization and education. Axtell, *The Invasion Within*; Cogley, *John Eliot's Mission*.
90. Nathaniel Whitaker to Eleazar Wheelock, July 5, 1765, Richardson, *An Indian Preacher in England*, 38.
91. Jasper Mauduit to Andrew Oliver, March 26, 1766, NEC LMA, Ms. 7927, 9b.
92. *CWSO*, 264–65. Richardson, *An Indian Preacher in England*, 105. Samuel Wood to Eleazar Wheelock, September 28, 1767, WP, 767528.4.
93. As Margaret Connell Szasz notes, £2,529 of this total figure was raised during the two short months Occom and Whitaker spent in Scotland. Szasz, *Scottish Highlanders and Native Americans*, 208. As a fascinating point of comparison, when Morgan Edwards traveled to Britain in 1767, he could only muster £888 for the nascent College in the English Colony of Rhode Island and Providence Plantations (Brown University). Columbia and Yale's fund-raising just three years prior, however, netted £16,200. See Jane Lancaster, "'A thing impracticable': The Founding of Brown University," 16.
94. Vaughan, *Transatlantic Encounters*, 165, 176, 177, 179, 247.
95. Vaughan, *Transatlantic Encounters*, 179.
96. Rev. Charles Beatty to Eleazar Wheelock, September 15, 1768, WP, 768515.2.
97. *LEWI*, 211–14.
98. *LEWI*, 216.
99. *PRCC*, 12:501.
100. "From the Minutes of the Connecticut Correspondents," March 12, 1765, Richardson, *An Indian Preacher in England*, 29.
101. On the lending of money to Mason, see Robert Keen to Eleazar Wheelock, September 14, 1767. Richardson, *An Indian Preacher in England*, 296 and n. 292. Regarding Occom's testimony, see letters from William Samuel Johnson on March 12, 1768, and April 29, 1768, in Trumbull, "The Trumbull Papers," in *CMHS*, ser. 5, vol. 9:269, 273. Before allowing Occom to go to England, Whitaker and Wheelock took great care to have Occom and Samuel Mason both promise to stay away from each other; Whitaker reported in February 1766 that Mason "concludes to have nothing to do with Mr. Occom"; and Occom "resolves not to meddle in any land controversies." Nathaniel Whitaker to Eleazar Wheelock, February 8, 1766, Richardson, *An Indian Preacher in England*, 91. See also *CWSO*, 20 and n. 19.
102. Henry Babcock to William Pitkin, January 18, 1769, *William Pitkin Papers, CCHS*, 14:160. Apparently Occom was behind an earlier petition. See Thomas Fitch to Richard Jackson, February 23, 1765, *William Pitkin Papers, CCHS*, 14:275.
103. As early as 1761, after seven years of running his Indian school, Wheelock confided to Whitefield about his personal frustrations with his undertaking: "None know, nor can any, without Experience, Well Conceive of, the difficulty of Educating an Indian." Eleazar

Wheelock to Thomas Foxcroft, June 18, 1761, WP, 761368.1. Sergeant had similar feelings. See Kidd, *The Great Awakening*, 193.

104. In theory, Moor's Indian Charity School was kept separate from Dartmouth until it closed in 1915, although Wheelock served as president of both, as did his son, John, who succeeded him upon his father's death. In the early years, however, things were not so clear, and there were not two separate physical spaces. At times it seems that the only indicator of who was in which school was that Indians were enrolled in Moor's and white students were at Dartmouth. There was enormous controversy from the 1770s into the second decade of the nineteenth century about which funds were being used for which school. See, for example, William Allen to Jedediah Morse, March 19, 1817, Papers of William Allen, Rauner Special Collections Library, Dartmouth College, ser. 3, box. 1, folder 28. Wheelock, *A Continuation of the Narrative of the Indian Charity-School*, 30–31.

105. Samson Occom to Eleazar Wheelock, July 24, 1771, *CWSO*, 98–99.

106. *CWSO*, 99, n. 70. James Manning reported that in the fall of 1770, there were only two Indians in residence, both Narragansetts. James Manning to Dr. Rev. Stennett, June 5, 1771, Guild, *Life, Times, and Correspondence of James Manning*, 184.

107. For a discussion of New England Natives at Dartmouth in the early years, see Calloway, *The Indian History of an American Institution*, 26, 36.

108. Love, *Samson Occom*, 93, n. 14.

109. Love, *Samson Occom*, 162.

110. July 27, 1767, Simmons and Simmons, *Old Light on Separate Ways*, 40.

111. May 22, 1769, Simmons and Simmons, *Old Light on Separate Ways*, 57–58.

112. Simmons and Simmons, *Old Light on Separate Ways*, 79–80.

113. January 22, 1776, Simmons and Simmons, *Old Light on Separate Ways*, 118.

114. January 22, 1776, Simmons and Simmons, *Old Light on Separate Ways*, 119.

115. The complaints of the Mohicans at Stockbridge in 1749 demonstrate that many of these issues were present early on. Frazier, *The Mohicans of Stockbridge*, 84–85; for the numbers, see p. 176.

116. Frazier, *The Mohicans of Stockbridge*, 48.

117. Frazier, *The Mohicans of Stockbridge*, 92.

118. Stiles, *The Literary Diary of Ezra Stiles*, 1:212.

119. Stiles, *The Literary Diary of Ezra Stiles*, 1:212, 413.

120. Jarvis, *The Brothertown Nation*, 13; Strong, "How the Montauk Lost Their Land," 92.

121. Szasz, *Indian Education in the American Colonies*, 253. Love, *Samson Occom*, 204. Strong, *The Montaukett Indians of Eastern Long Island*, 75.

122. Love, *Samson Occom*, 197. Clearly not all Indians were completely disaffected with Wheelock.

123. *LEWI*, 218. Love, *Samson Occom*, 348.

124. *LEWI*, 214–16. See also Vaughan, *Transatlantic Encounters*, 181; Joseph Fish, "Account of Journeys and Lectures," October 23, 1771; Miscellaneous Bound Manuscripts, MHS; "Rev. Joseph Fish Diary 1765–1776" (transcriptions), MPMRC.

125. "Rev. Joseph Fish Diary 1765–1776" (transcriptions), MPMRC.

126. Twenty-nine is my own count; Love says there were thirty-one. Love, *Samson Occom*, 70. In 1766, North Groton minister Jacob Johnson reported eighty-eight Native youth under the age of sixteen. Love, *Samson Occom*, 198.

127. Wheelock, *A Plain and Faithful Narrative*, 34, Jacob Johnson to Boston Commissioners (NEC), June 20, 1755, NEC LMA, Ms. 8011a.

128. McCallum provides a detailed listing of each student who attended the school based on the published reports of Wheelock and various kinds of correspondence and records relating to the school. David McClure, a one-time resident of the school and friend of Wheelock's, reported that the number was closer to 150. For the McClure reference, see *LEWI*, 298.

129. *LEWI*, 298. Once in Hanover, however, seven Natives went on to attend other four-year colleges such as Dartmouth and Princeton, and three of those seven eventually graduated. The three graduates were Daniel Simon (Narragansett; Dartmouth, 1777), Peter Pohuonnoppeet (Stockbridge; Dartmouth, 1780), and Lewis Sawwantawnan [Vincent] (Canadian; Dartmouth, 1781).

130. Brooks, *The Common Pot*; Wyss, *Writing Indians*; Brooks, *American Lazarus*.

Chapter 7

1. Joseph Johnson's Speech to the Oneidas, *WJJ*, 207.
2. *CWSO*, 165. See also Joseph Johnson's description of the meeting: *WJJ*, 182. Also Farmington Indians to "All our Indian Brethren," October 13, 1773, *WJJ*, 200.
3. For example, see Silverman, *Red Brethren*, 72. Also Jarvis, *The Brothertown Nation*.
4. Fisher, "'Traditionary Religion,'" 313–20.
5. Trumbull, "The Trumbull Papers," in *CMHS*, ser. 5, vol. 9:482.
6. Conroy, "The Defense of Indian Land Rights," 396. Walters, "*Mohegan Indians v. Connecticut* (1705–1773)," 826.
7. Samson Occom to Samuel Buell, [January] 1773, *CWSO*, 104.
8. Herndon and Sekatau, "The Right to a Name."
9. Love, *Samson Occom*, 64–65.
10. Report of William Hillhouse, May 17, 1769, IPCSL, ser. 1, vol. 2:286a, 286b. Hillhouse said that Occom's protest so depleted the number of attendees that there were insufficient hands to carry the remains of Ben Uncas III to the usual burial ground in Norwich. The body of Ben Uncas III was buried at Mohegan instead.
11. Peyer, *The Tutor'd Mind*, 82.
12. See, for example, IPCSL, ser. 2, vol. 1:312a.
13. By May 1785, however, the Mashantuckets submitted several complaints again. For the 1773 General Assembly decision, see *PRCC*, 14:130. The original petition can be found in IPCSL, ser. 1, vol. 2:243a. For the 1785 petition, see IPCSL, ser. 1, vol. 2:248.
14. Johnson, *The Papers of Sir William Johnson*, 8:879. Strong, *The Montaukett Indians of Eastern Long Island*, 76. Strong, "How the Montauk Lost Their Land," 92.
15. Joseph Johnson to Jonathan Trumbull, October 11, 1773, *WJJ*, 195–98.
16. *WJJ*, 195.
17. IPCSL, ser. 2, vol. 2:199.
18. Hopkins, *Historical Memoirs*, 78.
19. Although ideas about racial differences only developed slowly over time, in this time period, "mullato" usually referred to persons of white-black ethnicity; "mestizo" to white-Indian; and "mustee" to black-Indian.
20. For an excellent analysis of these trends, see Mandell, "Shifting Boundaries of Race and Ethnicity," 466–501.
21. Strong, *The Montaukett Indians of Eastern Long Island*, 60.
22. Strong, *The Montaukett Indians of Eastern Long Island*, 71.
23. Benjamin Uncas to Thomas Fitch, May 18, 1765, William Samuel Johnson Papers, CHS, as cited in *WJJ*, 173, 306 n. 112.
24. Edward Deake to Joseph Fish, December 5, 1765, Simmons and Simmons, *Old Light on Separate Ways*, 22.
25. "Memorial of Zachary Johnson, Simon Joyjoy, and the Rest of the Tribe of the Mohegan Indians," May 1774,. IPCSL, ser. 1, vol. 2:310.
26. IPCSL, ser. 1, vol. 2:312a. Also *PRCC*, 14:314.
27. June 6, 1779. *Norwich Packet*.
28. Joseph Johnson to Jonathan Trumbull, October 11, 1773, *WJJ*, 196–97.
29. Joseph Johnson to Jonathan Trumbull, October 11, 1773, *WJJ*, 196–97. In many ways, this prefigured by two hundred years the same policy that Indian Nations implemented in the twentieth century upon receiving US federal recognition and determining who should be considered official members and—more important—who receives earnings disbursements from casino profits.
30. Jarvis, *The Brothertown Nation*, 91. Strong, *The Montaukett Indians of Eastern Long Island*, 72.
31. Tobias Shattock to Eleazar Wheelock, October 2, 1767, WP, 767552. Also printed in *LEWI*, 207.
32. See, for example, William Samuel Johnson to William Pitkin, September 15, 1767, *CMHS*, ser. 5, vol. 9, 243. See also Nathaniel Whitaker to Eleazar Wheelock, January 20, 1767, Richardson, *An Indian Preacher in England*, 205–7.

33. In a letter to Robert Keen in November 1767, he reported that he had been "trying to collect a town of Christianized Indians, from the New England Colonies, & settle them in some suitable place, in the heart of the Indian Country." Eleazar Wheelock to Robert Keen, November 2, 1767, WP, 767602.1.

34. William Samuel Johnson to William Pitkin, September 15, 1767, Trumbull, "Trumbull Papers," *CMHS*, 243.

35. Some of these men formed the "Indian Council" of New England Indian refugees at New Stockbridge and petitioned the Connecticut General Assembly in October 1780, describing their situation and requesting aid. IPCSL, ser. 1, vol. 2:226a & 226b.

36. Wheelock stated in 1759 that Johnson was nine years old, so he might have been born in 1750. Joseph Johnson writing fragment, Bodleian Library, Oxford University, Ms. Montagu d. 16, fol. 219v, 220r.

37. Laura Murray, "Reading Joseph Johnson," in *WJJ*, 11. Much of the biographical sketch that follows is taken in part from Murray's helpful summary of Johnson's life.

38. Manuscript Records of the First Church of Christ in New London, CSL, vol. 1:34, 42, 46. Joseph was baptized on Mohegan lands and he was brought forward by his nonmember father; both of these occurrences are a bit unusual. Perhaps this was part of a transitional compromise as Native Separate churches became stronger on Native lands. This also might explain why the Johnsons' third and fourth children were apparently not baptized in association with the New London Church, if at all.

39. Bodleian Library, Oxford University, Ms., Montagu d. 16, fol. 219v, 220r. Thanks to Faith Davison for alerting me to the presence of this important manuscript fragment.

40. Joseph Johnson to Eleazar Wheelock, December 28, 1768; Samuel Kirkland to Eleazar Wheelock, December 29, 1768, *WJJ*, 76–77.

41. Joseph Johnson to Enquiring friends, or to Strangers, undated, but perhaps c. 1773. *WJJ*, 192.

42. See Johnson's journals, which begin in October 1771, *WJJ*, 92ff.

43. Szasz, *Indian Education in the American Colonies*, 254.

44. *WJJ*, 137.

45. Johnson's mother, Elizabeth, was a Garrett before she married Joseph Johnson, Sr. Although it is not clear, Benjamin Garrett was possibly Elizabeth's brother and was therefore a Pequot.

46. February 2, 1772, *WJJ*, 133.

47. November 18, 1772, *WJJ*, 151.

48. November 27, 1772, *WJJ*, 153.

49. On Sunday, December 20, 1772, for example, Joseph Sunsaman (Pequot) and Robert Ashpo (Mohegan) arrived and participated in services in the forenoon and afternoon. *WJJ*, 162.

50. Farmington Indians to "All Our Indian Brethren," October 13, 1773, *WJJ*, 198–99.

51. *WJJ*, 230–31. The actual document is dated May 2, 1774, IPCSL, ser. 1 (A), vol. 2:193.

52. May 1774, *PRCC*, 14:292.

53. Entry for August 22, 1774, Simmons and Simmons, *Old Light on Separate Ways*, 107. Ironically enough, however, Samuel Niles must not have liked what he saw, for he ended up staying in Rhode Island.

54. Deed to Oneida Lands, October 4, 1774, *WJJ*, 242–43.

55. Joseph Johnson to John Rodgers, February 15, 1775, *LEWI*, 189.

56. Joseph Johnson to John Rodgers, February 15, 1775, *LEWI*, 189.

57. IPCSL, ser. 1, vol. 2:306, 309.

58. Johnson, *The Papers of Sir William Johnson*, 13:684, deed to Oneida Lands, October 4, 1774, *WJJ*, 242–43. For the acreage, see Bickford, *Farmington in Connecticut*, 164.

59. In part, however, this was a bit of artful posturing, since the accompanying listing of nineteen heads of household "now Living in Mohegan that are not properly Mohegans" included notable Mohegans like Samson Occom, Samuel Ashpo, and John Cooper. Lynch, "Historical Chronology of the Eastern Pequot/Pawcatuck Pequot, 1638–1993," 27. For a related 1773 petition, see Mandell, *Tribe, Race, History*, 53.

60. Kirkland and Pilkington, *The Journals of Samuel Kirkland*, 24, 38.

61. Greene and Harrington, *American Population before the Federal Census of 1790*, 102. William DeLoss Love believed that Occom himself had introduced the clause into the lease. Love, "Samson Occom: The Founding of Brothertown by Christian Indians," 3. Strong also suggests that the British were keen to keep Africans and Indians apart on the frontier in order to reduce the chance of collaborative uprisings. Strong, *The Montaukett Indians of Eastern Long Island*, 77. However, the Oneidas were equally adamant about keeping whites off their lands, although such concerns did not make it into the land deed in 1774. In a 1770 letter from the Oneida sachems at Kanonwalohale to the Boston commissioners of the NEC, the Oneidas asserted that "we have firmly resolved never to admit any white People to settle amongst us or near us except a Minister & Schoolmaster, who are as one of us. We have seen the fate of Stockbridge, which loudly warns us." Samuel Kirkland to Ebenezer (?) Pemberton, March 5, 1771, Miscellaneous Bound Manuscripts, MHS.

62. *WJJ*, 230–31.

63. "To the Officers of the English Trust for Moor's Indian Charity School," November 10, 1773, *CWSO*, 108.

64. Stiles, *The Literary Diary of Ezra Stiles*, 1:401.

65. Letter of Samuel Kirkland, March 5, 1771, Miscellaneous Bound Manuscripts, MHS.

66. Samuel Kirkland to Andrew Eliot, March 28, 1775, Miscellaneous Bound Manuscripts, MHS.

67. Joseph Johnson to Guy Johnson, March 25, 1775, *WJJ*, 255.

68. David Fowler to Guy Johnson, April 8, 1775, *WJJ*, 260.

69. Joseph Johnson to Guy Johnson, March 25, 1775, *WJJ*, 258.

70. *WJJ*, 275.

71. *WJJ*, 266, 269.

72. The best single overview of Natives in the American Revolution is Calloway, *The American Revolution in Indian Country*. For New England, see Mandell, "'The times are exceedingly altered.'"

73. Taylor, *The Divided Ground*, 96–97.

74. Samson Occom to John Thornton, January 1, 1777, *CWSO*, 115.

75. Calloway, *The American Revolution in Indian Country*, 51–52.

76. New Hampshire Assembly's recommendation of Joseph Johnson, January 16, 1776, *WJJ*, 280.

77. George Washington to Joseph Johnson [February 20, 1776], *WJJ*, 281.

78. Mandell, "'The times are exceedingly altered,'" 171.

79. *WJJ*, 238.

80. Mandell, "'The times are exceedingly altered,'" 171; *WJJ*, 274–75. Cognehew also shows up in the Massachusetts muster rolls in 1787.

81. D'Agostino, "Leader of the Broken Tribes—Samson Occom," 57–58. David's last name is not listed.

82. "Patriots of Color at the Battle of Bunker Hill" (National Park Service, www.nps.gov/bost/forteachers/upload/Boston%20Lesson.pdf, n.d.), 10, 17. Accessed September 19, 2010.

83. Love, *Samson Occom*, 231.

84. Calloway, *The American Revolution in Indian Country*, 100–101.

85. The date of Johnson's death is unknown; various scholars give it within this time range. For the 1777 date, see Bickford, *Farmington in Connecticut*, 165. Also *WJJ*, xvii.

86. Samson Occom to John Thornton, 1776 (no month given), *CWSO*, 113.

87. PCRN, box 2, folder 1770–1779.

88. *East Hampton Trustees Journal, 1725–1772*, 1:21. Ales, "A History of the Indians on Montauk, Long Island," 59.

89. Samson Occom to John Bailey, [June or July] 1783, *CWSO*, 118.

90. McClure and Dexter, *Diary of David McClure*, 192.

91. Zachary Johnson to Richard Law, May 30, 1781, Indians—Collected Papers, CHS, 0286.

92. Samson Occom to the Easthampton Trustees, 1784, Stone, *The History and Archaeology of the Montauk*, 513.

93. Occom's journal entries for May 8–17, 1784, *CWSO*, 285–86. See also D'Agostino, "Leader of the Broken Tribes—Samson Occom," 58.

94. Journal entry for Monday, November 7, 1785, *CWSO*, 308. Although it is unclear whether there was a definite connection, it is interesting that a Christian Delaware settlement in New Jersey founded in 1759 was also named "Brotherton." Flemming, *Brotherton*, ch. 4.
95. In September 1784, Occom noted that the Stockbridge Indians had been to Oneida during the summer "and Planted much Corne," and were planning a larger move in the fall of 1784. Samson Occom to Solomon Welles, September 26, 1784, *CWSO*, 125.
96. Love, *Samson Occom*, 243–46. See also Wheeler, "Women and Christian Practice in a Mahican Village"; Wheeler, "Living upon Hope"; Dally-Starna and Starna, "A Comment on 'Mahican Life and Moravian Missions.'"
97. William DeLoss Love is the fountainhead of this tradition. See Love, *Samson Occom*.
98. Two recent books firmly cement this narrative arc, but the historiography has been heading in this direction for a decade or more. See Jarvis, *The Brothertown Nation*; Silverman, *Red Brethren*.
99. Indians—Collected Papers, CHS, 0281.
100. PCRN, box 2, folder 1770–1779.
101. Brad Jarvis has a helpful graph of this breakdown. See Jarvis, *The Brothertown Nation*, 114.
102. Greene and Harrington, *American Population before the Federal Census of 1790*, 69.
103. "The Number of Indians in Connecticut," in *CMHS*, ser. 1, vol. 10, 117.
104. McBride, *Transformation by Degree*, 51–52.
105. Strong, *The Montaukett Indians of Eastern Long Island*, 79.
106. Strong, "How the Montauk Lost Their Land," 92. Kirkland and Pilkington, *The Journals of Samuel Kirkland*, 162.
107. Entry for March 13, 1775, Simmons and Simmons, *Old Light on Separate Ways*, 112. See also *WJJ*, 133 and note.
108. Frazier, *The Mohicans of Stockbridge*, 240–41.
109. Petition of John and Daniel Skesuck, March 1787, PCRN, box 2, folder 1770–1779.
110. Brown and Rose, *Black Roots*, 276. Love, *Samson Occom*, 354. Benoni was also listed with his family on the 1799 Mohegan census. Holmes, "Memoir of the Mohegan Indians," *CMHS*, ser. 1, vol. 9:76.
111. Love, *Samson Occom*, 354. Sally was possibly Occom's granddaughter, as Love notes.
112. Brown and Rose, *Black Roots*, 276.
113. Joseph Johnson's Second Speech to the Oneidas, January 24, 1774, *WJJ*, 221 and note. This extra quotation comes from the Occom Papers copy of this speech, according to Laura Murray.
114. Backus, *A History of New-England*, 2:510.
115. Love, *Samson Occom*, 74–77, 204.
116. Love, *Samson Occom*, 309–10.
117. November 12, 1795. *Norwich Packet* (Norwich, Conn.). There seems to be some disagreement regarding the date of his death.
118. Abiel Holmes, "Memoir of the Mohegan Indians," in *CMHS*, ser. 1, vol. 9:76.
119. Henry Quaquaquid's family is listed on the 1799 Mohegan tribal census. Holmes, "Memoir of the Mohegan Indians," 76. Additionally, in Occom's journals post-1785, Quaquaquid is always associated with the Connecticut Mohegans.
120. Laura Murray, "Introduction," in *WJJ*, 2, 105, footnote.
121. Hannah Cooper, who was a widow at the Montville (New London North Parish) Church, died in Groton in February 1791. Jacob Cooper (Mohegan) married Lucy Poquiantup (Pequot) in Groton on October 10, 1782, and the couple was in residence on Mashantucket lands as late as November 1799, as Ebenezer Punderson's account books show. John Cooper, Jr., lived off the reservation in Lebanon in May 1827 with his three children, Peter, David, and Jacob. Brown and Rose, *Black Roots*, 92.
122. On April 1, 1787, James Nedson (presumably Edward's son) was married to Tyra Apes by the North Stonington Justice of the Peace. In 1820, James Nedson—still residing in North Stonington—applied for a pension for his years of military service and claimed that he and his wife (aged 63 and 66, respectively) had eleven children and supported two of them in their house plus two young grandchildren. After Nedson's estate was probated a few years later in 1826, his wife Tyra was given a small allowance to support herself. Brown and Rose, *Black Roots*, 265.
123. Love, *Samson Occom*, 202–3.

124. Bickford, *Farmington in Connecticut*, 165–66.
125. Jones, *Stockbridge, Past and Present*, 87.
126. Early American Newspapers, 8/1/1792. Issue: 1292, page 3. Love, "Samson Occom: The Founding of Brothertown by Christian Indians," 4.
127. Brothertown Tribe to the New York State Assembly, January 1791, *CWSO*, 157–58.
128. March 10, 1792, *Windham Herald*. See also February 18, 1792, *The New-York Journal, & Patriotic Register*.
129. For more on the New York and Wisconsin aspects of Brothertown and New Stockbridge, see Jarvis, *The Brothertown Nation*; Silverman, *Red Brethren*.
130. Holmes, "Memoir of the Mohegan Indians," *CMHS*, ser. 1, vol. 9:90.

Chapter 8

1. August 18, Curtis Coe, Third Journal, 1811, SPGNA PEM, box 1, folder 21.
2. November 13, Curtis Coe, Second Journal, 1810, SPGNA PEM, box 1, folder 21.
3. Tobias Ross and the Narragansett Indians to Frederick Baylies, July 22, 1820, SPGNA PEM, box 6, folder 5.
4. Curtis Coe, September 16, 1810, Second Journal, SPGNA PEM, box 1, folder 21.
5. Curtis Coe, October 14, 1810, Second Journal, SPGNA PEM, box 1, folder 21.
6. The Narragansetts to the SPGNA, November 26, 1810, SPGNA PEM, box 6, folder 3.
7. Gardiner, "Notes and Observations on the Town of East Hampton," 257.
8. For nineteenth-century notions of disappearance, see O'Brien, *Firsting and Lasting*.
9. See, for example, an 1810 statement regarding Thomas Commuck's imprisonment. PCRN, box 2, folder 1770–1779.
10. Petition from the Narragansetts, March 1787; also "Be it enacted . . .," March 17, 1787, PCRN, box 2, folder 1770–1779. See also an Act of the Assembly in October 1801 that prohibited sale of alcohol to any Narragansett or person of color married to a Narragansett.
11. August 30, 1797, *The Bee*.
12. Apess and O'Connell, *On Our Own Ground*, xxx–xxxi.
13. January 30, 1805, *Connecticut Gazette*.
14. Shinnecock Tribe to the State of New York [1787 or 1788], *CWSO*, 152–53.
15. Brown and Rose, *Black Roots*, 157.
16. A good summary of New England Native lives in the postwar period is Mandell, *Tribe, Race, History*.
17. As Jason Mancini argues, these reservation communities were increasingly supplemented by other important social—and increasingly less-visibly urban—nodes of Native and black communities. Mancini, "Beyond Reservation."
18. Mohegan and Niantic Tribes to the Connecticut General Assembly, May 1785, *CWSO*, 147–48.
19. Strong, *The Montaukett Indians of Eastern Long Island*, 83.
20. Strong, "How the Montauk Lost Their Land," 92–93.
21. IPCSL, ser. 1, vol. 2:252–252b.
22. Curtis Coe, First Journal, 1809, Appendix, SPGNA PEM. The same was true at Mohegan, as early as 1774. See October 1774 Committee Report, IPCSL, ser. 1, vol. 2, 313.
23. Petition of Samuel Mott, John M. Simons, and Josiah Charles, May 1811, IPCSL, ser. 2, vol. 2, 36a. Transcription by the MPMRC. Thanks to Jason Mancini for this reference.
24. "Rules and Regulations Respecting the Narragansetts," June 1792, PCRN, box 2, folder 1770–1779.
25. PRSC, 9:438.
26. "Report of a Committee to determine the disputes at Narragansett," June 1792, PCRN, box 2, folder 1770–1779.
27. Narragansetts to the General Assembly, January 20, 1813, PCRN, box 2, folder 1770–1779.
28. Curtis Coe, First Journal, 1809, SPGNA PEM, box 1, folder 21.
29. "Progress of Civilization," January 1, 1820, *Concord Observer*, vol. 2, issue 2, 2. Jarvis, *The Brothertown Nation*, 156. The Brothertown Indians had more people and land, of course, but the contrast is still striking.

30. Mancini, "Beyond Reservation," 160. For a discussion of Pequot mobility, particularly in the case of William Apess, see Apess and O'Connell, *On Our Own Ground*, xxvi–xxxv.
31. Mandell, *Tribe, Race, History*, 7.
32. Mandell, *Tribe, Race, History*, 8.
33. Mandell, *Tribe, Race, History*, 15.
34. William Apess, "Son of the Forest," in *On Our Own Ground*.
35. Porter, *A Historical Discourse*, 44.
36. Woodbridge, *The Autobiography of a Blind Minister*, 11, 37. Frazier, *The Mohicans of Stockbridge*, 244.
37. *CWSO*, 300.
38. Norwich Free Academy Records, Box 2, 1679–1941, CSL, Yale Indian Papers Project, http://images.library.yale.edu:8080/neips/data/html/1830.00.00.00/1830.00.00.00. html. Accessed April 15, 2011.
39. Tobias Ross and the Narragansett Indians to Frederick Baylies, July 22, 1820, SPGNA PEM, box 6, folder 5.
40. See, for example, the letter from the Narragansetts to the SPGNA on June 19, 1811, SPGNA PEM, box 6, folder 2.
41. Mandell, *Tribe, Race, History*, 36.
42. Petition of Augustus Harry, Tobias Ross, Joseph Primas, Joseph Commuck, and Joseph Hazard, February 1817, PCRN, box 2, folder 1770–1779.
43. Silas Shores to Abiel Holmes, November 19, 1814, SPGNA PEM, box 5, folder 2.
44. Petition of Samuel Mott, John M. Simons, and Josiah Charles, May 1811, IPCSL, ser. 2, vol. 2, 36a. Transcription by the MPMRC.
45. Lynch, "Historical Chronology of the Eastern Pequot /Pawcatuck Pequot, 1638–1993," 26.
46. Mohegan Indians to Richard Law, December 5, 1789, Indians—Collected Papers, CHS, 0288.
47. As quoted in Simmons, *The Narragansetts*, 61.
48. Curtis Coe, First Journal, 1809, Appendix, SPGNA PEM.
49. "The claim of Sarah Pendleton" and "Statement of the Brothertons Regarding Sarah Pendleton," in a folder titled "(Guy Johnson) Brotherton Indians" at the Hamilton College Archives, Hamilton, NY. See also Silverman, *Red Brethren*, 154–55.
50. Love, *Samson Occom*, 339.
51. Commuck, "Sketch of the Brothertown Indians."
52. Many of the original subscribers to the 1762 society were still living in 1787 and were enlisted to support the new society. See Samuel Dexter to Peter Thacher, June 14, 1788, SPGNA MHS, box 2, Correspondence, August 5, 1782–October 18, 1788. A listing of the SPGNA missionaries is given in *The Society for Propagating the Gospel*, 40. See also Mandell, "Eager Partners in Reform," 44.
53. *The Society for Propagating the Gospel*, 24.
54. The Second Great Awakening was even more amorphous than the First Great Awakening in many ways. At minimum, it had at least two different components: the first (from 1800 on) was centered more in the south and western backcountry and manifested in camp meetings; the second (1820s–1830s) was focused more in the northeast and associated with the revivals of Charles Grandison Finney. For more on antebellum reform and awakenings, see Abzug, *Cosmos Crumbling*; Hatch, *The Democratization of American Christianity*.
55. *The Home Missionary, for the Year Ending April, 1895*, 566.
56. *The Home Missionary, for the Year Ending April, 1895*, 562.
57. *The Home Missionary, for the Year Ending April, 1895*, 567. For the papers for the Rhode Island Home Missionary Society, see box 6 of the Rhode Island Congregational Christian Conference Records, Rhode Island Historical Society.
58. SPGNA MHS, box 2, folder September 18, 1813–April 22, 1815; box 2, folder June 2, 1812–July 25, 1812; also box 19, "SP Gospel Records," vol. 1, 142.
59. For more on the ABCFM and North American Protestant missions in the nineteenth century, see Shenk, *North American Foreign Missions, 1810–1914*.
60. See, for example, Makdisi, *Artillery of Heaven*, ch. 1.
61. Such was the case with David Bacon, who was sent by the Connecticut Missionary Society in 1800 to "travel among the Indian tribes south and west of Lake Erie, to explore their

situation and learn their feelings with respect to Christianity, and, so far as he has opportunity, to teach them its doctrines and duties." Punchard, *History of Congregationalism*, 300.

62. Holmes, *A Discourse*, 31.
63. *The Society for Propagating the Gospel*, 40.
64. As indicated, at least, by the treasurers' accounts and the missionary lists of the SPGNA through the first decade of the nineteenth century. *The Society for Propagating the Gospel*, 40, SPGNA MHS, box 2, various folders containing treasurers' accounts, c. 1790–1810. There were some exceptions, of course. In November 1790 the society noted that they had funded an Indian schoolmaster on Martha's Vineyard under the supervision of Zechariah Mayhew for £12 per year. Minutes of the select committee meetings, SPGNA MHS, box 19, "SP Gospel Records," vol. 1, 28.
65. Holmes, *A Discourse*, 32.
66. See especially the journals and letters in the SPGNA Collection at the Peabody Essex Museum, SPGNA PEM. The records go past 1820 as well. See Mandell, *Tribe, Race, History*.
67. Denison, *Westerly (Rhode Island) and Its Witnesses*, 81.
68. Curtis Coe, Third Journal, 1811, SPGNA PEM, box 1, folder 21.
69. James Kendall, "A Sermon Delivered before the Society for Propagating the Gospel among the Indians . . . 1812," PCRN, box 2, folder 1770–1779.
70. See, for example, Susan Juster's descriptions of the anti-democratic movements in the First Baptist Church of Providence during this same time period. Juster, *Disorderly Women*.
71. June 29, 1811, Curtis Coe, Third Journal, 1811, SPGNA PEM, box 1, folder 21.
72. June 29, 1811, Curtis Coe, Third Journal, 1811, SPGNA PEM, box 1, folder 21.
73. Morse, *A Report to the Secretary of War of the United States, on Indian affairs*, 75.
74. Curtis Coe, Second Journal, 1810, SPGNA PEM, box 1, folder 21.
75. July 21, 1811, Curtis Coe, Third Journal, 1811, SPGNA PEM, box 1, folder 21.
76. July 21, 1811, Curtis Coe, Third Journal, 1811, SPGNA PEM, box 1, folder 21.
77. Curtis Coe, Second Journal, 1810, SPGNA PEM, box 1, folder 21.
78. June 9, 1811, Curtis Coe, Third Journal, 1810, SPGNA PEM, box 1, folder 21.
79. Curtis Coe, Second Journal, 1810, SPGNA PEM, box 1, folder 21.
80. Curtis Coe, Third Journal, June 4, 1811, SPGNA PEM, box 1, folder 21.
81. Curtis Coe, Third Journal, June 29, 1811, SPGNA PEM, box 1, folder 21.
82. Tucker, *Historical Sketch of the Town of Charlestown*, 65.
83. The Narragansetts to the SPGNA, 1810, SPGNA PEM, box 6, folder 3.
84. Curtis Coe, Second Journal, 1810, SPGNA PEM, box 1, folder 21.
85. October 28, 1810, Curtis Coe, Second Journal, 1810, SPGNA PEM, box 1, folder 21.
86. June 29, 1811, Curtis Coe, Third Journal, 1810, SPGNA PEM, box 1, folder 21.
87. Curtis Coe, Second Journal, 1810, SPGNA PEM, box 1, folder 21.
88. "Report of the SPGNA on the Narragansett Indians," 1810, SPGNA PEM, box 6, folder 3.
89. Secretary's Incoming Correspondence, SPGNA PEM, box 6, folder 3.
90. July 1, 1811, Curtis Coe, Third Journal, 1811, SPGNA PEM, box 1, folder 21.
91. Curtis Coe, Second Journal, 1810, SPGNA PEM, box 1, folder 21.
92. Curtis Coe, Third Journal, 1811, SPGNA PEM, box 1, folder 21.
93. Curtis Coe, Fourth Journal, 1812, and Fifth Journal, 1814, SPGNA PEM, box 1, folder 21.
94. Jeremiah Niles to Abiel Holmes, October 27, 1812, SPGNA PEM, box 3, folder 12.
95. Silas Shores to Abiel Holmes, June 17, 1814, SPGNA PEM, box 5, folder 2.
96. Jeremiah Niles to Abiel Holmes, May 20, 1813, SPGNA PEM, box 3, folder 12.
97. "SP Gospel Records," vol. 1, 165. SPGNA MHS, box 19.
98. Mandell, *Tribe, Race, History*, 111–13.
99. Commuck, "Sketch of the Brothertown Indians."
100. Commuck, *Indian Melodies*. I am grateful to Bill Simmons for alerting me to the existence of this book. Samson Occom's hymnal, *A Choice Collection of Hymns and Spiritual Songs* (1774), is far more conventional when compared with Commuck's *Indian Melodies*.
101. See also the discussion of this tradition in Simmons, *Spirit of the New England Tribes*, 71.
102. For more on Cuffee's genealogy, see "Wading River Congregational Church," Digitized Newspaper Clippings, Southold Free Library, clipping 2007.0082.0009. Also *History of the Shinnecock Church*, 20. Some nineteenth-century commentators believed that this was the

Paul Cuffee that Harriet Beecher Stowe referenced in *Uncle Tom's Cabin*. But given the relative popularity of the Paul Cuffee from Massachusetts—of Wampanoag and African ancestry who was a famous ship captain in his day—in the same time period, along with the context of the phrase she used—"as grand as Cuffee," meaning with regard to dress and ornamentation—this hardly seems to be the case. Nonetheless, Harriet Beecher Stowe may well have heard about both Paul Cuffees since her father, Lyman Beecher, started his ministerial career in East Hampton on Long Island (1799–1810), not far from where the minister Paul Cuffee was serving.

103. "Paul Cuffee at Wading River," Digitized Newspaper Clippings, Southold Free Library, clipping 2006.0053.0020.
104. "Reverend Paul Cuffee was an Outstanding L.I. Indian," Digitized Newspaper Clippings, Southold Free Library, clipping 2007.0071.0059.
105. Cuffee is mentioned in the annual reports of the New York Missionary Society, published in the *New-York Missionary Magazine*. See, for example, "At the Last Meeting of the New-York Missionary Society," the *New-York Missionary Magazine*, January 6, 1801. In 1810, his annual salary was $60. "Annual Report of the Board of Directors to the New-York Missionary Society," *The Christian's Magazine*, May 1, 1811.
106. "Annual Report of the Board of Directors to the New-York Missionary Society," 1811.
107. *History of the Shinnecock Church*, 22.
108. *History of the Shinnecock Church*, 24.
109. Eells, "Indian Missions on Long Island," 185; Hunter, *"The Shinnecock Indians."*
110. Thompson, *The History of Long Island*, 1:128.
111. Baker, "The Mohegans," 676.
112. Dwight, *Travels in New-England and New-York*, 3:29.
113. Apess, *On Our Own Ground*, 151. See also Mandell, *Tribe, Race, History*, 108.
114. Apess, *On Our Own Ground*, lx.
115. See, for example, "A Son of the Forest" and "The Experience of Five Christian Indians of the Pequot Tribe," in Apess, *On Our Own Ground*.
116. Strong, *The Montaukett Indians of Eastern Long Island*, 90.
117. Seraile, *Fire in His Heart*, 133.
118. Tobias Ross and the Narragansett Indians to Frederick Baylies, July 22, 1820, SPGNA PEM, box 6, folder 5.

Epilogue

1. Personal interview with Melissa Zobel, January 9, 2007, Mohegan, Connecticut.
2. Personal interview with Melissa Zobel, January 9, 2007, Mohegan, Connecticut.
3. Hooker, *Memoir of Mrs. Sarah L. Huntington Smith*, Ch. 6.
4. Morse, *A Report to the Secretary of War of the United States, on Indian affairs*. Huntington's own correspondence reveals that the threat was tangible: Hooker, *Memoir of Mrs. Sarah L. Huntington Smith*, 119.
5. Fawcett, *Medicine Trail*, 12.
6. Ryan, "A Huntington's Mohegan Mission," 14. See also Brooks, "Samson Occom at the Mohegan Sun"; Fawcett, *Medicine Trail*, 12. On Gleason, see Baker, *History of Montville*, 672.
7. Sarah Huntington to Lydia Sigourney, April 4, 1831, Autographs and Miscellaneous Letters, 1780–1831, CSL.
8. Gleason, "Gleason Report on Mohegan School," 1:363.
9. De Forest, *History of the Indians of Connecticut*, 487.
10. Personal interview with Melissa Zobel, January 9, 2007, Mohegan, Connecticut.
11. Simmons, *The Narragansetts*, 91, 94.
12. Tucker, *Historical Sketch of the Town of Charlestown*, 65.
13. See O'Brien, *Firsting and Lasting*.
14. Boissevain, *"The Detribalization of the Narragansett Indians."*
15. Mandell, *Tribe, Race, History*, 215.
16. Mulvaney, "From Church to Citadel, Narragansetts Endure."

17. *Southampton, Long Island: 1640/1965: 325th Anniversary*, 52.
18. After Cuffee's death, this and other Indian churches were attended to by local non-Indian preachers. In 1827, William Benjamin, who already had been preaching to the Shinnecocks for three years, was officially called as the Shinnecocks' minister, in which capacity he served for more than three decades. *History of the Shinnecock Church*, 24–27.
19. http://www.shinnecocknation.com/history.asp.
20. Personal interview with Laughing Woman, Mashantucket Pequot Spiritual Leader, May 5, 2011, Mashantucket, Connecticut.
21. Personal interview with Wayne Reels, Mashantucket Pequot Cultural Director, May 5, 2011, Mashantucket, Connecticut.
22. Personal interview with Laughing Woman, May 5, 2011, Mashantucket, Connecticut.
23. Personal interview with Tall Oak Weeden, April 8, 2011, Providence, Rhode Island,
24. http://www.shinnecocknation.com/culture.asp.
25. Personal interviews with Laughing Woman and Fatima Dames, May 5, 2011, Mashantucket, Connecticut.
26. Personal interview with Laughing Woman, May 5, 2011, Mashantucket, Connecticut.
27. Experience Mayhew, "1713 Journal," 101, 110.
28. Personal interview with Laughing Woman, May 5, 2011, Mashantucket, Connecticut.
29. Personal interview with Wayne Reels, May 5, 2011, Mashantucket, Connecticut.
30. Personal interview with Tall Oak Weeden, April 8, 2011, Providence, Rhode Island.
31. For one such directory, see "Native American Ministries Directory," at http://www.missionfinder.org/nativeamer.htm. Accessed on May 10, 2011.

BIBLIOGRAPHY

Manuscript Primary Sources

Allen, William. *Memoirs of Samson Occom*. Unpublished Ms., William Allen Papers, Rauner Special Collections Library. Dartmouth College, 1859.

Autographs and Miscellaneous Letters, 1780–1831. Connecticut State Library.

Benjamin Colman Papers. Massachusetts Historical Society. Boston, Mass.

College and Schools Manuscript Series. Connecticut State Library. Hartford, Conn.

Curwen Family Papers, American Antiquarian Society. Worcester, Mass.

Ecclesiastical Affairs. Connecticut State Archives. Hartford, Conn.

History of the Shinnecock Church. Southampton, N.Y.: Unpublished Manuscript, First Presbyterian Church of Southampton Archives.

Indian Affairs, vols. 30–33. Massachusetts State Archives. Boston, Mass.

Indian Papers. Connecticut State Library. Hartford, Conn.

Indians—Collected Papers. Connecticut Historical Society. Hartford, Conn.

Journal Book of Proceedings of the First Church of Christ. Southampton, N.Y.: Unpublished Manuscript. First Presbyterian Church of Southampton Archives.

Manuscript Records of the Columbia (Lebanon Crank) Congregational Church. Connecticut State Library. Hartford, Conn.

Manuscript Records of the Company for the Propagation of the Gospel in New England. New England Historical and Genealogical Society. Boston, Mass.

Manuscript Records of the East Lyme Baptist Church. Connecticut State Library. Hartford, Conn.

Manuscript Records of the East Stonington Congregational Church. Connecticut State Library. Hartford, Conn.

Manuscript Records of the First Baptist Church of Groton. Connecticut State Library. Hartford, Conn.

Manuscript Records of the First Church of Christ in New London. Connecticut State Library. Hartford, Conn.

Manuscript Records of the First Presbyterian Church of East Hampton. East Hampton Library. East Hampton, N.Y.

Manuscript Records of the First/West Stonington Congregational Church. Connecticut State Library. Hartford, Conn.

Manuscript Records of the Groton First Congregational Church. Connecticut State Library. Hartford, Conn.

Manuscript Records of the New England Company. London Metropolitan Archives. London, UK.

Manuscript Records of the New London, North Parish, Congregational Church. Connecticut State Library. Hartford, Conn.

Manuscript Records of the North Groton (Ledyard) Congregational Church. Connecticut State Library. Hartford, Conn.

Manuscript Records of the North Stonington Congregational Church. Connecticut State Library. Hartford, Conn.

Microfilm Edition of the Papers of Eleazar Wheelock. Hanover, N.H.: Dartmouth College Library, 1971.

Miscellaneous Bound Manuscripts. Massachusetts Historical Society. Boston, Mass.

Moor's Indian Charity School, Records, 1760–1915. Rauner Special Collections Library. Dartmouth College. Hanover, N.H.

New England Company Collection, 1649–1775. American Antiquarian Society. Worcester, Mass.

New London Association Records, 1708–1788. Connecticut Conference Archives. United Church of Christ. Hartford, Conn.

New London County Court Records, Native Americans Collections. Connecticut State Library. Hartford, Conn.

Norwich Free Academy Records. Yale Indian Papers Project. http://www.library.yale.edu/yipp/.

Papers of William Allen. Rauner Library. Dartmouth College. Hanover, N.H.

Paul Campbell Research Notes. Rhode Island Historical Society. Providence, R.I.

Records of the Society in Scotland for the Propagation of Christian Knowledge. National Archives of Scotland. Edinburgh, UK.

Rhode Island Congregational Christian Conference Records. Rhode Island Historical Society. Providence, R.I.

The Society for Propagating the Gospel among the Indians and Others in North America Records. Massachusetts Historical Society. Boston, Mass.

The Society for Propagating the Gospel among the Indians and Others in North America Records, 1791–1875. Phillips Library. Peabody Essex Museum. Salem, Mass.

Yale Indian Papers Project. http://www.library.yale.edu/yipp/.

Printed Primary Sources

"Account of an Indian Visitation, A.D. 1698." In *Collections of the Massachusetts Historical Society.* Boston, Mass.: Munroe, Francis, and Parker, 1809.

"Annual Report of the Board of Directors to the New-York Missionary Society." *The Christian's Magazine,* May 1, 1811.

Apess, William. *On Our Own Ground: The Complete Writings of William Apess, a Pequot.* Edited by Barry O'Connell. Amherst: University of Massachusetts Press, 1992.

"At the Last Meeting of the New-York Missionary Society." *The New-York Missionary Magazine,* January 6, 1801.

Backus, Isaac. *A History of New-England, with Particular Reference to the Denomination of Christians Called Baptists.* Vol. 2. Boston: Edward Draper, 1777–1784.

Backus, Isaac, and William G. McLoughlin. *The Diary of Isaac Backus.* Providence: Brown University Press, 1979.

Bartlett, John Russell. *Records of the Colony of Rhode Island and Providence Plantations in New England.* New York: AMS Press, 1968.

Beatty, Charles. *The Journal of a Two Months Tour.* London: W. Davenhill and G. Pearch, 1768.

The Bee. New London, Conn.

Boston-Evening Post. Boston, Mass.

Boston Post Boy. Boston, Mass.

Buell, Samuel. *The Excellence and Importance of the Saving Knowledge of the Lord Jesus Christ in the Gospel-Preacher.* New-York: James Parker, 1761.

Caner, Henry. *A Candid Examination of Dr. Mayhew's Observations on the Charter and Conduct of the Society for the Propagation of the Gospel in Foreign Parts.* Boston: Thomas and John Fleet, 1763.

The Christian History: Containing Accounts of the Revival and Propagation of Religion in Great Britain and America. Boston, Mass., various years.

The Christian Monthly History: Or, an Account of the Revival and Progress of Religion, Abroad, and at Home. Edinburgh: R. Fleming and A. Alison, various years.

Collections of the Massachusetts Historical Society. Boston: The Society.

Colman, Benjamin. *A Letter from the Revd Mr. Sergeant of Stockbridge, to Dr. Colman of Boston; Containing Mr. Sergeant's Proposal of a more Effectual Method for the Education of Indian Children*. Boston: Rogers and Fowle, 1743.

Commuck, Thomas. *Indian Melodies*. New York: G. Lane and C. B. Tippett, 1845.

———. "Sketch of the Brothertown Indians." In *Wisconsin Historical Collections*, 291–98. Manchester: Wisconsin Historical Society, 1859.

Connecticut Church Records, State Library Index, New London First Congregational Church, 1670–1888. Hartford: Connecticut State Library, 1949.

Connecticut Gazette. Hartford, Conn.

Connecticut, Uncas, and John Mason. *Governor and Company of Connecticut, and Moheagan Indians*. London, UK: W. and J. Richardson, 1769.

Cooper, Mary. *The Diary of Mary Cooper: Life on a Long Island Farm, 1768–1773*. Edited by Field Horne. New York: Oyster Bay Historical Society, 1981.

The Daily Journal. London, UK.

Dally-Starna, Corinna, and William A. Starna. *Gideon's People: Being a Chronicle of an American Indian Community in Colonial Connecticut and the Moravian Missionaries Who Served There*. 2 vols. Lincoln: University of Nebraska Press, 2009.

Documents Relative to the Colonial History of the State of New York. Albany: Weed, Parsons, Printers, 1853.

Dwight, Timothy. *Travels in New-England and New-York*. 4 vols. London: Printed for W. Baynes and Son, 1823.

East Hampton Trustees Journal, 1725–1772. Vol. 1. Riverhead, N.Y.: Harry Lee. [1926].

Edwards, Jonathan. *A Faithful Narrative of the Surprising Work of God* [1737]. In *The Works of Jonathan Edwards Online*. http://edwards.yale.edu/.

Eliot, John. "A Further Account of the Progress of the Gospel." In *The Eliot Tracts*. Edited by Michael Clark. Westport, Conn.: Praeger, 2003.

"Extracts from Westerly Church Records." In *New England Historical and Genealogical Register* 26 (July 1872): 327–37.

The First Annual Report of the American Society for Promoting the Civilization and General Improvement of the Indian Tribes in the United States. New Haven, Conn.: S. Converse, 1824.

Fish, Joseph. *The Church of Christ a Firm and Durable House: Shown in a Number of Sermons on Matth. XVI 18*. New London, Conn.: Timothy Green, 1767.

Franklin, Benjamin. *The Autobiography and Other Writings*. Edited by Kenneth Silverman. New York, N.Y.: Penguin Books, 1986.

Gardiner, John Lyon. "Notes and Observations on the Town of East Hampton." In *New York Historical Society: Publication Fund*. New York, 1870.

The Gentlemen's Magazine. London, UK.

Gillies, John, ed. *Historical Collections Relating to Remarkable Periods of the Success of the Gospel*. 2 vols. Glasgow: n.p., 1754.

Gleason, Anson. "Gleason Report on Mohegan School." In *Public Documents, Printed by Order of the Senate of the United States*. Washington: Gales and Seaton, 1844.

Gookin, Daniel. "An Historical Account of the Doings and Sufferings of the Christian Indians in New England." In *Archaeologia Americana: Transactions and Collections of the American Antiquarian Society*. Cambridge, Mass.: Folsom, Wells, and Thurston, 1836.

———. "Historical Collections of the Indians in New England." In *Collections of the Massachusetts Historical Society for the Year 1792*. Boston: Munroe and Francis, 1806.

———. *Historical Collections of the Indians in New England*. Edited by Jeffrey H. Fiske. [n.p.]: Towtaid, 1970.

Hempstead, Joshua. *Diary of Joshua Hempstead of New London, Connecticut*. New London, Conn.: New London County Historical Society, 1901.

Holmes, Abiel. *A Discourse, Delivered before the Society for Propagating the Gospel among the Indians and Others in North America*. Boston: Farrand, Mallory, 1808.

———. "Memoir of the Mohegan Indians." In *Collections of the Massachusetts Historical Society*. Boston: Massachusetts Historical Society, 1804.

The Home Missionary, for the Year Ending April, 1895. Vol. 67. New York: J. J. Little, 1895.

Hopkins, Samuel. *Historical Memoirs, Relating to the Housatunnuk Indians*. Boston, N.E.: Printed and sold by S. Kneeland, 1753.

Horton, Azariah. "First Journal of Mr. Azariah Horton, the Society's Missionary in Long-Island, Near New York, from August 5th 1741, to November 1st That Year." In *The History and Archaeology of the Montauk*. Edited by Gaynell Stone. Edinburgh, Scotland, 1993.

———. "Journal." In *The History and Archaeology of the Montauk*. Edited by Gaynell Stone. Stony Brook, N.Y.: Suffolk County Archaeological Association; Nassau County Archaeological Association, 1993.

Hubbard, William. *The History of the Indian Wars in New England, from the First Settlement to the Termination of the War with King Philip in 1677*. New York: Kraus Reprint Co., 1969.

Hutchinson, Thomas. *A Collection of Original Papers Relative to the History of the Colony of Massachusetts-Bay*. Boston: Printed by Thomas and John Fleet, 1769.

Johnson, Joseph. *To Do Good to My Indian Brethren: The Writings of Joseph Johnson, 1751–1776*. Edited by Laura Murray. Amherst: University of Massachusetts Press, 1998.

Johnson, William. *The Papers of Sir William Johnson*. 14 vols. Albany: University of the State of New York, 1921.

Kirkland, Samuel. *The Journals of Samuel Kirkland: 18th-century Missionary to the Iroquois, Government Agent, Father of Hamilton College*. Edited by Walter Pilkington. Clinton, N.Y.: Hamilton College, 1980.

Law, Jonathan. *The Law Papers: Correspondence and Documents during Jonathan Law's Governorship of the Colony of Connecticut, 1741–1750*. Hartford: Connecticut Historical Society, 1907.

Mather, Cotton. *Diary of Cotton Mather, 1681–1724*. Boston: The Society, 1911.

Mather, Increase. *Pray for the Rising Generation, or A Sermon Wherein Godly Parents Are Encouraged, to Pray and Believe for Their Children*. Cambridge [Mass.]: Printed by Samuel Green and sold by Edmund Ranger in Boston, 1678.

Mayhew, Experience. "A Brief Journal of My Visitation of the Pequot and Mohegin Indians . . . 1713." In *Some Correspondence between the Governors and Treasurers of the New England Company in London*. London, UK: E. Stock, 1897.

———. *Indian Converts, or, Some Account of the Lives and Dying Speeches of a Considerable Number of the Christianized Indians of Martha's Vineyard, in New-England*. London, 1727.

———. "Journal of the Rev. Experience Mayhew during Part of September and October 1714." In *Some Correspondence between the Governors and Treasurers of the New England Company in London*. London, UK: E. Stock, 1897.

Mayhew, Experience, and John Cotton. *The Indian Primer or the First Book. By Which Children May Know Truely to Read the Indian Language*. Boston: B. Green, 1720.

Mayhew, Jonathan. *Observations on the Charter and the Conduct of the Society for the Propagation of the Gospel in Foreign Parts*. Boston: n.p., 1763.

McCallum, James Dow. *The Letters of Eleazar Wheelock's Indians*. Hanover, N.H.: Dartmouth College Publications, 1932.

McClure, David, and Franklin Bowditch Dexter. *Diary of David McClure Doctor of Divinity, 1748–1820*. New York: Knickerbocker Press, 1899.

McSparran, James. *A Letter Book and Abstract of Out Services Written during the Years 1743–1751*.

———. "America Dissected [1752]." In *History of the Episcopal Church, in Naragansett, Rhode-Island*. Edited by Wilkins Updike. New York: Henry M. Onderdonk, 1847.

Morse, Jedidiah. *A Report to the Secretary of War of the United States, on Indian Affairs*. New Haven, Conn.: S. Converse, 1822.

New England's First Fruits. Early English Books Online ed. London, 1643.

The New-England Primer, Enlarged. Boston: S. Kneeland & T. Green, 1727.

New England Weekly Journal. Boston, Mass.

The New-York Journal, & Patriotic Register.

New York Observer and Chronicle.

New-York Weekly Journal. New York, N.Y.

Norwich Packet. Norwich, Conn.

Occom, Samson. "Account of the Montauk Indians, on Long Island." In *The Collected Writings of Samson Occom, Mohegan*. Edited by Joanna Brooks. New York: Oxford University Press, 2006.

———. *A Choice Collection of Hymns and Spiritual Songs*. Boston: Timothy Green, 1774.

———. *The Collected Writings of Samson Occom, Mohegan*. Edited by Joanna Brooks. New York: Oxford University Press, 2006.

The Pennsylvania Gazette. Philadelphia, Penn.

The Public Records of the Colony of Connecticut. Edited by Charles J. Hoadly. Hartford, Conn.: Case, Lockwood and Brainard.

The Public Records of the State of Connecticut. Hartford: Press of the Case Lockwood and Brainard Company.

Records of the Town of East Hampton. 5 vols. Sag Harbor, N.Y.: J. H. Hunt, 1905.

Saltonstall, Gurdon. *A Memorial Offered to the General Assembly of His Majesties Colony of Connecticut*. New London, Conn.: n.p., 1715.

The Society for Propagating the Gospel among the Indians and Others in North America. Boston: University Press, 1887.

Simmons, Cheryl L., and William S. Simmons, eds. *Old Light on Separate Ways: The Narragansett Diary of Joseph Fish, 1765–1776*. Hanover, N.H.: University Press of New England, 1982.

Stiles, Ezra. *The Literary Diary of Ezra Stiles*. Edited by Franklin Bowditch Dexter. 3 vols. New York: C. Scribner's Sons, 1901.

Stiles, Ezra, and Franklin Bowditch Dexter. *Extracts from the Itineraries and Other Miscellanies of Ezra Stiles*. New Haven, Conn.: Yale University Press, 1916.

Stoddard, Solomon. *Question: Whether God Is Not Angry with the Country for Doing so Little Towards the Conversion of the Indians?* Boston, Mass.: B. Green, 1723.

Talcott, Joseph. *The Talcott Papers*. 2 vols. Hartford: Connecticut Historical Society, 1895–1896.

Tennent, Gilbert. *The Danger of an Unconverted Ministry*. Philadelphia: Printed by Benjamin Franklin, 1740.

Trumbull, Jonathan. The Trumbull Papers. In *Collections of the Massachusetts Historical Society*. Boston: Massachusetts Historical Society, 1885.

Wheelock, Eleazar. *A Continuation of the Narrative of the Indian Charity-School, in Lebanon, in Connecticut; From the Year 1768, to the Incorporation of It with Dartmouth-College, and Removal and Settlement of It in Hanover*. London: Printed by J. and W. Oliver, 1771.

———. *A Plain and Faithful Narrative of the Original Design, Rise, Progress and Present State of the Indian Charity-School at Lebanon, in Connecticut*. Boston: Richard and Samuel Draper, 1763.

Whitefield, George. *A Continuation of the Reverend Mr. Whitefield's Journal, from a Few Days after His Arrival at Savannah, June the Fourth, to His Leaving Stanford, the Last Town in New-England, October 29, 1740*. Philadelphia: Printed and sold by B. Franklin, 1741.

William Pitkin Papers. In *Collections of the Connecticut Historical Society*, Vol. 19. Hartford: Connecticut Historical Society, 1921.

Williams, Roger. *A Key into the Language of America*. London: Gregory Dexter, 1643.

———. "To my Deare and Welbeloved Friends and Countrey-men." *A Key into the Language of America*. London: Gregory Dexter, 1643.

Windham Herald.

Works of Jonathan Edwards Online. http://edwards.yale.edu/.

Secondary Sources

Abrams, Elliot Marc, and Anncorinne Freter. *The Emergence of the Moundbuilders: The Archaeology of Tribal Societies in Southeastern Ohio*. Athens: Ohio University Press, 2005.

Abzug, Robert H. *Cosmos Crumbling: American Reform and the Religious Imagination.* New York: Oxford University Press, 1994.

Albanese, Catherine L. *America, Religions and Religion.* Belmont, Calif.: Wadsworth, 1981.

Ales, Marion Fisher. "A History of the Indians on Montauk, Long Island." In *The History and Archaeology of the Montauk.* Edited by Gaynell Stone. Stony Brook, N.Y.: Suffolk County Archaeological Association; Nassau County Archaeological Association, 1993.

Amory, Hugh, and David D. Hall. *Bibliography and the Book Trades: Studies in the Print Culture of Early New England.* Philadelphia: University of Pennsylvania Press, 2005.

Anderson, Emma. *The Betrayal of Faith: The Tragic Journey of a Colonial Native Convert.* Cambridge, Mass.: Harvard University Press, 2007.

Anderson, Virginia DeJohn. "King Philip's Herds: Indians, Colonists, and the Problem of Livestock in Early New England." *William and Mary Quarterly* Third Ser. 51, no. 4 (October 1994): 601–24.

Axtell, James. *After Columbus: Essays in the Ethnohistory of Colonial North America.* New York: Oxford University Press, 1988.

———. "Colonial America without the Indians." In *After Columbus: Essays in the Ethnohistory of Colonial North America.* Edited by James Axtell. New York: Oxford University Press, 1988.

———. *The Invasion Within: The Contest of Cultures in Colonial North America.* New York: Oxford University Press, 1985.

———. "Through Another Glass Darkly: Early Indian Views of Europeans." In *After Columbus: Essays in the Ethnohistory of Colonial North America.* Edited by James Axtell. New York: Oxford University Press, 1988.

———. "Were Indian Conversions Bona Fide?" In *After Columbus: Essays in the Ethnohistory of Colonial America.* Edited by James Axtell. New York: Oxford University Press, 1988.

Baker, Henry A. *History of Montville, Connecticut, Formerly the North Parish of New London from 1640 to 1896.* Hartford, Conn.: Press of the Case Lockwood and Brainard Company, 1896.

———. "The Mohegans: An Historical Sketch of this Famous Tribe, Part III." *The Bostonian.* Vol. 1. Boston: The Bostonian Publishing Company, 1894–1985: 671–81.

Bakhtin, M. M. *Rabelais and His World.* Translated by Helene Iswolsky. 1st Midland book ed. Bloomington: Indiana University Press, 1984.

Banner, Stuart. *How the Indians Lost Their Land: Law and Power on the Frontier.* Cambridge, Mass.: Harvard University Press, 2005.

Barbour, John D. *Versions of Deconversion: Autobiography and the Loss of Faith.* Charlottesville: University Press of Virginia, 1994.

Beardsley, E. Edwards. "The Mohegan Land Controversy." In *Papers of the New Haven Colony Historical Society.* New Haven, Conn.: The Society, 1882.

Benes, Peter, ed. *New England Meeting House and Church: 1630–1850.* In *The Dublin Seminar for New England Folklife Annual Proceedings.* Boston: Boston University, 1979.

Berkhofer, Robert F. *Salvation and the Savage: An Analysis of Protestant Missions and American Indian Response, 1787–1862.* [Lexington]: University of Kentucky Press, 1965.

Bickford, Christopher P. *Farmington in Connecticut.* Canaan, N.H.: Phoenix, 1982.

Bilder, Mary Sarah. *The Transatlantic Constitution: Colonial Legal Culture and the Empire.* Cambridge, Mass.: Harvard University Press, 2004.

Blake, S. Leroy. *The Later History of the First Church of Christ, New London, Connecticut.* New London: Day, 1900.

Blodgett, Harold William. *Samson Occom.* Hanover, N.H.: Dartmouth College Publications, 1935.

Boissevain, Ethel. "The Detribalization of the Narragansett Indians: A Case Study." *Ethnohistory* 3, no. 3 (Summer 1956): 225–45.

"Books and Tracts in the Indian Language or Designed for the Use of Indians, Printed at Cambridge and Boston, 1653–1721." *Proceedings of the American Antiquarian Society* (October 1873).

Bowden, Henry Warner. *American Indians and Christian Missions: Studies in Cultural Conflict.* Chicago: University of Chicago Press, 1981.

Brainerd, David. *An Account of the Life of the Late Reverend Mr. David Brainerd*. Edited by Jonathan Edwards. Boston, Mass.: D. Henchman, 1749.

Brooks, James. *Captives and Cousins: Slavery, Kinship, and Community in the Southwest Borderlands*. Chapel Hill: University of North Carolina Press, 2002.

Brooks, Joanna. *American Lazarus: Religion and the Rise of African-American and Native American Literatures*. New York: Oxford University Press, 2003.

———. "Samson Occom at the Mohegan Sun: Finding History at a New England Indian Casino." *Common-Place* 4, no. 4 (July 2004). http://www.common-place.org/vol-04/no-04/brooks/03.shtml.

———. "'This Indian World': An Introduction to the Writings of Samson Occom." In Occom, Samson. *The Collected Writings of Samson Occom, Mohegan*. Edited by Joanna Brooks. New York: Oxford University Press, 2006.

Brooks, Lisa. "The Common Pot: Indigenous Writing and the Reconstruction of Native Space in the Northeast." Ph.D. Dissertation, Cornell University, 2004.

———. *The Common Pot: The Recovery of Native Space in the Northeast*. Minneapolis: University of Minnesota Press, 2008.

Bross, Kristina. *Dry Bones and Indian Sermons: Praying Indians in Colonial America*. Ithaca, N.Y.: Cornell University Press, 2004.

Brown, Anne S., and David D. Hall. "Family Strategies and Religious Practice: Baptism and the Lord's Supper in Early New England." In *Lived Religion in America*. Edited by David D. Hall. Princeton, N.J.: Princeton, 1997.

Brown, Barbara W., and James M. Rose. *Black Roots in Southeastern Connecticut, 1650–1900*. Detroit, Mich.: Gale Research, 1980.

Browning, Amos A. "The Preston Separate Church." In *Records and Papers of the New London County Historical Society*. New London, Conn.: New London County Historical Society, 1896.

Bushman, Richard L. *From Puritan to Yankee: Character and the Social Order in Connecticut, 1690–1765*. Cambridge, Mass.: Harvard University Press, 1967.

Butler, Jon. "Enthusiasm Described and Decried: The Great Awakening as Interpretive Fiction." *Journal of American History* 69, no. 2 (October 1982): 305–25.

Callender, John. *An Historical Discourse on the Civil and Religious Affairs of the Colony of Rhode-Island*. Edited by Romeo Elton. 3rd ed. Boston: Thomas H. Webb; Bartlett and Welford, 1843.

Calloway, Colin G., ed., *After King Philip's War: Presence and Persistence in Indian New England*. Hanover, N.H.: University Press of New England, 1997.

———. *The American Revolution in Indian Country: Crisis and Diversity in Native American Communities*. New York: Cambridge University Press, 1995.

———. *The Indian History of an American Institution: Native Americans and Dartmouth*. Hanover, N.H.: Dartmouth College Press, 2010.

Calloway, Colin G., and Neal Salisbury, eds. *Reinterpreting New England Indians and the Colonial Experience*. Boston: Colonial Society of Massachusetts, 2003.

Cañizares-Esguerra, Jorge. *Puritan Conquistadors: Iberianizing the Atlantic, 1550–1700*. Stanford, Calif.: Stanford University Press, 2006.

Caulkins, Frances Manwaring. *History of New London, Connecticut*. New London: The author [Press of Case Tiffany and Company], 1852.

———. *History of Norwich, Connecticut*. Hartford, Conn.: H. P. Haven, 1874.

———. *Memoir of the Rev. William Adams, of Dedham, Mass: and of the Rev. Eliphalet Adams*. Cambridge: Metcalf, 1849.

Cave, Alfred A. *The Pequot War*. Amherst: University of Massachusetts Press, 1996.

———. *Prophets of the Great Spirit: Native American Revitalization Movements in Eastern North America*. Lincoln: University of Nebraska Press, 2006.

Clark, Michael, ed. *The Eliot Tracts: With Letters from John Eliot to Thomas Thorowgood and Richard Baxter*. Westport, Conn.: Praeger, 2003.

Cogley, Richard W. *John Eliot's Mission to the Indians before King Philip's War*. Cambridge, Mass.: Harvard University Press, 1999.

Cohen, Charles L. "Conversion among Puritans and Amerindians: A Theological and Cultural Perspective." In *Puritanism: Transatlantic Perspectives on a Seventeenth-Century Anglo-American Faith*. Edited by Francis Bremer. Boston: Massachusetts Historical Society, 1993.

Conkling, Robert. "Legitimacy and Conversion in Social Change: The Case of French Missionaries and the Northern Algonkian." *Ethnohistory* 21, no. 1 (1974): 1–24.

Conroy, David W. "The Defense of Indian Land Rights: William Bollan and the Mohegan Case in 1743." *Proceedings of the American Antiquarian Society* 103 (1993): 395–424.

Cook, Noble David. *Born to Die: Disease and New World Conquest, 1492–1650*. New York: Cambridge University Press, 1998.

Cothren, William. *History of Ancient Woodbury, Connecticut*. Waterbury, Conn.: Bronson Brothers, 1854.

Crawford, Michael J. *Seasons of Grace: Colonial New England's Revival Tradition in Its British Context*. New York: Oxford University Press, 1991.

Cronon, William. *Changes in the Land: Indians, Colonists, and the Ecology of New England*. New York: Hill and Wang, 1983.

D'Agostino, Muriel. "Leader of the Broken Tribes—Samson Occom." Thesis, Hamilton College, n.d.

Dally-Starna, Corinna, and William A. Starna. "A Comment on 'Mahican Life and Moravian Missions.'" *Northeast Anthropology* no. 65 (Spring 2003): 53–65.

———. "American Indians and Moravians in Southern New England." In *Germans and Indians: Fantasies, Encounters, Projections*. Edited by Colin G. Calloway, Gerd Gmünden, and Susanne Zantop. Lincoln: University of Nebraska Press, 2002.

Davison, Faith. "Sachem Mahomet /Weyonomon: Mohegan Hero or Mason Tool?" Paper presented at the Heroism, Nationalism, and Human Rights Conference, University of Connecticut, February 2006.

De Forest, John William. *History of the Indians of Connecticut from the Earliest Known Period to 1850*. Hartford, Conn.: W. J. Hammersley, 1853.

Den Ouden, Amy E. *Beyond Conquest: Native Peoples and the Struggle for History in New England*. Lincoln: University of Nebraska Press, 2005.

Denison, Frederic. *Westerly (Rhode Island) and Its Witnesses: For Two Hundred and Fifty Years*. Providence: J. A. & R. A. Reid, 1878.

Dowd, Gregory Evans. *A Spirited Resistance: The North American Indian Struggle for Unity, 1745–1815*. Baltimore, Md.: Johns Hopkins University Press, 1992.

Drake, James David. *King Philip's War: Civil War in New England, 1675–1676*. Amherst: University of Massachusetts Press, 1999.

Eckstorm, Fannie Hardy. "The Attack on Norridgewock 1724." *William and Mary Quarterly* 7, no. 3 (September 1934): 541–78.

Eells, Earnest Edward. "Indian Missions on Long Island." In *The History and Archaeology of the Montauk*. Edited by Gaynell Stone. Stony Brook, N.Y.: Suffolk County Archaeological Association; Nassau County Archaeological Association, 1993.

Fagan, Brian M. *Chaco Canyon: Archeologists Explore the Lives of an Ancient Society*. New York: University Press, 2005.

Fawcett, Melissa Jayne. *Medicine Trail: The Life and Lessons of Gladys Tantaquidgeon*. Tucson: University of Arizona Press, 2000.

Fisher, Linford D. "'I believe they are Papists!': Natives, Moravians, and the Politics of Conversion in Eighteenth-Century Connecticut." *New England Quarterly* 81, no. 3 (2008): 410–37.

———. "'In the practice and profession of the Christian Religion': Native Americans, Conversion, and Christian Practice in Colonial New England, 1640–1730." *Harvard Theological Review* 102, no. 1 (January 2009): 101–24.

———. "'Traditionary Religion': The Great Awakening and the Shaping of Native Cultures in Southern New England, 1736–1776." Th.D. Dissertation, Harvard University, 2008.

Fitch, John T. *Puritan in the Wilderness: A Biography of the Reverend James Fitch, 1622–1702*. Camden, Maine: Picton Press, 1993.

Flemming, George D. *Brotherton: New Jersey's First and Only Indian Reservation and the Communities of Shamong and Tabernacle that Followed*. Medford, N.J.: Plexus, 2005.

Foster, Stephen. *The Long Argument: English Puritanism and the Shaping of New England Culture, 1570–1700*. Chapel Hill: University of North Carolina Press, 1991.

Frazier, Patrick. *The Mohicans of Stockbridge*. Lincoln: University of Nebraska Press, 1992.

Gaustad, Edwin S. *The Great Awakening in New England*. Gloucester, Mass.: P. Smith, 1965.

Glasson, Travis. *Mastering Christianity: Missionary Anglicanism and Slavery in the Atlantic World*. New York: Oxford University Press, 2012.

Glatthaar, Joseph T., and James Kirby Martin. *Forgotten Allies: The Oneida Indians and the American Revolution*. 1st ed. New York: Hill and Wang, 2006.

Godbeer, Richard. *Sexual Revolution in Early America*. Baltimore, Md.: Johns Hopkins University Press, 2002.

Goen, C. C. *Revivalism and Separatism in New England, 1740–1800: Strict Congregationalists and Separate Baptists in the Great Awakening*. Hamden, Conn.: Archon Books, 1969.

Gow, Peter. "Forgetting Conversion: The Summer Institute of Linguistics Mission in the Piro Lived World." In *The Anthropology of Christianity*. Edited by Fenella Cannell. Durham, N.C.: Duke University Press, 2006.

Greene, Evarts Boutell, and Virginia D. Harrington. *American Population before the Federal Census of 1790*. New York: Columbia University Press, 1932.

Greer, Allan. *Mohawk Saint: Catherine Tekakwitha and the Jesuits*. New York: Oxford University Press, 2005.

Griffiths, Nicholas. "Introduction." In *Spiritual Encounters: Interactions between Christianity and Native Religions in Colonial America*. Edited by Nicholas Griffiths and Fernando Cervantes. Lincoln: University of Nebraska Press, 1999.

———. *Sacred Dialogues: Christianity and Native Religions in the Colonial Americas, 1492–1700*. England: Lulu Enterprises, 2006.

Griffiths, Nicholas, and Fernando Cervantes, eds. *Spiritual Encounters: Interactions between Christianity and Native Religions in Colonial America*. Lincoln: University of Nebraska Press, 1999.

Grigg, John A. "'How This Shall Be Brought About': The Development of the SSPCK's American Policy." *Itinerario* 32, no. 3 (2008): 43–60.

Guild, Reuben Aldridge. *Life, Times, and Correspondence of James Manning, and the Early History of Brown University*. Boston: Gould and Lincoln; Sheldon and company, 1864.

Gutiérrez, Ramón A. *When Jesus Came, the Corn Mothers Went Away: Marriage, Sexuality, and Power in New Mexico, 1500–1846*. Stanford, Calif.: Stanford University Press, 1991.

Haefeli, Evan, and Kevin Sweeney. *Captors and Captives: The 1704 French and Indian Raid on Deerfield*. Amherst: University of Massachusetts Press, 2003.

Hall, David D., ed. *Lived Religion in America: Toward a History of Practice*. Princeton, N.J.: Princeton University Press, 1997.

———. *Worlds of Wonder, Days of Judgment: Popular Religious Belief in Early New England*. New York: Knopf, 1989.

Hall, Timothy D. *Contested Boundaries: Itinerancy and the Reshaping of the Colonial American Religious World*. Durham, N.C.: Duke University Press, 1994.

Hamilton, Alexander, and Carl Bridenbaugh. *Gentleman's Progress: The Itinerarium of Dr. Alexander Hamilton, 1744*. Chapel Hill: University of North Carolina Press, 1948.

Hankins, Jean. "Solomon Briant and Joseph Johnson: Indian Teachers and Preachers in Colonial New England." *Connecticut History* 33, (1992): 38–60.

Hatch, Nathan O. *The Democratization of American Christianity*. New Haven: Yale University Press, 1989.

Herndon, Ruth Wallis, and Ella Wilcox Sekatau. "Colonizing the Children: Indian Youngsters in Servitude in Early New England." In *Reinterpreting New England Indians and the Colonial Experience*. Edited by Colin G. Calloway and Neal Salisbury. Boston: Colonial Society of Massachusetts, 2003.

———. "The Right to a Name: The Narragansett People and Rhode Island Officials in the Revolutionary Era." *Ethnohistory* 44, no. 3 (1997): 433–62.

Heyrman, Christine Leigh. *Southern Cross: The Beginnings of the Bible Belt*. Chapel Hill: University of North Carolina Press, 1997.

Hindmarsh, D. Bruce. *The Evangelical Conversion Narrative: Spiritual Autobiography in Early Modern England*. New York: Oxford University Press, 2005.

The History and Archaeology of the Montauk Indians. Lexington, Mass.: Ginn Custom Publishing, 1979.

The Holy Bible, King James Version. New York: American Bible Society, 1999.

Hooker, Edward William. *Memoir of Mrs. Sarah L. Huntington Smith, Late of the American Mission in Syria*. 3.d ed. Boston: T. R. Marvin, 1846.

Hunter, Lois Marie. *"The Shinnecock Indians."* Southampton, N.Y.: Southampton Public Library, Long Island Room.

Jarvis, Brad D. E. *The Brothertown Nation of Indians: Land Ownership and Nationalism in Early America, 1740–1840*. Lincoln: University of Nebraska Press, 2010.

Jennings, Francis. *The Invasion of America: Indians, Colonialism, and the Cant of Conquest*. Chapel Hill: University of North Carolina Press, 1975.

Jones, Electa F. *Stockbridge, Past and Present*. Springfield, Mass.: S. Bowles, 1854.

Juster, Susan. *Disorderly Women: Sexual Politics and Evangelicalism in Revolutionary New England*. Ithaca, N.Y.: Cornell University Press, 1994.

Karr, Ronald Dale. "'Why Should You Be So Furious?': The Violence of the Pequot War." *Journal of American History* 85 (December 1998): 876–909.

Kawashima, Yasuhide. *Igniting King Philip's War: The John Sassamon Murder Trial*. Lawrence: University Press of Kansas, 2001.

Kellaway, William. *The New England Company, 1649–1776: Missionary Society to the American Indians*. [London]: Longmans, 1961.

Kidd, Thomas S. *The Great Awakening: The Roots of Evangelical Christianity in Colonial America*. New Haven, Conn.: Yale University Press, 2007.

———. *The Protestant Interest: New England after Puritanism*. New Haven, Conn.: Yale University Press, 2004.

Kupperman, Karen Ordahl. *Indians and English: Facing Off in Early America*. Ithaca, NY: Cornell University Press, 2000.

LaFantasie, Glenn W. "Introduction." In *The Correspondence of Roger Williams*. Edited by Glenn W. LaFantasie. Hanover, N.H.: University Press of New England, 1988.

Lambert, Frank. *Inventing the "Great Awakening."* Princeton, N.J.: Princeton University Press, 1999.

Lancaster, Jane. "'A thing impracticable': The Founding of Brown University." Chapter draft in the author's possession, 2011.

Lawrence, H. Newman. *The Old Narragansett Church (St. Paul's)*. n.c.: n.p., 1915.

Lepore, Jill. "Dead Men Tell No Tales: John Sassamon and the Fatal Consequences of Literacy." *American Quarterly* 46, no. 4 (December 1994): 479–512.

———. *The Name of War: King Philip's War and the Origins of American Identity*. New York: Knopf, 1998.

———. "When Deer Island Was Turned into Devil's Island." *Bostonia* (Summer 1998): 14–19.

Little, Elizabeth A. *The Indian Contribution to Along-Shore Whaling at Nantucket*. Nantucket, Mass.: Nantucket Historical Association, 1981.

Love, William DeLoss. *Samson Occom and the Christian Indians of New England*. 1st Syracuse University Press ed. Syracuse, N.Y.: Syracuse University Press, 2000 [1899].

———. "Samson Occom: The Founding of Brothertown by Christian Indians." *Utica Morning Herald*, February 14, 1894.

Lovelace, Richard F. *The American Pietism of Cotton Mather: Origins of American Evangelicalism*. Grand Rapids, Mich.: Christian University Press, 1979.

Lynch, James P. "Historical Chronology of the Eastern Pequot/Pawcatuck Pequot, 1638–1993." Mashantucket Pequot Museum and Research Center, Mashantucket, Conn.

Makdisi, Ussama Samir. *Artillery of Heaven: American Missionaries and the Failed Conversion of the Middle East.* Ithaca. N.Y.: Cornell University Press, 2008.

Mancini, Jason R. "Beyond Reservation: Indian Survivance in Southern New England and Eastern Long Island, 1713–1861." Ph.D. Dissertation, University of Connecticut, 2009.

Mandell, Daniel R. *Behind the Frontier: Indians in Eighteenth-Century Eastern Massachusetts.* Lincoln: University of Nebraska Press, 1996.

———. "Eager Partners in Reform: Indians and Frederick Baylies in Southern New England, 1780–1840." In *Native Americans, Christianity, and the Reshaping of the American Religious Landscape.* Edited by Joel W. Martin and Mark A. Nicholas. Chapel Hill: University of North Carolina Press, 2010.

———. "Shifting Boundaries of Race and Ethnicity: Indian-Black Intermarriage in Southern New England, 1760–1880." *Journal of American History* 85, no. 2 (September 1998): 466–501.

———. "'The times are exceedingly altered': The Revolution and Southern New England Indians." In *Eighteenth Century Native Communities of Southern New England in Colonial Context.* Edited by Jack Campisi. Mashantucket, Conn.: MPMRC, 2005.

———. *Tribe, Race, History: Native Americans in Southern New England, 1780–1880.* Baltimore: Johns Hopkins University Press, 2008.

———. "'Turned Their Minds to Religion': Oquaga and the First Iroquois Protestant Church, 1748–1776." Under review, *William and Mary Quarterly.*

Martin, Joel W. *The Land Looks after Us: A History of Native American Religion.* New York: Oxford University Press, 2001.

Martin, Joel W., and Mark A. Nicholas. *Native Americans, Christianity, and the Reshaping of the American Religious Landscape.* Chapel Hill: University of North Carolina Press, 2010.

Martin, John Frederick. *Profits in the Wilderness: Entrepreneurship and the Founding of New England Towns in the Seventeenth Century.* Chapel Hill: University of North Carolina Press, 1991.

Mavor, James W., and Byron E. Dix. *Manitou: The Sacred Landscape of New England's Native Civilization.* Rochester, Vt.: Inner Traditions International, 1989.

McBride, Kevin. "Bundles, Bears, and Bibles: Interpreting Seventeenth-Century Native 'Texts.'" In *Early Native Literacies in New England.* Edited by Kristina Bross and Hillary Wyss. Amherst: University of Massachusetts Press, 2008.

———. "'Desirous to Improve after the European Manner': The Mashantucket Pequots in the Brotherton Indian Movement." Unpublished essay, 2007.

———. "Transformation by Degree: Eighteenth Century Native American Land Use." In *Eighteenth Century Native Communities of Southern New England in Colonial Context.* Edited by Jack Campisi. Mashantucket, Conn.: MPMRC, 2005.

McCarthy, Keely. "Conversion, Identity, and the Indian Missionary." *Early American Literature* 36, no. 3 (2001): 353–69.

Merritt, Jane T. "Dreaming of the Savior's Blood: Moravians and the Indian Great Awakening in Pennsylvania." *William and Mary Quarterly* 54, no. 4 (1997): 723–46.

Mills, Kenneth. *Idolatry and Its Enemies: Colonial Andean Religion and Extirpation, 1640–1750.* Princeton, N.J.: Princeton University Press, 1997.

Mills, Kenneth, and Anthony Grafton, eds. *Conversion in Late Antiquity and the Early Middle Ages: Seeing and Believing.* Rochester, N.Y.: University of Rochester Press, 2003.

———, eds. *Conversion: Old Worlds and New.* Rochester, N.Y.: University of Rochester Press, 2003.

Monaghan, E. Jennifer. *Learning to Read and Write in Early America.* Amherst: University of Massachusetts Press, 2005.

Moran, Gerald F. "Sisters in Christ: Women and the Church in Seventeenth-Century New England." In *Women in American Religion.* Edited by Janet Wilson James. Philadelphia: University of Pennsylvania, 1980.

Morrison, Kenneth M. *The Solidarity of Kin: Ethnohistory, Religious Studies, and the Algonkian-French Religious Encounter.* Albany: State University of New York Press, 2002.

Mulvaney, Katie. "From Church to Citadel, Narragansetts Endure." *Providence Journal,* August 4, 2004.

Newell, Margaret Ellen. "The Changing Nature of Slavery in New England, 1670–1720." In *Reinterpreting New England Indians and the Colonial Experience*. Edited by Colin G. Calloway and Neal Salisbury. Boston, Mass.: Colonial Society of Massachusetts, 2003.

———. "Indian Slavery in Colonial New England." In *Indian Slavery in Colonial America*. Edited by Allan Gallay. Lincoln: University of Nebraska Press, 2009.

O'Brien, Jean M. *Dispossession by Degrees: Indian Land and Identity in Natick, Massachusetts, 1650–1790*. New York: Cambridge University Press, 1997.

———. "Divorced from the Land: Resistance and Survival of Indian Women in Eighteenth Century New England." In *After King Philip's War: Presence and Persistence in Indian New England*. Edited by Colin G. Calloway. Hanover, N.H.: University Press of New England, 1997.

———. *Firsting and Lasting: Writing Indians Out of Existence in New England*. Minneapolis: University of Minnesota Press, 2010.

Olson, Paul A., ed. *The Struggle for the Land: Indigenous Insight and Industrial Empire in the Semiarid World*. Lincoln: University of Nebraska Press, 1990.

Onuf, Peter. "New Lights in New London: A Group Portrait of the Separatists." *William and Mary Quarterly* 37, no. 4 (October 1980): 627–43.

Orcutt, Samuel. *History of the Towns of New Milford and Bridgewater, Connecticut, 1703–1882*. Hartford, Conn.: Press of the Case Lockwood and Brainard Company, 1882.

Orsi, Robert. "Everyday Miracles: The Study of Lived Religion." In *Lived Religion in America: Toward a History of Practice*. Edited by David D. Hall. Princeton, N.J.: Princeton University Press, 1997.

Ottery, Will, and Rudi Ottery. *A Man Called Sampson*. Camden, Maine: Penobscot Press, 1989.

"Patriots of Color at the Battle of Bunker Hill." National Park Service. www.nps.gov/bost/forteachers/upload/Boston%20Lesson.pdf, n.d.

"Paul Cuffee at Wading River." Digitized Newspaper Clippings, Southold Free Library. Southold, N.Y.

Peyer, Bernd. *The Tutor'd Mind: Indian Missionary-Writers in Antebellum America*. Amherst: University of Massachusetts Press, 1997.

Pope, Robert G. *The Half-Way Covenant: Church Membership in Puritan New England*. Princeton, N.J.: Princeton University Press, 1969.

Porter, Noah. *A Historical Discourse, Delivered by Request, before the Citizens of Farmington, November 4, 1840*. Hartford: L. Skinner, 1841.

Porterfield, Amanda. "Women's Attraction to Puritanism." *Church History* 60, no. 2 (June 1991): 196–209.

Punchard, George. *History of Congregationalism from about a.d. 250 to the Present Time*. Vol. 5. Boston: Congregational Publishing Society, 1881.

Rambo, Lewis R. *Understanding Religious Conversion*. New Haven, Conn.: Yale University Press, 1993.

"Reverend Paul Cuffee was an Outstanding L.I. Indian." Digitized Newspaper Clippings, Southold Free Library. Southold, N.Y.

Richardson, Leon B. *An Indian Preacher in England*. Hanover, N.H.: Dartmouth College Publications, 1933.

Richter, Daniel K. *Before the Revolution: America's Ancient Pasts*. Cambridge, Mass.: Harvard University Press, 2011.

———. *Facing East from Indian Country: A Native History of Early America*. Cambridge, Mass.: Harvard University Press, 2001.

———. *The Ordeal of the Longhouse: The Peoples of the Iroquois League in the Era of European Colonization*. Chapel Hill: University of North Carolina Press, 1992.

Ronda, James P. "Generations of Faith: The Christian Indians of Martha's Vineyard." *William and Mary Quarterly* 38, no. 3 (1981): 369–94.

Rowlandson, Mary White, and Timothy Harrington. *A Narrative of the Captivity, Sufferings, and Removes, of Mrs. Mary Rowlandson*. Clinton, Mass.: Ballard and Bynner, 1853.

Ryan, Bill. "A Huntington's Mohegan Mission." *New York Times*. Sunday, October 6, 1996.

Sainsbury, John A. "Indian Labor in Early Rhode Island." *New England Quarterly* 48, no. 3 (September 1975): 378–93.

Salisbury, Neal. "Embracing Ambiguity: Native Peoples and Christianity in Seventeenth-Century North America." *Ethnohistory* 50, no. 2 (Spring 2003): 247–59.

———. *Manitou and Providence: Indians, Europeans, and the Making of New England, 1500–1643.* New York: Oxford University Press, 1982.

Schmidt, Leigh Eric. *Holy Fairs: Scottish Communions and American Revivals in the Early Modern Period.* Princeton, N.J.: Princeton University Press, 1989.

Seed, Patricia. *Ceremonies of Possession in Europe's Conquest of the New World, 1492–1640.* New York: Cambridge University Press, 1995.

Seeman, Erik R. *Pious Persuasions: Laity and Clergy in Eighteenth-Century New England.* Baltimore: Johns Hopkins University Press, 1999.

Sensbach, Jon F. *Rebecca's Revival: Creating Black Christianity in the Atlantic World.* Cambridge, Mass.: Harvard University Press, 2005.

Seraile, William. *Fire in His Heart: Bishop Benjamin Tanner and the A.M.E. Church.* Knoxville: University of Tennessee, 1998.

Shenk, Wilbert R. *North American Foreign Missions, 1810–1914: Theology, Theory, and Policy.* Grand Rapids, Mich.: William B. Eerdmans, 2004.

Shipton, Clifford Kenyon. *Sibley's Harvard Graduates: Biographical Sketches of Graduates of Harvard University, in Cambridge, Massachusetts.* Boston, Mass.: Massachusetts Historical Society.

Silverman, David J. "The Church in New England Indian Community Life: A View from the Islands and Cape Cod." In *Reinterpreting New England Indians and the Colonial Experience.* Edited by Colin G. Calloway and Neal Salisbury. Boston: Colonial Society of Massachusetts, 2003.

———. *Faith and Boundaries: Colonists, Christianity, and Community among the Wampanoag Indians of Martha's Vineyard, 1600–1871.* New York: Cambridge University Press, 2005.

———. "Indians, Missionaries, and Religious Translation: Creating Wampanoag Christianity in Seventeenth-Century Martha's Vineyard." *William and Mary Quarterly* 62, no. 2 (April 2005): 141–74.

———. *Red Brethren: The Brothertown and Stockbridge Indians and the Problem of Race in Early America.* Ithaca: Cornell University Press, 2010.

Simmons, William S. "Conversion from Indian to Puritan." *New England Quarterly* 52, (1979): 197–218.

———. "The Great Awakening and Indian Conversion in Southern New England." In *Papers of the Tenth Algonquian Conference.* Edited by William Cowan. Ottawa: Carleton University Press, 1979.

———. *The Narragansetts.* New York: Chelsea House, 1989.

———. "Red Yankees: Narragansett Conversion in the Great Awakening." *American Ethnologist* 10, no. 2 (May 1983): 253–71.

———. "Southern New England Shamanism: An Ethnographic Reconstruction." In *Papers of the Seventh Algonquian Conference, 1975.* Edited by William Cowan. Ottawa: Carleton University, 1976.

———. *Spirit of the New England Tribes: Indian History and Folklore, 1620–1984.* Hanover, N.H.: University Press of New England, 1986.

The Society for Propagating the Gospel among the Indians and Others in North America. Boston: University Press, 1887.

Southampton, Long Island: 1640/1965: 325th Anniversary. Southampton: Southampton Town Committee, 1965.

Sprague, William. *Annals of the American Pulpit: Presbyterian.* Vol. 3. New York: Robert Carter and Bros., 1858.

———. *Annals of the American Pulpit: Trinitarian Congregational.* Vol. 2. New York: Robert Carter and Bros., 1857.

Stevens, Laura M. *The Poor Indians: British Missionaries, Native Americans, and Colonial Sensibility.* Philadelphia: University of Pennsylvania Press, 2004.

Stone, Gaynell, ed. *The History and Archaeology of the Montauk.* 2nd ed. Vol. 3. Stony Brook, N.Y.: Suffolk County Archaeological Association; Nassau County Archaeological Association, 1993.

Stout, Harry S., and Peter Onuf. "James Davenport and the Great Awakening in New London." *Journal of American History* 70, no. 3 (December 1983): 556–78.

Strong, John. "How the Montauk Lost Their Land." In *The History and Archaeology of the Montauk.* Edited by Gaynell Stone. Stony Brook, N.Y.: Suffolk County Archaeological Association, 1993.

———. *The Montaukett Indians of Eastern Long Island.* Syracuse, N.Y.: Syracuse University Press, 2001.

Sweeney, Kevin. "River Gods and Related Minor Deities: The Williams Family and the Connecticut River Valley, 1637–1790." Ph.D. Dissertation, Yale University, 1986.

Sweet, John Wood. *Bodies Politic: Negotiating Race in the American North, 1730–1830.* Baltimore: Johns Hopkins University Press, 2003.

Szasz, Margaret. *Indian Education in the American Colonies, 1607–1783.* Albuquerque: University of New Mexico Press, 1988.

———. *Scottish Highlanders and Native Americans: Indigenous Education in the Eighteenth-Century Atlantic World.* Norman: University of Oklahoma Press, 2007.

Taylor, Alan. *The Divided Ground: Indians, Settlers, and the Northern Borderland of the American Revolution.* New York: Knopf, 2006.

Thompson, Benjamin Franklin. *The History of Long Island, From Its Discovery to the Present Time.* 3 vols. New York: Gould, Banks, 1843.

Thompson, Henry P. *Into All Lands: The History of the Society for the Propagation of the Gospel in Foreign Parts, 1701–1950.* London, UK: SPCK, 1951.

Thornton, John Kelly. *Africa and Africans in the Making of the Atlantic World, 1400–1800.* 2nd ed. New York: Cambridge University Press, 1998.

Tooker, William Wallace. *John Eliot's First Indian Teacher and Interpreter, Cockenoe-de-Long-Island.* New York: Francis P. Harper, 1896.

Tracy, Joseph. *The Great Awakening: A History of the Revival of Religion in the Time of Edwards and Whitefield.* Boston, Mass.: Tappan and Dennet and Josiah Adams, 1842.

Tucker, William Franklin. *Historical Sketch of the Town of Charlestown.* Westerly, R.I.: G. B. and J. H. Utter, 1877.

Ulrich, Laurel. *Good Wives: Image and Reality in the Lives of Women in Northern New England, 1650–1750.* New York: Knopf: Distributed by Random House, 1982.

———. *A Midwife's Tale: The Life of Martha Ballard, Based on her Diary, 1785–1812.* New York: Knopf: Distributed by Random House, 1990.

Updike, Wilkins. *A History of the Episcopal Church in Narragansett, Rhode Island.* 2 vols. Boston: Merrymount Press, 1907.

Van Lonkhuyzen, Harold W. "A Reappraisal of the Praying Indians: Acculturation, Conversion, and Identity at Natick, Massachusetts, 1646–1730." *New England Quarterly* 63, no. 3 (1990): 396–428.

Vaughan, Alden T. *Transatlantic Encounters: American Indians in Britain, 1500–1776.* New York: Cambridge University Press, 2006.

Vickers, Daniel. "The First Whalemen of Nantucket." In *After King Philip's War: Presence and Persistence in Indian New England.* Edited by Colin G. Calloway. Hanover, N.H.: University Press of New England, 1997.

Viswanathan, Gauri. *Outside the Fold: Conversion, Modernity, and Belief.* Princeton, N.J.: Princeton University Press, 1998.

"Wading River Congregational Church." Digitized Newspaper Clippings, Southold Free Library. Southold, N.Y.

Walker, George L. *Some Aspects of the Religious Life of New England.* Boston: Burdett, 1897.

Walters, Mark D. "*Mohegan Indians* v. *Connecticut* (1705–1773) and the Legal Status of Aboriginal Customary Laws and Government in British North America." *Osgoode Hall Law Journal* 33, no. 4 (1995): 785–829.

Weinstein-Farson, Laurie. "Land, Politics, Power: The Mohegan Indians in the Seventeenth and Eighteenth Centuries." *Man in the Northeast* 42 (1991): 9–16.

Weis, Frederick L. "The New England Company of 1649 and Its Missionary Enterprises." In *Publications of the Colonial Society of Massachusetts*. Boston, Mass.: Colonial Society of Massachusetts, 1959.

Westerkamp, Marilyn J. *Triumph of the Laity: Scots-Irish Piety and the Great Awakening, 1625–1760*. New York: Oxford University Press, 1988.

Wheeler, Rachel M. "Living upon Hope: Mahicans and Missionaries, 1730–1760." Ph.D. Dissertation, Yale University, 1999.

———. *To Live upon Hope: Mohicans and Missionaries in the Eighteenth-Century Northeast*. Ithaca: Cornell University Press, 2008.

———. "Women and Christian Practice in a Mahican Village." *Religion and American Culture* 13, no. 1 (2003): 26–67.

Wheeler, Richard Anson. *History of the First Congregational Church, Stonington, Conn., 1674–1874*. Norwich, Conn.: T.H. Davis, 1875.

Whitaker, Epher. *History of Southold, L.I.: Its First Century*. Southold, N.Y.: n.p., 1881.

Winiarski, Douglas L. "Jonathan Edwards, Enthusiast? Radical Revivalism and the Great Awakening in the Connecticut Valley." *Church History* 74, no. 4 (December 1, 2005): 683–739.

———. "Native American Popular Religion in New England's Old Colony, 1670–1770." *Religion and American Culture* 15, no. 2 (Summer 2005): 147–86.

Winslow, Ola E. *Master Roger Williams: A Biography*. New York: Macmillan, 1957.

Woodbridge, Timothy. *The Autobiography of a Blind Minister*. Boston: J. P. Jewett, 1856.

Wyss, Hilary E. "'Things That Do Accompany Salvation': Colonialism, Conversion, and Cultural Exchange in Experience Mayhew's Indian Converts." *Early American Literature* 33, no. 1 (1998): 39–61.

———. *Writing Indians: Literacy, Christianity, and Native Community in Early America*. Amherst: University of Massachusetts Press, 2000.

Young, Biloine W., and Melvin L. Fowler. *Cahokia, the Great Native American Metropolis*. Urbana: University of Illinois Press, 2000.

INDEX

Abenakis (Indians), 27
Ackery (black or mulatto), 94
Adams, Eliphalet, 48, 50, 57, 70, 142
  baptizing Indians, 102, 170
  church schism and, 68
  instructing Benjamin Uncas III, 60
  preaching to Indians, 48, 69, 109
  See also Mohegans; New London
Adams, John, 170
Adams, Samuel, 172
Adams, William, 48
affiliation, 8–9, 240n38–40, 240n42–44, 241n69
  ambivalence of Indian, 12, 89
  defined, 8, 10, 86
  Indian, ceasing after the First Great
    Awakening, 108, 111–12, 114
  Indian, during First Great Awakening, 84, 87,
    89–97
  interpreting Indian, 98–106
  material benefits of Christian, 56, 62
  patterns of Indian, 87, 90–94
  present-day Indian, 212, 214, 220–21, 223
  See also conversion, deaffiliation, Indian
    Christianity, Indian Great Awakening
Africans. See blacks, mulattos, negroes
afterlife, 7, 16, 19, 59, 221
agriculture, 22, 24, 30, 56, 171
  Indian practices of, 15, 143, 201
  production of Brothertown Indians, 12, 195
Albany, New York, 39, 141, 173–74, 181
alcohol, 80, 122, 186
  alcoholism, of Indians, 32–33, 37, 61, 119, 122,
    164, 191
  attempts to restrict sale of, on Indian lands, 42,
    60, 149, 191, 255n10
  drunkenness, of Indians, 42, 80, 93, 109, 119,
    134, 157, 191, 203
  effects of, in Indian communities, 32–33, 191,
    222

excessive drinking, 74, 94, 99, 122, 162
  sin of drunkenness, 73, 80, 93–94, 119, 138,
    151
Alderman (Indian, shot King Philip/Metacom),
    27
Algonquians, 15–16, 19–20, 88–89, 131, 146, 171.
    See also Indians
Amauhzeen (Niantic Indian), 44
American Board of Commissioners for Foreign
    Missions (ABCFM), 200, 215, 256n59
American Indians. See Indians, specific tribal
    names
Anabaptist, 115
Anasazis (Indians), 14
Anglicans, 30, 42, 67, 110, 117, 128, 199
  controversies with dissenting colonists, 45,
    144–45
  Indian disinterest in, 204
  Indian interest in, 81, 101, 117, 152
  Indian non-affiliations at Narragansett church,
    96
  missionary activity, 38–39, 45–46
  See also James McSparran, Society for the
    Propagation of the Gospel in Foreign Parts
Anglicization, of Indians, 88, 195
  burial practices, 58
  colonial designs for, 37, 42, 51–52, 59
  cultural appropriation, 43
  Indian rejection of, 100
  See also Christianization, evangelization,
    Indian Christianity
Anglo-American. See Euroamericans
Ann (cousin of Mahomet II), 62, 235n124
Antigua, 171
antirevivalism, 68–69, 125
Apess, William, 191, 195, 210
Arrowsic Island, Maine, 38
Ashbow (Ashpo), Joshua, 191
Ashpo, Hannah, 119, 185